❖ Women's Access to Political Power in
Post-Communist Europe

Gender and Politics represents the most recent scholarship in the areas of women, gender, and politics, and is explicitly cross-national in its organization and orientation. Recognizing the contribution of women's studies to gendered political analysis, the goal of *Gender and Politics* is to develop, and to publish, frontier analysis, the empirical research exemplary of the intersection between political studies and women's studies.

The series is edited by Professor Karen Beckwith at the Department of Political Science, College of Wooster and Professor Joni Lovenduski, Department of Politics and Sociology, Birkbeck College.

❖ Women's Access to Political Power in Post-Communist Europe

edited by
RICHARD E. MATLAND
AND
KATHLEEN A. MONTGOMERY

OXFORD
UNIVERSITY PRESS

OXFORD

UNIVERSITY PRESS

Great Clarendon Street, Oxford OX2 6DP

Oxford University Press is a department of the University of Oxford.
It furthers the University's objective of excellence in research, scholarship,
and education by publishing worldwide in

Oxford New York

Auckland Bangkok Buenos Aires Cape Town Chennai
Dar es Salaam Delhi Hong Kong Istanbul Karachi Kolkata
Kuala Lumpur Madrid Melbourne Mexico City Mumbai Nairobi
São Paulo Shanghai Taipei Tokyo Toronto

Oxford is a registered trade mark of Oxford University Press
in the UK and in certain other countries

Published in the United States
by Oxford University Press Inc., New York

© the several contributors, 2003

British Library Cataloguing in Publication Data

Data available

Library of Congress Cataloging in Publication Data

Women's access to political power in post-communist Europe / edited by Richard E.
Matland and Kathleen A. Montgomery.
p. cm.—(Gender and politics)
Includes bibliographical references and index.
1. Women in politics—Europe, Eastern. 2. Women in politics—Europe, Central.
3. Europe, Eastern—Politics and government—1989– 4. Europe, Central—Politics and
government—1989– 5. Women—Europe, Eastern—Social conditions. 6. Women—Europe,
Central—Social conditions. I. Matland, Richard E. II. Montgomery, Kathleen A.
III. Series.
HQ1236 .W651717 2003   320′.082′0947—dc21   2002035582

ISBN 0-19-924685-8 (hbk)
ISBN 0-19-924686-6 (pbk)

1 3 5 7 9 10 8 6 4 2

Typeset by Newgen Imaging Systems (P) Ltd., Chennai, India
Printed in Great Britain
on acid-free paper by
T. J. International Ltd., Padstow, Cornwall

This book is dedicated to my daughters, Nora and Emma

Richard E. Matland

This book is dedicated to my first and best teacher, my mother

Kathleen A. Montgomery

❖ Contents

viii

❖ Preface

We began our odyssey with this book nearly five years ago in Chicago at a panel on 'Electoral Rules and Female Representation in Post-Communist Europe' that Kathleen had organized for the Midwest Political Science Association's annual meeting. Richard had been working on issues of institutional design and women's representation and was eager to explore the implications of his research in a novel context. Kathleen came at the material from an interest in democratization processes and post-communism more generally. These different backgrounds proved complementary. As discussant, Richard pointed the panel toward the rich body of general theory regarding female legislative recruitment. Kathleen and the other panelists sought to test the applicability of those theories in the unique circumstances of post-communist democratization. The possibility of a book exploring these themes developed over the exchange generated by the panel. Over the ensuing years we have fleshed out the basic structure and approach in an iterative process. It has been a fully collaborative effort at every stage.

When we began, we were both struck by the dearth of writing about women's participation in Eastern European politics and by the emphasis, in the writing that did exist, on the failure of East European women to form Western-style pro-equality feminist movements. Important as we believe that was (and is), we agreed that existing studies had paid too little attention to the possibility of *institutional remedies* to women's under-representation. We also agreed it was time to look at the post-communist European countries as (developing) democracies, to test whether factors identified by Western scholars would explain variations in women's access to political power. Our aim was twofold: to better understand developments in the individual countries of Eastern Europe, and to test the robustness of the existing theories in a new set of countries.

One of the crucial beliefs driving our work is that institutions matter. They do not matter exclusively, but they do matter. Much of the writing on women and politics in Eastern Europe has emphasized the importance of post-communist political culture, a culture that combines a strong patriarchal tradition with the residual effects of directive emancipation. The analyses in this book suggest culture plays a role in determining the relative supply of and demand for female candidates, but those effects are tempered by political institutions—in particular, the design of electoral system and the characteristics of the emerging parties and party systems.

We do not believe that institutions exclusively determine outcomes. Furthermore, this is not what the chapters in this volume show. We do believe, however, that institutional choices can noticeably improve or weaken the chances for women to gain access to political power. This message has not been considered sufficiently often when analysing the new democracies of Eastern Europe, though it does much to explain the wide diversity in recruitment outcomes across the region. Like other studies, we find evidence of some broad cultural effects that are common across all of these countries, but there is also considerable evidence that political factors alter the impact of this legacy. This book contains important contributions concerning the contemporary situation in individual countries and seeks to inspire investigators to undertake further investigation of the internal political dynamics in all of these nascent democracies.

In the course of developing a project of this scope, we have naturally accumulated a number of intellectual and personal debts. This book stands on the shoulders of the many scholars cited in its pages. In addition, a crucial step in the process of developing this book was a conference organized by Richard and held at the University of Bergen in Norway 28–29 May 1999. This international conference on Women's Representation in Eastern Europe brought together some 50 scholars from Eastern Europe, Western Europe, and the United States. Without the conference this book would not have been possible. We wish to thank the Research Council of Norway (NFR), the Nordic Academy for Advanced Study (NorFA), the city of Bergen and the University of Bergen for their support. At the University of Bergen we would especially like to thank the university rector, Kirsti Koch Christensen, who provided economic support and opened the conference. After listening to 25 papers presented over the two days, we approached a dozen of the scholars present at the conference and asked if they would be willing to participate in the development of this book. They all agreed, and this book represents the end product of those efforts. Along the way we have added two scholars from countries that were not represented at the conference to provide as broad a spectrum of countries as possible.

We have in no small measure also benefited from tolerant and understanding authors, editors, research assistants, and family. We would first like to thank our chapter authors. The chapter authors were willing to go more than the extra mile, even when it meant four or five drafts, to produce the strongest product possible. We have developed friendships and collaborative relationships that we expect to carry well into the future. We also would like to thank the series editors, Karen Beckwith and Joni Lovenduski, for their support.

Kathleen would like to thank Sarah Fuller, Josip Glaurdic, Gretchen Grabowski, and Justin Taylor for their research and editorial assistance at Illinois Wesleyan University. She would also like to thank the Faculty Development Committee at Illinois Wesleyan University for their generous research support. Richard would like to thank Adrian Shepherd, Crys Lewis, and Michelle LeBlanc at the University of Houston for their assistance. He would also like to thank the University of Houston Women's Studies Program for summer support that helped provide the time to finish the manuscript.

Finally, we want to thank our families. Kathleen would like to thank her husband Frank Boyd, as a partner (for giving her the time and freedom to pursue this project) and as a political scientist (for listening to and critiquing the arguments set forth in the book). She'd also like to thank her children, who came into being coterminously with the book. Alston was born just before the Midwest conference and Bronwen attended the Bergen conference three months before she was born. They have provided a poignant reminder of why gender politics and this project should have occupied her time and imagination over the past several years. Richard would like to thank his wife, Aud, for her patience and understanding. He would like to thank his daughters, Nora and Emma, for providing relief from and inspiration for the project. As citizens of both the US and Europe they have impressed him with their ability to adapt, to understand, and to appreciate the diversity they face across countries. Hopefully, their future will be one of increased progress for women throughout Europe and the rest of the world.

❖ List of Figures

❖ List of Tables

❖ LIST OF TABLES

❖ List of Abbreviations

General Abbreviations

CPSU	Communist Party of the Soviet Union
ENP	Effective Number of Parties
EU	European Union
GDP	Gross Domestic Product
KPRF	Communist Party of the Russian Federation
LDCs	Lesser Developed Countries
MMP	Mixed Member Proportional
LR-Hare	Largest Remainder-Hare Formula
MP	Member of Parliament
NGOs	Non-Governmental Organizations
PR	Proportional representation
SMD	Single Member District

Bulgaria

BBB	Bulgarian Business Block
BCP	Bulgarian Communist Party
BSP	Bulgarian Socialist Party
BWP	Bulgarian Women's Party
MRF	Movement for Rights and Freedoms
NMSII	National Movement Simeon II
UDF	Union of Democratic Forces

Croatia

BaBe	Be Active, Be Emancipated
HDS	Croatian Democratic Party
HDZ	Croatian Democratic Union
HKDU	Croatian Christian Democratic Union
HND	Croatian Independent Democrats
HNS	Croatian People's Party
HSLS	Croatian Social Liberal Party
HSP	Croatian Rights Party
HSS	Croatian Peasants' Party

SDFZ	Social Democratic Women's Forum
SDP	Social Democratic Party
SDU	Social Democratic Union

Czech Republic

ČSSD	Czech Social Democratic Party
ČSZ	Czech Union of Women
KDU-ČSL	Christian Democratic Union—Czech People's Party
KSČM	Communist Party of Bohemia and Moravia
ODS	Civic Democratic Forum
SDZ	Social Democratic Women's Organization
SPR-RSČ	Republicans
US	Freedom Union

Germany

CDU	Christian Democrats
CSU	Christian Social Union
FDP	Free Democrats
GDR	German Democratic Republic (East Germany)
PDS	Democratic Socialists
SPD	Social Democrats

Hungary

AFD	Alliance of Free Democrats
CDPP	Christian Democratic People's Party
Fidesz-MPP	Young Democrats-Civic Party
FKgP	Independent Smallholder's Party
HDF	Hungarian Democratic Forum
HJLP	Hungarian Justice and Life Party
HSP	Hungarian Socialist Party
ISP	Independent Smallholders' Party
KDNP	Christian Democratic People's Party
MDF	Hungarian Democratic Forum
MIÉP	Hungarian Justice and Life Party
MONA	Foundation of the Women of Hungary
MSzP	Hungarian Socialist Party
SzDSz	Free Democrats/Alliance of Free Democrats Party

Lithuania

HU	Homeland Union
LC	Lithuanian Conservatives
LCDP	Lithuanian Christian Democratic Party
LCU	Lithuanian Central Union

LCWA	Lithuanian Catholic Women's Association
LDLP	Lithuanian Democratic Labour Party
LLU	Lithuanian Liberal Union
LSDP	Lithuanian Social Democratic Party
ULR	Union of Lithuanian Russians
WP	Women's Party

Macedonia

PDP	Party for Democratic Prosperity
PDPA	Party for Democratic Prosperity of the Albanians
SDSM	Social-Democratic Alliance of Macedonia
SDYM	Social-Democratic Youth of Macedonia
VMRO-DPMNE	International Macedonian Revolutionary Organization–Democratic Party for Macedonian National Unity

Poland

AWS	Electoral Action Solidarity
BBWR	Non-Party Block in Support of Reforms
BdP	National Christian Bloc for Poland
KLD	Liberal-Democratic Congress
KPN	Confederation of Independent Poland
LPR	League of Polish Families
MN	Social and Cultural Society of the German Minority in Silesia
PC	Civic Centre Alliance
PChD	Party of Christian Democrats
PiS	Law and Justice
PO	Civic Platform
PSL	Polish Peasant Party
PSL-PL	Polish Peasant Party–Popular Agreement
PUWP	Polish United Worker's Party
ROP	Movement for the Reconstruction of Poland
SdRP	Social Democracy of the Republic of Poland
SLD	Democratic Left Alliance
SLD-UP	Alliance of Democratic Left/Labour Union
SO	Self-Defense of the Polish Republic
UD	Democratic Union
UP	Labour Union/Union of Labour
UPR	Union of the Republic Right
UW	Freedom Union
WPG	Women's Parliamentary Group
WAK	Electoral Catholic Action

Russia

CPSU	Communist Party of the Soviet Union
LDPR	Liberal Democratic Party of Russia
non-KPRF	Other Communist Parties
NPSR	People's Party of Free Russia
KPRF	Communist Party of the Russian Federation
RKRP	Russian Communist Workers Party
URW	Union of Russia's Women
WOR	Women of Russia

Slovenia

DeSUS	Democratic Pensioners Party of Slovenia
DS	Democrats of Slovenia
LDS	Liberal Democracy of Slovenia
LS	Liberal Party
NSi	New Slovenia
SDS	Social Democratic Party
SDZ	Slovenian Democratic Alliance
SKD	Slovenian Christian Democrats
SLS	Slovenian People's Party
SMS	Party of Young People
SNS	Slovenian National Party
SZS	Socialist Alliance of Slovenia
ZLSD	United List of Social Democrats
ZS	Greens of Slovenia

Ukraine

NDP	Popular Democratic Party
SDP(u)	Social Democratic Party United
SelPU	Rural Party
SLOn	Social Liberal Union

❖ Notes on Contributors

MILICA ANTIĆ is Assistant Professor in the Faculty of Arts (Sociology Department) and a researcher at the Peace Institute at the University of Ljubljana, Slovenia. She also teaches in the Department of Gender Studies at the Central European University in Budapest, Hungary. She is co-founder of the interdisciplinary graduate studies program in Women's Studies and Feminist Theory at the University of Ljubljana. She has published widely in English and Slovenian on a range of contemporary women's issues and feminist thought. She is currently engaged in research projects dealing with strategies for enhancing the position of women in Slovene politics and a comparison of equal opportunity policies in East and Central Europe.

SARAH BIRCH is currently a Lecturer in the Department of Government, University of Essex. Her research interests include electoral systems and democratization (with special reference to Eastern Europe). She has published widely on these topics. Her most recent publications include *Embodying Democracy: Electoral System Design in Post-Communist Europe* (co-author, Palgrave, 2002); 'Two-Round Electoral Systems and Democracy', *Comparative Political Studies*, 2003; and *Elections and Democratization in Ukraine* (Macmillan 2000). She was awarded the Lord Bryce Prize for best doctoral dissertation in Comparative Politics in 1998 by the Political Studies Association of the United Kingdom (1999).

JOANNE BAY BRZINSKI is currently Associate Dean of Academic Affairs and Adjunct Professor of Political Science at Emory University in Atlanta, Georgia. She has recently co-edited special issues on federalism and representation in Western Europe in *Publius: The Journal of Federalism* (December 1999) and *West European Politics* (April 1999). She has published on developing federalist structures in Europe and the role of the European Union.

JOSIP GLAURDIC is a Sterling Fellow in Yale University's doctoral program in political science. His research interests include comparative politics, institutions and democratic transitions, and Eastern European politics. He is Research Assistant for the project, 'Global Data Set of Political Institutions,' funded by the Carnegie Globalization Project and Yale Centre for International and Area Studies.

GABRIELLA ILONSZKI is Associate Professor in the Department of Political Science at the Budapest University of Economic Sciences. Her research has emphasized issues of party development in new democracies including candidate recruitment and representational roles. She is the author of numerous articles and book chapters in both Hungarian and English. Her research has appeared in the *Journal of Communist and Post-Communist Studies*, *Journal of Theoretical Politics* and *Legislative Studies Quarterly*. In 1999, she served as Mellon Research Fellow at the Institute of Human Sciences, Vienna. From 1997 to 1999, she held a NATO Research Grant.

TATIANA KOSTADINOVA is Assistant Professor in Political Science at the University of Minnesota Duluth. Among her main research interests are institutional reform and the effects of electoral systems on representation and voter behaviour. Her publications include *Bulgaria 1879–1946: The Challenge of Choice* (Columbia University Press, 1995) and a chapter on institutional design and ethnic strife in *Diversity in Adversity: Propensities for Ethno-National Conflict in Contemporary Eastern Europe* (University of Bologna, 2001). She has also published articles on mixed electoral systems and East European support for international institutions in *Electoral Studies* and *Journal of Peace Research*.

ALGIS KRUPAVIČIUS is Associate Professor at the Kaunas University of Technology and Vytautas Magnus University in Kaunas, Lithuania. From 1991 to 1995 he served as President and co-founder of the Lithuanian Political Science Foundation. He has been a Visiting Professor at Northwestern University in the United States and the Copenhagen Peace Research Institute. He has published in *Political Studies*, *Electoral Studies*, and the *European Journal of Political Research*. He has also written and edited books on Lithuanian politics. His most recent book is *Party Systems in Central East Europe: Dimensions of System Stability* (University of Strathclyde, 1999).

RICHARD MATLAND is Associate Professor of Political Science at the University of Houston and adjunct Professor in the Department of Administration and Organization Theory at the University of Bergen in Bergen, Norway. He has written extensively on Women and Politics with an emphasis on the role of electoral institutions on women's representation. His work has appeared in the *American Journal of Political Science*, *British Journal of Political Science*, *Journal of Politics*, *Canadian Journal of Political Science*. *Comparative Political Studies*, *Political Research Quarterly*, and *Legislative Studies Quarterly*. He has also served on the executive committee of the Women and Politics section of the American Political Science Association and presently serves on the editorial board of *Women and Politics*.

IRMINA MATONYTĖ is Associate Professor of Political Science at Kaunas University of Technology. She received her doctorate in political sociology in 1999 from Vytautas Magnus University in Kaunas, Lithuania. Among her research interests are questions of women's integration in politics in the Baltic region, the democratization process in the Baltic states, and the role of economic and political elites in the newly democratizing countries.

KATHLEEN MONTGOMERY is Associate Professor of Political Science at Illinois Wesleyan University in Bloomington, Illinois. Her research focuses on legislative politics, particularly institutional development in the new post-communist democracies. Her articles have been published in *Party Politics* and *The Journal of Communist Studies and Transition Politics*. She also contributes a chapter on Hungarian politics to Gabriel A. Almond, Russell J. Dalton, and G. Bingham Powell, Jr. (eds), *European Politics Today*.

ROBERT MOSER is Associate Professor of Government at the University of Texas at Austin. His primary research interests are electoral systems, political parties, and representation in Russia and other post-communist states. He is the author of *Unexpected Outcomes: Electoral Systems, Political Parties, and Representation in Russia* (Pittsburgh: University of Pittsburgh Press, 2001) and the co-editor (with Zoltan Barany) of *Russian Politics: Challenges of Democratization* (Cambridge: Cambridge University Press, 2001). His articles have appeared in *World Politics, Comparative Politics, Electoral Studies*, and *Post-Soviet Affairs*. He has also contributed chapters to several edited volumes.

DAWN NOWACKI is Associate Professor of Political Science at Linfield College in McMinnville, Oregon. Her research interests include the recruitment and representation of marginalized groups (women and minorities) in the regional parliaments of the Russian Federation and comparative nationalism in the post-Soviet states. She formerly worked as a research analyst for Radio Free Europe/Radio Liberty and as the assistant editor of *Central Asian Survey*.

KAROLINA RISTOVA is a junior assistant professor at the Faculty of Law 'Justnijan Prvi' Skopje, University St. Cyril and Methodius in Skopje, Macedonia. She has published in scholarly journals and popular press on a range of issues, including EU enlargement toward Central and Eastern Europe, transition to democracy, and gender issues. She also serves as a member of parliament, having been elected to parliament in the fall 2002 elections.

STEVEN SAXONBERG is Associate Professor of political science at Dalarna University in Sweden. He is author of *The Fall: A Comparative Study of the End of Communism in Czechoslovakia, East Germany, Hungary and Poland* (Harwood Academic/Routledge, 2001) and *The Czech Republic Before the New Millennium* (forthcoming in East European Monographs/Columbia University Press). His work has appeared in the *Journal of Democracy, East European Politics and Society, Problems of Post-Communism,* and *Czech*

Sociological Review. He has also been a regular contributor to journals such as *New Presence: The Prague Journal of Central European Affairs, Briské Listy,* and *Central European Review.*

RENATA SIEMIEŃSKA is Professor and Head of the Department of Sociology of Education, Institute of Sociology, University of Warsaw. She also holds the titles 'UNESCO Chair of Women, Society, and Development' and 'Head of the Interdisciplinary Research Division of Gender Studies' at the Institute of Social Studies. She publishes widely on gender issues and Polish politics in international journals, edited volumes, monograph series, and reports for international organizations (UNESCO, United Nations, Council of Europe, and OECD).

BETH STARK is an American government doctoral candidate at Georgetown University. Her dissertation research focuses on the role of civic culture in women's political participation.

SUE THOMAS, formerly Associate Professor and Director of Women's Studies at Georgetown University, is currently a researcher in Santa Cruz, California. Her scholarly interests centre on women and politics. She has published widely in professional journals and her books include *How Women Legislate* and *Elective Office: Past, Present, and Future,* both by Oxford University Press. Most recently, she has concentrated on women's health issues, including fetal alcohol syndrome.

CLYDE WILCOX is Professor of Government at Georgetown University. He has written and edited numerous books and published articles on gender politics, religion and politics, and campaign finance. His work in the gender politics area includes research on gender differences in public opinion, abortion rights, and feminism in both the American and the comparative European areas. His work has appeared in *Comparative Political Studies, European Journal of Political Research, International Journal of Public Opinion Research, Journal of Politics, Political Research Quarterly,* and *Women and Politics* among other journals. Since 1990, he has served on the editorial board of *Women and Politics.*

1 ❖ Introduction

Kathleen A. Montgomery

The last decade of the twentieth century began with multi-party elections throughout what had once seemed an immutable communist-authoritarian bloc. That moment offered the hope of establishing truly representative and gender-equal democracy in the region. After all, the state socialist regimes had accomplished high levels of female education, labour force participation, and political representation, achievements that might have been expected to endow women with the resources necessary to compete in free elections. Moreover, the stakes seemed clear. If women did not demand and achieve a significant presence in the new centres of decision-making power, emergent nationalist and neo-conservative forces would shape democracy according to patriarchal assumptions; and women would lose the reproductive, employment, and social welfare rights granted under communism.

With hindsight, it is clear that women in the state socialist regimes were poorly placed to '... influence the State and the newly active political parties during the very rapid collapse of the old order...' (Waylen 1994: 347). Men founded and assumed leadership of the new political parties. Men negotiated the rules of the democratic game, and men filled the new halls of power. Women's share in national parliaments plummeted from a regional average of around 30 per cent to less than 10 per cent, in several countries below 5 per cent (see Fig. 1.1).

This decline signified more than a one-time rejection of those with experience in politics, among them women who had served in parliament, or a voter backlash against communist policies that included the 'directive emancipation' of women. More than a decade after founding democratic elections in the region, the mean level of female representation, at around 12 per cent, remained slightly below the world average (14 per cent) and well below the Western European mean (25 per cent).[1] Women also remain virtually absent from party leaderships, cabinet positions, key ministries,[2] and institutions of social bargaining (Iankova 1996).

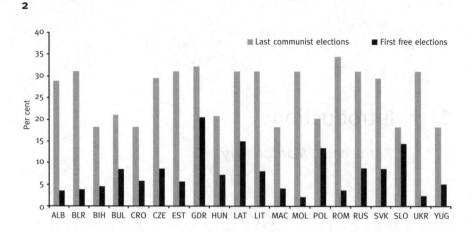

Figure 1.1. Democracy and the decline in female legislative representation

Countries included are Albania, Belarus, Bosnia-Herzegovina, Bulgaria, Croatia, Czech Republic, Estonia, Germany, Hungary, Latvia, Lithuania, Macedonia, Moldova, Poland, Romania, Russia, Slovakia, Slovenia, Ukraine, Yugoslavia

Notes:

(1) Figure includes all countries that emerged from the Soviet Bloc except the Central Asian and Trans-Caucasian states of the Former Soviet Union.

(2) For Belarus, Estonia, Latvia, Lithuania, Moldova, the Russian Federation, and Ukraine, the 'last communist elections' figure represents the 1984 elections for the lower chamber of the USSR's Supreme Soviet.

(3) The figures for Czech Republic and Slovakia are for united Czechoslovakia.

(4) For Bosnia and Herzegovina, Croatia, the Former Yugoslav Republic of Macedonia, Slovenia, and the Federal Republic of Yugoslavia, the 'last communist elections' figure represents the elections to the joint Yugoslav legislature.

The research compiled in this volume seeks to explain these trends in the period that, for want of a better term, we will refer to as 'democratic consolidation'.[3] This emphasis sets our work apart from previous studies that have focused explicitly (or by default) on the period that includes the old regime's collapse and the advent of multi-party elections (e.g. Einhorn 1993; Funk and Mueller 1993; Waylen 1994; Jaquette and Wolchik 1998). We also differ from existing studies in the extent to which we draw upon the extensive Western literature on women's legislative recruitment. All individual case studies test the propositions set forth in a common theoretical framework derived from that literature; and all use a combination of quantitative and qualitative research methods to analyse novel empirical data. This approach allows us to extend our current understanding about the general factors that help and hinder female representation. The book therefore stands as a significant contribution to the empirical political science literature and to the general study of legislatures, recruitment, and gender politics. It also provides unprecedented leverage on intra-region comparisons and thereby enhances our accounts of

❖ KATHLEEN A. MONTGOMERY

gender politics in societies that are undergoing profound social, political, and economic transformations.

❖ THE PRESENCE OF WOMEN IN PARLIAMENT MATTERS

Most students of democratization have either overlooked gender entirely or treated the decline in female representation as a return to 'normal politics' in the region.[4] When communist parties lost hegemonic control over recruitment, voters used their franchise to select candidates with desirable socio-economic and political capital—as it turns out, the same kinds of candidates valued by Western electorates. Early surveys in the region suggest that post-communist citizens did not see the decline in female faces as a real loss in terms of women's effective voice in politics (Buckley 1992; Einhorn 1993; Lapidus 1993).

Western feminists were hardly so sanguine. Very early on, they decried the establishment of 'male democracy' in the region (Eisenstein 1993) and 'reproached East Central European women for being apolitical and not understanding their own oppression and interests' (Gal and Kligman 2000: 99–100). Much of the early feminist debate revolved around the puzzle that East European women had failed to mobilize a proper feminist movement. Since then, differences between Eastern and Western definitions of feminism have been thoroughly analysed (Funk and Mueller 1993; Marody 1993; Renne 1997); and feminist scholarship has turned to the question of whether women are better off now—with liberal economic and political structures—than they were under state socialist rule.

We argue that both interpretations fail to apprehend important aspects of the relationship between democratization and women's access to power in the post-communist systems. It is self-evident that opportunities for political access are greater in a democratic regime than an authoritarian one. The issue is whether the apertures are relatively generous or penurious for women. In other words, what determines the extent to which a newly emerging democracy is 'woman-friendly'? This is a question about the *quality* of democracy that is taking root after socialism; and here the feminist warnings about 'male democracy' ought to resonate.

Studies in the Western democracies show that women's presence in legislatures makes a difference. Perhaps the most expansive claim is that a substantial level of women in elected office leads to the enactment of woman-friendly policies (Lijphart 1991; Thomas 1991). This position is controversial, because correlation does not prove causality and definitions of 'woman-friendliness' vary widely. What is clearer is the presence of women shapes the legislative agenda. Women may differ widely among themselves about the desirability of particular policies, but they share a common emphasis on family and child-related issues, and they tend to focus more on issues of gender equality than do men. When women reach a critical mass in legislatures, they can help to get those issues onto the agenda (Norris and Lovenduski 1989; Saint-Germain 1989; Skjeie 1991; Welch and Thomas 1991; Tamerius 1995; Dodson 1998; Bratton and Ray 2002).

Transitions from communist authoritarianism lead to a significant restructuring of relations between citizens and the state. Since post-communist women occupy distinct social roles and structural positions in the economy, they can be expected to prioritize a distinct set of policies. Without a substantial female presence in elected offices, however, those issues are not being treated seriously; they are being pushed aside as irrelevant compared to the exigencies of dual economic and political transitions. Male dominated party hierarchies often reduce women's issues to a set of consumer demands. As a result, party platforms exhort women to be patient and wait for the fruits of successful marketization to relieve their dual burdens, presumably with a wider availability of consumer goods. Meanwhile, women's reproductive rights are being curtailed, state welfare is being rolled back, women are being left behind or on the periphery of economic growth, and the numbers of women and children in poverty are growing (e.g. Corrin 1992, 1994*a,b*; Moghadam 1992; Funk and Mueller 1993; Matynia 1994; Wejnert 1996; Meurs 1998; Rueschemeyer 1998*a*; LaFont 1999, 2001; Goven 2000).

The absence of women in parliament has systemic consequences as well. Where '...all citizens are seen to have an equal opportunity to participate in the decision-making that affects their lives, there is a greater likelihood that the polity will be stable and that citizens will have a reasonable degree of trust in and support for it' (Thomas 1998). Where women do not have access to that kind of participation, a clear message is sent about the value of their citizenship. Political exclusion infantilizes women (Phillips 1993), compounds gender stereotypes, and retards progress toward social equality more generally (Reynolds 1999). That, in turn, raises questions about the accountability, responsiveness, and legitimacy of democratic governance.

We should not be much comforted by the observation that eastern European women are 'becoming political' below the national level (Regulska 1998) and outside of formal arenas, via non-governmental organizations (NGOs) and behind the scenes in party hierarchies (Corrin 1994; Racioppi and See 1995; Haney 1997; Gal and Kligman 2000). While it is certainly true that women are political in many unheralded ways, and women's informal political activity may produce tectonic changes in attitudes toward gender roles, it is nevertheless also the case that political power in a democracy resides in formal institutions. In Eastern Europe, parliaments have served as *the central sites* for the resolution of major national issues (Ágh 1994; Judge 1994; Olson and Norton 1996) and have been the focus of popular expectations for

❖ KATHLEEN A. MONTGOMERY

democratization (Mishler and Rose 1994). Parliaments matter and women's representation in them makes a difference. We should not passively accept that Eastern Europe has somehow returned to normal when that equilibrium involves the significant political exclusion of women.

Neither, however, should we treat female under-representation as a phenomenon sui generis to post-communism, as some feminists and area scholars do. Only a handful of Western countries consistently produce greater than one-third female legislative representation. Furthermore, women worldwide are under-represented in executives, party leaderships, and prestige ministries and committees (IPU 1997; Reynolds 1999). Critics have long charged that 'liberal democracy does not serve women well' (Phillips 1993: 103), and all of the post-communist countries have embraced liberal political and economic models. Why, then, should we blame the presence of political inequality in the post-communist democracies on the 'backwardness' of East European women or any other peculiar legacy of communist gender politics?

To do so is not only unfair—large feminist movements are rare in the world[5]—it also diverts our attention away from important questions about what is helping and hindering women's access to political power across the region. Rather than continuing to lament male democracy or rehearse all that women have lost in transition, we want to know: 'What specific rules, arrangements, or practices are most likely to provide women with access to significant positions of political authority...' as democracy consolidates in the region (Schmitter 1998: 223). What explains the wide and growing differences in women's access to power across post-communist cases and across elections over time? Answers to these questions will extend our existing theories about women's representation and will help answer a question of classical interest to political scientists: What can be done?

❖ GENDER EQUALITY IN POLITICS: PREREQUISITES OR POLITICAL CHOICES?

The general literature on women and politics employs three major sets of variables to explain cross-national variations in the level of female legislative representation: political, socioeconomic, and cultural. Most studies focus on the twenty-five or so most affluent and long-standing democracies and find that political factors (the design of electoral rules and party characteristics) hold the greatest explanatory power (for a critique, see Kenworthy and Malami 1999). Studies of lesser developed countries (LDCs), by contrast, tend to emphasize socioeconomic and cultural barriers to women's representation, such as low levels of female education and workforce participation, poverty,[6] and inegalitarian social values that may be reinforced through powerful Catholic, Muslim, or Orthodox churches. Recent large-N studies that sample across regions, however, find evidence in support of all three clusters (Kenworthy and Malami 1999; Reynolds 1999). Norris and Inglehart (2000) have recently argued for the independent effects of cultural variables across a sample of 55 countries.

The relative emphasis placed on different sets of factors depends in large measure on whether the researcher sees political equality as a product of certain social and cultural prerequisites or as primarily the consequence of incentives created by institutional and political choices.[7] Most likely, the two interact and shape one another. Once adopted, political institutions such as electoral rules may develop inertia or become 'sticky', but they are still far more malleable than the cultural and developmental attributes of a nation. If we want to 'fix' male democracy in the new democracies of Eastern Europe, adopting woman-friendly institutions may be one way to do that. Institutions, however, do not operate in a vacuum. Their selection is shaped by cultural and historical trajectories of development; and the same institutions may perform very differently when planted in different soil.

The way that politics, culture, and socioeconomic development interact deserves greater attention in the literature, and the consolidating post-communist democracies would seem to offer an ideal laboratory in which to weigh their effects. That discussion, however, is notably absent in the post-communist region, where area scholars and feminists have focussed almost exclusively on the cultural and socioeconomic legacies of communist gender policies.[8]

Those policies were never homogeneous. Communist leaders (and ideology) were deeply ambivalent and often contradictory on the so-called 'woman question,' and policies varied widely according to local conditions. Nevertheless, most scholars agree that communist gender policies failed to uproot traditional gender hierarchies. Extensive welfare programs allowed women to work, but female labour was concentrated in lower pay and lower prestige sectors; and women were still expected to perform the bulk of household and childrearing duties. Political participation was mandatory and quotas ensured that there would be female faces in parliament; but the legislatures themselves served as rubber stamps for decisions made in the top echelons of party and state power, places where women were notably absent. Communism usurped the language of feminist emancipation, but in praxis women were marginalized across economic, political, and social spheres (Scott 1973, 1976; Heitlinger 1979; Wolchik 1981; Wolchik and Meyer 1985). As a result, women found themselves at a structural disadvantage vis-à-vis men in competitive elections; and feminism was thoroughly discredited as an ideology and basis for political action.

Taken together, this multi-faceted legacy does much to explain the failure of women to mobilize during the critical window of opportunity presented by the collapse of the old order. It also helps us to account for the initial decline

❖ Kathleen A. Montgomery

in female legislative representation in the post-communist region. Women, eager to shed one of their many burdens and primed in some cases by anti-political roles in the democratic opposition,[9] voluntarily withdrew from the public sphere. At the same time, voters regarded women who aspired to elected office with suspicion, as lacking the time, experience, and skills to do the job.[10]

Those two central hypotheses (that women do not want to enter the candidate pool and that voters reject women at the ballot box) seem plausible enough, but they have yet to be tested systematically. Moreover, the emphasis on a common socialist inheritance leaves some important questions unanswered. How, for example, can this common 'push-jump' response account for considerable variations within the region? One answer is that communist countries varied in the degree they could deliver on their promises of female emancipation. Directive emancipation was far more successful in the GDR than it was in the Balkans.

To be sure, countries emerged from socialist rule in different economic and political positions, and that has had implications for the nature and extent of gender inequality in the post-communist period. Women fare worse in poor countries, in places where the nation-State has ceased to function, and where there is no working party system. But, those factors may inhibit women in any poor capitalist system. They do not need to be understood primarily in terms of post-communism.

The emphasis on a common legacy provides even less traction on the problem of change over time. Jaquette and Wolchik (1998), noting the overall trend of improvement in the region, predict a convergence between the levels of representation achieved in Eastern Europe and those accomplished in the new democracies of Latin America, where a mobilized women's movement placed pressure on the state and newly organized parties to recruit women. Barbara Einhorn (1993) similarly suggests that once women realize that what they have lost constitutes citizenship rights, they will mobilize to demand a greater share of political power. These authors, however, focus primarily on the early transition period. As a result, they do not have much to say about why some post-communist countries are improving more than others or *the specific mechanisms and practices* that are leading to improvement.

These are matters of central concern to this study. Table 1.1 presents data on the percentage of seats held by women in the lower (or only) chamber of parliament over the past decade. Since the demise of the Soviet Bloc, the share of female MPs in Croatia, Bulgaria, and Poland have improved to the point that they better the level in many affluent and long-standing Western democracies.[11] In most places, however, the record is less even. Women in Russia have lost ground, and many countries in Table 1.1 show fluctuations over time. Still, the very fact that some post-communist countries have been able to post relatively high levels of female representation provides a hopeful indication that something can be done to make neo-democracies more woman-friendly.

Table 1.1. Female parliamentary representation across post-communist elections (%)

Country	First election	Second election	Third election	Fourth election	Fifth election	Change from first to most recent
Albania	3.6	5.7	12.1	5.7		+2.1
Armenia	3.7	6.3	3.1			−0.6
Azerbaijan	2.0	10.5	10.5			+8.5
Belarus[1]	3.8	?	10.3			+6.5
Bosnia–Herzegovina	4.5	?	7.1	28.6	7.1	+2.6
Bulgaria	8.8	13.8	12.9	10.4	26.3	+17.5
Croatia	5.8	7.9	20.5			+14.7
Czech Rep.	10.0	10.0	15.0	15.0	17.0	+7.0
Estonia	5.7	12.9	17.8			+12.1
Georgia	6.3	6.8	7.2			+0.9
Germany (w/former GDR)	20.5	26.2	30.9	31.7		+11.2
Hungary	7.3	11.4	8.3	9.1		+1.8
Kazakhstan[1]	6.7	11.9	10.4			+3.7
Kyrgyzstan	6.3	4.9	1.4	10.0		+3.7
Latvia	15.0	9.0	17.0			+2.0
Lithuania	9.9	7.1	17.5	10.6		+0.7
Macedonia	4.2	3.3	7.5			+3.2
Moldova	2.1	4.8	12.9	8.9		+6.8
Poland	13.5	9.1	13.0	13.0	20.2	+6.7
Romania	3.6	4.1	7.0	10.7		+7.1
Russian Federation	8.7	13.4	10.2	7.6		−1.1
Tajikistan[1]	3.0	2.8	12.7			+9.7
Turkmenistan[1]	4.6	18.0	26.0			+21.4
Slovakia	12.0[2]	15.0	13.0	14.0		+5.3
Slovenia	13.3	7.8	13.3			0.0
Ukraine	3.0	4.3	7.9	4.9		+1.9
Uzbekistan[1]	9.6	6.0	7.2			−2.4
Yugoslavia	2.5	2.8	7.3			+4.8

Sources: Inter-Parliamentary Union, 'Reports and Documents' No. 23, on-line data updated June 2002.

Notes:
Bold indicates the case is included in this volume.
? data were not available.
First election: Russia (1990 Supreme Soviet election), other countries of former Soviet Union (Supreme Soviet of SSR elections in 1990), Slovakia (1990 election of Slovak National Council), Poland (partly free elections of 1989), countries of former Yugoslav Federation (first post-independence elections).
[1] Countries deemed 'not free' in Freedom House Survey of Freedom Country Scores, 1999–2000.
[2] This was the 1990 election to the Slovak National Council. Slovakia was still a part of the Czechoslovak Federation until 1993.

✧ KATHLEEN A. MONTGOMERY

The real question, then, is *what?* What electoral institutions work to promote equality for women as democracy consolidates in the post-communist countries? Do our predictions for the woman-friendliness of particular electoral rules hold in the novel context of post-communist democracy? What role (if any) are non-governmental organizations having on the demand for women in office and the ability of women to penetrate male-dominated party and legislative hierarchies? What affect does the desire to enter Western institutions have on attitudes and practices regarding gender equity in politics? Are women, in fact, being rejected by voters at the ballot box, as so much of the area literature suggests? Or, are there other more significant obstacles to women's representation in the region? As party systems develop and parties institutionalize, are some parties emerging as more woman-friendly than others are? Are these the same kinds of parties that we would consider 'women friendly' in the West? Finally, how do the answers to these questions vary across the countries of post-communist Europe, influenced perhaps by growing socio-cultural differences and wide disparities in the success of economic and political transition?

It is tempting to treat the post-communist region as homogeneous, to compare it with the West and conclude that it lags behind due to the experience of communist gender policies; but post-communism is not a static condition. If the countries of the region ever shared an approach to gender, it is clear they no longer do. Cultural, religious, and economic differences, once masked by the appearance of a monolithic bloc, have come into the open and grown wide, accompanied by new institutional diversity. How do those differences shape the attitudes of voters and party gatekeepers and the opportunities for women across this increasingly diverse region? What is the relative role of political choice as opposed to socio-cultural and economic prerequisites in explaining the level of political inequality in post-communist Europe?

❖ STRUCTURE AND PLAN OF THE VOLUME

In order to address those questions, the present volume begins by elaborating a general framework on legislative recruitment, drawn primarily from the Western political science literature. Stated briefly, the framework posits that the level of female recruitment in a particular legislature is a function of the relative supply of qualified female aspirants and the demand for female candidates among those empowered to confer a party's nomination (party gatekeepers) and voters. Relative levels of supply and demand are determined by a combination of political, cultural, and socioeconomic development factors noted earlier.

Central to the model is the prediction that, *ceteris paribus*, women will fare best in proportional representation (PR) elections with large magnitude multi-member constituencies, a high electoral threshold, and affirmative action (quotas). We expect to find this in the post-communist context, though it is clear that gender was not a foremost concern in the debates surrounding institutional design in the region.[12]

Institutions, however, can only do so much. PR electoral rules introduce the logic of ticket balancing and reduce the zero-sum nature of political contests, but parties will only choose to balance their tickets with women if there is significant pressure for them to do so. The level of pressure may depend on characteristics of the party system and given parties within it, as well as a variety of developmental and cultural factors. This is where a country's pathway from communism and its specific experiences of communist gender policies may be applied. These experiences and the way they have shaped gender attitudes and practices, as well as the country's position in the world economy, may be expected to affect both the supply and demand sides of the equation.

Chapter 3 takes up the issue of demand directly by analysing cross-national data on attitudes toward feminism in the region. The authors confirm what feminists have already lamented: in terms of the attitudes Westerners typically associate with feminism, East European electorates are far less egalitarian than their Western counterparts. This would seem to bode ill for the formation of pro-equality women's movements and by extension the improvement of women's representation in the region. Yet, we are faced with the empirical fact that some countries are improving their levels of female representation.

We can interpret these apparently dissonant findings in a variety of ways. It is possible that women are mobilizing in some countries more effectively than they are in others or that voters in some countries are becoming less sexist. It may be that sexist voters matter far less than we might expect and that other factors—the recruitment practices of parties and the structure of political opportunities—matter far more. Perhaps the linkage between organized feminism and female legislative representation is simply less fixed than early feminist studies in the region suggested. The authors of Chapter 3 juxtapose widespread anti-feminist attitudes with high levels of support for 'the women's movement' across the region and suggest that women may be mobilizing from the political right. This would be consistent with the different definition of feminism found in the region and with the Western experience, where women first gained gender consciousness through conservative and religious issues and later developed feminist consciousness.

The 12 case studies selected for inclusion in this volume shed light on this puzzle. They each address the same dependent variable: the proportion of female representation in the lower (or only) chamber of the national legislature (the Chapter on Russian regional legislatures provides the only exception). The case studies concentrate on the explanatory factors identified in the general framework. Given the importance of electoral system for this investigation, the volume begins with the cases that currently employ mixed electoral

❖ KATHLEEN A. MONTGOMERY

systems (some single member districts along with a proportional component), moving from North to South and East to West. Thus, a chapter on Germany is followed by chapters on Lithuania, Hungary, Ukraine, Russia (Duma and regional), and Macedonia. We then look at those countries that currently use some form of proportional representation: Poland, Czech Republic, Slovenia, Croatia, and Bulgaria.

The new post-communist democracies have been willing to tinker with their electoral rules to a much higher degree than most established democracies, and so they display wide variation on the characteristics most likely to affect female representation—size of legislature, method of seat allocation, district magnitude, and threshold. As Table 1.2 shows, Slovenia's 80-seat

Table 1.2. Electoral rules in 12 post-communist countries (1990–2002)

Country	Year	Size	Method	Magnitude	Threshold
Bulgaria	1990	400	Mixed (two systems—single-member, absolute majority constituencies, with run-off provision; multi-member constituencies, filled by PR)	200 MPs elected from SMDs, 200 elected from 28 MMDs (mean magnitude = 7.14)	4%
	1991	240	Multi-member local constituencies, filled by mixture of PR [for parties] and quota [for independent candidates]	All 240 MPs elected from 31 MMDs; magnitude = 7.74	4%
	1994	240	As in 1991	As in 1991	4%
	1997	240	As in 1991	As in 1991	4%
	2001	240	As in 1991	As in 1991	4%
Croatia	1990				
	1992	138	Mixed (two systems—single-member, simple majority constituencies; nationwide multi-member constituency filled by PR, plus votes for diaspora and minorities)	60 MPs elected from SMDs; 60 MPs from national PR lists	3%
	1995	127	Mixed (two systems—single-member, simple majority constituencies; nationwide multi-member	28 MPs elected from SMDs; 80 MPs from	5% single parties 8% two-party blocs

Table 1.2. continued

Country	Year	Size	Method	Magnitude	Threshold
			constituency filled by PR, plus votes for diaspora and minorities)	national PR lists	11% 3+ blocs
	2000	151	Multi-member local constituencies, filled by PR, plus votes for diaspora and minorities	10 MMDs with magnitude = 14	5%
Czech Republic	1996	200	PR (two systems— multi-member local constituencies filled by PR; nationwide multi-member constituency, filled by PR)	8 MMDs with magnitude of 12 to 39	5% single parties 7–11% blocs
	1998	200	As in 1996	As in 1996	As in 1996
Czechoslovakia	1990	150	Multi-member local constituencies, filled by PR		5%
	1992	150	As in 1990		5%
GDR	1990	400	Multi-member local constituencies, filled by PR		None
Hungary	1990	386	Mixed (three systems— single-member, absolute majority constituencies with run-off provision; multi-member local constituencies filled by PR; nationwide multi-member constituency filled by proportional distribution of 'scrap votes')	176 SMDs territorial lists magnitude of 3–28; approx. 90 national list seats	4%
	1994	386	As in 1990	As in 1990	5%
	1998	386	As in 1990	As in 1990	As in 1994
	2002	386	As in 1990	As in 1990	As in 1994
Lithuania	1990	141	Single-member districts—simple plurality	Magnitude = 1	

❖ Kathleen A. Montgomery

Table 1.2. continued

Country	Year	Size	Method	Magnitude	Threshold
	1992	141	Mixed (two systems—single-member absolute majority constituencies; nationwide multi-member constituency filled by PR)	71 MPs elected from SMDs; 70 elected from national PR lists	4%
	1996	141	As in 1992	As in 1992	5% single parties 7% blocs
	2000	141	Mixed (two systems—single-member simple plurality; nationwide multi-member constituency filled by PR)	As in 1992	As in 1996
Macedonia	1990	120	Single-member, absolute majority constituencies with run-off provision	Magnitude = 1	
	1994	120	As in 1990	Magnitude = 1	
	1998	120	Mixed (two systems—single-member, absolute majority constituencies; nationwide multi-member constituency filled by PR)	35 MPs elected from national PR lists; 85 elected in SMDs	5%
Poland	1991	460	PR (two systems—multi-member local constituencies filled by PR; nationwide multi-member constituency filled by PR)	391 MP elected from 37 MMDs; magnitude 7–17 (mean 10.5); 69 national lists	None for MMDs; 5% for national lists
	1993	460	As in 1991	391 MP elected from 51 MMDs of magnitude from 3 to 17 (mean 7.5); 69 from national PR	MMDs: 5% parties 8% blocs National PR: 7%
	1997	460	As in 1991	As in 1993	As in 1993
	2001	460	As in 1991	51 MMDs reduced to 42	As in 1993

Table 1.2. continued

Country	Year	Size	Method	Magnitude	Threshold
Russia	1993	450	Mixed (two systems— single-member constituencies, simple majority with 25% turnout requirement; nationwide multi-member constituency filled by PR)	225 MPs elected from national PR lists; 225 from SMDs	5%
	1995	450	As in 1993	As in 1993	5%
	1999	450	As in 1993	As in 1993	5%
Slovenia	1990	80	Single-member, absolute majority constituencies with run-off provision		
	1992	90	PR (two systems— multi-member local constituencies filled by PR; remainder votes used for nationwide multi-member constituency or 'best loser' system) 2 SMD seats for ethnic minorities	8 MMDs; magnitude = 11; Second national tier uses remainder votes	3%
	1996	90	As in 1992	8 MMDs; magnitude = 11; second national tier uses remainder votes	3%
	2000	90	PR in multi-member local constituencies, second national lists eliminated, best loser system only	Second national tier is eliminated	4%
Ukraine	1994	450	Single-member, absolute majority constituencies with run-off provision and 50% turnout requirement		
	1998	450	Mixed (two systems— single-member constituencies; nationwide multi-member	225 MPs elected from SMDs; 225 from national PR lists	4%

❖ KATHLEEN A. MONTGOMERY

Table 1.2. continued

Country	Year	Size	Method	Magnitude	Threshold
			constituency filled by PR)		

Leslie Holmes, *Post-Communism: An Introduction* (Durham: Duke University Press, 1997, pp. 157–65); Lijphart Elections Archive, UCSD Social Sciences and Humanities Library (http://dodgson.ucsd.edu/lij/); and the contributing authors in this volume.

legislature offers fewer electoral opportunities than Poland's 460-seat Sejm. Electoral rules of virtually every stripe have been tried, from Hungary's highly complicated three-tier mixed system to the single member absolute majority elections used during 1990 in Ukraine and Macedonia. Electoral thresholds have ranged from zero (in Poland's multi-member districts in 1990) to as much as 11 per cent for party-blocs in some countries. District magnitude (the number of seats allocated through a given district) ranges from as little as three in some regional constituencies to as much as 90 on some national lists. The latter ought to maximize women's access to parliament, but does it? This is the sort of empirical question that the case chapters address.

The study does not include any countries that are deemed 'not free' according to the Freedom House ranking system. It is also limited to post-communist *European* states; we do not consider the Central Asian former republics of the Soviet Union. Though not exhaustive, the case selection in this volume does encompass the wide diversity in 'pathways' from communist rule. Five rank as lower-middle income (Bulgaria, Lithuania, Macedonia, the Russian Federation, and Ukraine), four as upper middle-income (Croatia, Czech Republic, Hungary, and Poland), and two as high-income (Germany and Slovenia). Three cases (Macedonia, Russia, and Ukraine) are still considered only 'partly free'; and party systems vary from volatile and highly fragmented (Russia and Ukraine have been described as a 'no party' party systems) to relatively stable and moderately fragmented (Hungary, Czech Republic). A cursory review of the data reveals no clear pattern of correlation between economic development factors and the level of female recruitment. Slovenia, with one of the highest GDP per capita ($10,050 in 2000) in the East, has generated no improvement in women's representation in the dozen years since transition. Bulgaria, on the other hand, has one of the lowest GDP per capita ($1520), yet has one of the very highest levels of representation.

The picture remains murky when we look at variation in levels of social and cultural egalitarianism. Standard measures, such as women's labour force participation and education levels, do not vary widely among the post-communist cases. Women continue to work outside the home (either by choice or necessity) and female literacy rates and education levels remain high across the region; but other cultural patterns, such as religious affiliation and year of female suffrage, do vary. We might expect to find a more egalitarian climate in the Czech Republic and Germany than Bulgaria or Croatia. Yet, the latter two countries recently posted some of the most impressive increases in female representation in the region.

All of this points to the complexity of the problem in the post-communist region and calls for nuanced efforts to link the specific characteristics of post-communism with general factors that affect recruitment. In this spirit, contributing authors have adapted the general framework to the specifics of their cases. Authors test the hypotheses set forth in the framework to explain change over time within their given country. Each chapter addresses a slightly different puzzle. In Ukraine, the question is how well do women do when there is only the barest outlines of a party system. The Slovenian chapter asks why one of the most affluent and Western orientated countries in the region does not recruit more women. What works in Croatia, Bulgaria, and Poland? Why do women in Russia fare better in the majoritarian element of the electoral system? Moreover, what explains the up and down pattern of female recruitment in places like Hungary and Lithuania? Taken together the answers to these questions provide leverage on many of the broad puzzles raised earlier in this chapter.

The concluding chapter provides a synthesis of the findings of the empirical chapters. The findings of the country cases are compared with the expectations of the general theoretical model in order to draw conclusions about the region as a whole, and then compared with the experiences of the established Western democracies. This evaluation finds that many of the theoretical predictions based on the existing literature from industrialized democracies hold true in Eastern Europe. It seems reasonable on the bases of these findings to assert our theories are robust, as they operate in a similar fashion in distinctly different cultural and developmental settings. There are, however, a number of instances where uniquely Eastern European phenomena are found. These are identified and described. The book ends with a discussion of the next steps that need to be taken in understanding women's access to political power in post-communist Europe.

❖ NOTES

1 Data from June 2002, based on the Inter-Parliamentary Union's on-line database (www.ipu.org). The figure for post-communist countries includes all countries of the region, except those deemed unfree by the Freedom House ranking system. The figure for Western Europe includes 18 major European countries.

❖ KATHLEEN A. MONTGOMERY

2 There are a few notable exceptions, such as the brief periods with female Prime Ministers in Poland (Hanna Suchocka), Lithuania (Kazmiera Prunskiené), and Bulgaria (Renate Indzhova).

3 The metaphor of transition is subject to criticism on a number of fronts, not the least of which is that it suggests a complete discontinuity with the political and developmental trajectories that led up to multi-party elections. It also leads to the problematic conclusion that progress through consolidation—a borderless stage on the way to stable democracy and functioning markets—is continuous. Experience clearly demonstrates the contrary. Countries follow different 'pathways' from authoritarianism and the entire process may be sporadic, uneven, and filled with reversals and side excursions (see review in Gal and Kligman 2000). With those problems clearly in view, we nonetheless use the term 'consolidation', because it provides convenient shorthand for the period that comes after a founding democratic election.

4 This position appears in a number of early analyses of democratization in the region. For a representative example, see Loewenberg 1994.

5 Gal and Kligman (2000) raise this point in *The Politics of Gender after Socialism*, p. 99.

6 A recent USAID report concludes that 'of the factors limiting women's ability to participate in politics, poverty is perhaps the most pervasive. Women carry primary responsibility for household and family maintenance...These dual obligations...leave most women with little time for politics' pp. 1–2 in 'Women's Political Participation: The Missing Half of Democracy.' *Gender Matters Information Bulletin* No. 3, July 1999: A publication of USAID's Office of Women in Development.

7 This characterization derives from two debates: one within the women and politics literature over the relative role of political culture and electoral institutions in explaining variations in the level of female legislative representation (Norris and Inglehart 2000); the other over the relative importance of preconditions and institutional crafting in the successful establishment of stable and lasting democracy (Montgomery and Remington 1994).

8 With the fall of communism in Eastern Europe, neo-institutional scholars rushed to the new democracies to debate the relative merits of different electoral systems; but those debates centred on the presumed trade-off between the representativeness of the party system achieved through PR systems and the ability to produce stable and efficient governments. Gender inequality did not impress transitologists as a threat to democratic longevity and stability.

9 Einhorn (1993) cites Barbara Jancar and Renata Siemieńska on these points, pp. 159–60; see also Matynia (1993) and Goven (1993).

10 Einhorn (1993) is the first to outline this 'jump and push' model, but the central hypotheses have been more or less accepted in subsequent literature.

11 Turkmenistan also has posted impressive gains, though this may be seen more as a continuation of the old system with single party rule, 99 per cent voter turnout, and no voter choice on the ballot. As in the old Eastern bloc, women are well

represented, but Turkmenistan is a country that Freedom House defines as being at the very bottom of their scale in terms of political freedom.

12 Despite localized participation in anti-communist opposition movements, women were largely excluded from transitional negotiations. In those countries where Roundtable Talks brought an end to communist rule (the most unambiguous example of institutional crafting), transitional actors were primarily concerned with issues of *party* representation. That consideration has continued to be important, as countries have modified their rules. Where the issue of descriptive representation has been raised, it has usually been in connection with ethnic minorities.

❖ KATHLEEN A. MONTGOMERY

2 ❖ Recruiting Women to National Legislatures: A General Framework with Applications to Post-Communist Democracies

Richard E. Matland and Kathleen A. Montgomery

In this chapter, we present a general model of legislative recruitment drawn primarily from literature on established Western democracies (Rule 1981, 1987; Norris 1985; Darcy, Welch, and Clark 1994; Matland 1998*a*). The framework incorporates important findings about socio-cultural and developmental determinants of women's representation, but it places special emphasis on the role of formal institutions—the electoral system and party rules for selecting candidates. We argue that institutions matter for female legislative recruitment, but they matter in specific ways and under specific conditions. They cannot be treated as a recipe that can be pulled out of a drawer and used to 'cook up' gender equity in legislatures. Rather, outcomes are a function of the supply of and demand for female candidates and the manner in which the institutions translate these factors into recruitment outcomes.

After extensive study, researchers have identified a set of variables that strongly influence the level of women's representation in advanced industrialized democracies. Western models of recruitment perform poorly, however, in explaining levels of female representation in lesser developed countries that may lack a minimum threshold of socio-economic development (Matland 1998*b*). The new post-communist democracies provide a third and novel setting in which to test theories about female legislative recruitment. The communist experiment with directive emancipation created a cultural and developmental legacy that differs in key respects from the Western democracies and countries in the developing world. At the same time, democratizing post-communist countries are drawing heavily on constitutional models and institutional designs pioneered in Western Europe. Do those institutions perform for women in the same ways when planted in post-communist soil? The final part of this chapter details the central features of a broad post-communist legacy and suggests ways in which that legacy fits within the general expectations of our framework.

Extant research provides a fairly clear menu of conditions that can improve women's representation, as well as a few obvious impediments. Following Norris (1996) we consider these factors in the form of a stages model that goes through the process of legislative recruitment. After describing the legislative recruitment process, we then provide an extended discussion of the role that we believe institutions play in female recruitment.

While the recruitment process is described as linear, clearly, there are interactions and feedback loops in the process. Factors that make it more likely that gatekeepers will be interested in nominating female candidates, for example an organized women's movement lobbying party gatekeepers to increase the number of women running, make it also likely there will be an increased supply, as potential female aspirants react to the party's newfound interest in finding female candidates. Institutions, for their part, influence the separate stages by providing greater or lesser incentive for women to become aspirants and for parties to nominate women.

❖ THE LEGISLATIVE RECRUITMENT PROCESS AND WOMEN

In their classic formulation Loewenberg and Patterson (1979: 77) depict the legislative recruitment process as a funnel that winnows a large pool of eligibles at the mouth of the funnel down to a small set of elected representatives at the end of the process. In any given country there will typically exist a large pool of eligibles (citizens that fulfill the legal and formal requirements for becoming legislators); but only a subset of these individuals will consider putting themselves forward as possible candidates. An even smaller number will be able to secure the nomination of a political party and thus become candidates. Those candidates in turn must garner a sufficient level of support from the voters to win a legislative seat. This process, depicted in Fig. 2.1, is highly influenced by the cultural and political contexts within which it occurs (Norris 1987, 1997).

At each stage in this process, women can face gender specific impediments. Understanding why, and under what circumstances, women are disproportionately 'winnowed out' helps us to account for levels of female representation across a variety of political systems. In general women are not formally discriminated against at the start of the process. An Inter Parliamentary Union (1995) survey of their 188 member states found there are virtually no *formal*, in the sense of legal, barriers to women's participation in the national legislatures. If women are formally just as 'eligible' as men, then their under-representation must be explained by de-selection at other points in the process. In almost all

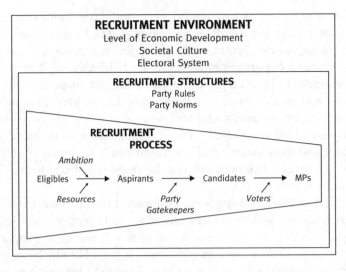

Figure 2.1. Legislative recruitment system

Source: Adapted from P. Norris: *Legislative Recruitment* in L. Leduc, R. Niemi, and P. Norris, *Comparing Democracies: Elections and Voting in Global Perspective*, London: Sage, 1996, p. 196.

countries at the start of the legislative recruitment process the eligibility pool is slightly greater than 50 per cent female. By the end of the process, however, the proportion has dropped dramatically and the final outcome is national legislatures that are overwhelmingly male.

❖ From eligibles to aspirants

The decision to openly aspire for office is the calculation of a rational thinker, albeit a boundedly rational one. There are many factors that impact a potential aspirant's evaluation of whether she wants to campaign for a nomination. They include an assessment of the costs in time, energy, and financial commitment to both run and serve if elected, and the benefits in terms of the attractiveness of the job with respect to remuneration, status, and/or political power. Ambition is a necessary prerequisite for a possible candidate (Schlesinger 1966), but ambition is constrained by the electoral opportunity structure; that is, the chances to gain office within the existing political system. Even among individuals very high on personal ambition, few choose to run if they believe there is little or no chance of getting nominated or winning election (Abramson, Aldrich, and Rohde 1987; Maisel and Stone 1997). The individual's calculations are affected by their perception of whether there are substantial openings for new candidates, by how friendly the political environment will be to their candidacy, and by an estimation of the resources they can generate in comparison to the resources needed to run an effective campaign (Fowler and McClure 1989; Prinz 1993).

The relative openness of a system to new candidates varies dramatically from nation to nation. In Costa Rica, for example, MPs are not allowed to run for re-election. Every new election results in 100 per cent turnover in the parliament. The electoral opportunities are relatively rich in Costa Rica and that, prima facie, ought to increase the openness of the system to women. In the United States, on the other hand, on average more than 90 per cent of members of Congress run for re-election and well over 90 per cent of them win. The opportunity structure is relatively poor for Congressional aspirants in the United States, and since incumbents have traditionally been male, female representation has lagged. Relative openness, however, is just one formal aspect of opportunity structure.

The cultural context also influences the perception of how friendly the political environment will be to one's candidacy and therefore the likelihood of success. If running for office is something that is not quite proper for a woman to do, or is likely to be met with scorn, it would hardly be surprising if relatively few women were willing to run. To the degree women face discrimination, whether direct or indirect, they may be hesitant to come forth as candidates. A country's culture need not be overtly discriminatory to differentially influence men and women in the move from eligible to aspirant. Socialization in most societies emphasizes politics as a male domain. We find lower levels of knowledge about and interest in politics among women than men in countries as diverse as the United States and Norway (Strømsnes 1995; Delli Carpini and Keeter 2000). Georgia Duerst-Lahti (1998) reports the results of a national survey of 1000 voters in the United States and finds that 18 per cent of the men polled had considered running for office, while only eight per cent of the women had considered running. In other words, there is a clear gender gap in terms of political ambition.

Furthermore, women typically have access to less power and fewer resources than the men in their societies. As a result, women may believe they lack the crucial material resources necessary to launch a successful campaign. This should be most problematic in electoral systems that place the burden of campaigning on the individual rather than the party. Time is also a resource and because women often have more complicated family and work roles, they may believe they lack the time for a career in politics. This phenomenon, sometimes referred to as the 'three job problem', occurs when a woman has a full-time job in her profession and a full-time job at home with her family, so that becoming politically active and running for office effectively requires her to take on a third job. Many professional women are reluctant to take the step into politics, even if they are qualified, because of the tremendous time commitment that it implies on their already over-extended day. One can see the consequences of this problem when looking at the women who have been elected to national legislatures. A number of individual studies have found

❖ R. E. MATLAND AND K. A. MONTGOMERY

women who are elected officials tend to be older than men when they become active in politics, have no children, or have fewer children than their male counterparts (Carroll 1989; Dodson and Carroll 1991; Thomas 1997).

A related problem is the match between a woman's attributes and attributes desired by the parties. These concerns affect both the move from eligible to aspirant and from aspirant to candidate. Possible aspirants rightly perceive that parties are interested in a specific set of characteristics. It is axiomatic that political parties in democratic systems want to win votes. To achieve that end, a party tries to field the most attractive slate of candidates possible. A problem occurs for women when the characteristics parties believe are important to winning votes are characteristics disproportionately held by males. For example, parties in all countries field candidates who have high socio-economic status. Candidates usually have extensive education at the university level and work in high-status professions, such as medicine or law. In many countries, another implicit prerequisite is that major party candidates for parliament have served the party previously in political office at the local level. If men dominate the professions, higher education, and local elected offices, then there will be fewer women likely to aspire to national office and the parties will exhibit a lower demand for women.

The availability of 'qualified' female aspirants is strongly linked with levels of socio-economic and political development. Average levels of representation are considerably higher among the advanced industrialized countries than the developing democracies (Matland 1998b). Even among the OECD countries women are better represented in those countries with higher levels of GDP. Several processes that accompany economic development should increase women's political resources and decrease existing barriers to political activity. Development leads to weakening of traditional values, decreased fertility rates, increased urbanization, greater education and labour force participation for women, and attitudinal changes in perceptions of the appropriate roles for women.

Increasing female labour force participation rates have proven especially important for improving women's political representation in the Western countries (Andersen 1975; Welch 1977; Togeby 1994). It appears that moving out of the house and into the workforce has a consciousness raising effect on women; they become politicized and discover decisions made in the political sphere directly impact them, both at work and at home. Workforce participation also increases the number of women who hold high status positions and experience, characteristics that make an aspirant attractive to party gatekeepers.

❖ From aspirant to candidate

Moving from aspirant to actual party candidate is the next stage of the model. At this stage the party gatekeepers determine the individual aspirant's fate.

The parties face both external and internal pressures that affect their decisions as to which candidates to nominate.

External pressures refer to party concerns with how their nominees will be evaluated by the voters. Under any democratic system an overriding consideration for parties is presenting candidates the party believes will maximize their vote.[1] If certain types of candidates are seen as a liability, gatekeepers will shy away from nominating these candidates. If the political culture in a country is such that the general public believes politics is not a proper sphere for women to participate in, not only does this diminish the likelihood that women will step forward, it also makes party gatekeepers reluctant to select women, even if they personally believe women are as capable as men.

Gallagher argues there is a set of characteristics party selectors look for in possible candidates across virtually all of the Western democracies he studied. He notes (1988: 248) 'The most widely valued (characteristics) are aspirant's track records in the party organization and in the constituency'. Even for new candidates a past history of party participation and activism is important. Visibility in the community through one's profession, holding public office, or other activity is also highly desirable. Aspirants who have held office at the local level or community leadership positions are disproportionately male, therefore these criteria tend to hurt women.

While external pressures influence the selection process, there are also clear internal pressures that impinge upon the selection process. Across parties, there is an expectation that political ideology will affect women's access to viable slots. Women are expected to be less common in rightist parties due to the traditional views of the leadership and of the women who are active in the party. Women, when they are active, will typically take a backstage role. The assertion is often made that leftist parties, with a basis in the underprivileged classes in society have a natural affinity for women's plight and therefore provide a more hospitable environment in which women can pursue office. This perspective oversimplifies reality. Many of the leaders of long established leftist parties come out of labour movements that are overwhelmingly male; these individuals often have very traditional views on women's roles. At least initially, many of these parties were not particularly open to women's demands for representation. Caul (1999) finds that women do best first and foremost in New Left parties with post-materialist values. Green parties that share an explicit commitment to gender equality and are willing to back that with explicit quotas and other New Left parties have tended to provide women with their most equal representation.

While ideology may influence the openness of parties to women's demands, party responsiveness and perception of women as a legitimate constituency first happens when internal pressure for better representation comes from elements within the party. This happens primarily when women are organized effectively and make increased representation in the legislature and party and chamber leaderships an explicit goal. It is not sufficient to merely organize. Increased political access must be an explicit goal before significant legislative gains are realized. Women auxiliaries have existed in political parties for quite some time. If these groups do not lobby for significant representation, it is unlikely to occur. Israel, for example, uses a woman-friendly set of electoral institutions to select members to the Knesset; yet there are very few female members. Brichta and Brichta (1994) conclude that a major impediment to female recruitment is the unwillingness of women to organize as an effective lobby, despite the presence of women's organizations in the parties. Those organizations have engaged in a tacit agreement with party leaders to reserve a couple of safe seats on the lists for women. In return, the women's caucuses have not pressed for more equitable representation in the legislature and have not unified to lobby for greater presence in the central decision-making bodies of the parties.

The most effective conditions for increased women's representation are when there is both internal and external pressure for better representation. Popular attitudes in support of gender equality affect the calculus of party gatekeepers in the nomination stage. If party gatekeepers perceive that voters see political equality as an important aim, they will seek to prove they are aware of and sympathetic to these concerns. For party leaders, nominating female candidates can help build the party image on issues of equality. When those pressures appear in society, if there is an effective internal organization also pushing the issue, then significant changes can occur quickly.

In a competitive electoral environment, party gatekeepers need to worry about what other parties are doing with reference to women. Research has shown that parties respond to cues from other ideologically similar parties through a contagion effect (Matland and Studlar 1996). When a small party of the left, for instance, starts nominating sizable numbers of women or adopts gender-based quota rules, a larger leftist party may feel compelled to respond and do the same, fearing the loss of an important sector of voters to the competition. Significant increases in representation start to occur when the more mainstream parties adopt the equality policies first promoted by smaller fringe parties (Matland and Studlar 1996).

❖ From candidate to MP

One might expect sexism by voters at the final stage to serve as a brick wall, making it almost impossible for women to penetrate the halls of power. The evidence is mixed, however, on this point. Studies of elections in advanced industrialized democracies suggest that voters primarily vote for the party label rather than individual candidates (Leduc, Niemi, and Norris 1996). This is certainly true of electoral systems using closed list proportional representation where studies find that most voters can identify the national party leaders, but cannot identify the individual candidates who are on the ballot in their local constituency (Valen 1988). Under these conditions, the crucial stage of the process is nomination by the party.

There are, nevertheless, countries where the candidate's personal vote is considered important (Cain, Ferejohn, and Fiorina 1987). Being female could be a liability in systems where there are personal votes, but voters do not seem to be the primary obstacle. There is mounting evidence that when female candidates face the voters directly, they do about as well as their male counterparts (Darcy and Schramm 1977; Welch and Studlar 1986; Darcy, Welch and Clark 1994; Seltzer, Newman and Voorhees Leighton 1997). Hence, even in single member district (SMD) systems, getting the party nod may still be the crucial stage.

The precise impact of voters on female legislative representation requires further investigation. It should, nonetheless, be apparent from this cursory review that women are not primarily winnowed out at the election stage. Rather, among advanced industrial democracies, the crucial points are getting women to run and getting the party selectorate to choose women as their candidates. The framework presented in Fig. 2.1 posits the level of female representation (understood here as the per cent of legislative seats held by women) is a function of the supply of qualified female candidates and the level of demand for such candidates. This relationship, in turn, is mediated by political institutions that form a key element of the opportunity structure that faces female eligibles and constrains the nomination strategies of party gatekeepers. It is the *interaction* of institutions, supply, and demand that ultimately determines how many women sit in parliament.

❖ THE ROLE OF INSTITUTIONS

❖ Electoral rules

In the advanced industrial democracies, there is overwhelming evidence that women fare better in various types of proportional representation systems than under majoritarian rules. Furthermore, the differences are substantial. Among European Union member states, the legislatures with the highest levels of female representation all use some form of proportional representation (PR), while those with the lowest levels (France, Italy, and the United Kingdom) all employ majoritarian or mixed systems. The evidence is even clearer when we examine variations within systems that combine PR and majoritarian rules. Nearly twice as many women are recruited to the German Bundestag through the PR half of the electoral system as through the SMD component.

❖ R. E. MATLAND AND K. A. MONTGOMERY

Why should PR systems be so much more woman-friendly? Perhaps the foremost reason is that such systems have higher district magnitudes, and this typically produces higher party magnitudes. District magnitude is the number of seats per district; party magnitude refers to the number of seats a party wins in a district. Party and district magnitudes are important because they *affect party strategy when choosing candidates* (Matland 1995). The party gatekeepers who must consider which aspirants to choose as candidates will have a different set of concerns and incentives depending upon the expected party magnitude.

When district magnitude is one, as it is in majoritarian systems, the party can win, at most, one seat in a district. By definition, the party has no chance to balance the party ticket in a single district. If nomination decisions are made at the district level, as they generally are, they become strictly zero-sum in nature. Female candidates must compete directly against men, and when nominating a woman, a party must explicitly deny the aspirations of all men in the same district. When district magnitude increases, the chances that a party will win several seats in the district increases. When a party expects to win several seats, party leaders are much more conscious of trying to balance their tickets. Gatekeepers will divide winning slots on the party list among various internal party interests.

Parties have several incentives to balance the ticket when given the opportunity to do so (Valen 1988). First, balance can be a means of attracting voters. Rather than looking for a single candidate who can appeal to a broad range of voters, party gatekeepers think in terms of different candidates' appeal to specific sectors of voters. A woman candidate can be seen as a benefit to the party by attracting a certain sector of voters, without having the significant costs to intra-party peace of requiring powerful interests represented by men to step aside as they would in a majoritarian system. Conversely, failing to provide some balance could have the undesirable effect of driving voters away. A second reason for balancing is that, inside the party, ticket balancing is often seen as a matter of equity; different party factions argue that it is only fair that one of their representatives be among those candidates who have a genuine chance of winning. When a woman's branch of the party has been established and is active in doing a significant amount of the party's work, women can be one of those groups demanding to be included on the list in winnable positions. A third reason for balancing the slate is that dividing safe seats among the various factions in the party is a way of maintaining party peace and assuring the continued support of the various groups within the party. In short, when given the opportunity, parties try to balance their ticket.

Furthermore, contagion processes, whereby a party responds to a competing party's policy of supporting women by adopting the same policy, is more likely to occur in PR systems than in majoritarian ones (Matland and Studlar 1996). The costs of responding to a challenge from another party on the issue of women's representation are lower in PR than in majoritarian systems, and the gains may be greater. Because PR systems give major party leaders several slots from which they might find room to nominate a woman, as opposed to only one under majoritarian rules, the party has an easier time finding room for female candidates. Furthermore, in an SMD system, when a party that is dominant in an individual district is challenged on the issue of candidate diversity, it can often safely ignore such a threat, because it is very unlikely to lose the seat. In a PR system, on the other hand, even the loss of a few votes can lead to a loss of seats in parliament. Furthermore, since PR systems tend to produce more parties and the political distance between parties is often small (Downs 1957), a threat by women to shift allegiances to another party is more plausible. As a result, party leaders may feel a greater need to respond when another party starts to promote women candidates.

While proportional representation systems are generally considered superior for women, not all proportional arrangements are equally advantageous. PR systems vary in the degree to which they provide ticket-balancing opportunities. If women are to win seats in parliament, the parties must win multiple seats so they go down into the party list when selecting MPs. In designing electoral rules, women will be helped both by having high district magnitudes and by electoral thresholds, because of their effects on average party magnitude. Not surprisingly, there is generally a strong positive correlation between average district magnitude and average party magnitude. As the number of seats per district increases, parties will go deeper on their lists (i.e. win more seats) and more parties will have multi-member delegations. Both should increase women's representation. The limiting case, and the one that may be the most advantageous for women, is if the whole country is one electoral district.

This is the system used in the Netherlands, which has a very high level of women's representation (34.0 per cent) and in Israel, which has a low level of women's representation (14.2 per cent). In Israel the level of voter support needed for a party to win a seat in the Knesset has been extremely low (it was raised to 1.5 per cent in the mid 1990s). This has encouraged the creation of many mini-parties, which often elect only one or two representatives. Parties usually have male leaders, and party leaders inevitably take the first few slots on the list. Women tend to show up a little farther down the list when party concerns turn to ensuring ticket balance. If the party only elects one or two representatives, however, even though many of their candidates in mid-list positions are women, women will not win any representation.

The Israeli case reminds us that electoral systems cannot guarantee high levels of female representation. It also suggests that, when designing electoral systems, there is a tradeoff between representing the voters who choose small parties and increasing the descriptive representation of the legislature by having more women from the larger parties. It is sometimes argued that maximizing proportionality will help women, because small pro-female parties, such as Greens, will have easier legislative access. Simulations using data from two countries that use electoral thresholds—Costa Rica (Matland and Taylor 1997) and Sweden (Matland 1998c)—challenge this assumption. They show quite clearly that higher thresholds have the effect of reducing party fragmentation and thereby improving the chances of women by increasing average party magnitude.

Another characteristic that distinguishes proportional representation systems from each other is whether they use closed party lists, where the party determines the rank ordering of candidates, or open party lists, where the voters are able to influence which of the party's candidates are elected via preferential voting. While there is always a temptation to recommend open party lists, because this would allow women voters to move women up through preferential voting, there is some evidence that open lists disadvantage women. The experience in Norway shows the effects of preferential voting are generally negative. While preferential voting provides the opportunity for some voters to promote women, this can easily be outweighed by the opportunity for other voters to demote women. If this can happen in places like Norway, which has a deserved reputation for being highly progressive on issues of gender equality, it would hardly be surprising to find similar phenomena in countries with more traditional views on the proper role for women. Voters with very traditional views might go out of their way to strike or lower women's names on the party list.

Preferential voting also lets the parties off the hook by blurring accountability for final electoral outcomes. Parties cannot ultimately control how their supporters vote. If thousands of individual voters making individual decisions vote women down and out of parliament, the parties can hardly be held culpable. With closed party lists, however, it is quite clearly the party's responsibility to insure there is balance in the delegation. If representation fails to grow, women can identify and support parties more willing to consider their demands for representation. Closed lists also seem to have an impact on the efficacy of quota rules. Jones (1998) finds that quotas work most effectively in the case of Argentine local elections when they are employed in conjunction with closed lists.

What should be clear from the foregoing discussion is that woman friendly institutions—PR ballot structure, high district magnitude, closed party lists, and high electoral thresholds—facilitate higher levels of female representation. This occurs, however, only if women enjoy some minimum level of cultural standing, possess the qualifications party gatekeepers find attractive, and are sufficiently organized to place pressure on party gatekeepers to nominate women.

These necessary preconditions are often tied to development. Development leads to an increased supply of qualified female candidates. When the number of women with the necessary resources becomes substantial, they may then start to form movements to demand greater representation, both within and outside the political parties. Whether those movements are likely to be successful, however, depends crucially upon the political institutions. Figures 2.2 and 2.3 show the level of women's representation as of 1 June 2000 on the Y-axis and a per capita GDP measure on the X-axis.[2] Figure 2.2 presents a scatterplot and a simple bivariate regression for majoritarian electoral systems, while Fig. 2.3 presents the same analyses for proportional representation electoral systems.

The figures show the effect of development under the two different electoral systems.[3] The regression shows that while the effect of development on women's representation across countries with majoritarian electoral systems is positive, it is very modest and is not statistically significant. Development has only a very limited effect when there is a majoritarian

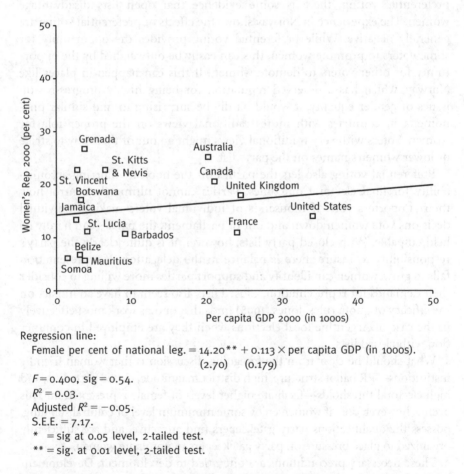

Regression line:

Female per cent of national leg. = 14.20** + 0.113 × per capita GDP (in 1000s).
                                    (2.70)   (0.179)

$F = 0.400$, sig = 0.54.

$R^2 = 0.03$.

Adjusted $R^2 = -0.05$.

S.E.E. = 7.17.

* = sig at 0.05 level, 2-tailed test.

** = sig. at 0.01 level, 2-tailed test.

Figure 2.2. Relationship between development and women's representation in free countries with majoritarian electoral systems, 2000

❖ R. E. MATLAND AND K. A. MONTGOMERY

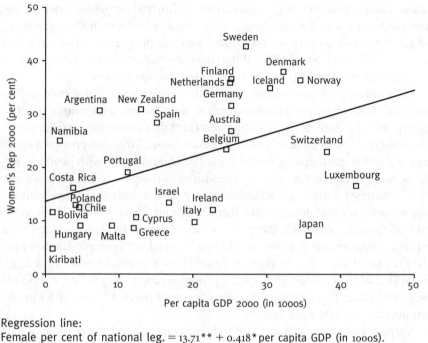

Regression line:
Female per cent of national leg. = 13.71** + 0.418*per capita GDP (in 1000s).
$$(3.46) \quad (0.159)$$

$F = 6.94$; sig = 0.014.
$R^2 = 0.20$
Adjusted $R^2 = 0.19$
S.E.E. = 8.51
* = sig at 0.05 level, 2-tailed test.
** = sig at 0.01 level, 2-tailed test.

Figure 2.3. Relationship between development and women's representation in free countries with PR electoral systems, 2000

electoral system. When a country has a proportional representation electoral system, on the other hand, development has a considerably stronger effect. The effect is statistically significant and the unstandardized regression coefficient, which measures the effect of the variable, is more than three times what it is for majoritarian systems. There is an interaction effect, when both high levels of development and a PR electoral system exist simultaneously, then significant levels of representation are consistently achieved, if either of these elements is missing the expected levels of representation are more modest.

❖ *Party institutions*

The electoral system directly effects female legislative representation, because it shapes the recruitment strategies of party gatekeepers at the nomination phase. Parties, however, vary substantially within and across national settings and electoral systems with regard to the number of women they nominate, where they rank women on party lists, and the proportion of women they send to parliament. Some of the differences across parties are produced by the institutional mechanisms in place within the various parties.

Party nomination procedures can be differentiated on a number of characteristics. Gallagher (1988) distinguishes nomination procedures on two dimensions: breadth of participation and centralization or decentralization of the process. At one end are those nomination procedures that provide a broad opportunity to participate for members. The United States, with primary elections, is at the extreme in terms of breadth of participation, but there are several countries where all-member party caucuses provide substantial opportunity for significant input from rank and file members. At the other end are systems in which the party leader, national faction leaders, or the national executive chooses the candidates. In Israel, for example, the complete list for one of the religious parties, Degel Hatora, is put together by a single rabbi (Rahat 1999). Depending on the procedure used, the gatekeeper role will be played either by party leaders, a broader set of party officials, or a significant portion of party rank and file.

Norris (1996), like Gallagher, differentiates recruitment structures based on whether they use centralized or localized decision making. She also considers a second dimension, whether the recruitment system is patronage-oriented or bureaucratic in form. Her description of a bureaucratic system of candidate selection within a party adheres closely to the Weberian paradigm. Rules are detailed, explicit, standardized, and followed, regardless of the person who is in a position of power. The concept of bureaucratic form, as Norris uses it, has clear antecedents to the concept of institutionalization of the candidate selection process as described by Czudnowski (1975). Authority is based on legalistic principles. In a patronage-based system, rules are far less clear, and even when rules exist there is a distinct possibility they are not followed. Authority is based either on traditionalist or charismatic leadership, rather than legal-rational authority. Loyalty to those in power in the party is paramount. These different systems emphasize different factors as important in choosing candidates.

In terms of women's representation, it is clear that bureaucratically based systems that have incorporated rules guaranteeing women's representation, *that are followed,* are a huge advantage. In many of the Nordic countries, parties have explicitly adopted quotas guaranteeing that at least 40 per cent of the party's list will consist of women. In Argentina, a one-third quota was established in the early 1990s and written into the constitution (Jones 1996). In South Africa the ANC established quotas for all its candidates (Ballington 1998). While the importance of quotas in the Nordic case can be debated,[4] in

Argentina and South Africa they have had a dramatic and positive effect on women's representation.

While quotas can have significant positive effects, the outcome is far from guaranteed. First, quotas are hard to enact. One must have a situation in which men in power are actively interested in giving away power. This does happen, but it is rare. In the Norwegian case the Labour party was pushed and pulled into adopting quotas because of internal pressure from their women's organizations and external pressure from competing parties (Matland and Studlar 1996). In the Argentinian case, the leader of the Peronistas, Carlos Menem, knew he was facing a serious gender gap with women pulling away from his party. To try and woo back female voters, he cajoled the legislature into enacting quotas, despite objections of some of the male deputies of his own party. In the South African case, the women in the party fought very hard and were able to establish quotas *before* any ANC representative had actually been elected to the South African parliament.

A second concern with quotas is they can be written so that they are *ineffective*, providing the appearance of power sharing, but in fact continuing to lead to male dominated legislative bodies (Jones 1998; Htun and Jones 2002). Meier (1999) provides an excellent example of this in evaluating the effects of the Belgian quota law. The Belgian law requires that each party nominate a minimum of one-third of each gender on their lists. In simulations of the 1995 national elections, Meier shows that even if a stricter version of the law had been applied, requiring every third name to be female, the practical effect of the law would have been nil. No more women would have been elected to the parliament.

If we look beyond institutional arrangements that guarantee representation, the effects of various institutional arrangements depend upon the context in the individual countries. Nevertheless, there are some general predictions that can be made. Patronage based selection systems where decisions are made by a lim-ited number of elites are generally dominated by small groups that have tended to control power for some time. Women, *as a group*, have tended to be on the outside. While it is not uncommon, in patronage systems, for there to be some women who are on the inside, they are likely to be few in number, and promot-ing greater representation of women is rarely seen as a party goal. Patronage sys-tems are fairly closed systems that are likely to be unfavourable to women.

Furthermore, bureaucratic systems, which Norris posits as the alternative to patronage systems, offer important advantages to women. When there are explicit and clear bureaucratic procedures by which candidates are chosen, it is possible to monitor the system to make sure decisions are made according to the rules. When bureaucratized procedures exist, party congresses will often debate what rules are to be followed. Even when quotas are not adopted, internal debate that points out the gross under-representation of women often pressures parties to take representation more seriously. Clear and open rules also provide women the opportunity to develop strategies to take advantage of those rules. For example if party caucuses are officially open to all party members, it is possible for women to mobilize to elect women either as delegates to the party congress or as actual candidates. When patronage oriented procedures dominate, it is much harder to gain access to the place where decisions are actually made.

The second characteristic on which Norris and Gallagher distinguish party nomination procedures is whether nomination decisions are made at a local or centralized level. Women are advantaged by decisions being made at a more centralized level. This is true for two reasons. First, the logic of party magnitude also applies when looking at the level at which nomination decisions are made. The more centralized the process, the larger the number of slots considered simultaneously. The more slots considered, the easier it will be for women to gain some representation. Second, if the process is centralized and women are able to convince party leadership of the need for significant representation, that decision can be fairly quickly effectuated with significant gains in representation occurring quickly. In a highly decentralized system, individual battles arguing for greater representation would have to be fought at many different localities and progress could be quite slow.

❖ LESSONS FROM ESTABLISHED DEMOCRACIES

If we return to Fig. 2.1 we see the crucial stages of legislative recruitment for women in advanced industrialized democracies are the stages from eligible to aspirant and from aspirant to candidate. Women are on equal footing with men in terms of eligibility and, at least tentatively, in terms of being selected once they are candidates. The dramatic drop off occurs when moving from eligibles to aspirants and when the parties determine which aspirants they will select as candidates. Just how great that drop off is depends upon a number of characteristics of the political and social systems, including the level of development, the level of women's organization, and the existing political institutions.

One clear lesson is that *development matters*. Development affects representation because it leads to an increase in the pool of qualified aspirants who are female. With development comes increased resources and increased political ambition among women. It also, hopefully, leads to a greater willingness to accept women as leaders both by party gatekeepers and the general electorate. Closely tied to, but independent of development, is political culture. Societal culture, especially in terms of the proper public role for women, will influence women's success at each stage of the recruitment process.

A second lesson from Western democracies is that significant gains for women first started occurring when second wave feminism led to women getting organized and demanding greater representation. Organized lobbying

❖ R. E. MATLAND AND K. A. MONTGOMERY

groups both inside and outside political parties provided women with the experience and power base necessary to become serious aspirants for office and to increase the likelihood that the party selectorate would choose women. In many parties women traditionally have done a considerable amount of the essential party work; yet, until they actively started demanding greater representation, representation remained at very low levels. Formal organization of women within the parties increases the visibility and legitimacy of women as a constituency and improves their representation chances.

A third lesson is that *institutions matter*. This is important not just from a descriptive pattern, but also from a prescriptive focus. While development levels and political culture are quite difficult to change, institutions are considerably more malleable. The electoral system is a central concern. Women's representation is improved, *ceteris paribus*, by the use of proportional representation. In considering various other characteristics of electoral system design, plans that are likely to lead to high party magnitudes should help women. A large number of seats in the national chamber, relatively few electoral districts, and significant electoral threshold should all help women by increasing party magnitudes.

In terms of internal party institutions, parties that have explicit bureaucratic procedures for selecting candidates provide the best opportunities. When the nomination processes are institutionalized it is possible for women to develop strategies to improve representation. When the process is dominated by patronage, rules can be murky, and decisions are often made by a limited number of persons, typically men.

The lessons from Western democracies indicate women will be helped by moves to specific electoral institutions. Such moves, however, cannot *guarantee* increased representation of women immediately. While PR systems *on average* have higher proportions of women than majoritarian systems, that will not be true for every case. Rules can advantage one group or another, but an effect will appear only if the group is sufficiently well organized to take advantage of the rules. If the forces interested in women's representation are not effectively organized, then the electoral system is expected to have only limited effect. The central concern of the remainder of the book is whether these findings from the West also hold in Central and Eastern Europe.

❖ APPLYING THE FRAMEWORK IN A POST-COMMUNIST SETTING

We contend these same general lessons should apply in the post-communist countries, despite some important differences between those cases and the countries that have been most thoroughly examined in the empirical literature. There is little doubt that the post-communist systems emerged from a gender regime that differed in key respects from the Western countries that experienced second-wave feminism and from lesser developed countries that lack minimal levels of development for women. These were regimes that, for all their regional and longitudinal variations, generally provided women with the overt characteristics of emancipation. By 1983, some 92 per cent of working age women in the Soviet Union either worked or studied; Poland and Hungary nearly matched this figure, and women actually outnumbered men among university-enrolled students in the Soviet Union and several East European countries (Wejnert 1996). At least initially, we might expect that Eastern party gatekeepers would be faced with aspirant pools where women were largely men's equals. This is not, however, what we find.

Much ink has been devoted to describing the common cultural and developmental legacies of communist gender policies (Einhorn 1993; Funk and Mueller 1993; Matynia 1994; Havelkova 1996; Siemieńska 1996; Wejnert and Spencer 1996; Jacquette and Wolchik 1998; Rueschemeyer 1998a). Several features of this common legacy may be expected to dampen both the supply of female aspirants and the demand (among party gatekeepers and voters) for female candidates.

At an ideological level, the so-called 'woman question' in the party-states was relegated to secondary status. Linked as it was to the question of capitalist property relations, the emancipation of women was to be achieved, first and foremost, through socialist revolution. Once that revolution took place, however, women still had to be liberated from subordination and unpaid labour in men's kitchens. This was to be accomplished by simultaneously moving women into the paid labour force and socializing domestic chores (child-rearing, cooking, caring for the elderly and infirm).

The state-socialist regimes did accomplish a high degree of social, economic, and political participation for women, but that participation came at a high price. The centrally planned economies, with their institutionalized preferences for heavy industry, proved unable to provide household conveniences on the scale found in the West. At the same time, the quality of the socialized domestic services was often low and access limited. Extensive maternity and sick leave policies made employers view women as expensive and unreliable labour. Socialist laws that enshrined the dual 'worker-mother' role produced nothing equivalent for men (Heitlinger 1979; Jancar 1978; Meyer 1985; Wolchik 1985; Einhorn 1993). In theory and in praxis, the household remained the primary responsibility of women; men were sometimes exhorted to 'help out more' but their essential role within the family was never officially challenged (Einhorn 1993; Rueschemeyer 1998a).

All this resulted in an extreme 'double burden' in which women would work extended shifts often in low-paying, menial work and then return home to a disproportionate burden of household and child-rearing duties. The severity of the burden varied from country to country and by class and ethnic factors. Research has shown, however, that working women throughout the region did far more cooking and cleaning than their working husbands, three times as much in Czechoslovakia according to one study (Heitlinger 1979; Corrin 1993; Waylen 1994; Wejnert 1996).

The replacement of the traditional 'patriarchal bargain'—in which women accept an essentially unequal status in return for protections and material support from individual males—by a state socialist version of that bargain had profound social consequences. In this new bargain, women came to see themselves as '...coping with very difficult demands, which brought on exhaustion but also...a sense of moral superiority, and power in the household from their...apparent indispensability' (Gal and Kligman 2000: 54–5). Socialist men, who were better paid and dominant at work, reacted to the 'superwoman martyr' by becoming the 'big child' at home, '...disorganized, needy, dependent, vulnerable, demanding to be taken care of and...to be humored as he occasionally acted out with aggression and alcoholism, womanizing, or absenteeism' (Gal and Kligman 2000: 54). Single motherhood, divorce, abortion, and spousal abuse became pandemic. During the breakdown of the state socialist regimes, nationalist opposition picked up on these trends, accusing women of being in cahoots with the communists to undermine the family, emasculate men, and destroy the nation through declining fertility.

Women had political experience in the state-socialist regimes. Indeed, political activism, like paid employment, was mandatory. Yet these women did not emerge from transition as a ready pool of aspirants for the democratizing legislatures. Rather than being viewed as highly educated and qualified candidates, women have been seen as lacking the time and commitment necessary for participation in full-time working legislatures. Surveys of citizens and members of parliament in Eastern Europe consistently cite 'lack of time' and 'need to care for family' as primary obstacles to female legislative participation (Reuschemeyer 1998). At the same time, traditional values about the role of women were never really transformed in the socialist ideology or practice (Waylen 1994; Reuschemeyer 1998); and the tokenism of female representation in the communist party-states, rather than providing women with credible political credentials, actually created a number of negative stereotypes about the 'woman representative' (Goven 1993).

While it is difficult to demonstrate empirically, it has been suggested that many women simply chose to withdraw to the private sphere when they finally had the opportunity to do so (Einhorn 1993). Given the sham nature of their communist-era participation, the expectation of intense 'second shift'

RECRUITMENT THEORIES AND EASTERN EUROPE ❖

work, and the anticipation of hostile voters, it would hardly be surprising if women were reluctant to enter the 'funnel of recruitment' in the new democracies. This is ultimately a question for empirical testing. What we do know is that those women who have chosen to enter democratic politics rarely label themselves 'feminist'.

It is by now redundant to say that post-communist women are allergic to Western-style feminism. A number of articles and anthologies examine the differences between Western and Eastern perceptions of feminism; and several scholars cite this particular legacy of communism as a chief barrier to women's formal political power in the region (Einhorn 1993; Goven 1993; Marody 1993; Matynia 1994; Smejkalova 1994; Waylen 1994; Chamberlayne 1995; Havelkova 1996; Siklova 1996; Jacquette and Wolchik 1998).[5] State-socialist appropriation of the goals and rhetoric of Western feminism leaves post-communist women without an acceptable discourse in which to press equity demands. When women do lobby aggressively for their interests or try to bring more women into politics, they may be accused of being 'fame crazed', 'man-haters', 'anti-family', 'lesbian', and 'communist.' We might reasonably expect these kinds of hostile reactions would make it unattractive for possible female candidates to aspire to political office or for gatekeepers to select women as the party's candidates.

Women's limited success at organizing effectively to place pressure on politically powerful actors in the post-communist period may also be a 'hangover' from the paternalistic and atomized aspects of communist political culture more generally. In the communist party-states, the hegemonic position of the Party was constitutionally enshrined, factions and autonomous social organizations banned. What few social organizations (trade unions, women's, and youth groups) were maintained were thoroughly co-opted and controlled by the Party. Civil society, understood as autonomous social self-organization, had little opportunity to develop, and when it did, it typically took the form of a hidden or parallel sphere located within family and friendship networks. Reform efforts, such as Kádárism in Hungary, Gierek's 'sausage stuffing strategy' in Poland, and Brezhnev's consumerist policies only exacerbated the problem. At an ideological level, citizens were still educated in the socialist values of anti-individualism, anti-nationalism, and anti-Westernism. At a practical level, however, they were encouraged to withdraw from public life in return for the promise of greater access to Western-style consumerism. The end result was a post-communist culture that placed family life and personal well being over civic association and political activism (Hankiss 1990).

Waylen (1994) and Jacquette and Wolchik (1998) compare the role of women in the Latin American and East European transitions from authoritarianism and find crucial differences that lead to divergent levels and types of mobilization. In both settings, women participated in the opposition movements. In Latin America, however, women joined autonomous organizations designed to protest economic conditions, undermine regime authority, and create democracy anew with much broader social representation. Women mobilized, as women, around what Molyneaux (1985) terms practical needs—food prices, employment, housing—but came to see those needs as linked to the strategic interest of increasing the female voice in politics. In turn, women were granted a surprising amount of political space by the rightist authoritarian regimes, perhaps because the male leaders did not see the activities of women as a true threat to their hegemony. The product of this type of mobilization, at least in the short term, was that gender issues found their way into the new constitutions of Brazil, Peru, and Argentina.

East and Central European women, by contrast, worked to undermine authoritarian rule by fostering regime-subverting values in the home. They had little opportunity to develop organizational skills and experience and were generally reluctant to identify with any sort of ideological position, including feminism. As a result, women did not organize effectively in the transition period and have been reluctant to identify any particular 'women's problems'. Some women's groups did form around economic survival and religious issues, but often they have consciously avoided actions in the political sphere. Furthermore, they have not seen their interests as fundamentally advanced by increasing female legislative representation.

Parties, therefore, have experienced neither intense external nor internal pressure to place women on the ballot, nor have they provided a particularly favourable environment for the advancement of female candidates. As communist authoritarianism disintegrated, it might have been a time of great opportunity for women. Founding elections produced extremely high rates of elite turnover in most countries. Women, however, were not substantially involved in the formation of new parties or the transformation of grassroots movements into formal political entities that would compete in popular elections. For reasons described above, women may not have felt they had the time, resources, or popular support to become active in electoral politics; and freshly legitimated dissident men may have been just as happy to see women recede from the public sphere (Heinen 1992; Watson 1993).

Parties initially formed around the macro-issues of democratization, economic reform/stabilization, and nationalism. Public and scholarly attention concentrated almost exclusively on national parties and legislatures as the central sites of democratic transition. Matters of greatest concern to women were swept aside as tertiary issues that could be dealt with once the 'real issues' of transition had been resolved. In this environment, there was little opportunity to launch alternative platforms, and women quickly found themselves political subjects, rather than agents, in their new party systems. Rightist and Christian-conservative parties made political hay of blaming working mothers for a range of social ills inherited from the communist era; and communist rhetoric was replaced by the nationalist view of women as 'mothers of the nation', the literal and symbolic reproducers of the ethnic community. For many post-communist citizens, nationalism emerged as a far more legitimate replacement for communist ideology than liberalism or certainly feminism. This was particularly true in places where statehood was in question (e.g. Czechoslovakia and Yugoslavia) but also had appeal in other East European states and former Soviet republics that saw themselves as victims of long-term foreign domination.[6]

❖ LEGACY AND CHANGE IN THE POST-COMMUNIST SYSTEMS

Examined through our framework, this legacy translates into a low supply of female aspirants and weak demand for female candidates. The post-communist democracies display a wide range of institutional choices, including some that ought to provide parties with the opportunity and incentive to nominate women. We would expect women in countries that have adopted large legislative chambers and use high magnitude PR electoral systems to fare better than women in less woman-friendly systems, but as long as women are inadequately organized and public attitudes anti-feminist, women will be unable to fully utilize favourable rules.

Some of the features of the new party systems will also work against women at least in the short term. Many of the party systems that emerged in the region are highly fragmented, and nearly all of the parties (with the possible exception of reformed communists) initially emerged as personality based organizations. Early nomination practices were marked by murky rules and patronage based decisions in the hands of a few select party leaders. These characteristics of fledgling party systems clearly disadvantage women, even where electoral rules are favourable. Numerous parties competing for seats reduces party magnitudes, and women will rarely have the patronage links that men enjoy.

Over time, many of these factors may be expected to change. The nations that comprised the former Soviet bloc differ from one another in key respects, and they are changing over time. Already, the relevance of a common policy legacy is being replaced by differences in levels of socio-economic development. The region is increasingly cleaved between countries that have hopes of eventually gaining membership in the European Union and those struggling with the problems of poor capitalism (often the partial and uneven collapse of the party-state system without any clear replacement). In the latter group, women face structural and cultural barriers to political action. These barriers may act as a ceiling on the degree to which women's representation can advance even where more woman-friendly rules are adopted.

❖ R. E. MATLAND AND K. A. MONTGOMERY

Even countries that have experienced relative economic success may face a backlash against the loss of social welfare benefits associated with neo-liberal reforms. That backlash could strengthen the appeal of populist and nationalist parties that define female roles in very traditional ways and thereby discourage greater female participation in formal politics. Alternatively, it could mobilize women from the right and the old left. Parties that wish to align themselves with the protection of social safety nets may find female candidates attractive, as women are often attributed special expertise with and concern about 'ethic of care' issues.

Finally, we should not expect the anti-feminist and atomized aspects of post-communist political culture to remain static. A new generation educated after the fall of communism is coming of age. Presumably their worldview will differ from that of their parents' generation. Young educated women may become dissatisfied with political inequality, and in those countries where the party system has become more institutionalized (and women possess adequate resources), women may be able to identify points of access and strategies for seeking nomination. The post-communist transitions to democracy are perhaps unparalleled in the extent to which they have attracted international funding for the development of women's political participation. These efforts draw upon the substantial international literature on women in politics. They focus on increasing supply, by identifying and training potential female candidates, and on increasing demand on the parties to make structural changes that help promote women. Those efforts ought to pay dividends in the post-communist countries where they occur.

❖ NOTES

1 Clearly this is not the only concern and sometimes not even the primary concern. Concern for party unity (purity?), or intra-party factional fights may from time to time trump the vote maximizing desire, but in the long-run parties in democracies are forced to be concerned about winning votes. If not, they run the risk of disappearing from the political stage.

2 The representation numbers are from the Inter-Parliamentary Union's website: www.ipu.org; GDP numbers are from the CIA World Fact book various editions.

3 The countries included in the analyses in Figs 2.2 and 2.3 are all nations that were defined by Freedom House as politically free in 1990, 1995, and 2000.

4 While quotas are often credited with being responsible for Nordic countries leading the world in women's representation, the Nordic countries were generally world leaders, *before* such rules were adopted.

5 It should be noted that, while many East European scholars highlight anti-feminism as a strand of post-communist political culture and a barrier to women's participation, they also express frustration over the perception that Western feminists

seem to hold about East European women. They do not want the different conception of feminism expressed by East European women to be treated as a deficiency, and they are uncomfortable with the perceived attempt by the Western feminist community to impose their models of female emancipation on the post-communist countries.

6 There is a history of radical women subordinating their interests to the interests of the national struggle in countries where nation-building was of primary concern—for example, Poland, Slovenia, Ireland (Meyer 1985). Julie Mertus makes this point in her research on Kosovar women and cites an interview with a young representative of the women's branch of the Democratic League of Kosovo/a (LDK) who declares, 'After we have freedom, women will have freedom'. See: 'Gender in the Service of Nation: Female Citizenship in Kosovar Society' in *Social Politics* (Summer/Fall 1996 p. 261).

3 ❖ Popular Support for Electing Women in Eastern Europe

Clyde Wilcox, Beth Stark and Sue Thomas

The number of women in legislatures is a function of the supply of women candidates, public demand for women policymakers, and the political institutions in which supply and demand interact. There has been a great deal of scholarship on the supply of women candidates (Andersen 1975; Welch 1977; Togeby 1994; Norrander and Wilcox 1998; Thomas and Wilcox 1998). Yet it is also important to consider the demand side of the equation.

There are two types of demand for women candidates—women's (and especially feminist) groups' organized demand and the general public's unorganized, diffuse demand. In many countries, organized feminists have pressed parties to nominate more women, and have rallied to help recruit, support, and even fund women candidates (Duerst-Lahti 1998). In Western Europe, feminist groups have pushed to alter the opportunity structure in political parties to allow women to advance (Katzenstein and Mueller 1987).

Diffuse demand is a function of general societal attitudes about the roles of women in the family, in society, and especially in politics. Voters may vary in the degree to which they believe women are able to perform as political leaders. In most countries, at least some voters believe men are better suited for politics than women, and that men make more able executives and legislators. The traditional stereotype of women is they are too moralistic to engage in the backroom dealmaking that often allows legislatures to reach compromise, and they are not sufficiently tough to manage the rough and tumble world of politics.

On the other hand, in some countries, women (and some men) believe that women have unique political interests that can best be served by having significant numbers of female representatives in national legislatures. In the United States in 1992, men and women in many states told pollsters, 'It is important to elect more women to the US Senate'. (Cook 1994). A majority of women in California and Washington states, and more than 40 per cent of men in those states, indicated that it was 'very important' to elect more women to the Senate. In this case, diffuse demand for women legislatures was positive, but in countries where traditional stereotypes hold sway, there may be no unorganized demand for electing more women to public office.

Demand and supply interact through political institutions. Central to this interaction are party leaders, who interpret the direction and extent of organized and unorganized demand for women candidates, and choose candidates accordingly. If party leaders believe their party will win more seats if they nominate more women, they will be more likely to do so. They will also seek to increase the supply of women candidates through active recruitment. If they believe women candidates hurt their party's chances, then they are more likely to bypass women and choose men to run.

This chapter examines unorganized demand for women in the legislatures of post-communist Central and Eastern European countries. We begin by examining the extent to which electorates in these countries may hold traditional gender stereotypes—that men are better political leaders than women. We find that large numbers of men and women in Central and Eastern Europe believe that men are better political leaders than women, suggesting there is little diffuse demand for more women in legislatures and that traditional stereotypes are likely to make it more difficult to elect more women.

Although these data suggest that demand for women political leaders is low, it is possible this represents a short-term reaction against the legislated gender equality of the discredited communist system—a reaction that may fade with time. In the United States, the past 30 years have seen a remarkable increase in the percentage of Americans willing to vote for women for elected office. This change occurred because general beliefs in equality in society were applied to gender politics, thanks in part to organized feminist efforts.

We start with a consideration of general gender attitudes, in the workplace and family, and the level of support for a women's movement that might mobilize those attitudes into support for women in legislative office. We conclude with some multivariate analyses to help us sort through the differences among the countries and to identify the sources of attitudes.

Our data come from the World Values Studies in 1995–7 and an earlier survey in 1991–3, which polled citizens in a number of Central and Eastern European countries, as well as a few Western European countries. The 1995–7 survey asked a more concrete question about attitudes toward women in politics, but it was not administered in several Central and Eastern European countries including Hungary, the Czech Republic, and Slovakia. The 1991–3 survey was administered in more countries, but its questions are less directly related to women in politics.[1] We have excluded from our analysis Central and Eastern European countries that are clearly undemocratic. For comparison, we include data from Western European countries, although it should be

❖ C. WILCOX, B. STARK AND S. THOMAS

noted these countries are among the most affluent and best educated in the world and therefore set a high standard for comparison.

❖ DEMAND FOR WOMEN IN PUBLIC OFFICE

Unfortunately, no cross-national survey in Eastern or Central Europe has asked voters directly whether it was important to elect more women to national legislatures. Yet, we know demand for women candidates is rooted in fundamental views of the political abilities of men and women. If women believe that men are better politicians or leaders than women, they are unlikely to press for gender equality in representation in legislatures and may be less likely to run for office. Attitudes on women's abilities as political leaders are empirically related to the proportion of women serving in legislatures worldwide (Norris and Inglehart 2000). Thus, an important starting point in any discussion of public demand for female legislators is to investigate lingering support for this stereotype.

The 1995–7 wave of the World Values Study included an item that asked respondents to strongly agree, agree, disagree, or strongly disagree with this statement: 'On the whole, men make better political leaders than women do'. Fig. 3.1 shows the percentage of men and women in several Eastern and Central European countries who believed that men made better leaders, with comparative data on men and women in a few Western European countries. The data reveal a striking regional contrast: in every Western European country, a large majority of men and women reject the belief that men are better political leaders. More than three quarters of men and women disagreed with the statement, and many objected strongly.

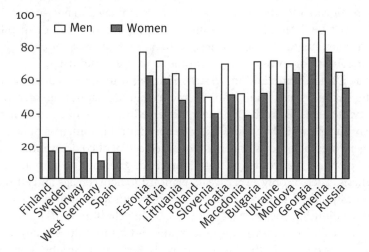

Figure 3.1. Per cent who agree that 'men make better political leaders'.

Source: 1995–7 World Values Study.

In contrast, a majority of men in every Eastern and Central European country believe that men make better leaders than women, as do a majority of women in most of these countries. Only in Slovenia, Macedonia, and Lithuania do the majority of women disagree, and only in Macedonia does opposition approach that in the West. In Bulgaria, Ukraine, and Estonia, more than 30 per cent of men *strongly* agreed that men make better leaders.

The portion of the public that believes that men make better political leaders in these countries is striking. Ninety per cent of men in Armenia hold this belief, as do 86 per cent of men in Georgia, 65 per cent in Russia, and 67 per cent of men in Poland. Three-quarters of the women in Georgia agree that men make better leaders, as do more than half of the women in Poland and the Baltic countries. It is evident from these data that not only is there little demand for electing more women in Central and Eastern Europe, but also that public stereotypes of women's abilities are a significant barrier to electing women.

These data paint a relatively bleak portrait of demand for women legislators in Central and Eastern European countries.[2] In many countries, an outright majority of women believe that men make better leaders. In others, the proportion is sufficiently sizable that it poses a significant electoral barrier. Clearly, there is currently little unorganized demand for electing more women to legislatures in Eastern and Central Europe.

The widespread belief that men make better leaders limits women's election in many ways. Most importantly, it is likely that many who hold this view will be less likely to vote for a woman candidate for public office, although, the exact relationship between abstract belief and concrete behaviour in this instance is not entirely clear.[3] Party leaders may find similar results in their own surveys and conclude their party would lose seats if it nominated many women. Finally, women may be deterred from running for office because they, or members of their families, may hold these beliefs, or because they interpret public opinion in their country or constituency as hostile to women candidates.

In the United States and in Western Europe, young, well-educated women led the second-wave feminist movement that demanded greater political equality. It seems likely that younger, better-educated women in Central and Eastern Europe would be more likely to have faith in women as political leaders. Therefore, the process of generational replacement could eventually lead to greater demand for women in legislatures. Yet, the data do not support this hypothesis. There is only a very weak relationship between age and attitudes on women as political leaders in post-communist Europe, compared with a very robust relationship in the West (Norris and Inglehart 2000). The correlation between age and attitudes about gender and leadership is three times as high in the West ($r = 0.15$) as in the East ($r = 0.05$).[4] Moreover, a very high proportion of the most educated women in Eastern and Central European countries believe that men make better political leaders.

❖ C. WILCOX, B. STARK AND S. THOMAS

Overall, these data yield little hope that demand for electing women to legislatures in Eastern and Central Europe will increase soon. Yet, because of the rapid pace of political and social change in many of these countries, it is premature to suggest that demand for women legislators will always be low. Political cleavages are in flux in post-communist Europe, parties may come and go, and issues may arise that might increase the demand for women in elected office. If there is general support for gender equality in Central and Eastern Europe and significant support for a feminist movement, it is possible the women's movement will mold those general equality values into support for women candidates among women voters. In addition, it may directly pressure party officials to respond to the generalized support for gender equality.

❖ Support for Gender Equality in Central and Eastern Europe

If support for political equality among women is to grow in Central and Eastern Europe, it might come from general ideas of equality between men and women. In the United States and Western Europe, general attitudes about gender equality are highly correlated with support for women in elected office. Americans who believe that women should stay home and care for their families or that preschool children suffer if their mothers work are less likely to report they would support a woman for president than are men and women who support basic gender equality. Moreover, there are strong aggregate regional relationships between these attitudes. Areas in which citizens voice low levels of support for general women's equality are also the lowest in support for women's political equality. Finally, the states in which surveys have shown the greatest support for electing more women to the US Senate (Cook 1994) are also states with relatively egalitarian attitudes on general gender equality.

In the United States, attitudes towards women in political life became more egalitarian *before* attitudes on family life, and the same appears to be true in Western Europe (Wilcox 1991a). The dynamic may well be different in Eastern and Central Europe, however, where gender equality in employment and education were official government policies and where some kind of state-funded childcare was widely available. It is possible that attitudes that are more egalitarian were shaped in the areas of employment, education, and family life. Moreover, these values might provide the basis for a future increase in support for women in elected office.

❖ *Attitudes towards work and education*

Table 3.1 shows selected attitudes on employment and education in the two waves of the World Values Study. The first two columns show the percentage

Table 3.1. Attitudes towards employment and education

	1991–3		1995–7			
	Scarce jobs to men		Scarce jobs to men		Boys to college	
	Men (%)	Women (%)	Men (%)	Women (%)	Men(%)	Women (%)
Sweden	7	9	8	7	10	8
Finland	16	15	17	12	15	19
Norway	17	15	15	14	21	19
Netherlands	26	21	na	na	na	na
Germany	37	27	24	21	13	9
Spain	32	30	27	27	18	6
France	35	31	na	na	na	na
Britain	31	36	na	na	na	na
Italy	38	33	na	na	na	na
Average West	25	24	18	16	15	12
Latvia	46	43	33	19	16	10
Slovenia	34	25	28	25	8	5
Lithuania	71	63	41	24	18	18
Bulgaria	57	35	42	29	7	6
Ukraine	na	na	47	31	16	16
Romania	46	38	na	na	na	na
Hungary	41	44	na	na	na	na
Croatia	na	na	47	38	14	12
Estonia	46	43	na	na	na	na
Poland	58	52	48	41	7	7
Macedonia	na	na	56	42	6	6
Russia	47	38	54	46	17	17
Moldova	na	na	56	48	14	8
Czech Rep.	57	52	na	na	na	na
Armenia	na	na	71	50	31	10
Georgia	na	na	72	55	20	9
Average East	50	43	50	37	15	11

Percentage who agreed that when jobs are scarce, men have more right to a job; and that a university education is more important for a boy than a girl.

who agreed that when jobs are scarce, men have first right to the job (in both waves of the survey). The final column shows the percentage who agreed that a university education is more important for a boy than a girl. The top part of the table provides data for some selected West European countries for comparative purposes.

The data show that in Western Europe, an average of one in four men and women believed that scarce jobs should go to men in 1991–3. The rate was

❖ C. WILCOX, B. STARK AND S. THOMAS

higher in Britain and in countries with larger Catholic populations, reaching 38 per cent of men in Italy and 36 per cent of women in Britain. In contrast, support was much lower in Scandinavian countries.

Support for reserving scarce jobs for men was much higher in Eastern and Central Europe. Seventy-one per cent of men in Lithuania thought that men should get scarce jobs, as did 63 per cent of women. Among men, only Slovenians fell within the range of attitudes in the West; among women, those of Slovenia, Romania, and Bulgaria would have fit within attitudes of the Catholic countries of Western Europe.

This question was repeated in the 1995–7 wave, with a somewhat different set of countries. In the West, attitudes were generally stable between waves, although German attitudes moved in a more egalitarian direction. In the East, attitudes changed especially in Latvia and Lithuania. In Latvia, support for reserving jobs for men dropped among women from 43 per cent to 19 per cent over this short period. In Lithuania, it dropped from 63 per cent to 24 per cent among women, and from 71 per cent to 41 per cent among men. The magnitude of this change is remarkable. Polish and Bulgarian men also became somewhat more egalitarian, while Russians become somewhat less so.

In the final column, there is much less regional difference in the belief that a university education is more important for a boy than a girl. Only men in Armenia stand out as especially non-egalitarian. The residents of Poland, Slovenia, Croatia, and Macedonia are even less likely to agree to this statement than respondents from the three Scandinavian countries.

The data in this table raise a number of questions. Why are men and women in the East more willing to reserve scarce jobs for men? Why did attitudes on this question move so remarkably in Latvia and Lithuania? Why are attitudes towards gender preference in education so different from those in employment?

That both men and women in Eastern and Central Europe support reserving scarce jobs for men is especially striking. It is possible that the explanation lies in the double burden of paid employment coupled with household and childrearing chores. As economic fortunes have declined, these household tasks have expanded to include additional work for barter or as part of an underground economy. Writing of the Hungarian situation, Fodor (1985) noted that 'the only possible solution to women's double burden they saw was a return to the traditional distribution of chores, so that women could work less outside the home or not take a job at all' (p. 185). Support for reserving jobs for men may reflect a desire to escape this double burden to retreat from the paid labour force in order to escape the crushing load of domestic and paid work. Thus, perhaps women and men in Eastern Europe agree on this question for very different reasons.

It is also possible that support for reserving jobs for men reflects a belief that in times of economic scarcity, jobs should be rationed for greater equality—one to a family. The question on reserving jobs for men was part of a larger battery about job allocation in periods of high unemployment, a phenomenon that many in the Central and Eastern European countries were experiencing for the first time. These data show that Central and Eastern European women are far more likely than their Western counterparts to believe, not only that men should get scarce jobs, but also, that the elderly should be forced to retire to open up jobs, nationals should be hired before immigrants, and that it is unfair to give jobs to the handicapped when able-bodied workers are unemployed. Thus, the preference for selecting men might be seen as part of a more general egalitarian belief that jobs should be rationed one to a family in hard times.

A third possibility is that women in Eastern Europe find their jobs unfulfilling and are thus more willing to leave the labour force. Additional analysis (not shown) suggests that women in the West and in Eastern and Central Europe differ in the nature of their jobs and their fulfillment from those jobs. Women in Eastern and Central Europe are significantly more likely to say they work primarily for pay and are less likely to say that they always do their best at work, that they enjoy their work, that they have pride in their work, that their jobs are satisfying, or that they have decision-making freedom. The nature of the work experience for women in the East appears to be markedly less fulfilling than in the West and this may account for the willingness of women in the East to agree to reserve scarce jobs for men.

The remarkable change in women's attitudes in Lithuania and Latvia deserves additional scrutiny, but there is nothing in these data that permit us to better understand these changes. It is possible that the frequent contact between women of these countries and those of Sweden, Denmark, and Norway sparked this change. When the 2000–2 wave of the World Values surveys are complete, it will be interesting to see if this trend has continued.

Finally, why are attitudes so much more egalitarian on education than on employment? Future research is needed here as well to unpack this discrepancy. The Communist governments that once ran these countries had considerable success in equalizing educational access below the college level, but differences persisted in college education. It may be that a college education is seen as essential to the new economy. Thus, men and women alike want their daughters to have an equal chance at good future jobs. Even women who seek to escape a double burden by leaving the paid labour force may imagine their daughters with more fulfilling and higher paid jobs than their own if they receive a university education. In addition, the question about college education does not force respondents to make a choice. It is possible that higher education is less a scarce good than are steady jobs in Eastern Europe. Respondents might have answered differently to a question that asked if university student slots were scarce, whether boys should get first choice.

❖ C. WILCOX, B. STARK AND S. THOMAS

❖ *Attitudes towards family roles*

Table 3.2 shows attitudes on select questions about family roles. The first column shows the percentage of respondents in 1991–3 who agreed that being a housewife is as fulfilling as working for pay. Majorities in most countries agreed that being a housewife was fulfilling, but this belief was especially common in Estonia, Lithuania, Bulgaria, and Russia. It was especially uncommon in

Table 3.2. Traditional attitudes towards family roles

	1991–3		1995–7			
	Housewife fulfilling		Both contribute		Want boy	
	Men (%)	Women (%)	Men (%)	Women (%)	Men (%)	Women (%)
Sweden	63	63	10	9	18	10
Finland	56	51	23	19	28	15
Norway	54	53	21	19	23	9
Netherlands	56	52	na	na	na	na
Germany	56	53	24	23	26	15
Spain	62	58	12	6	23	13
France	63	57	na	na	na	na
Italy	57	46	na	na	na	na
Britain	56	63	na	na	na	na
Average West	*58*	*55*	*18*	*15*	*24*	*12*
Latvia	62	66	16	10	47	22
Lithuania	87	83	18	18	40	15
Slovenia	69	57	8	5	32	22
Bulgaria	86	88	7	6	43	19
Ukraine	na	na	16	12	42	22
Romania	52	45	na	na	na	na
Croatia	na	na	14	12	39	16
Poland	na	na	7	14	28	10
Macedonia	na	na	6	6	36	28
Estonia	75	67	9	6	45	20
Hungary	79	73	na	na	na	na
Russia	90	83	17	9	51	23
Moldova	na	na	14	8	54	30
Armenia	na	na	31	10	60	40
Czech Rep.	42	37	na	na	na	na
Georgia	na	na	20	9	63	35
Average East	*71*	*67*	*14*	*10*	*64*	*23*

Percentage who agreed that being a housewife is as fulfilling as working for wages; that *disagreed* both husband and wife should contribute to household income; and that if they had one child they would want it to be a boy.

then-united Czechoslovakia.[5] In general, support for the housewife role was higher in the East than in the West, although country differences are complex.

The second column shows the percentage in 1995–7 who *disagreed* that both husband and wife should contribute to household income. In Western Europe disagreement was higher in Finland, Germany, and Norway, and much lower in Sweden and Spain. In the East, disagreement was highest in Georgia and Armenia among men, and in Lithuania among both men and women. However, agreement was high in both regions. The norm of two-income households appears to be near universal in all regions of Europe. The extra contributions of many women in Eastern and Central Europe to non-monetary family income may mean that Eastern and Central European attitudes are even more egalitarian than this question suggests.

The final column shows the percentage of respondents in 1995–7 who indicated that, if they had one child, they would prefer a boy (other options were to prefer a girl, or to have no preference). On this item Eastern European men and women are far more traditional than those in the West. In Moldova, Georgia, Armenia, and Russia, more than half of men expressed this view, as did more than 40 per cent of men in Estonia, Latvia, Lithuania, Bulgaria, and the Ukraine. There is a sizable gender gap in all countries on this item, but women in the East were also generally more likely than those in the West to express preference for a baby boy. The men and women in Poland and the women in Lithuania are the least likely to voice this sentiment.

These data provide a mixed picture, in part because of the complex nature of gender attitudes about families (Sapiro 2002), and in part because none of these questions ask specifically about equality in the family. In general, these data show there is slightly higher support in the East for women performing the housewife role, and greater support for the traditional preference for a baby boy.

❖ Attitudes on motherhood

In the United States, the 'politics of motherhood' have become highly contested (Luker 1984). Large symbolic debates occur between feminists and antifeminists over whether young children benefit from a mother's close attention in early years and whether childcare stunts children's emotional growth. Many feminists in the United States have argued that women have no special advantages as caregivers to children. Moreover, they believe some childcare centres provide as much emotional support for children as some mothers who stay home full-time to care for their children. In Western Europe, many feminists have instead maintained that children do benefit from the close attention of mothers *and* fathers, and have pushed for extended, paid family leave for women and for men, with laws guaranteeing they can return to their job at the end of that period.

❖ C. WILCOX, B. STARK AND S. THOMAS

Table 3.3 shows attitudes on motherhood and childcare in West and Eastern Europe. The first column shows the percentage that disagreed that a working mother can establish as warm a relationship with her child as a mother in the labour force. The third column shows responses to this same question in 1995–7. In the West, German attitudes were quite distinctive in the first

Table 3.3. Attitudes towards motherhood

| | 1991–3 | | | | 1995–7 | | | |
| | Mother warm | | Preschool child | | Mother warm | | Need child | |
	Men (%)	Women (%)	Men (%)	Women (%)	Men (%)	Women (%)	Men (%)	Women (%)
Sweden	35	18	81	66	30	13	20	14
Finland	7	4	60	40	10	3	26	16
Norway	38	23	54	36	36	24	21	17
Netherlands	38	21	73	50	na	na	na	na
Germany	63	55	86	82	41	22	30	25
Spain	36	31	56	56	33	35	45	44
France	27	27	68	63	na	na	na	na
Italy	35	31	74	76	na	na	na	na
Britain	33	27	57	52	na	na	na	na
Average West	*35*	*26*	*68*	*58*	*30*	*19*	*28*	*23*
Latvia	*57*	*50*	*90*	*93*	*29*	*25*	*71*	*75*
Lithuania	*56*	*59*	*87*	*92*	*31*	*21*	*72*	*78*
Slovenia	29	23	70	64	25	22	49	52
Bulgaria	40	39	73	79	22	20	69	72
Ukraine	na	na	na	na	24	21	78	81
Romania	17	15	57	59	na	na	na	na
Croatia	na	na	na	na	31	27	57	59
Poland	na	na	na	na	55	47	69	70
Macedonia	na	na	na	na	37	29	66	68
Estonia	19	17	89	91	22	13	80	81
Hungary	33	28	71	70	na	na	na	na
Russia	37	36	71	70	25	22	80	86
Moldova	na	na	na	na	22	19	85	86
Armenia	na	na	na	na	23	13	83	83
Czech Rep.	47	36	80	76	na	na	na	na
Georgia	na	na	na	na	29	17	82	84
Average East	*37*	*34*	*76*	*77*	*29*	*23*	*72*	*75*

Percentage who disagreed that a working mother can establish as warm a relationship with her child as a mother in the labourforce, in 1991–3 and 1995–7; who believe preschool children suffer when their mother is in the workforce; and who believe that a woman needs a child to be fulfilled.

survey: well over half of men and women do not believe that working women can establish as warm a relationship with their children. Finns were also distinctive in their belief that working mothers *can* establish warm relationships. In the East, attitudes varied widely, but Latvia and Lithuania were distinctive in their belief that working women cannot establish a warm relationship. Men and women in Estonia were much more likely to think that this could occur.

In the second wave of surveys, German attitudes had changed markedly on this question, as had attitudes in Latvia and Lithuania. In this later survey, attitudes in the East appear to be generally more liberal than in the West, with Polish men and women the most likely to believe that working women cannot establish as warm a relationship.

The second column shows the percentage in 1991–3 who believed that pre-school children suffer when their mother works for wages. Note this is a different question in several respects: it identifies the child as young, and it does not specifically focus on the mother–child bond. Thus, it is possible to believe that mothers can establish warm, loving relationships, but that the quality of childcare is so poor that children suffer as a result of extended childcare.

On this item, that was not repeated in the later survey, national patterns in the West signal this item taps into far more than simple gender politics. Agreement is highest in Germany and Sweden, and lowest in Norway and Spain—both unlikely pairings. In Eastern Europe, agreement is highest again in Lithuania and Latvia, although we cannot tell if these attitudes had changed by the second survey because the question was not repeated.

The final column shows agreement with the statement that a woman needs a child to be fulfilled. Here there is a sharp regional difference in responses: men and women in every western country are more likely to disagree with this statement than are men and women in every eastern and central European country. The gaps here are large: in Germany and northern Europe a quarter or fewer of women agreed with this statement, but in most Central and Eastern European countries the figure was closer to 85 per cent.

There is a second, subtler, pattern in these data as well. In every Western European country in this set, men were more likely than women to agree with this statement, and the difference was statistically significant everywhere but in Spain. In every Eastern or Central European country, women were more likely than men to agree with the statement; even the apparent tie in Armenia reflects a slightly larger level of agreement among women. The difference is statistically significant in only a few Eastern and Central European countries, but when the nations of the region are combined, the difference is quite significant.

The most straightforward interpretation of these results is that women in the East are far more centred on their roles as mothers than are women in the West. This is consistent with the greater support for the role of housewife in

❖ C. WILCOX, B. STARK AND S. THOMAS

Table 3.3 as well. This may be the function of many factors—a more traditional culture, less parental involvement by men, and less rewarding jobs to offer competing sources of fulfillment. It is also possible, however, that the data overstates this regional difference. In the West, many men and women who find their children to be a critical element of their own fulfillment may hesitate to say yes to a blanket statement that seems to imply that *all* women need children, for the culture now rejects such sweeping statements about any group. It is also possible that there exists a widely accepted 'correct' answer to this question in the West. It is openly acknowledged, by all groups, that not all women desire motherhood.

Taken together, the data in these three tables provide us with a complicated pattern of gender attitudes in Eastern and Central Europe. Eastern attitudes are most distinctive on whether to reserve scarce jobs for men, whether a boy child is preferred when a family has only one child, and whether a woman needs a child to be fulfilled. The simplest interpretation of these patterns is that men and women in East and Central Europe tend to hold views of gender roles that are more traditional, with a preference for women to focus on their roles as mothers and homemakers and for men to focus on paid employment. At first glance, this would seem to bode ill for the prospects of electing more women in Eastern Europe. Housewives generally make less successful political candidates than women who have been active in politics or in business or civic leadership. Yet, in the United States, the feminist movement carefully crafted arguments to increase support for gender equality, and if there is support for a women's movement in Eastern and Central Europe, it is possible that feminists could move opinion there as well.

❖ SUPPORT FOR THE WOMEN'S MOVEMENT IN EASTERN EUROPE

In the West, feminist movements have spearheaded the demand for women in public office. These movements have sought to identify opportunity structures and to recruit and train candidates to exploit those structures. Moreover, feminist movements in western societies have made strong arguments in favour of gender equality in politics and public life. These efforts have been a likely source of the increased support for equality in Western Europe (Wilcox 1991a,b, Morgan and Wilcox 1992). Thus even if there is currently little unorganized demand for women candidates in Eastern and Central Europe, and even if traditional gender stereotypes are common there, a strong feminist movement could potentially change all of that in a generation.

The World Values Study in 1991–3 asked respondents whether they approved of the women's movement. In 1995–7, respondents were asked their level of confidence in the women's movement. These two questions are not identical, for it is possible to support a movement in which you have little confidence but much hope, and it is also possible, if less likely, to have confidence in a movement that you do not support. Table 3.4 shows these data for each country. At first glance, these items would seem to be adequate measures of support for feminist style organizations.[6]

Yet, the data in Table 3.4 show some puzzling patterns. In the data from 1991–3, we see stronger approval of the women's movement in Eastern Europe than in the West, reaching a remarkable 92 per cent among Bulgarian women.

Table 3.4. Approval of and confidence in the women's movement

	1991–3		1995–7	
	Approve of women's movement		Confident in movement	
	Men (%)	Women (%)	Men (%)	Women (%)
Sweden	72	80	28	37
Finland	57	73	31	40
Norway	66	76	21	37
Netherlands	68	68	na	na
Germany	63	79	44	55
Spain	64	72	42	47
France	69	68	na	na
Italy	45	55	na	na
Britain	79	79	na	na
Average West	*65*	*72*	*33*	*43*
Latvia	86	92	45	47
Lithuania	87	92	58	58
Slovenia	na	na	na	37
Bulgaria	83	92	43	40
Ukraine	na	na	49	42
Romania	67	84	na	na
Croatia	na	na	33	32
Poland	86	92	37	38
Macedonia	na	na	28	20
Estonia	82	88	na	na
Hungary	76	79	na	na
Russia	84	93	50	42
Moldova	na	na	35	34
Armenia	na	na	71	54
Czech Rep.	59	70	na	na
Georgia	na	na	59	48
Belarus	89	89	51	42
Serbia	na	na	39	28
Average East	*80*	*87*	*46*	*40*

Entries are percentage who approved or strongly approved of the women's movement in 1991–3, or who had a great deal of confidence in or were quite confident in the women's movement in 1995–7.

❖ C. WILCOX, B. STARK AND S. THOMAS

Indeed, Bulgarian *men* are more supportive of the women's movement in these data than are Swedish women, a result that is especially unlikely given the strong consensus among Bulgarian men that they make better politicians than women. Within the Eastern and Central European countries, the ranking of countries on this measure is also counterintuitive. In data from 1995–7, Georgian women were more confident in the women's movement than women in Macedonia, a pattern inconsistent with the data in Fig. 3.1.

How might we explain these surprising results? It seems unlikely that a nascent feminist movement has gathered considerable strength without affecting attitudes on gender equality in politics. Instead, these data suggest that the meaning of the 'women's movement' is different in Eastern Europe than it is in the West. In the East, the 'women's movement' has little to do with feminism.

Among Central and Eastern European women in 1991–3, the correlation between approving of the women's movement and disapproving of reserving scarce jobs for men was 0.02.[7] In the 1995–7 data, the correlation among Eastern and Central European women between confidence in the women's movement and disagreement that men make better political leaders was a scant 0.06. Clearly, in Eastern and Central Europe, many women who feel close to 'the women's movement' support non-feminist organizations. Writing before the fall of the Wall, Wolchik (1986) noted 'many of the new women's groups do not call for greater equality, but in fact are explicitly devoted to fostering women's domestic roles. Most deny that they are feminist... feminism is for the most part a dirty word in these countries, as most citizens associate the term with radical, man-hating activists' (p. 11). These data suggest that her conclusion is also true today. For many in the East, the 'women's movement' refers to groups that promote traditional gender and maternal roles. Indeed, in the 1991–3 data, the single strongest attitudinal predictor of Eastern and Central European women's approval of the women's movement was the belief that a woman needs a child to be fulfilled. Clearly, these data present a cautionary tale for scholars who seek to compare political values and movements across cultures.

Yet, this does suggest that women in Eastern and Central Europe are supportive of a variety of types of women's groups. Regardless of whether these groups are actually feminist, they can help women develop important political skills and can form alliances with political parties. Moreover, there are many ways to build support for women's candidacies, and if women in Eastern Europe come to believe they have special interests relating to motherhood and childrearing that only women can understand, then it might be possible for maternalist women's movements to build support for women in elected office. Women might also come to see common interest in family-centred policies relating to prevention of violence against women and children, in maintaining government programmes that provide social welfare benefits, or even in fighting alcohol abuse.[8]

❖ SOURCES OF SUPPORT FOR WOMEN LEADERS

Figure 3.1 showed considerable variation among men and women in Eastern and Central Europe in their evaluation of women as political leaders. Of course, the electorates in these countries differ in many ways: in Poland 94 per cent of respondents are Catholic, whereas in Bulgaria the figure is one per cent. Nearly one in four respondents in Macedonia are Muslim, but that figure is zero per cent in Estonia. Only six per cent of women in the Ukraine consider themselves to be housewives, but 29 per cent of Croatian women report that labour-force status. All of these variables are known to influence support for women in politics in the West.

Table 3.5 shows the sources of attitudes toward women as political leaders, among men and women of Eastern and Central Europe. We have estimated a logistic regression equation, predicting the belief that men make better political leaders. In the first equation, we include both men and women, using sex as the independent variable; in the second equation, we include only women, and in the third, we include only men. We have identified residents of each country with a dummy variable, with Russia as the excluded country. Russia's average attitude is the median of all countries in this set. We include as predictors characteristics and attitudes that predict support for gender equality in the West—age, education, religion, marital status, motherhood, labour-force participation, and left-right self-placement. For religion, we have identified Catholics, Muslims, and members of Orthodox churches with dummy variables, assessing them against members of other faiths and especially against secular citizens. We also included a measure of the frequency of attendance. For labour-force participation, we have identified those who work for wages, and those who are full-time housewives. Each was assessed relative to those who are unemployed or retired.[9] Our measure of marital status included those who indicated they lived together as married, and our measure of motherhood is a count of the number of children.

The basic demographic variables are not strong predictors of attitudes. Women are significantly less likely than men to believe that men make better political leaders, and gender is the single strongest predictor in the model. Older, less educated respondents are more likely to hold traditional gender stereotypes, as are Muslims and those who place themselves on the political right. The patterns for men and women are similar, but there are notable differences. Age and education are much stronger predictors for women than for men, suggesting that generational replacement and increasing access to higher education will be more likely to change attitudes of women than men. Islam matters more for men than women, the difference is significant at 0.10. Finally, ideology matters for men but not for women.

After controlling for religious, educational, and ideological differences, the data show that significant country differences exist. Men and women in

❖ C. WILCOX, B. STARK AND S. THOMAS

Table 3.5. Sources of belief that men make better political leaders

	All		Women		Men	
	B	Wald	B	Wald	B	Wald
Latvia	0.29	6.80**	0.24	2.72	0.35	4.20*
Lithuania	−0.31	5.09*	−0.39	4.26*	−0.20	1.04
Slovenia	−0.77	31.86**	−0.80	18.33**	−0.69	12.36**
Bulgaria	−0.01	0.00	−0.27	3.63	0.33	4.30*
Ukraine	0.21	4.73*	−0.04	0.10	0.54	13.04**
Croatia	−0.36	6.50*	−0.63	10.11**	−0.04	0.04
Poland	−0.10	0.47	−0.22	1.17	0.08	0.13
Macedonia	−0.65	32.65**	−0.69	17.12**	−0.53	11.63**
Estonia	0.39	11.35**	0.25	2.45	0.53	8.84**
Moldova	0.42	12.61**	0.39	6.06*	0.44	6.65**
Armenia	1.25	105.29**	0.94	34.30	1.63	73.07**
Georgia	1.12	122.56**	0.89	45.37**	1.46	82.30**
Woman	−0.62	179.39**	na	na	na	na
Married	0.00	0.00	0.05	0.63	−0.03	0.11
Number of children	0.02	1.09	0.04	1.58	0.02	0.29
Age	0.01	23.93**	0.01	23.99**	0.01	4.50*
Education	−0.03	4.56*	−0.05	6.33*	−0.00	0.01
Works for wages	−0.01	0.05	−0.10	2.16	0.10	1.71
Housewife	0.08	1.34	0.10	0.83	na	na
Catholic	0.08	0.68	−0.08	0.33	0.27	3.29
Muslim	0.75	24.77**	0.67	9.25**	0.86	17.25**
Orthodox	−0.10	2.49	−0.16	3.15	−0.05	0.29
Church Attendance	0.02	1.16	−0.03	1.66	0.02	0.00
Right ideology	0.04	13.71**	0.02	3.54	0.05	10.47**
Constant	1.19	38.43**	−0.00	0.00	0.19	0.53
N	19074		10442		8629	
Model chi-square	951.93,24df**		429,23df**		394,23df**	
−2 log likelihood	12612.43		7000.08		5569.23	
Nagelkerke R^2	0.12		0.10		0.11	

* = sig. at 0.05
** = sig. at 0.01

Georgia and Armenia are distinctly more likely than Russians to agree that men make better political leaders. Men and women in Moldova and men in Ukraine, Estonia and Latvia are also significantly more likely to agree that men make better political leaders. Men and women in Slovenia, Croatia, and Macedonia are all likely to disagree. The same can be said of Lithuanian women.

There is a clear geography to some of these patterns: support for women as political leaders is lowest in Georgia and Armenia, and highest in Slovenia, Croatia, and Macedonia. National differences in the Baltic region are interesting: men in Estonia and Latvia are more likely than Russians to agree that men make better political leaders, but women in Lithuania are significantly less likely to think this than are women in Russia. As we have seen, more general gender attitudes have been changing rapidly in the Baltic region.

We also estimated models for women in Western Europe and those in the East separately, including only the demographic and social sources of attitudes (not shown). It is important not to generalize too far from these data, since the set of Western European nations is quite limited, but there are intriguing differences. First, the demographic variables do a far better job of explaining variation in the West than in the East: the Nagelkerke R^2 was twice as high in the West (0.08) as in the East (0.04). Most intriguing was the impact of Catholicism; Catholicism was weakly associated with support for women political leaders in the East, and strongly associated with the belief that men make better leaders in the West. Indeed, many of the Eastern European countries with the highest portion of Catholics—Croatia, Slovenia, and Lithuania, but not Poland, are among the most supportive of women as elected leaders in all of Europe. The difference in the impact of Catholicism on attitudes between these two regions was statistically significant.

Frequency of church attendance, marriage, the number of children, labour force attachment, and left-right identification all matter in the West but not in the East. Age and education are far stronger predictors of attitudes of Western women than among those in Eastern and Central Europe. This suggests that many of the cultural divisions in the West—between married and single women, between mothers and those without children, between highly religious and non-religious women—are not helpful in understanding Eastern European attitudes toward women as politicians.

❖ CONCLUSIONS

Our analysis suggests there is currently little demand for female legislators, and that large majorities in many countries believe that men make better political leaders. This view is more prevalent among older and less educated citizens, but it is sufficiently widespread among even younger and better-educated women that it is unlikely that generational replacement offers much hope for increasing demand for female legislators. Moreover, although there is significant support for a 'women's movement' in Eastern and Central Europe, that support appears to be for a non-feminist, maternalist movement. Women and men who believe that women need children to be fulfilled are especially likely to support the movement.

❖ C. WILCOX, B. STARK AND S. THOMAS

Women and men in Eastern and Central Europe are generally more likely to believe that the role of homemaker and mother is fulfilling and that motherhood is essential to a woman's happiness than are citizens in the West. They are more likely to believe that men should get scarce jobs, and more likely to want a baby boy if they have only one child.

Taken together, these data would seem to offer scant hope that demand will increase in Eastern or Central Europe in the near future. However, these countries are undergoing rapid social, economic, and political change, and we think it is possible that demand will increase in the near future. First, with fluid party politics and candidate-centred factions, a strong woman political leader might rise quickly in any of these countries, and if she is successful, she might change attitudes by force of her example.

A non-feminist women's movement also might lead to greater demand for female political leaders. If women in Eastern and Central Europe share a common concern with home and family, and if they come to believe that male politicians are ignoring important issues like education, childcare, family violence, and other issues that they find important, this might lead to calls for female politicians to articulate women's distinctive issues. The lack of social cleavages so politicized in the West—between women in the labour force and housewives, between Catholics and secular women, and even between older and younger women—raises the intriguing possibility that feminist and non-feminist women's groups might work together towards a common goal of electing women in legislatures.

❖ NOTES

1 While the questions asked in the World Values Surveys are not ideal for our purposes, few other surveys in this region ask any questions about gender politics.

2 Our conclusion is not definitive, because of the ambiguity of the meaning of the term 'political leader'. In some countries, voters may have agreed with this statement because they think that men make better executives, but still supported women in important legislative roles. Based on the evidence in the remainder of the paper, however, we think this is unlikely.

3 Women have been elected to public office even as president or prime minister in countries where traditional gender stereotypes dominate. For at least some voters, traditional stereotypes in the abstract do not deter them from supporting particular women in some elections.

4 It is worth noting, however, that older women were more likely to hold the traditional stereotype.

5 A later version of these data permit us to pull apart those who lived in what later became the Czech Republic and those who lived in what became Slovakia. There was no significant difference in attitudes on this item.

6 For a discussion of question wording relating to women's groups in the United States, see Cook and Wilcox (1992).

7 Interestingly, it was 0.09 for Eastern European men, but it was much higher in the West—0.12 for women and 0.18 for men.

8 In the United States, first wave feminism developed close ties with the temperance movement, as women sought to ban the sale of alcohol at least in part to prevent family violence and to preserve the spending power of workers' families.

9 We also estimated a model in which we identified only women who are employed full time; the results were substantively identical.

❖ C. WILCOX, B. STARK AND S. THOMAS

4 ❖ Women's Representation in Germany: A Comparison of East and West

Joanne Bay Brzinski

The process of democratization in East Germany is unique among post-communist states. East Germany joined a working democratic state with an established set of parties, creating very different political challenges than faced by other east European states. This political amalgam provides interesting comparisons for those studying the effects of political institutions. Both regions of Germany share the same electoral rules, but the contexts of political competition differ in important ways.

These contrasts are especially interesting when considering women's representation. After the 1998 election Germany ranked seventh in the world in the percentage of parliamentary seats held by women at 30.6 per cent.[1] In the election of 1987 (the last West German election), 15 per cent of those elected to the Bundestag were women; by 1998, the proportion had more than doubled. These changes in women's representation have not been uniform across regions and parties. Differences in party competition and nature of electoral districts lead to varying electoral contexts in eastern and western *Länder*. In addition, party competition in East and West Germany involves different actors, with differing concern about and sensitivity to women's representation.

In the 1990 election, the euphoria of unification dominated every other issue and resulted in electoral outcomes that were not a reflection of 'normal' party preferences and levels of support. Though electoral behaviour was less volatile in 1994, party competition was still unsettled. Particularly in East Germany, the electoral support for the Free Democrats (FDP), the Greens, and the Democratic Socialists (PDS) fluctuated widely between the first two national elections, and across the five regional and one European election held in 1994 (Rueschemeyer 1998*b*: 104–5). In the 1998 election, in contrast, a predictable constellation of parties competed for support, and election discussion focused primarily on coalition politics. The vast swings of party support that had characterized the first two elections have settled into more stable patterns in the two regions. For these reasons, 1998 represents the first 'normal' election in a unified Germany and therefore is where I concentrate my effort.

The data used for this analysis are 1998 election data on candidates and elected MPs (Statistisches Bundesamt 1999a). The chapter is divided into three parts. The first part looks at differences across parties in the representation of women, and at party efforts to recruit women. Regional differences in party systems and party support are quite important in understanding women's representation in Germany. The second part of the chapter considers the effects of electoral rules and structures on women's success. The final section of the chapter looks at the joint effects of region, parties, and electoral rules.

❖ PARTY RECRUITMENT AND THE REPRESENTATION OF WOMEN

One of the most important influences on women's representation is the behaviour of political parties. Parties' decisions that representation of women is important, and changes in party rules to facilitate this, have significant consequences for women's representation. Germany's unification created very different party contexts for the recruitment of women compared to other East European states. The political institutions of the Federal Republic of Germany were largely retained in the united Germany, and many key political actors have also been retained. Although the PDS has succeeded as a mostly East German party, the largest political parties in united Germany are West German parties. These parties brought to East Germany a set of party policies and a West German history of women's inclusion that have influenced the presence of women in the united German *Bundestag*.

❖ Women's representation in West Germany

Before 1987, there were few women in the *Bundestag*. Between 1949 and 1990, on average seven per cent of the *Bundestag*'s seats were held by women (Dalton 1993: 215). That percentage has increased continuously from 1983, when women held only 9.8 per cent of the seats, to the present. The reasons for the change in the proportion of women in the *Bundestag* have a great deal to do with party politics and the process of selecting candidates.

German political parties and the candidate selection process are regulated by law, and create similar processes in different parties. Scarrow (1998: 300) notes 'In the German context, these [legal structures] of the framework of electoral competition have shaped the development of parties' organization and electoral strategies'. The German Basic Law, Article 21, carefully lays out

❖ JOANNE BAY BRZINSKI

the rights and responsibilities of parties, and specifies the general process of candidate selection. Candidate selection must take place at the regional (*Länder*) level, rather than by a central party apparatus, and 'democratic principles' must guide candidate selection. For all the parties this internal democratic selection takes place either through party conventions or party caucuses.

Legally, regional party organizations are independent from both the central party organization and from other regional organizations of the same party (Poguntke 1994: 187). This creates conditions for stratarchic rather than hierarchical parties. As a consequence of this system, all candidates must have a strong base of support in the *Länd*, or local party. Within regions, there is centralization of decision-making; regional party leaders have a great deal of leverage over local party leaders. This is true even in the Green Party, arguably the most loosely organized of German parties (Kitschelt 1989: 204).

For much of the post-war period, this system of choosing candidates led all of the parties to select few women. The major parties had no formal policy about women's inclusion until 1988. The consequence was very low numbers of women in the national parliament. The entry of the Green Party into national politics changed the prospects for women because of the Green Party's commitment to gender equity. Women and women's organizations have been extremely active in the Green Party, and have consistently pushed for equal representation of women on candidate lists. In 1985, the Green Party adopted a rule mandating equal representation of men and women on the party lists. The Greens alternate men and women on the party lists, and women are given the first position. The consequence of this has been gender parity in representation within the Green Party and considerable consistency across *Länder* and time. In 1994, 28 of 49 Green Party seats in the *Bundestag* were held by women (57.1 per cent); in 1998, women held 27 of 47 party seats (57.4 per cent).

The Greens have made this policy a political issue, pushing the major parties to justify the absence of women in their candidate lists. Lemke (1993: 155) notes the effect of this policy '[The Greens'] bold approach to increasing the political representation of women in parliaments has had a major impact on the German party system. Due to electoral competition, the other major parties started to redesign their policies towards women voters and to increase the number of women in their organizations'. The result in Germany has been similar to that found elsewhere, a process of contagion has occurred whereby one by one the major parties are forced to deal with the issue of representation and increase representation in response to innovative behaviour by a smaller party (Matland and Studlar 1996). In 1988, the Social Democrats (SPD) adopted a flexible quota of 33 per cent women candidates and officers (raised to 40 per cent in 1992), and a goal that no fewer than 30 per cent of SPD *Bundestag* deputies should be female (Kolinsky 1996: 275). In 1988, the

Christian Democrats (CDU) and FDP also approved goals of having women candidates and officers in the same proportion as in their party membership. The CDU goal is currently 25 per cent (Kolinsky 1996: 277). The FDP has been notably reluctant to enforce their goals, however. The Christian Social Union (CSU), the Bavarian wing of the CDU, is alone among the traditional four parties in having failed to endorse any party goals about women's representation (Lemke 1993: 155–6). The Democratic Socialists (PDS) have set a goal of gender parity, but without specific quotas.

West German parties built party organizations in the East based on the West German model, rather than responding to the special circumstances and situation of the Eastern region (Rueschemeyer 1998*b*). There are therefore no substantial regional differences within the other parties in party structures or candidate selection processes.

An exception to this rule is the East German Green Party. This party insisted on retaining its own name (*Bündnis '90*) when the parties combined, and East German leaders and activists have a stronger position in the party than East Germans do in the other Western parties. The unexpected loss by West German Greens in 1990 (and the success of the *Bündnis '90*) gave the East German Greens a great deal of power in their unification with the West German party. In fact, the Greens and *Bündnis '90* remained separate parties until 1993, and the West German Greens had to accept several organizational changes during their merger with *Bündnis '90*. Nonetheless, policies on recruitment of women in the unified Green/*Bündnis '90* party are essentially the same as used by the West German Greens because of a shared commitment on this issue (Poguntke 1994: 209–10).

Table 4.1 shows the overall level of representation across parties and divided into East and West Germany. The PDS has the highest levels of representation at an amazing 62 per cent. This is probably the highest level of women's representation of any parliamentary party in the world, outside of a few small all women's parties that have won seats in some national legislatures. The Greens have the best record among the pre-unification parties, while the CSU and FDP have the fewest women. Although the CDU has not met its goal for inclusion of women, the introduction of quotas (soft or hard) and informal goals for recruiting women has clearly made a difference across all parties in Germany.

❖ *Party and regional variation in women's inclusion, 1998*

Table 4.1 indicates that the percentage of women elected in West Germany is 29.0 per cent while women hold 36.5 per cent of East German seats. Although this represents a large difference in proportion, it is not a consequence of fundamental differences in the support for women's inclusion in the two regions.

❖ JOANNE BAY BRZINSKI

Table 4.1. Regional differences in women's representation: percentage of regional party seats held by women

| | Number of seats held by women | | | Difference of proportions: |
	Total (%)	West (%)	East (%)	t-value (significance)
All parties	30.6	29.0	36.5	1.75
	(205)	(150)	(55)	(p = 0.08)
PDS	62.2	83.3	58.1	−1.16
	(23)	(5)	(18)	(p = 0.26)
Greens	57.4	53.8	75.0	1.09
	(27)	(21)	(6)	(p = 0.28)
SPD	34.2	35.2	30.8	−0.66
	(102)	(82)	(20)	(p = 0.51)
FDP	21.4	21.6	20.0	−0.08
	(9)	(8)	(1)	(p = 0.94)
CDU	19.2	17.9	23.8	0.85
	(38)	(28)	(10)	(p = 0.40)
CSU	12.8	12.8	na	na
	(6)	(6)		

Cell values for columns three and four are the percentage of party's seats within the specified region that are held by women.

The *t-value* provides for an equality of proportions test. In this case it indicates whether the percentage of women represented in the West is significantly different from the percentage of women in the same party (or in all parties) in the East.

As the *t*-tests in Table 4.1 show, within each party there is no significant difference in the proportion of women selected in the West or the East. The regional differences are due instead to the relative strength of different parties in the two regions. Most significant of these regional differences is the PDS' strength in the East and weakness in the West. In the five Eastern *Länder*, the PDS receives about 20 per cent of the vote, and is clearly a potent political force. In the Western *Länder*, the PDS has a much more limited role.

West Germany has been known traditionally as a two-and-a-half party system. Two large parties, the CDU, together with its sister party CSU, and the SPD have alternated in power, with the smaller FDP as a coalition partner. The addition of the Green Party in 1983 changed the underlying electoral dynamic of the party system only slightly. Using Laakso and Taagepera's (1979), measure of the effective number of parties, West German *Länder* averaged 2.57 parties per *Länder*.[2] The primary competition is between the CDU/CSU and the SPD in all Western *Länder*. In contrast, the effective number of parties in the five Eastern *Länder* is on average 3.11. As this indicates, the primary party competition in these *Länder* involves the SPD, CDU, and PDS, a very different dynamic. Where the CDU and SPD dominate, the parties which have been promoting women most actively are either largely absent (PDS) or hold only a small number of seats (Greens).

This higher level of party fragmentation in East Germany has important consequences. Because the margins of victory are lower in the East, parties have fewer district seats they are certain of winning. Anderson (1993) noted that as early as 1990 there were fewer safe seats in the East than in the West. He attributes this mostly to high levels of volatility in new democracies, but these differences in party competition suggest that it is an enduring difference between East and West Germany.

❖ PDS policies on women's representation

While the Greens and the PDS have similar high levels of women's representation, there are striking differences in party policies. The Green Party produced important changes in other parties' policies towards women in the 1980s because they made gender equity a political issue and had clear policies and consistent results in recruiting and electing women. The PDS has not consciously campaigned on women's issues, nor internally institutionalized equality.

The PDS does not have rules guaranteeing women every other slot on the party list. The PDS has a goal that 40 per cent of its candidates are women, but this is not uniformly applied. In fact, there is substantial variability across *Länder*. In Brandenburg and Saxony-Anhalt, half of the PDS party list candidates were women. In Thuringen, however, only two of twelve candidates were women. The PDS also shows considerable variability over time in the success of women. Although women held 62.2 per cent of PDS *Bundestag* seats in 1998, in 1994 women held close to 20 per cent less, 14 of 31 PDS seats (45.2 per cent).

The high proportion of women in the PDS is somewhat puzzling because it runs counter to many of the descriptions of the party by political observers. Initially, the PDS was seen as the party of East German (GDR) officeholders, a group that was predominantly male (Zelle 1998: 224). Moreover, public opinion surveys and exit polls have consistently shown that among voters, East German women are no more likely than men to vote for the PDS (Kolinsky 1998; Zelle 1998). The PDS does not focus specifically on women's issues (unlike the Greens), but rather on a regional identity and the problems for East Germans created by unification. This absence of deliberate action and policy in favour of women's election makes the success of PDS women surprising. In looking for a possible explanation for women's strong showing in the PDS, it is useful to look at the primary policy message the party presents.

❖ JOANNE BAY BRZINSKI

Among political activists in East Germany, women may be disproportion-ately drawn to the PDS because Eastern women have paid a particularly heavy price for unification, in both economic status and societal security. East German women differed from West German women in their economic role before unification, and they differed from East German men in how they were affected by unification. In the GDR, women were much more integrated into the economy than in the West. Before unification, virtually all East German women, by one estimate nearly 90 per cent, were employed or attending school full time (Rueschemeyer 1998b). Though West German women also entered the workforce and universities, they did so in smaller numbers. In 1984, 48 per cent of the East German workforce was female; in the West, only 38 per cent of the workforce was female (Press and Information Office 1985).

This presence in the workforce did not indicate gender equality. Like all women in communist societies, this simply placed a double burden on women. East German women bore primary responsibility for the family, in addition to their work responsibilities. There were a variety of social services available to working women: child care, paid time off for parents with sick children, liberal parental leave policies, and preferential access for single mothers to apartments and child care (Rueschemeyer 1998b). Though family supports and leave pol-icies existed in the Federal Republic, they were far less extensive than those found in the GDR.

With the end of the communist system, women lost many of the social sup-ports that permitted them to work. The double burden of job and family responsibilities that East German women had carried meant that women keenly felt this loss of social services. Moreover, the economic costs of unifica-tion fell disproportionately on women. After unification women lost jobs at a higher rate then men, and have been slower to return to the workforce. The effects are still apparent. In 1998, the monthly unemployment rates for women in eastern *Länder* were on average 4.2 per cent points higher than for men in the same regions (averaging 21.6 per cent for women, 16.2 per cent for men). In contrast, not only were unemployment rates lower overall in western *Länder*, but women's and men's rates were nearly indistinguishable (Statistisches Bundesamt 1999b). The disproportionate effects of the economic shock poten-tially provide a source of political mobilization for women. East German women may be drawn to the PDS because they have been particularly hurt by unification.

The PDS' behaviour supports this interpretation of women's participation. Since unification, the PDS has chosen to emphasize social equality (of which women's equality is a key part) rather than class identity as the basis of its socialist philosophy (Krisch 1996: 113–14). The PDS' emphasis on its East German identity leads it to present itself as the protector of those who lost in the unification process, a group that includes women. This is evident in the party's discussion of women and women's issues. On the PDS website in 1998, the party's policy statement on women focused on women's economic role and on the decline of social services supporting women's work, rather than on gender equity as a goal in and of itself (PDS 1999). As the successor party to the East German Communist party, the PDS has also emphasized the positive accomplishments of the GDR, including its employment and social policy for women. Voters have responded to this message. Zelle (1998) found that a combination of Eastern identity and a preference for socialism over a market economy were related to support for the PDS among voters (pp. 233–43). These themes are likely to attract East German women activists.

One of the most striking and memorable elements of the PDS's 1998 campaign was a television commercial which vividly illustrates these themes. The commercial shows two escalators. On the right is an escalator with well-dressed prosperous-looking people (representing the West). The escalator is going up, allowing these people to move forward quickly. On the left, a line of people is also trying to mount an escalator, but an escalator that is going down. This line makes no progress trying to climb the down escalator—the people end up staying in the same place although they walk continuously. A woman in red (the PDS color) walks past this row of people, defying the policemen trying to stop her. She turns off the escalator, allowing the formerly stationary line to move forward. In this commercial, the PDS emphasized its role as protector of the dispossessed, but also women as party activists. These images emphasize women's role in the PDS, and underline how central women have become to the party's image and to its message.

A second factor that explains the success of women in the PDS is ideology. Cross-national studies of women's representation have demonstrated that parties of the left are more likely to recruit and elect women than are parties of the right (Caul 1999). The three parties with the highest percentages of women in Germany are the three parties of the left: the SPD, the Greens, and the PDS. Nevertheless, there are significant enough differences in behaviour among these leftist parties to suggest that ideology alone is an insufficient explanation. The Green Party has actively taken steps to ensure gender parity in its parliamentary fraction; neither the SPD nor the PDS have been similarly proactive. The Greens also have been more assertive in focusing on gender equity as a political issue. The SPD changed its policies mainly in reaction to the Green Party. The PDS subsumes the discussion of the status of women under its broader emphasis on its regional identity. To lump these parties together as 'leftist' parties misses the important differences in behaviour, and the way in which these parties raise issues of gender.

Summary National law governs candidate selection and therefore the broad outlines of candidate selection are the same in all parties. Nevertheless, the individual parties still have considerable leeway to map out individual strategies. As such, the role of parties and party policy in increasing the percentage of women in the *Bundestag* is undeniable. Quotas and policies on list placement of women have led to a tripling of the proportion of women in less than 20 years. The high proportion of *Bundestag* seats held by women is part of a trend that began in 1983 when the Green Party made women's representation a key issue and encouraged other parties to follow suit. Over time, and under pressure from the Greens, the major Western parties changed their policies on women's recruitment and representation and became increasingly open to women. The consistent emphasis on women's representation and the institutionalization of rules to guarantee women's representation strongly suggests that the Greens will continue to elect women at the same high rates in the future.

The huge percentage of PDS seats held by women has also contributed to the strong results for women in the 1998 election. East German *Länder* have a substantially larger proportion of women than West German *Länder* because of the PDS. Unlike the Greens, the PDS has not made women's representation a key issue, nor created party policies to ensure that women continue to be elected at high rates. Therefore, although the PDS has a higher proportion of women than any other party, continuation of this trend is questionable. The PDS also differs from the Greens in the disjunction between its electorate and its activists. Although a majority of PDS deputies are female, women in the electorate are no more likely to support the party than are men. Whether this result is an anomaly or the beginning of a shift in the base of support for the PDS will not be clear for a number of years. The PDS will likely continue to have high numbers of women, but at less consistent rates than the Greens.

❖ ELECTORAL RULES AND WOMEN'S REPRESENTATION

❖ Germany's electoral system

Party efforts and party policies clearly are important in election of women to national office. However, the electoral rules, which structure opportunities, can have an equally important role in encouraging the election of women. In a unified Germany, the electoral rules have carried over unchanged from West Germany. The election of women to the *Bundestag* takes place under a mixed electoral system, which includes both proportional representation through party lists, and direct selection of deputies in single member districts.

German voters have two votes. The first vote (*Erststimme*) selects one individual to represent a defined geographic district. The winner is chosen by plurality vote in the district. Three hundred and twenty-eight members are chosen in these single member district races. The second vote (*Zweitstimme*) is a vote for regional party lists (at the state or *Länd* level) in multi-member districts. The party lists are closed; Germany does not offer preferential voting. The list seats are allocated proportionally, taking into consideration the number of seats won by parties in the district races. The total number of seats a party receives in the *Bundestag* from an individual *Länd*, is at least equal to the percentage of the vote the party received in this second vote. First, the number of seats earned in the party vote is determined, and then the number of seats won in district races is deducted from this number to determine how many list seats are won by a party.[3]

Although district votes and party list votes are cast separately, the process of allocating seats in Germany links the two types of electoral systems. When a party is very successful in winning districts, relatively few of its candidates on the regional party list are likely to be chosen. In 1998, in eight *Länder*, the SPD had no party list seats because it won as many or more district seats than it earned in the party vote. Because of this link between list and district voting, German parties tend to have candidates run both in individual districts as well as on the party list. Almost all of those winning seats in 1998 (85.7 per cent) involved candidates on both district ballots and party lists. Only 72 of the winning deputies ran exclusively in districts, and only 24 ran exclusively on party lists.

Two aspects of electoral systems are expected to affect opportunity structures for women: the ballot structure and the district magnitude. The ballot structure distinguishes between plurality single-member district seats and proportional party list seats. Measures of district magnitude focus on how many seats are distributed. Mixed electoral systems are especially interesting because they allow comparison of the results of representation within one country and at one point in time, but under two sets of electoral rules.

❖ German ballot type and district size

In the 1998 election, the result in Germany matched the theoretical expectation concerning ballot type. Table 4.2 shows women held 22.3 per cent of single member district seats and 38.7 per cent of party list seats, a statistically significant difference. By dividing the sample into East and West, Table 4.2 shows this distinction between ballot types holds in both regions. It is also true that all four parties that won both district seats and party list seats have the same result for women's representation: a higher proportion of party list seats are held by women. The Greens and FDP won only party list seats, but for the CDU/CSU there are dramatic differences. The CDU elected women to 26.6 per cent of their party list seats, but only 6.8 per cent of their single member district (SMD) seats. The CSU exhibited a similar pattern; women won

Table 4.2. Ballot type and women's representation: total and regional differences in percentage of single member district and party list seats held by women

	West (%)	East (%)	Total (%)
Single member districts	21.0	26.3	22.3
Party list (multi-member districts)	36.3	47.9	38.7
District size: 2–9 seats	27.3	50.0	35.3
10–19 seats	38.7	47.7	44.8
20–29 seats	20.0	—	20.0
30–39 seats	32.4	—	32.4
>40 seats	39.8	—	39.8

Cell values are the percentage of seats in each district category held by women.
Difference in proportions by ballot type: t-value $= 3.76$, $p = 0.001$.
Difference in proportions by region: t-value $= 4.68$, $p = 0.000$.

33.3 per cent of the party list seats, but only 7.9 per cent of the district seats. The SPD elected substantially more women at the district level (29.7 per cent), but women did even better on the SPD *Länder* lists (45.3 per cent). Finally, even in the PDS, women did better on the *Länder* lists than in district seats won by the PDS (50.0 per cent vs. 62.6 per cent). This consistent result among all *Bundestag* deputies and across parties and regions gives strong support for the idea that ballot type matters for women's representation.

The effect of district magnitude is less clear. District magnitude is coded using the number of seats in the district in which the parliamentarian won. For an individual running in a single member district, district magnitude is always one. For those running on party lists, districts are always multi-member and the number of seats available ranges from 2 to 77. Theoretically, in multi-member districts, a larger district size should have a larger percentage of women (Rule 1987). The results in Germany do not indicate this. In Table 4.2, there is a clear difference in representation between the one seat available in a single member district, and the many party list seats, but beyond that, more seats do not seem to offer women better opportunities.

One explanation for the absence of a strong relationship between district magnitude and women's representation may be the regional differences in district size. East German districts tend to be small to medium-sized, while all of the largest districts are West German districts. Because the East also produces a higher proportion of women deputies, region may distort the effects of district size. When district magnitude is considered by region, however, the results are equally murky. As can be seen in Table 4.2, the differences between single member districts and multi-member districts are large in both regions. When comparing multi-member districts, however, larger districts do not have higher percentages of women in either the East or the West. The results in Germany suggest it does matter whether the district has some seats or one seat, but that beyond this simple distinction, women do not benefit from larger district sizes.

A cautionary note is worth inserting here: care needs to be taken when looking at district magnitude in mixed electoral systems. A simple comparison of the results for single member districts and for multi-member districts ignores the linkages between the systems. In Germany, the prevalence of dual mandates, that is, running simultaneously in a district and on the regional party list, creates strong connections between the results on one type of ballot and the other. Candidates who are elected from districts also run on party lists and could have won in their multi-member district if they did poorly in the district balloting. Furthermore, because the distributions from the party list are compensating and take the results at the district level into account, changes on first ballot district voting sufficient to change who wins at the district level could still lead, at least in theory, to a Bundestag that had exactly the same membership, but with some MPs now being elected off party lists rather than in their districts.[4]

Matland (1993) argues it is not district size, but party magnitude that is crucial. An alternative specification of the variable of interest is the size of the party delegation elected (party magnitude), rather than the overall size of the district. Furthermore, Matland argues that party magnitude's importance for women is likely to vary across time and parties. When there are no pressures on a party to elect women, party magnitude will not help women. When women play a central role in the party, their demands for representation are likely to be met from the outset and the assistance of large party magnitude is not needed. It is at those points in a party's development that women and women's representation are seen as a legitimate concern, but where women are one of the weaker interests within the party, that large party magnitudes can help. In this situation the more powerful, and predominately male, interests will claim the first slots on a party list. If the party only elects a few people off the lists, they will be the top names and the delegation will be predominately male. If the party has a substantial number of winning slots to fill, however, it is likely the names lower down on the list will include women. Therefore, if the party is able to win sufficient seats to go well down onto the party list, they will elect women.

In considering women's role in the German parties, women are probably past the point at which party magnitude is likely to matter for both the Greens and the PDS. On the other hand, party magnitude should matter quite a bit for the parties with the lowest levels of representation, the CDU–CSU and the FDP. The SPD is in an ambiguous position, women do well in the party, but they are still a significant distance from equal power in the party.

❖ JOANNE BAY BRZINSKI

Table 4.3. Party magnitude and women's representation: party differences in percentage of seats held by women as party magnitude increases

Party/party magnitude	1 seat (%)	2–3 seats (%)	4–5 seats (%)	6–7 seats (%)	8–9 seats (%)	10+ seats (%)
CDU–CSU/ FDP	7.7 (9 of 117)	16.7 (2 of 12)	22.7 (5 of 22)	31.3 (10 of 32)	30.8 (8 of 26)	24.4 (19 of 78)
SPD	29.6 (63 of 213)	33.3 (1 of 3)	77.8 (7 of 9)		25.0 (2 of 8)	44.6 (29 of 65)
Greens/ PDS	71.4 (10 of 14)	63.6 (7 of 11)	53.8 (14 of 26)	50.0 (3 of 6)	62.5 (10 of 16)	54.5 (6 of 11)

Cell values are the percentage of seats in each category held by women.
Statistical significance:

CDU–CSU/FDP: tau-b = 0.19, gamma = 0.37, sig. = 0.00.
        SPD: tau-b = 0.14, gamma = 0.30, sig. = 0.01.
  Greens/PDS: tau-b = −0.07, gamma = −0.12, sig. = 0.45.
Tau-b and gamma are measures of association used for ordinal data.

Table 4.3 considers the effects of party magnitude for these six parties grouped into three separate categories based on expected effects of party magnitude.

The results provide support for the party magnitude hypothesis. As expected, party magnitude does not have any significant effects for the Greens/PDS. It has a clear effect for the CDU/CSU and FDP combination. The proportion of seats won by women increases gradually with party magnitude, although there is a slight drop for the largest category. The statistical tests return powerful evidence of the effect party magnitude has on the female proportion of the district delegation for the centre-right end of the political scale. The statistical results show that party magnitude also matters for the SPD, although inspection of the data shows the effects are not as clear cut as they are for the CDU/CSU–FDP grouping.[5]

Summary Electoral structures influence women's representation in the *Bundestag*, but the greatest effects are a consequence of the two types of ballots on which candidates may run. Party lists have offered the greatest opportunities for women in Germany. In part, this is because the Greens and PDS win, almost exclusively, list seats not district seats (Kolinsky 1996). Even among the four traditional parties, however, women are significantly less likely to hold single member district seats, and women almost never run only for a district seat. To reach their quota goals parties do not ensure they elect women equally on both types of ballots, but rather, parties achieve those goals by placing and electing most women on party lists.

While district magnitude appears to have no effect beyond the distinction between single member districts and list seats, there was evidence of an effect for party magnitude. Women got a higher proportion of seats when party magnitude increased for the FDP and CDU–CSU delegations. Party magnitude had a weaker but positive effect for the SPD, but did not matter for the Greens and PDS. As such, it would appear the relevance of party magnitude is greatest when women are trying to establish their legitimacy within the party.

❖ MULTIVARIATE ANALYSIS OF WOMEN'S REPRESENTATION

The preceding discussion of women's representation in Germany suggests that two types of influences affect the percentage of seats held by women: party recruitment policies and electoral structures and rules. Thus far, these two types of effects have been considered independently. This section looks at their joint effects. The dependent variable is whether a woman or a man holds a seat. Probit models are used to estimate the effects of the independent variables.

The leftist parties, the Greens, PDS, and the SPD, would be expected to recruit more women because of their ideology. Furthermore, the Green Party and the SPD have firm quotas for women of 50 per cent and 30 per cent, respectively, and the PDS has a party goal of 40 per cent. The Green Party alone alternates men and women on the party list. Ideally, to model recruitment practices, three party-related variables would be used: a measure of quota levels used by parties, a measure indicating party list placement policies, and a measure of leftist party ideology. Because of practical problems in measuring these concepts of party practices separately, due to high multicolinearity, I instead use dummy variables for the Green Party, SPD, and PDS, indicating which party holds the *Bundestag* seat.

The important electoral system variables distinguish between type of ballot and district and party magnitude. BALLOT indicates whether the deputy won in a single member district or on the party list. I also use separate measures of district magnitude and party magnitude. Furthermore, an interaction term is tested. Inspection of the data showed that party magnitude does not appear to matter for the leftist parties. Therefore, an interaction term of non-leftist party magnitude was created to see if this held up in a multi-variate analysis.

In addition to these core variables, I have included a measure for urbanization. CITY indicates seats in districts of cities of 500,000 or more. Because cities are generally less traditional than small towns or rural areas, one would expect a higher proportion of women to be chosen from urban districts. For candidates running in single member districts, this measure is relatively accurate because these districts are small in size. Three *Länder* represent cities: Berlin, Hamburg, and Bremen. However, the other regional party lists represent a mix of rural, suburban, and urban areas. In Bavaria, for example, district seats representing Munich are coded as urban (1). However, the party list seats that represent Munich, but also rural areas of Bavaria, are coded as non-urban (0). I have also included a dummy variable, EAST, indicating whether the district is in East Germany.

Table 4.4 reports the results of three separate multi-variate models. The most robust measures are the party variables, reflecting the effects of party recruitment practices and party characteristics. Each of the leftist parties has

Table 4.4. Multivariate probit analysis: women in the *Bundestag*, 1998

Variables	Model 1	Model 2	Model 3
Constant	−1.30***	−1.30***	−1.39***
	(0.13)	(0.13)	(0.16)
PDS	1.03***	1.02***	1.10***
	(0.25)	(0.25)	(0.26)
GREEN	0.91***	0.89***	0.97***
	(0.21)	(0.22)	(0.23)
SPD	0.70***	0.71***	0.84***
	(0.13)	(0.13)	(0.18)
CITY	−0.05	−0.06	−0.07
	(0.18)	(0.18)	(0.18)
EAST	0.10	0.09	0.08
	(0.15)	(0.14)	(0.14)
BALLOT	0.56***	0.60***	0.66***
	(0.21)	(0.17)	(0.18)
District magnitude	0.000		
	(0.005)		
Party magnitude		−0.002	−0.011
		(0.008)	(0.012)
Interaction term			0.013
			(0.012)
−2 Log likelihood	748.40	748.37	747.16
Chi-Square	76.1***	76.1***	77.3***

*$p<0.05$, **$p<0.01$, ***$p<0.001$. Standard Error for each coefficient is listed in parentheses.

CITY codes as 1 all those who are elected in single member districts in cities of 500,000 or more, and those on party lists from Berlin, Hamburg or Bremen, 0 for others.

EAST East German districts are coded as 1, those in West Germany as 0.

For BALLOT, Party list = 1, single member district = 0.

District magnitude measures the number of seats available in that district. For all those running in single member districts, that number is one. For those in multi-member districts, it is the number of seats available.

Party magnitude codes the actual number of seats won by the deputy's party in his or her district.

Interaction term interacts non-leftists with party magnitude (i.e., for non-leftist parties the interaction term is equivalent to party magnitude, for leftist parties the interaction term is equal to zero).

a significant effect on the probability that a woman holds a seat. In no model does urbanization have a statistically significant result, and the small size of the coefficient suggests that this conceptual variable is not significant in Germany. Similarly, as suggested by the descriptive results, a district being in the EAST does not have a statistically significant effect when electoral system and party characteristics are considered.

The one set of variables that are varied across the three models are the electoral system variables. What the three equations show consistently is that ballot structure has a significant effect. Women are much more likely to be elected on a party list than in a district. District magnitude and party magnitude do not appear to have significant add-on effects.[6] In Model 3 the interaction effect tests whether party magnitude has an effect exclusively for non-leftist parties. The results show a stronger effect of party magnitude for the non-leftist parties, but it is still not significant.

❖ CONCLUSIONS

When I began work on this project, I assumed the forty-year division of Germany and the strikingly different experiences of women in the two Germanies *must* play a role in post-unification representation of women. I expected fundamental cultural differences and expectations in the two regions about the role of women in economics and politics to show up in the data. What is fascinating in Germany, however, are the similarities between the regions.

In Germany as a whole, the variables that are helpful in explaining when and where women achieve representation in established democracies work as well in the East as in the West. In both regions, proportional party lists produce more women deputies than do single member districts. Each party tends to elect similar proportions of women in both regions. This suggests that party recruitment and election policies have a similar effect in both regions.

Nonetheless, the high proportion of women elected by the PDS is not fully explained in this analysis. The PDS elected a substantially higher proportion of women than either of the other two leftist parties in Germany, even without clear recruitment policies that would account for that result. The 1998 election may simply be an anomaly. It may, however, indicate that women's experiences in the German Democratic Republic and/or in unification do play a role in the representation of women in East Germany. The emphasis by the PDS on the pain of unification and of the value of some policies in the GDR may find a receptive audience among East German women. This result may be a harbinger of that trend. In the next election, a continuation of high percentages of PDS deputies and a growing gender gap in the electorate would be consistent with this explanation. If this is evident, the success of the PDS in electing women may become an important influence in encouraging other German parties to increase their proportion of women as well.

❖ NOTES

1 After the autumn 2002 elections, Germany ranks eighth in the world with women winning 32.2 per cent of the seats in the new Bundestag.

2 Laakso and Taagera's (1979) formula is used as a means of evaluating the effective number of parties in any electoral system. In a pure two party system, both parties will receive a little more or a little less then 50% of the vote and ENP will be close to 2.0. The equation they use is as follows:

$$\text{Effective Number of Parties (ENP)} = 1/\sum_{i=1}^{n} (p_i)^2,$$

Where p = the proportion of the vote received by party i, and the parties are numbered $i = 1$ to n.

3 In some cases, parties win more district races than the number of seats to which they are entitled. To compensate for the disproportionality caused by these extra seats, called *Überhangmandate*, additional equalizing seats are simply added to the *Bundestag*. This means the number of seats in the *Bundestag* can vary from election to election. In 1998, 669 *Bundestag* delegates were elected, and there were 13 *Überhangmandaten*.

4 To take account of dual mandates I developed a modified district magnitude measure. For deputies who ran in both districts and on regional lists, party magnitude was set to the size of the regional list, that is, the larger multi-member party even if the person won a district seat. Seventy-two, or 11%, of those deputies winning single member district seats did not run on party lists as well, and only one of those deputies was a woman. This modified measure showed an even larger discrepancy in the percentage of women elected from single member and multi-member districts. It did not result, however, in a stronger relationship between women's representation and district size among multi-member districts (table not shown).

5 In looking at the SPD results, there is a marked spike up at the 4–5 seat category that seems to indicate that women do quite well even when the delegation size is reasonably modest. Inspection of the data, however, shows that where the party magnitude is 5, list seats in Rheinland-Pfalz, the SPD also won 10 district seats. The five MPs, four of who were women, elected from the party list in Rheinland-Pfalz had list positions 7, 9, 11, 12, and 14. We therefore see that even though party magnitude was only 5, because of dual listings and the ability of the names at the top of the regional party list to win their district seats, the party was able to go quite deep into the list for winning candidates.

6 A problem for these probits is the high multi-colinearity between BALLOT and district magnitude or party magnitude. Conceptually these variables are distinct, but in measuring them there is significant overlapping and we must be cautious in interpreting the results. For example if we drop BALLOT from the equation, the effect of district magnitude or party magnitude shoots up to strong statistically significant positive results. (Such a strategy would be entirely defensible as it can be argued that both district and party magnitude are just more finely grained measures of the electoral system than BALLOT, rather than distinct factors. I believe they are distinct and therefore include both measures.)

5 ❖ Women in Lithuanian Politics: From Nomenklatura Selection to Representation

Algis Krupavičius and Irmina Matonytė

The Baltic States, including Lithuania, were at the forefront of the movement to sever ties with the old Soviet regime and establish independent democratic status. Since 1989, the reintroduction of democratic principles has transformed the social and political environment. In the 1990s, Lithuania led the post-Communist European countries in political development and female representation. In 1996, women won 18.2 per cent of the seats in the Lithuanian Parliament (the Seimas). In the 2000 elections, however, there was a dramatic drop in representation to 10.6 per cent, placing Lithuania below Eastern Europe's average. This chapter describes how representation in Lithuania has changed over time and looks at possible explanations for the fluctuation in women's representation.

❖ HISTORICAL LEGACIES AND CONSOLIDATING DEMOCRACY

Lithuania was one of the first countries in Europe to grant political rights to women. This is somewhat surprising given that Lithuania has historically been a deeply Catholic and agrarian country. European countries with a predominately Catholic citizenship tended to provide women voting rights much later than Protestant countries (Human Development Report 1999: 238–9). Despite this, and despite the low levels of female literacy and low levels of participation in higher education that prevailed in Lithuania around the turn of the century, inclusive rules for female participation were extended in 1918, when Lithuania gained independent statehood.

The Lithuanian Catholic Women's Association (LCWA) was founded in 1907 and played a significant role in opening gates for women's political activity. The LCWA was a significant political force responsible for the small, but visible female presence in the earliest Lithuanian parliaments. LCWA members were elected to Parliament on Catholic Organizations' joint lists. From 1920 to 1926, women made up about 4 per cent of each of independent Lithuania's Parliaments (Trinkūnienė and Trinkūnas 1999).

There was considerable opposition, however, to women's participation in politics. On 3 November 1926, the Cabinet of Ministers decided to remove married women from public offices. While women MPs protested, noting this decision directly contradicted the Lithuanian Constitution, their demands were not respected (Kaukėnas 1995: 31). An autocratic *coup d'etat* led by the Nationalists' Union and A. Smetona occurred one month later. Smetona's authoritarian nationalist regime suspended many civil and political rights. It restricted the freedom of all political parties except the Nationalists' Union, stopping the development of women's political expression.

Lithuania fell under Soviet control in the 1940s. The Soviet regime (1940–1, 1944–90) with its emphasis on modernization, industrialization, and urbanization, introduced dramatic changes in the Lithuanian socioeconomic structure. All these changes, positive from a structural point of view, took place under heavy Communist ideological domination. In Parliament, the communist regime introduced a quota selection system; and from a quantitative point of view the absolute numbers of women were quite high. In the Supreme Soviet of Lithuania, female representation reached 30 per cent by the early 1950s and was more than 35 per cent after the last Communist-controlled elections in 1985 (see Table 5.1). These were not, however, competitive elections. It is therefore impossible to speak of 'electing representatives', but only of 'approving of candidate selection' to all political positions in governing institutions.

A turning point from the Soviet *façade* to *competitive* female representation came with democratization in Lithuania, which started in 1988. The period of *selection without representation* was over with a re-introduction of competitive elections in Lithuania in 1989. Women's reaction to the opening for true political opportunities was initially surprising. After a long period of indoctrination, during which women had been told they should prioritize their social rather than family roles, they took the emerging democracy as an opportunity to return to the family.

While this was the general trend throughout the region, there were efforts to establish independent women's organizations from 1989 to 1992. A majority of the 63 women's organizations that functioned in the late 1990s, however, were founded only after Lithuania entered into a phase of democratic consolidation and macroeconomic stabilization between 1994 and 1997. According to Kazimiera Prunskienė, leader of the Women's Party, these organizations serve an important role because 'women's organizations allow women to be closer to politics, to be involved in social processes, and in the life of the state without being connected with a clear political orientation.'[1] While the desire to stay at arms

✣ ALGIS KRUPAVIČIUS AND IRMINA MATONYTĖ

Table 5.1. Legislative institutions of Lithuania and their political composition since 1920

Parliament	Electoral formula	Total MPs	Date of election	Party winner— number of seats	Number of women	Per cent female
Constituent Seimas	Proportional	112	14–15.04.1920	Coalition of Christian Democrats—59	4	3.6
First Seimas	Proportional	78	10–11.10.1922	Coalition of Christian Democrats—38	2	2.6
Second Seimas	Proportional	78	12–13.05.1923	Coalition of Christian Democrats—40	3	3.9
Third Seimas	Proportional	85	9–10.06.1926	Left-wing coalition—37	4	4.7
Fourth Seimas	Proportional	49	9–10.06.1936	LNU—42	–	–
Peoples' Seimas	Non-competitive list system	79	14–15.07.1940	Lithuanian Peoples' Labour Union	8	10.1
II Supreme Soviet	Non-competitive majority	180	09.02.1947	CPSU—117	39	21.7
III Supreme Soviet	Non-competitive majority	205	18.02.1951	No data	61	29.7
IV Supreme Soviet	Non-competitive majority	209	27.02.1955	CPSU—156	62	29.7
V Supreme Soviet	Non-competitive majority	209	15.03.1959	CPSU—152	58	27.8
VI Supreme Soviet	Non-competitive majority	290	17.03.1963	CPSU—189	96	33.1
VII Supreme Soviet	Non-competitive majority	290	19.03.1967	CPSU—193	94	32.4
VIII Supreme Soviet	Non-competitive majority	300	13.06.1971	CPSU—203	97	32.3
IX Supreme Soviet	Non-competitive majority	320	15.06.1974	CPSU—216	109	34.1
X Supreme Soviet	Non-competitive majority	350	24.02.1980	CPSU—235	125	35.7
XI Supreme Soviet	Non-competitive majority	350	24.02.1985	CPSU—235	125	35.7
Supreme Council-Constituent Seimas	Majority-plurality	141	24.02.1990	Sąjūdis—96	14	9.9
Seimas	Mixed[1]	141	25.10.1992	LDLP—73	10	7.1
Seimas	Mixed[1]	141	20.10.1996	HU(LC)—70	25	18.1
Seimas	Mixed[1]	141	08.10.2000	Social Democrat Coalition—51	15	10.6

[1] For the 1992, 1996, and 2000 elections a mixed member proportional electoral system was used with 71 single member districts and 70 proportional list seats based on national lists.

length from political parties is important for establishing an organization's independence, it also means that most women's organizations have very little influence on the processes that determine the extent of their political representation.

❖ ELECTORAL RULES AS INSTITUTIONAL CONDITIONS OF WOMEN'S POLITICAL REPRESENTATION

After 1945, the Soviet electoral system was introduced in Lithuania. Soviet ideology maintained that voting itself is democratic, but that it was possible to vote only for those candidates chosen by the communist councils. As elsewhere, a complicated quota system was introduced along gender, ethnic, and occupation lines. The electorate faced a ballot, however, with a single candidate in a single-member district.

The first democratic parliamentary elections were held in 1990, and they partially used inherited Soviet electoral rules. The process was different, however, as 'other interested parties' were free to nominate candidates. These 'other interested parties' included social and political organizations, social movements, workers' groups, community meetings and political parties. The number of candidates was unlimited.

The electoral system was revamped shortly after the 1990 parliamentary elections. The new Seimas Election Law, passed on 9 July 1992, created a mixed electoral system. The law established 71 single-member constituencies based on the number of inhabitants and existing administrative-territorial divisions and one nationwide multi-member district with 70 seats. The seats awarded in the multi-member district are not compensatory, meaning they do not take into consideration how many seats the party wins in single-member constituencies. In order to win the first round in a single-member constituency, a candidate had to get over 50 per cent of the valid votes and turnout had to exceed 40 per cent. If no candidate was elected in the first round, the top two finishers met in a runoff. For the proportionally based national constituency, 70 members were elected by LR-Hare formula on the basis of list votes. There was a four per cent threshold for national parties, and a two per cent threshold for ethnic minority parties.[2]

The Election Law was amended again in 1996. Political movements lost the right to nominate candidates and the electoral threshold was changed. The electoral threshold was divided into two parts, for single parties it was raised to five per cent and for party coalitions seven per cent. The higher threshold increased disproportionality and made it more difficult for small parties to win.

Finally, in 2000, new amendments were passed dropping the requirement of runoff elections when a candidate won less than an absolute majority. Henceforth, a simple plurality would be sufficient. The result was that a large number of the winners in the 2000 election had well below 50 per cent of the votes in their constituency. Candidates with less than 30 per cent of the vote won 47 of the 71 single-member constituencies. Six of these winning MPs won less than 20 per cent of the vote.

What are the consequences for women's political representation of moving from a strictly majoritarian system to a mixed system? In the first election with a new system, there was little difference between the majoritarian and proportional portions of the electoral system. As Table 5.2 shows, in 1992, women were 11.7 per cent of the candidates appearing on party lists and 8.9 per cent of all candidates in single-member districts. In terms of electing women, there were no differences. Each portion of the electoral system supplied five female MPs to the 1992 Seimas. The 1996 electoral statistics show a significant overall increase in the number of female candidates, and a continuing small gap between the different electoral systems. Women were 21.3 per cent of the candidates on party lists and 19.4 per cent of the single member district (SMD) candidates. The gap between the two portions was somewhat larger in terms of elected MPs, as women captured 20 per cent of the multi-member seats and 16.2 per cent of the SMD seats. In 2000, women comprised 17.6 per cent of the multi-member seat candidates and 15.2 per cent of the SMD candidates. They comprised 8.4 per cent of the MPs elected in SMDs and 12.8 per cent of the candidates elected off the lists. In all cases, the differences are small. They reflect, however, more female candidates and MPs in the proportional section of the electoral system.

Large parties benefit from the high threshold of participation in proportional seat distribution. At each election, only four or five lists have been able to get seats through the PR portion of the electoral system.[3] Furthermore, the small parties that enter the parliament do so only via the SMD. Their nominees, in their strongest districts, tend to be party leaders and overwhelmingly male.

Table 5.2. Electoral formula and women MPs in 1992–2000

	1992 Seimas elections				1996 Seimas elections				2000 Seimas elections			
	Candidates		MPs		Candidates		MPs		Candidates		MPS	
	N	%	N	%	N	%	N	%	N	%	N	%
Multi-member electoral district (party lists)	87	11.7	5	7.1	264	21.3	14	20.0	203	17.6	9	12.8
Single-member electoral district	42[1]	8.9	5	7.0	170	19.4	11	16.2[2]	107	15.2	6	8.4
Total	101	11.9	10	7.1	279	20.7	25	18.1	232	18.4	15	10.6

[1] Independent candidates are not included.
[2] Among 68 MPs actually elected.

In such a situation, broad women's political representation can be facilitated best through the major parties. All 10 female MPs elected to the Seimas in 1992 were members of the Lithuanian Democratic Labour Party (LDLP), Sąjūdis (a broad coalition of anti-communist parties, the right wing of which became the Homeland Union (LC)), or the Christian Democratic coalition. In 1996, 23 out of 25 female MPs got into the parliament as representatives of the five major parties that cleared the PR threshold. In 2000, all 15 female MPs were elected from lists or parties that passed the threshold for PR representation. When comparing women's representation between the non-threshold and independent parties on the one hand and the threshold parties on the other, women have been better represented in the threshold parties in every election (7.6 per cent vs. 0.0 per cent in 1992, 18.7 per cent vs. 14.3 per cent in 1996, 12.1 per cent vs. 0.0 per cent in 2000).

❖ POLITICAL PARTIES AND WOMEN'S REPRESENTATION

On 12 March 1990, the day after the restoration of Lithuanian independence, Ms. Kazimiera Prunskienė, Professor of Economics at the University of Vilnius and well-known leader of Sąjūdis, became the country's Prime Minister. At the time, Lithuania was the only transforming country in all of Eastern and Central Europe in which a woman led the Cabinet of Ministers. This was a dramatic shift from the old Communist traditions and motivated individuals with relatively conservative opinions to appreciate women as viable political leaders. Prunskienė, called 'The Amber Lady', became the most popular Lithuanian politician only a few months after her appointment. Nonetheless, the Prunskienė phenomenon was more an individual achievement than a major movement in favour of women's political involvement. She was the lone woman in the 17-member Cabinet.

The salience of women's issues and representation is very much dependent upon the transitional settings in new democracies. Figure 5.1 presents a model that shows how the relevance of these issues changes over time. Looking at the transition from communist rule to representative democracy from the perspective of dominant political actors and issues, it is clear the politically relevant players and issues differ substantially during different phases of transition.

In the initial phases of transition, structural conditions (stable electoral and party system, independent women organizations, and democratic political culture) were non-existent or, at best, just starting to be established and undergoing constant change. Initially, broad political issues dominated the agenda as women's issues went to the backburner. Furthermore, there were no actors encouraging broad female political involvement.

Under these conditions, it was not surprising that the first democratic parliamentary elections resulted in a tremendous decrease in the number of

❖ ALGIS KRUPAVIČIUS AND IRMINA MATONYTĖ

Character of elections:

	Non-competitive	Competitive, non-party	Competitive and multi-party	Competitive and multi-party
Selection system:				
	Nomenklatura and quota system	No formal rules	No formal rules	Women's quotas in some parties
Articulated issues:				
	Communist ideology	Macro-political issues: independence, democracy, etc.	Medium-range political issues: privatization, institutional building, etc.	Medium-range political issues, including women's problems
Degree of representation:				
	35% of MPs	10% of MPs	7% of MPs	10.6–18.2% of MPs
Trend of representation:				
	Stable high quota	Decline	Stabilization on the lowest edge	Volatile
Phase of transition and time frame:				
	Prior to 1988, ends with Liberalization	Transition: new system-building, 1990	Consolidation of democracy, 1992–96	From consolidation of democracy to consolidated democracy, 1996–present

Figure 5.1. Transitional framework and logic of women representation: Lithuania's case

women MPs. In 1990, only 14 women (9.9 per cent of all MPs) were elected to the Supreme Council/Reconstituted Seimas. In the 1992 elections, the returns were even lower; only 10 women were elected. The initial political discourse in Lithuania, as in other democratizing countries, revolved around macro-political issues (national independence, institutional democracy, rule of law, market economy, etc.). Therefore, women's and other social groups' issues were left off of the political agenda. There were additional factors that worked to make the initial elections in Lithuania and other countries especially punitive for women. The 1990 founding elections in Lithuania were run under a majoritarian electoral system inherited from the Soviets, but by 1992, the former women's quota system was replaced by free competition. The social costs of transition to market economy affected women to a greater extent than men, increasing their 'double burden' of social and family responsibilities and leading to a withdrawal by many women from the public sphere (Einhorn 1993).

The situation changed rapidly following democratic consolidation. The stabilization of the social and economic environment in the mid-1990s led to a steady improvement in the social conditions of life for both genders. Political discourse became more focused on medium- and short-range issues. Politicians began to articulate women's specific concerns. After achieving a certain level of stability, the major political parties had to accommodate the needs of most modern parties, specifically the need to mobilize supporters on a continuous basis, to encourage and develop party loyalties among new voters. These needs led parties to address salient women's issues more extensively. Internal party building forced and encouraged parties to attract women as new members. Therefore, while most parties were created as male-dominated organizations, changes were made beginning in the mid-1990s.

Since 1992, Lithuania has had 3.0–3.3 effective political parties. The relatively high thresholds for participation in the PR portion of the electoral system have prevented more than four or five lists from winning seats in the PR portion of the election. The parliamentary elections under this system have resulted in one dominant party, three or four moderate-sized opposition parties, and a smattering of mini-parties.[4]

The political pendulum's recurrent shift from the right to the left in each new set of parliamentary elections since 1990 is typical for Lithuania. The shift has not, however, led to radical change in terms of the main political players. The Christian Democratic Party was far weaker in 2000 than in previous elections, and the new millennia brought with it a dramatic rise for a new party, New Union/Social Liberals, and a breakthrough for the Liberal Union. Nevertheless, the Lithuanian party system has for the most part had the same players since independence.

Another feature of the Lithuanian party system is that politics reflect a traditional left-right division (Krupavičius 1998, 1999). The Homeland Union

❖ ALGIS KRUPAVIČIUS AND IRMINA MATONYTĖ

(LC) represents the conservative wing of the political spectrum. They went from being the main opposition party from 1992 to 1996 to being the dominant party in the ruling coalition from 1996 to 2000. They were, however, soundly beaten in the 2000 election and initially replaced by a more centrist coalition in which the Liberal Union and the New Union/Social Liberals played major roles. This minority government was quickly replaced by a Centre-Left majority coalition in which the major leftist party, the United Lithuanian Social Democratic Party (LSDP) formed a governing majority with the New Union/Social Liberals. The Lithuanian Democratic Labour Party (LDLP), which was the largest party to merge into the United Lithuanian Social Democratic Party had previously been the ruling party from 1992 to 1996.

❖ Candidacies

Table 5.3 shows the number of candidates and percentage of female candidates across the major political parties. The seven major parties listed in Table 5.3 have won 84–90 per cent of the seats in each of the past three parliamentary elections. A couple of questions follow from the data. First, what explains the overall pattern of a significant increase in the number of female candidates among most parties in 1996, followed by a drop in terms of candidates in the year 2000? Second, what explains the variations across the parties in their willingness to nominate women?

There are several plausible explanations for why women gained access to the political system as candidates in the mid-1990s. First, as democratic stability increased, politics turned to mid-range issues. Among them were concerns about female representation. Although far from becoming a central issue, representation issues did at least appear on the agenda. Second, the parties needed to pay attention to women simply because of demographic realities. A majority of the populace is female, and women have voted at much higher rates than men in every election since 1989. In fact, women have made up between 55 and 60 per cent of the electorate in each of the national elections since independence. In order to achieve electoral success under these conditions, every serious party needs to pay attention to female voters.

One of the ways parties acknowledged the significance of women and women's issues was by establishing separate women's organizations. The two major left wing parties, the LDLP and LSDP, established women's organizations as part of their party structure as early as 1991. The LSDP founded the Social Democratic Women's Union using as inspiration the Socialist International (organization of Social Democratic parties). The Christian Democrats established their women's section in 1993, copying the practice of their Nordic sister parties.[5] At least partially in response to the creation of the Women's Party in 1995, two leading Lithuanian parties on the right, the Centre Union and HU-Conservative Party, both established women's sections in their national organizations in 1996.

LITHUANIAN WOMEN'S RECRUITMENT ❖

Table 5.3. Major party candidates by sex in the 1992, 1996, and 2000
Seimas elections

	Total cands. 1992	Per cent female 1992	Total cands. 1996	Per cent female 1996	Total cands. 2000	Per cent female 2000	Percentage change 1992–6	Percentage change 1996–2000
Homeland Union/ Lithuanian Conservatives	101	15.8	114	16.7	125	18.4	+ 0.9	+ 1.7
Lithuanian Liberal Union	44	2.3	41	9.8	131	13.0	+ 7.5	+ 3.2
New Union/ Social Liberals	—	—	—	—	135	17.8	—	—
Christian Democratic Party	56	16.1	86	20.9	64	17.2	+ 4.8	− 3.7
Lithuanian Centre Union	37	10.8	81	16.0	97	18.6	+ 5.2	+ 2.6
Lithuanian Social Democratic Party	76	9.2	95	24.2	54	24.1	+ 15.0	− 0.1
Lithuanian Democratic Labour Party	83	4.8	105	14.3	58	13.8	+ 9.5	− 0.5
Major parties	397	10.3	523	17.6	664	17.1	+ 7.2	+ 0.5
Women's Party/ New Democracy	—	—	67	85.1	14	78.6	—	− 6.5
Other Parties and Independents	428	12.6	772	16.2	589	18.3	+ 3.6	+ 2.1
Totals/average	825	11.5	1352	20.3	1267	18.4	+ 8.8	− 1.9

The establishment of the Women's Party (WP) in early 1995 encouraged all Lithuanian political parties to expand women's representation in the party elite and better articulate women's interests. The WP was led by Prunskienė, the former Prime Minister, and represented a clear native-born impulse to better represent women on the political scene. Prunskienė explained the goals of the WP in the following way: 'Our aim was to decrease political domination by one gender. Therefore, we founded a party with a majority of women. In thinking about the democratic process, we wanted to balance out the many male-dominated parties that did not recognize they were male parties. While women were dominant, from the very beginning our party included men. Speaking generally, a female-dominated party permitted us to develop a party program that reflected women's political priorities'.[6] The Women's party, even in its revised form as New Democracy, continues to centre on Prunskienė. I. Šiaulienė, a leader of the Lithuanian Democratic Women's Collegium affiliated with the LDLP, stressed that 'all women who enter and who will enter politics in the future, will have [Prunskienė's] example in front of them'.[7]

✣ Algis Krupavičius and Irmina Matonytė

To understand why Prunskienė started the WP, we need to look at the Lithuanian political context of the time. In an internal political battle within Sąjūdis, Prunskienė found herself on the losing end of a crucial political debate on how to deal with Russia. Party opponents effectively squeezed her out in 1992. She still had a strong desire to actively participate in politics, but to do so effectively she had to have a party base. None of the existing parties provided a satisfactory base. Therefore, she established the WP. Prunskienė said the WP was a 'more humane and safe shelter' for women interested in politics. Ideologically, while the party has espoused a policy of social liberalism with an emphasis on women's issues, it does not espouse an explicitly feminist perspective (at least what Western feminists might perceive of as feminist).

The WP was a fringe party, winning only one seat in the 1996 parliamentary elections, when Prunskienė won her single-member district. Despite this, the WP did influence the other parties. They perceived the WP as a challenger in terms of women-specific issues and as a potentially important competitor for women's votes. Prunskienė described the other parties' reaction to the WP in the following way:

> I think that our party really contributed to the democratic dialogue in Lithuania. Some of the male-dominated parties saw our popularity climbing before the elections. They felt threatened—women could vote for a party that better represents women, first of all, by its composition. A few years ago, quotas were unthinkable. Now parties opt for them to increase their popularity among women voters. This happens not because men understand the need to give positions to women, but because party leadership finds out their party could win more total seats if it presents female and male candidates.[8]

In the 2000 elections the WP (renamed New Democracy) made a strategic decision to join the Social Democratic coalition in order to broaden the party's electorate and increase their influence. It won three seats and, ironically, one of its elected MPs was male.

If we turn to the question concerning variations across parties, we see from Table 5.3 that the strongest support for female representation among the major parties has consistently come from the LSDP. Close to 25 per cent of its candidates in the last two elections have been women. The LDLP, the other major leftist party in the 1990s, has been less supportive of women. Only 14 per cent of its candidates in the 1996 and 2000 elections were women. In 2000, these two leftist parties, along with New Democracy/Women's Party and the Union of Lithuanian Russians, were part of an electoral coalition. The overall coalition gave 25 per cent of its nominations to women. The Christian Democratic Party (LCDP) also had a very strong showing in terms of nominating women candidates in the mid-1990s, with 20.9 per cent of its candidates being female in 1996. They slipped slightly to 17.2 per cent in 2000.

The conservatives (Homeland Union) have consistently had a significant number of women candidates, with women holding 16–18 per cent of their nominations for each of the three elections. The Lithuanian Liberal Union is the only true laggard among the major parties. The party has consistently had the lowest level of female representation. Less than 10 per cent of their candidates both in 1992 and 1996, and only 13.0 per cent in 2000 were women.

Why do these variations exist? One place to look for an explanation is to the voters of the various parties. The Liberal party tends to get its votes predominately from male voters, while the Christian Democrats rely heavily on female support (R. Ališauskienė and G. Purvaneckienė 1998: 65). In both cases, however, supporters' party choice is based on factors other than gender. For the Christian Democrats, there is a connection between sex and religiosity. Females, and especially older females, are more religious, and as a consequence more supportive of the LCDP. The Liberal Union, on the other hand, is the most pro-private business party in Lithuania, therefore attractive to the many males engaged in private business. Furthermore, the core of the Liberal Union's support comes from the strongest believers in free enterprise, a predominately male group. The other major Lithuanian parties tend to draw fairly equally from male and female voters.

Which candidates are chosen depends on the parties' nomination procedures and formal rules. Nomination procedures are generally centralized and patronage-based via national executives in the leading parties. In choosing candidates, loyalty to national executives is crucial, but service at the local level can also be a valuable attribute and an important stepping-stone to positions in the national Parliament. When we look at local-level politics in Lithuania, we see substantial numbers of female officials (see Table 5.4). As the political role of municipal authorities is less important and prestigious, there is less competition for political positions at the local level. The election results for the last three local elections show that women consistently do better in local elections than parliamentary elections. In 1995, 302 women were elected to local councils. They represented 20.3 per cent of all members in local authorities. In 1997, these figures increased to 318, or 21.8 per cent. In 2000, there was a drop to 275 (17.6 per cent).

When we compare the proportion of women elected across parties, we see patterns that mimic the national level. A significant number of the councilors are women elected from both the Homeland Union (LC) and the LSDP parties. Their support is weakest among the parties in the centre, including the Liberal Union, Lithuanian Centre Union, and the New Union (Social Liberals). The drop in local councilors seen in 2000 is largely due to a dramatic increase in the number of councilors from parties that have traditionally nominated few women (LLU, LCU), causing losses among those parties that traditionally nominate substantial numbers of women (HU(LC), LCDP).

❖ ALGIS KRUPAVIČIUS AND IRMINA MATONYTĖ

Table 5.4. Number and percentage of female local councilors, major parties, 1995–2000

	1995 local councils		1997 local councils		2000 local councils	
	Number	%	Number	%	Number	%
Homeland Union (Lithuanian Conservatives)	107	25	125	25	40	20.1
Lithuanian Liberal Union	—	—	1	2	18	10.8
New Union (Social Liberals)	—	—	—	—	47	17.5
Lithuanian Centre Union	4	5	17	13	22	12.7
Lithuanian Christian Democratic Party	58	23	37	21	18	18.2
Lithuanian Democratic Labour Party	62	21	53	25	29	17.2
Lithuanian Social Democratic Party	7	10	27	20	21	20.2
Others	51	17.6	59	23	80	26.7
Total	302	20.3	318	21.9	275	17.6

In the long run, the significant number of women elected to local political offices would appear to be a good starting position to increase representation on the national political stage. There are, however, a couple of obstacles to this seemingly straightforward conclusion. The Lithuanian political elite in general and parliamentary elite in particular (more than 80 per cent of all MPs since 1990), are greatly over-represented by politicians from the five largest cities (Vilnius, Kaunas, Klaipėda, Šiauliai, and Panevėžys). In general, women have done best in local municipalities that are rural. These are less likely to produce candidates for national elections. Moreover, women's representation on the municipal council of Vilnius (which supplies more than 50 per cent of Lithuania's parliamentary elite) has been well below the national average. In 1995 women made up 19.6 per cent of local councilors in Vilnius, but in 1997 their share of local councilors dipped to 9.8 per cent. It rose again in 2000, when women claimed 15.5 per cent of the seats, but this is still below the national average.

The issue of gender quotas has been raised from time to time. There has been, however, significant skepticism about quotas. Lithuanians are familiar with quotas because they were used during the Soviet era. Memory of the Soviet era quotas, however, impedes the public's ability to perceive women as having a legitimate role in the political sphere. As one LCDP MP noted, 'quotas for women in the Soviet legislature, which existed and which were preserved at any price, spurred a social prejudice that women are incompetent on political matters'.[9] In 1999, 10 years after the collapse of Communism, most of the leaders of influential Lithuanian political parties were still critical to quotas for increasing women's representation. Furthermore, in spite of differences in their ideological leanings, most of the interviewed political leaders agreed 'there should not be any artificial formula, or re-arranged conditions'[10] for female political participation and representation. They referred to the 'negative experience in the Soviet system'[11] and stressed that a quota system 'contradicts the principle of free competition'.[12] In this case, negative memories about the Communist practices of female quota selection to political office serve as an argument against introducing formal rules for female selection and representation in new political parties.

The only party to introduce a form of quota in conjunction with their candidate selection procedure is the Lithuanian Social Democratic Party. In 1996, the LSDP introduced a 20 per cent female quota on all party electoral lists. Later on, the LSDP increased this quota and formulated a principle requiring each gender to comprise at least 30 per cent of a party list. While no other party passed any formal regulations on female representation, at least some parties felt pressured by the LSDP adopting quotas. Č. Juršėnas, the LDLP (other leftist party) leader, pointed out the Labour Democrats 'are very concerned about female and male equality, [but] our party should function as the British constitution—rules are unwritten but efficient'.[13]

The LSDP has consistently shown itself to be the most woman-friendly party in Lithuania. There are several possible reasons for this. One very important reason is ties to the Socialist International. The strong emphasis on ensuring equitable female representation among Western European parties in the Socialist International strengthened the position of women within the LSDP who were arguing for representation guarantees. Furthermore, the LSDP may have seemed a more attractive option to women with political ambitions than the LDLP. The LDLP has direct ties back to the old Lithuanian Communist party. This had a couple of effects. For one, the LDLP was hesitant to establish quotas because members wanted to distance themselves from the Communist past. Secondly, the LDLP in many ways looked like the Communist party of old. There were a considerable number of women in the party, but men overwhelmingly held the positions of true power. It is quite telling, for example, that none of the ministers that sat in the initial LDLP government from 1992–6 were women. After the 2000 elections, the LDLP and the LSDP merged, and have agreed to continue with the use of quotas in nominating candidates. It will be interesting to see how the different party cultures in the LSDP and LDLP blend.

It has become easier for women within the various parties to raise the issue of quotas as the memory of the Soviet period fades. R. Melnikienė, Centre Union MP, was firm that '[women in the LCU] will certainly raise the quota issue in the party Congress. Perhaps not to formally regulate it, but to encourage proportional representation of our party members, both men and women'.[14] Even the Christian Democrats, who hold conservative positions on women's roles, are changing their minds and feel 'this time we will talk about women's quotas. Some time ago we thought that we, Christian Democratic women, were strong enough to compete with our peer men and that Lithuanians naturally would soon modernize their understanding about gender roles in society. But life has shown us that this hope for a 'natural' evolution will take too long. . .'[15]

This view is not universal among women. Women in the Homeland Union (LC) are skeptical about the need for quotas. As R. Juknevičienė recalled:

> Quotas? I mentioned this issue once. Leaders of the Conservative Party asked, "How much do you need? We will write it down". It appears that for our party it is not a problem. We have enough women working in important positions because of their professional qualities, not because they are women. We don't have women sitting on the working group on NATO enlargement because of a gentlemanly attitude towards including women. It happens because of a pure appreciation of our competence.[16]

Women are already well represented in the central institutions of the HU (LC), and as this quote indicates, they are confident in their abilities to encourage party leadership to nominate many active women for municipal and parliamentary candidacies.

❖ Female membership in the Seimas

While candidacies are a crucial step towards greater influence, actual election to the parliament is obviously a more meaningful measure of greater influence. When we look at women's representation in the Lithuanian Seimas, we see the overall pattern shows a modest 7.1 per cent women were elected in 1992, with a dramatic jump to 18.1 per cent in 1996 and a precipitous drop to 10.8 per cent in the 2000 election. When we look at these numbers alongside the ideological shifts in the Parliament, we see the big growth in the number of women representatives in the 1996 Seimas coincides with an ideological shift from the left to the political right. The 2000 elections resulted in a huge drop in support for the Lithuanian Conservatives and simultaneously a dramatic fall in women's representation. At first glance, it would appear as if women are helped by winning conservatives and hurt by winning leftists. Before coming to this conclusion, however, we should take a closer look at the data (see Table 5.5).

In trying to interpret the dramatic drop in representation in the 2000 election, a number of trends can be identified. The Homeland Union (LC) has been number one or two in the proportion of the delegation that is female in every Parliament. The coefficient of representation, the proportion of women elected divided by the proportion of women nominated, being over 1.00 in

Table 5.5. Parliamentary delegation by party, number of and per cent female MPs, 1992–2000

	1992 Seimas			1996 Seimas[1]				2000 Seimas			
	Number of MPs	Number of Fem. MPs	Per cent Fem. MPs	Number of MPs	Number of Fem. MPs	Per cent Fem. MPs	Coeff. of representation	Number of MPs	Number of Fem. MPs	Per cent Fem. MPs	Coeff. of representation
Homeland Union (Lithuanian Conservatives) HU(LC)	28	4	14.3	70	15	21.4	1.28	9	2	22.2	1.21
Lithuanian Liberal Union (LLU)	0	0	—	1	0	0	0.00	33	3	9.4	0.72
New Union (Social Liberals)	—	—	—	—	—	—	—	28	2	7.1	0.40
Lithuanian Centre Union (LCU)	2	0	—	13	3	23.1	1.44	2	0	0	0.00
Lithuanian Christian Democratic Party (LCDP)	9	0	0	16	1	6.3	0.30	2	0	0	0.00
Lithuanian Democratic Labour Party (LDLP)	73	3	4.1	12	2	16.7	1.17	27	2	7.4	0.54
Lithuanian Social Democratic Party (LSDP)	8	0	0	12	2	16.7	0.69	18	4	22.2	0.92
Others[2]	21	3	14.3	16	2	12.5		22	2	9.1	0.57
Total	141	10	7.1	137	25	18.2		141	15	10.6	

[1] The Lithuanian electoral law requires that a minimum of 40% of voters participate in a parliamentary election for a district's results to be valid. In 1996, the vote total in four districts was below this, and consequently, no MP was elected. New elections were held and validated with the local elections in the spring of 1997.

[2] In 1992, the largest parties in the 'other' category were The Union of Lithuanian Political Prisoners and Deportees with five representatives, three of which were women, followed by the Union of Lithuanian Poles, an ethnic-based party that won four seats, and the Lithuanian Democratic Party, also with four seats. In 1996, the Lithuanian Democratic Party was the only 'other' party to win more than a single seat; it won two. In 2000, the Lithuanian Peasant's Party won four seats, while the Union of Lithuanian Russians, Party of New Democracy (formerly the Women's Party), and Union of Modern Christian Democrats each won three seats. Both the female MPs elected in this 'other' category were from the Party of New Democracy.

both 1996 and 2000 is especially striking. This provides a numerical indicator of the overall quality of the nominations women are getting. If women are facing a situation of equality, the coefficient of representation would equal 1.00. The proportion of female MPs would equal the proportion of female candidates. A ratio greater than 1.00 indicates that women have higher quality nominations than men. Ratios lower than 1.00 indicate that women are getting poorer-quality nominations. In both 1996 and 2000, women received better-quality placements on lists and in single member districts than men in the Homeland Union (coefficients of representation = 1.28 and 1.21).

There is a divergent pattern among parties on the left. In 1996, the LSDP nominated more women, but failed to elect any more so the LSDP has a noticeably lower coefficient of representation than the LDLP has. In 2000, the LSDP coefficient of representation shows their establishment of quotas and increase in female candidates has not been purely symbolic. Women had significant numbers both in terms of nominations and in terms of winning seats. The relatively high coefficient of representation in 2000 (0.92) indicates that women are not being placed in unwinnable districts or at the bottom of the party list. When we evaluate the LDLP in 2000, however, women not only had a lower per cent of nominations (see Table 5.3), but also received poorer-quality nominations. The low 0.54 coefficient of representation indicates the nominations women received were systematically inferior to those men received. It will be quite interesting to see the consequences of the LSDP and LDLP's aforementioned merger. As already noted, the new party is to continue using quotas. If it maintains a coefficient of representation in the range practiced by the old LSDP, it is reasonable to expect a noticeable increase in the number of women in the next parliament among the representatives of the left.

The 2000 elections saw a significant jump in the seats won by the Social Liberals and the Liberal Union, two liberal parties on the centre-right with low levels of female candidates and weak coefficients of representation. This further depressed the number of women they elected. Among the centre block, the one party that has had significant levels of female candidates, at least at the local level, is the Christian Democratic Party. The Christian Democratic vote, however, was split among three different Christian Democratic parties, and none of them crossed the five per cent threshold needed to participate in the PR tier of seat allocation. In short, a significant part of the explanation for the drop in 2000 was that parties that have traditionally had significant female representation lost seats to parties with lower levels of representation.

Perhaps most surprising is the strong position of women in the Homeland Union (Lithuanian Conservatives), and its predecessor—the right wing of Sąjūdis (led by V. Landsbergis). This party has been one of the most influential parties in post-communist Lithuania. It was also one of the first parties to provide women with significant representation. As early as 1992, they started not only running women as candidates, but also including significant numbers of women in the party leadership.

When we consider the Western literature, a strong positive relationship between right-wing parties and female representation is an unexpected finding. One possible explanation is in the paradigms these newly formed parties looked to follow. The right-wing parties in most of the transforming countries carried the major burden of system reforms. The end goals of this work were known from the beginning: development of democratic institutions and the introduction of market economies. The existing institutions in western societies were blueprints for this work. Eastern European architects used western blueprints in constructing their internal party organizations as well. The *instinctive imitation* of their western counterparts was a successful way to deal with the issue of party building. In doing so, they came to recognize women's legitimate interests in politics and the significant party-building advantages gained by party organizations' involving women in politics. In addition, allowing women political access helped party leaders develop and stabilize party electorates in competition with other political organizations. Ideologically, right-wing parties' openness to women was a formal sign of being democratic, different than the preceding regime, and a point that could be used in political campaigning.

An influential female MP from the HU (LC), N. Oželytė, notes 'paradoxically, women from the "right" do not have clear boundaries in terms of women's representation. Our concern is to promote women into politics, but only women who have the "right" economic values. This means, women who support large-scale privatization, private initiative, private property, and a reduction in the state's economic role'.[17] Women within the HU (LC) also recognize that impulses to open doors to women in 1992–3 'came from our European and American conservative partners, especially the British Conservative party, and the European Democratic Union'.[18]

Ironically, while the HU (LC) is a pro-women party in terms of representation, the 1996 party programs' content study showed the conservatives did not include policy statements supportive of women's issues (Purvaneckienė 1998: 37). The most women-oriented programs were those of the LSDP and the LDLP, with the Centre Union falling in between. Most parties included women's issues in their programs in a very superficial way just to ensure they had mentioned them. Sometimes, their statements concerning women contradicted other policy positions. The issue of women's representation, however, has become part of party programmes and is unlikely to be completely neglected on the political agenda. However, its significance is likely to wax and wane over time.

In this context, it is worth noting that in the run up to the 2000 election there were serious problems in the Lithuanian economy indirectly tied to difficulties in the Russian economy. Serious economic problems tended to dominate the political debate, pushing mid-range issues such as women's representation off the agenda. This may partially explain the relatively weak showing women had in the 2000 general elections.

❖ Women in governmental and parliamentary elite

When we go beyond considering membership in Parliament to looking at the composition of the government, we see there has been a steady incremental increase in the number of women with ministerial portfolios. Although a woman, Kazimiera Prunskienė, led the Lithuanian government immediately after independence, she was the only woman in the government. The first conservative cabinet from 1991 to 1992 had only one female minister. From 1992 to 1995, the leftist LDLP governments had no women in a ministerial position. Only in February 1996, when there was a reshuffling of cabinet posts, and only 10 months prior to the expiration of their parliamentary mandate, was a woman finally appointed in the LDLP Cabinet led by M. Stankevičius. Shortly after the 1996 elections, in the second G. Vagnorius' government, women held two ministerial posts (European Affairs, and Social Affairs and Labour). At 11 per cent of the cabinet, women were still well below their 18 per cent representation in the Parliament. There were two short-lived centre-right governments from mid-1999 until the election in the fall of 2000 which each had only one female minister. Immediately after the 2000 election a centre-dominated minority coalition took over for eight months. Two of the 13 ministers (15.3 per cent) were female. Finally, in June 2001, Algirdas Brazauskas formed a coalition government led by the United Lithuanian Social Democratic Party, formed from the LDLP and LSDP, joining with the union of Lithuanian Russians and the centrist New Union/Social Liberals. In the newly formed government women's representation expanded to new levels. Three women were given ministerial posts (Ministers of Culture, Social Affairs and Labour, and Finance). With these appointments, women now hold 23.1 per cent of the portfolios in the government. This is well above their representation in Parliament.

In November 1999, Conservative R. Juknevičienė became the first woman appointed Deputy Chair of Seimas. A positional analysis of women in the Lithuanian parliament reveals this as the exception; the rule is that women are generally placed in lower and less significant political positions than are men. During the 1996–2000 parliamentary term, every fifth Seimas member was a woman. Despite this, a woman chaired only one of the standing committees, and only one had a deputy chair. Among 10 Seimas commissions established, only one was headed by a woman and only one had a female deputy chair. Among 14 Seimas political fractions, a woman headed only one. K. Prunskienė chaired the Independent fraction, and two fractions (Conservatives and Democratic Labour party) have female deputy chairs.

Women remained underrepresented after the 2000 elections, chairing none of the parliamentary committees and having only two of 17 deputy chairs

(11.8 per cent). The picture is not entirely bleak, however. Women chair five of the 14 parliamentary commissions and hold five of the deputy chairs (35.7 per cent). While less influential than the parliamentary committees, the commissions have significant powers and deal with important issues (i.e. NATO, constitutional revisions, anti-corruption, etc.).

❖ Women's caucus in parliament

There has been a parliamentary women's caucus in the Seimas since 1997. Women from all parties are welcome and the chairperson is appointed for six months, according to a rotation procedure. Only 15 of the 25 female parliamentarians joined initially. However, additional MPs joined over time. The caucus serves as a meeting point where Seimas women can exchange their opinions about different matters of interest to women. It is clear, however, that the female members of the Parliament are first and foremost members of their party and only secondarily women.

The parliamentary women's caucus officially encompasses the whole political spectrum and has no explicit political agenda. Nevertheless, it is well known that this parliamentary group is a result of joint efforts from the left and the centre. The caucus was established on Prunskienė's initiative, with active support from women in the Lithuanian Democratic Labour Party, the Social Democrats, and the Centre Union. The Conservatives and Christian Democrats were largely inactive in the women's caucus. While the Conservatives were in power, the Conservative women had a ready explanation for their failure to participate. We were told in interviews that 'Women from the Conservative Party were much less active in the parliamentary women's group because this group does not have any real decision power, and it functions more as a consciousness raising group. The Conservative party being in power, women from it have had more formal duties and responsibilities and could not take active part in general discussions about women's fate in Lithuania'.[19]

Significantly, after the 2000 election, the caucus continued and has become more inclusive. Fourteen of the 15 female MPs in the Seimas and all parties are now members of the caucus. While the need to encompass the whole political spectrum has made it hard to find issues on which they could agree, the Caucus was able to agree on, and was a crucial player in passing, the Equal Gender Opportunity Law.

Equal Gender Opportunity Law. In 1998, after 10 years of transition to democracy and market economy, women represented 47.5 per cent of the Lithuanian Labour market. The Lithuanian Labour market is vertically and horizontally segmented along gender lines: women work in the less prestigious and the least-paid branches of the economy. Women's average salary in 1998 was only 77.2 per cent of men's salary. According to a Gallup survey on 'Gender and

❖ Algis Krupavičius and Irmina Matonytė

Society: Statuses and Stereotypes' conducted in 1996, only 28 per cent of women and 46 per cent of men think that both genders have equal opportunities to get a job. However, 89 per cent of women and 79 per cent of men claimed these opportunities should be made equal (Melnikienė 1997).

Upon the initiative of the parliamentary women's group, the Board of Seimas on 17 June 1997 appointed a working group to prepare the Law on Equal Opportunities. The group was composed of parliamentarians from different political parties, including a chairwoman (N. Oželytė) from the Conservatives and representatives from the Ministry of Justice, the Seimas Ombudsmen Office, and the Institute of Free Market (a private research institute).

The Equal Opportunity Law project and debates were intensive, but they did not mobilize broad political and public interest. As one of the promoters of the law, R. Melnikienė, explains: 'Since this law does not concern money issues directly and immediately, it was only weakly affected by public opinion. When the Seimas debated the law on compulsory drivers' insurance—the story was very different'.[20] Non-governmental women's organizations organized conferences, meetings, and debates in the workplaces about equal opportunities. The Lithuanian trade union leaders say this was a watershed period in which employed women began talking openly about the differences in women and men's life chances.[21] Overall, however, the Seimas working group did not receive much feedback from either women's organizations or individual citizens.

The most active MPs working for the law's passage within the women's caucus were Centre and Women's party members. The Equal Opportunity Law was not an issue of great significance for any political party except for the Women's Party, which, in the period of discussion in the Seimas, worked behind the scenes to ensure passage. The perception among most political parties is that the law is a positive and an important part of the modernization and Europeanization of Lithuania.

Some Conservative women, however, were quite reluctant to support the bill. As R. Melnikienė, one of the central supporters of the law noted,

> The Conservative Party has attracted women with strong personalities and rich career experiences. When they come to Seimas, they compete according to male principles of the political battle. Any rules of women's solidarity are unnecessary for them. They are able to compete and win. These Conservative women criticized us and denied the need for such a law. The fiercest critiques of the bill, [that it was] a complete nonsense, came from a Conservative female deputy.[22]

Leaders from both the Women's Party and the Centre Union talked about their belief that Conservative women had a misperception of their philosophy of female representation. 'Women from the Conservative party participated very little in the [parliamentary women's] group and preparation of the law [on equal opportunities]. It was as if they were afraid to identify themselves with women and to express their otherness in politics. They do not under-stand that it is useful for men too, to be democratic and civilized and follow European trends, where such laws on gender equality exist.'[23]

The 'Equal Women and Men's Opportunity Law' was passed by the Seimas with only token opposition in 1998 and took effect in March 1999. In the end, the vote for passage was 48-2 with seven members abstaining. The low vote totals show that perhaps the modal reaction was one of indifference. Nevertheless, the bill does have consequences: The government created an Ombuds' office to implement this law. In an in-depth interview, A. Burneikienė, the Ombudswoman, explained the purpose of the law in the following way:

> The most important thing about this law is not the possibility to punish certain employers and harassers. The most important thing is the long-term educative influence. It will teach us to respect our Constitution and not to publish labour announcements where recruitment criterion is not personal competence, but a candidate's gender. Institutions of education cannot establish special entry con-ditions based on gender as happened in the Soviet time and sometimes happens now. Labour relations should become based on professional grounds not on an individual's sex.[24]

As the law has only recently been enacted, it is too early to see its long-term effect. It does create, however, the possibility of significant changes in women's economic position.

While the law passed with substantial support from most actors involved in the process, the bill is not without its critics. R. Smetona, leader of the National Democratic Party, argues: 'I do not think we really needed such a law. Perhaps it happened because of our Lithuanian habit to catch up and to bypass others. As far as I know, there are only a few states in Europe where such a law exists . . . It is not a law with significant consequences. It legitimates a situation that practic-ally exists in Lithuania already . . . This is largely a Western propaganda tool'.[25]

❖ CONCLUSIONS

Lithuanian women have never been excluded from public life. Women's acces-sion to political representation and positions of power has been favoured by national independence movements that marked Lithuania in the first and last decades of the twentieth century. The Soviet regime introduced important ideological changes and, to a certain extent, led to economic modernization. Meanwhile, gender roles and female political interests underwent serious communist distortions that transformed these issues into empty political slo-gans and left behind a cultural stigma against women's political participation.

Reopening for political freedom in the post-communist Lithuania has taken place under qualitatively different circumstances. While the number of women in formal positions of power has dropped precipitously from the

Soviet period, the women who are active in politics have been able to carve out more authentic places for themselves, with meaningful power. Furthermore, as the democratic system begins to stabilize and recovers from the initial chaos of regime change, the mid-range issues of women's representation and recruitment are increasingly included on the political agenda as a part of the democratic process and discourse.

The opening up of the political process has not been a linear movement towards greater female influence. At the outset of the new democratic period, there were a number of situations in Lithuania that advantaged Lithuanian women vis-à-vis their sisters in other Eastern European countries. The leadership of Prunskienė, the close ties that very quickly developed between Lithuanian parties and their European sister parties, especially those in Scandinavia, and the relatively quick development of a reasonably stable party system were all factors in Lithuania's leading levels of female representation in the region.

Nevertheless, the 2000 elections cannot be seen as anything other than a serious setback for women's interests. Despite this, there are reasons to believe women will once again make significant inroads in their quest for political power. The electoral system is advantageous; parties on both the right and left have shown considerable willingness to nominate women; recent mergers of parties on the left and in the centre (Christian Democratic parties), where women have received favourable list placements in the past, should strengthen these pro-women parties; and, in addition, large numbers of women are presently serving 'apprenticeships' on local city councils. All these factors point in the direction of greater female representation over time.

❖ NOTES

1 Prunskienė K. (1995), Women's Party/New Democracy, In-depth interview on 19 October 1999.

2 The costs of registering candidates were sufficent that parties may have hesitated to register candidates where they saw little chance of winning. In single-mandate constituencies registered political parties, after presenting petitions showing support of no less than 1000 eligible voters, had to pay a security deposit equal to one average monthly salary. This sum was reimbursed only if the individual candidate won a seat. The multi-mandate national constituency lists were to include no less than 20 candidates with a security deposit equal to 20 average monthly salaries. This deposit was reimbursed if the list passed the threshold of 4% of the national vote cast.

3 Smaller parties do have a possibility of getting in via the PR portion of the election if they can join a major party in a list coalition. In 2000, the Union of Lithuanian Russians was able to win three list seats through its membership in the Social Democratic Electoral Coalition, headed by the LDLP and the LSDP.

4 One might argue this is not true for the 2000 elections, in which all of the parties appear to be of moderate size. If we consider the LDLP and LSDP, which ran

together as a coalition in 2000 and merged into a single party in 2001, as a single party, however, the argument still holds.

5 Paliokienė G., Lithuanian Christian Democratic Party, in-depth interview on 11 August 1999.

6 Prunskienė K., Women's Party/New Democracy, in-depth interview on 19 October 1999.

7 Šiaulienė I., Lithuanian Democratic Labour Party, in-depth interview on 19 October 1999.

8 Prunskienė K., Women's Party/New Democracy, in-depth interview on 19 October 1999.

9 Paliokienė, G. Lithuanian Christian Democratic Party, in-depth interview on 11 August 1999.

10 Smetona R., Lithuanian National Democratic Party, in-depth interview on 19 October 1999.

11 Šiaulienė I., Lithuanian Democratic Labour Party, in-depth interview on 19 October 1999.

12 Ozolas R., Lithuanian Centre Union, in-depth interview on 12 October 1999.

13 Juršėnas Č., Lithuanian Democratic Labour Party, in-depth interview on 10 December 1999.

14 Melnikienė R., Lithuanian Centre Union, in-depth interview on 10 December 1999.

15 Paliokienė G., Lithuanian Christian Democratic Party, in-depth interview on 11 August 1999.

16 Juknevičienė R., Homeland Union (Lithuanian Conservatives), in-depth interview on 30 November 1999.

17 Oželytė N., Homeland Union (Lithuanian Conservatives), in-depth interview on 30 November 1999.

18 Juknevičienė R., Homeland Union (Lithuanian Conservatives), in-depth interview on 30 November 1999.

19 Juknevičienė R., Homeland Union (Lithuanian Conservatives), in-depth interview on 30 November 1999.

20 Melnikienė R., Lithuanian Centre Union, in-depth interview on 12 October 1999.

21 Baublytė A., Lithuanian Trade Union Confederation, Women' Section. In-depth interview on 26 October 1999.

22 Melnikienė R., Lithuanian Centre Union, in depth interview on 10 October 1999.

23 Prunskienė D., Women's Party/New Democracy, in-depth interview on 19 October 1999.

24 Burneikienė A., in-depth interview on 26 October 1999.

25 Smetona R., Lithuanian National Democratic Party, in-depth interview on 19 October 1999.

❖ ALGIS KRUPAVIČIUS AND IRMINA MATONYTĖ

6 ❖ Weak Mobilization, Hidden Majoritarianism, and Resurgence of the Right: A Recipe for Female Under-Representation in Hungary

Kathleen A. Montgomery and Gabriella Ilonszki

For nearly 40 years, elections in Hungary provided little suspense about who would sit in the legislature. The Hungarian Socialist Workers' Party controlled the candidate selection process and electoral machinery. As in other communist countries, quotas ensured women a presence in parliament while men filled the positions of real authority. In 1985, only one woman was a member of the Council of Ministers (government). The ministers were overwhelmingly male, as was the membership of the highest decision-making body in the Party, the Politburo (Heinrich 1986; Fodor 1994; Peto 1994; Morondo 1997).

With the introduction of multi-party elections in 1990, voters rejected the old communist representatives and endorsed a new elite that looked strikingly familiar to observers of Western parliaments. Educated, middle-aged men filled the ranks of the 386 member unicameral National Assembly. Women managed to secure only seven per cent of the seats, a dramatic decline from the communist-era norm of around 30 per cent (Fodor 1994). In the decade since, female legislative representation reached an apogee of 11 per cent in 1994 but fell again to around 8 per cent in 1998 and 9 per cent in 2002. This places Hungary among the lowest tier of European countries and well below several of its nearest post-communist neighbours.[1]

The question raised by the Hungarian experience is not so much why did women's representation decline with the advent of democracy. Rather, the question is why do women continue to be so severely under-represented in a country that is arguably one of the most consolidated and prosperous of the post-communist democracies.

Studies that emphasize the cultural bases of support for women in politics might answer this question with evidence of anti-feminist attitudes. Institutionalist scholars might point to the majoritarian element of Hungary's mixed electoral system. Still others might emphasize the strength of conservative-nationalist forces in the emerging multi-party system. We examine each of these approaches in turn using a combination of electoral and public opinion data, as well as in-depth interviews with women in the parliamentary parties.[2] We conclude that women fare best when non-rightist parties are able to engage in ticket balancing strategies. The unique features of the Hungarian mixed electoral system, however, produce fewer incentives for such strategies than we might expect from a mixed electoral system. Moreover, a lack of organized demand for political equality means that, even when parties have the opportunity to balance the ticket with women, other interests receive priority.

❖ ANTI-FEMINISM AND THE MISSING WOMEN'S MOVEMENT

Public opinion surveys show that Hungarians hold more traditional gender role conceptions than citizens in many of the Western democracies, a finding that coincides with broad patterns of post-communist culture (see Chapter 3). In places like Poland and Slovakia, traditionalism coincides with highly observant Catholic populations. This is not the case in Hungary, where Catholics form only a slim majority, and some 66 per cent of survey respondents say that they 'rarely or never attend' church.[3]

These comparisons suggest that anti-feminism reflects more than a return to pre-communist cultural patterns or a simple backlash against communism. In Hungary, 'an . . . explicitly anti-feminist discourse' resulted from 'the particular conditions of state socialism' there (Goven 1994: 225). Those conditions include (from 1956) a set of policies that came to be known as Kádárism. Kádárism promised citizens the freedom to pursue a higher standard of living in return for political quiescence. The emphasis on consumerism was intended to stimulate economic growth and raise levels of citizen satisfaction.

In the end, it did neither; and by the 1980s, the critique of state socialism in Hungary had become entwined with a critique of social breakdown. Sociological studies revealed an exhausted and atomized populace and a widespread 'crisis of the family' (Bollobás 1993; Simon 1993; Andorka 1999). To fulfill the lifestyle demands unleashed by Kádárism, most men worked extra jobs in the unofficial 'gray' economy, while most women participated in the paid labour force and supplied hours of unpaid labour to maintain the home. Universal social welfare benefits transferred the dependence of women on individual men to dependence on the state; but benefits, such as state-sponsored daycare, were widely viewed as inadequate.

❖ K. A. MONTGOMERY AND G. ILONSZKI

With rates of divorce, suicide, alcoholism, and single motherhood well above the European average, it is little wonder that Hungarians rejected the model of female emancipation held forth by the socialist regime. That rejection has tangible consequences for post-communist political culture. When asked to characterize what they look for in a candidate, survey respondents in the early 1990s either said they prefer male candidates or that gender is irrelevant (Fodor 1994). These attitudes, however, do not appear to translate into direct voter discrimination at the ballot box. Women consistently comprise around nine per cent of 'strong' candidates (those with a mathematical possibility of entering the legislature) and consistently manage to obtain between 7 and 11 per cent of seats (Tóka 1995). The perception that women do not belong in politics, however, may discourage female aspirants. The women we interviewed believe female politicians face greater obstacles than their male counterparts. Several expressed the opinion that female politicians must be two or three times more qualified than male candidates are. It helps, they say, to be highly educated, to have personal connections to politics (e.g. through a husband), and to have either a non-conventional family arrangement or the full support of husband and children.

Several of these anecdotes are supported by 1998 data from Hungary's Central Statistical Office.[4] A recent survey suggests that, while female candidates match the educational levels of their male counterparts, they often have more extensive political backgrounds, particularly in the local party (26 per cent of female candidates and only 16 per cent of male candidates claimed to have held a local party position before running for office). In addition, a higher percentage of the female candidates in the survey sample had small families (one child or none). This is consistent with the notion that women with family responsibilities lack the time and ambition to launch a political career. It may also reflect the cultural bias against mothers assuming non-traditional roles. Female survey respondents more frequently claimed to be living in a non-traditional family arrangement (single, divorced, or in a partnership).

All of this suggests that the costs of aspiring to parliament are higher for women; yet we find that over time the percentage of women in the candidate pool has moved steadily upward. In 1990, every twelfth candidate was a woman. That figure rose to every tenth candidate in 1994 and every eighth in 1998. Preliminary calculations suggest that in the 2002 elections, approximately every sixth candidate was a woman. With time, it appears that women are beginning to regard politics as an attractive and realistic goal. The problem is getting parties to nominate strong female candidates; and this is where anti-feminist cultural values may be most detrimental.

In 1998, the six main parties put forth 1099 strong male candidates and only 127 strong female candidates (Sebestény 1999). We may assume that parties operating in a competitive electoral environment will place women on the ballot when they believe that women can bring votes. In Hungary, unfortunately, party gatekeepers have ample reason to believe that female candidates may lose votes. Popular opinion is anti-feminist, and there is currently no women's movement that specifically seeks to increase political equality, either by supporting female aspirants or pressuring parties to recruit more women. The small Feminista Halozat (Feminist Network) is by all accounts politically ineffective, maintained largely through foreign interest and support (Pigniczky 1997). The larger Magyar Nők Szövetsége (Hungarian Women's Association), founded by former members of the official women's organization, has rejected both feminism and politics. In 1992, a handful of women in the liberal Alliance of Free Democrats Party formed the Foundation of the Women of Hungary (MONA), but as we discuss later, the group has not had a significant impact on party policy.

Occasionally Hungarian women engage in direct citizen action. In 1995, for example, a group of mothers took over a local welfare office demanding that benefits continue to be provided on the basis of 'motherhood right' (Haney 1997); and women came together to block church efforts to restrict abortion rights (Gal 1994). There is not a strong protest culture in Hungary, however, and anomic responses to single issues do not provide a basis for the development of a broader pro-equality movement.

Where women are organized, they tend to be on the right of the ideological spectrum. Some of the conservative parties in Hungary receive support from large women's auxiliaries. A group of conservative women formed the National Party of Hungarian Mothers in 1993 to lobby for the promotion of better conditions for full-time motherhood; and some of the most prominent female politicians have been conservatives like Agnes Maczo, who served as Speaker of the Assembly. These organizations and politicians do not define gender equality as an ideological goal and do not actively work to recruit more women into political leadership.

In the absence of an effectively organized pro-equality women's movement, increased female representation depends on the magnanimity of party gatekeepers. The degree to which gatekeepers are willing to take the risk of recruiting women depends, in part, on the structure of incentives provided by the electoral rules; and Hungary's complicated electoral system offers a mixed bag.

❖ A MIXED-MAJORITARIAN SYSTEM

The details of Hungary's electoral system have been thoroughly elaborated elsewhere (see Benoit 1996). For our purposes, a simple summary of the main features affecting women is sufficient. There are three methods of translating votes into seats in the Hungarian National Assembly. Approximately one half of the seats (176) are filled through a two-round, majority vote system in single member districts. If no candidate wins a majority in the first round, the top three candidates (and any candidate with more than 15 per cent of the vote) compete in a second round where a mere plurality is required to secure the seat. The remaining seats are distributed proportionally to party lists in two types of multi-member constituencies. In the 19 historical counties and Budapest, 152 seats are distributed on closed party lists according to a special variant of the largest remainder formula. Whenever the quota for a seat cannot be met in a territorial constituency, that seat is added to a pool of 52 seats awarded to parties on the basis of a proportional allocation of remainder votes (tőredék szavazatok) on nationwide party lists.[5]

In terms of female recruitment, the winner-take-all district contests should be the least friendly component of the system. Parties have incentives to choose candidates with the broadest electoral appeal in order to win or at least qualify for the second round. Even parties that do not expect to win a given seat cannot afford to endorse a candidate who may lose votes, since votes cast for a losing candidate in the first round will be applied to the party's national list.

The PR component of the system, by way of contrast, should provide opportunities for party gatekeepers to recruit women. The lists are closed, so gatekeepers exert control over which candidates will be placed in winnable positions. If they wish to recruit women, they have the power to do so. More importantly, district magnitude ranges from 3 to 28 (in the counties) to as much as 90 (on the national lists). Large district magnitudes help to ensure that parties will send parliamentary delegations larger than one, and this hypothetically shifts the calculus from winner-take-all to ticket-balancing. The larger a party expects its delegation to be, the greater the opportunities and incentives for a balancing strategy. National lists, by this reasoning, should provide the ideal opportunity to recruit women.

Table 6.1 tests this by dividing the sex of seatholders (man = 0, woman = 1) in the Hungarian Assembly by type of mandate (SMD, county list, and national list) in the three post-communist elections. In 1990, approximately 21 per cent of the women elected came from single-member districts, 29 per cent entered through county lists, and fully 50 per cent gained their seats via national lists. If we were to look only at the 1990 election, we would have to conclude that Hungary would recruit far more women if it shifted to a pure PR system in a single nationwide constituency.

The 1994 and 1998 elections, however, complicate the picture. While female representation increased in 1994 (from 7.3 to 11.1 per cent), gains did not come through the national lists. The number of women recruited from regional lists *and* districts doubled, while the number from national lists actually declined. This trend continued in 1998. Nearly the same number of women entered

Table 6.1. Distribution of seats in 1990, 1994, and 1998 elections by sex

Mandate	Male		Female		Total	
1990						
SMD	170	(96.6%)	6	(3.4%)	176	(45.7%)
County list	111	(93.3%)	8	(6.7%)	119	(30.9%)
National list	76	(84.4%)	14	(15.6%)	90	(23.4%)
	357	(92.7%)	28	(7.3%)	385	(100%)
Kendall's tau-β	0.164		Significance level = 0.002			
1994						
SMD	161	(91.5%)	15	(8.5%)	176	(45.6%)
County list	109	(87.2%)	16	(12.8%)	125	(32.4%)
National list	73	(85.9%)	12	(14.1%)	85	(22.0%)
	343	(88.9%)	43	(11.1%)	386	(100%)
Kendall's tau-β	0.072		Significance level = 0.136			
1998						
SMD	163	(93.1%)	12	(6.9%)	175	(45.5%)
County list	115	(89.8%)	13	(10.2%)	128	(33.2%)
National list	75	(91.5%)	7	(8.5%)	82	(21.3%)
	353	(91.7%)	32	(8.3%)	385	(100%)
Kendall's tau-β	0.035		Significance level = 0.456			

parliament through SMDs as county lists (12 and 13, respectively), but the number elected via national lists declined by half.

If we compare the proportion of men and women recruited from each category across elections, the trend becomes even clearer. In 1990, the proportion of women recruited to the Assembly through national lists was more than twice the proportion of male candidates who entered through that method. By 1998, women were *no more likely* to have entered parliament through national lists than their male counterparts.

❖ Ballot structure, district magnitude, and party magnitude

The expectation of the literature is that party list PR in multi-member districts will outperform winner-take-all district contests. To examine this hypothesis directly, we test for a correlation between various measures of the electoral system and women's representation. Ballot structure distinguishes between MPs elected from district seats and party lists seats. District magnitude is coded for each seatholder and logged to adjust for extreme values that can occur for members elected through the national lists. Since PR ballot structure and high district magnitude are expected to improve women's representation by ensuring larger *party delegations* (Matland 1993), we also look directly at the log of *party magnitude* (the delegation size of each party in each regional constituency and national list for the given election year).

When looking at female recruitment over the three post-communist elections pooled together, the electoral rules produce the predicted effect. The relationships between the three electoral system variables and sex of the seatholder are in the expected direction and statistically significant (at the 0.01 level). The tau-β coefficient for Ballot Structure is 0.085, for district magnitude it is 0.090, and for party magnitude it is 0.093. Note that party magnitude performs marginally better than either district magnitude or ballot structure taken alone.

Looking at each election individually, however, the electoral system explanation works well only in the founding democratic election of 1990. Ballot structure presents tau-β of 0.137 in 1990 (sig. <0.01), 0.076 in 1994 (n.s.), and a paltry 0.035 (n.s.) in 1998. District magnitude similarly fades in strength from a tau-β of 0.183 in 1990 (sig. <0.01), to 0.086 (sig. <0.05), to an anemic and insignificant 0.037 in 1998. The effect of party magnitude on women's representation also disintegrates over time tau-β = 0.199 (sig. <0.01) in 1990, 0.082 (sig. <0.05) in 1994, and 0.029 (n.s.) in 1998.

One problem with the electoral system explanation is there are fewer *de facto* incentives for ticket balancing in the Hungarian system than the literature would predict. Several factors mitigate against balancing. In the first place, parties may put forth the same candidate in more than one component of the system. This practice of dual or even triple listings, which has been increasing steadily over the post-communist period, makes it very difficult for party gatekeepers to predict which slots on the lists represent winnable positions.

In most party list systems, we expect that the top positions on the list will go to the most powerful intra-party interests. The second tier slots provide gatekeepers with opportunities to balance the ticket with less powerful but legitimate interests within the party and electorate. Everything below these winnable slots is purely ornamental. When it is possible for a candidate to run in more than one component of the system, the top-listed candidate on, for instance, the national list could win in another component of the system and choose to have his name stricken from the national list. The party will then drop down to the next name. Party leaders cannot know in advance how many of the names at the top will be stricken, so they cannot meaningfully engage in (or be held accountable for) ticket balancing. In 1998, the MSzP, for example, sent a woman to the Assembly from slot 71 on its national list. There was no way for MSzP gatekeepers to know that the party delegation would include names that far down on the list.

The inability of party gatekeepers to predict which slots are competitive poses a problem on both types of party lists, but uncertainty is exacerbated for the national lists by the use of remainder votes. To predict the proportion of national list seats it will receive, a party would have to know how many district and territorial contests it will lose and by how much. If gate-keepers cannot predict which seats are winnable, the incentive will be to pursue strategies that protect the most powerful constituencies in the party at all levels.

Parties can maximize a party leader's chances for success by running that candidate simultaneously in all three components of the system. The upper-most party leaders, however, often choose to run only on the regional and national party lists, because they do not want to perform the constituency service functions expected of district MPs (Ilonszki 1999). What this means for women is that, if their party does poorly and the male leaders do not win in their regional contests, then the national list seats will be used to perpetu-ate the (largely male) party leadership in parliament. If the party does well, it will have fewer remainder votes from the territorial contests and will therefore receive fewer national list seats. The party will not go as deep into its national list, down to the slots where women are more likely to be placed.

A second important point about the Hungarian electoral system is that while the second tier of the electoral system, the county level, is proportional in theory, in practice it generates very low party magnitudes. The use of a high electoral threshold (initially 4 per cent, raised to 5 per cent) has encouraged the formation of a less fragmented party system in Hungary than we find in several of the post-communist systems. Even so, six parties have consistently divided seats in county constituencies that range in magnitude from 3 to 28. Consequently, many of the smaller magnitude county constituencies have become de facto SMDs. In 1994, when the Socialist Party (MSzP) won a land-slide victory, only three counties (Budapest, Pest, and Borsod-Abauj-Zemplen) produced party magnitudes consistently larger than one. In 1998, the vote was divided more evenly between the MSzP and the Young Democrats-Civic Party (Fidesz-MPP). Only one of the county constituencies became a *de facto* SMD, but 13 yielded party magnitudes of *no more than two for any party*. Across all three elections, we find that fully 70 per cent of party delegations number three or less.

Add to this the fact that average party seat change has been over 80 per cent in the post-communist period, and it is little wonder that party gatekeepers emphasize recruitment strategies that ensure the perpetuation of the national party leadership. There are, for all practical purposes, no safe seats for party leaders to allocate. Only the top slot on the large magnitude Budapest list has ever been guaranteed, and only for a few of the largest parties. Those rare safe slots have never been allocated to women.[6] When we look at all regional lists for 1998, we find that women were placed in the top position only 7.5 per cent of the time—nearly half of these from insignificant parties. If, in most cases, a party will only be able to send the top name on its list, women are clearly at a disadvantage.

The situation for women becomes worse when we look at the patterns of candidate placement by gender. Among those candidates who ran in only one component of the system, men were more likely to run 'district only' and women were more likely to appear as 'regional list only'. This reflects the concerns party gatekeepers have about the winner-take-all nature of the districts and has negative consequences for women. A female candidate who runs solely on a regional list gets only one chance to enter parliament; and that chance may not be very strong when we take into consideration low party magnitudes. Virtually everything depends on where parties are willing to place women on the lists; and in this way, the strong presence of rightist and national-conservative parties in post-communist Hungary exacerbates the problem of female under-representation. See Table 6.2 for party details.

Table 6.2. Hungary's post-communist party system

Party name and acronym (Hungarian/English translation)	Government participation	Ideological affiliation
Fiatal Demokraták Szövetsége (Fidesz-MPP)/Alliance of Young Democrats–Civic Party (officially recognized as independent political organization on 30 March 1988)	1998–2002 led coalition that included FKgP and MDF. 2002–present, in opposition	Began as liberal youth party but has moved to centre-right
Független Kisgazda-, Földmunkás és Polgari Párt or Független Kisgazdapárt (FKgP)/Independent Smallholders' Party (ISP) (originally founded in 1930, reactivated 12 November 1988)	In MDF-led coalition 1990–4, in Fidesz-led coalition 1998–2002	Conservative Nationalist
Kereszténydemokrata Néppárt (KDNP)/ Christian Democratic People's Party (CDPP) (originally active in the interwar period, reactivated in April 1989)	In MDF-led coalition 1990–4	Christian Conservative
Magyar Demokrata Fórum (MDF)/ Hungarian Democratic Forum (HDF) (officially founded on 27 September 1987)	Led 1990–4 coalition, a minor member of Fidesz-led coalition 1998–2002	Moderate Conservative
Magyar Igazság és Élet Pártja (MIÉP)/ Hungarian Justice and Life Party (HJLP) (founded in 1993)	During first parliament became an opposition fraction after expulsion of key leaders from	Populist Nationalist

Table 6.2. continued

Party name and acronym (Hungarian/English translation)	Government participation	Ideological affiliation
	the MDF. Cleared 5% threshold in 1998 but was not invited to join the rightist coalition led by Fidesz	
Magyar Szocialista Párt (MSzP)/ Hungarian Socialist Party (HSP) (founded in 1989 from the reform wing of the communist party)	Led coalition from 1994–8, 2002–present	Moderate Left Social Democrats
Szabad Demokraták Szövetsége (SzDSz)/Alliance of Free Democrats (AFD) (formed in November 1988 out of the Network of Free Initiatives, a coordinating centre for a Number of oppositional movements)	Coalition with MSzP 1994–8, 2002–present	Liberal

❖ POST-COMMUNIST POLITICAL PARTIES AND FEMALE LEGISLATIVE RECRUITMENT

None of the parties that have made it into the National Assembly may be described as strongly pro-female. Men dominated the party formation and institutional negotiation phases of the transition from communist rule. They, in turn, became the gatekeepers for recruitment. Table 6.3 shows that, since the transition, only one woman has served as a party president. Women are also severely under-represented across party presidiums. All five of the women who served on the Fidesz presidium did so prior to or during 1990, and the same is true for the one female member listed for the Christian Democrats (KDNP) and several of the MSzP women.

Male dominance in the parties carries over into party-apportioned positions in the chamber. In 2001, among 22 chairs in the Standing committees, only one (the Minister of Justice) was a woman; out of 51 vice chairs, only four were female. Women we interviewed suggested their male colleagues support the notion of women in politics as long as women are content to remain active at the local level or in the backbenches. As soon as a woman expresses higher ambitions, however, she becomes suspect to her male colleagues. Women do not try to press too overtly for advancement, for fear they will be labelled as 'aggressive.' This appears to be a particular concern among women in the major parties.

❖ K. A. MONTGOMERY AND G. ILONSZKI

Table 6.3. Women in the leadership of the parliamentary parties (# women/total)[1]

Party acronym	Presidents	Vice Presidents/ Party managers	Members of presidium	Total
Fidesz-MPP	0/1	1/15	5/27	6/42 (14%)[2]
FKgP	0/4	N/A[3]	3/73	3/77 (4%)
KDNP	0/3	2/24	1/13	3/40 (7%)
MDF	1/5[4]	2/21	3/39	6/65 (9%)
MIÉP	0/1	0/6	2/23	2/30 (7%)
MSzP	0/3	3/13	6/38	9/54 (17%)
SzDSz	0/4	N/A	2/31	2/35 (6%)
Totals	1/21 4.8%	8/79 10.1%	22/244 9.01%	31/344 9.01%

[1] The period covered is from the foundation of the given party to 1998.
[2] Since 1990, this figure is only 3%.
[3] The FKgP and SzDSz have only two levels of leadership, party president and members of the presidium.
[4] Recently Ibolya David became president of the party. She is the first female president in any major political party in Hungary.

Indeed, the upward trajectory in female candidates over the post-communist period can be accounted for largely through the recruitment practices of the non-parliamentary parties. Non-competitive parties like the Worker's Party and the Green Party maintain an explicit ideological commitment to gender equity and use affirmative action to improve female recruitment. In 1998, for example, the Green Party was only able to field a single regional list. That list contained 24 names, 23 of which belonged to women.

Even among less ideologically committed minor parties, women tend to fare better than in the major parties. Recruitment to a non-competitive party is less appealing to male aspirants, so there is less competition for those candidacies. The Christian Democratic Party (KDNP), for example, trebled its number of female candidates in 1998 after the party virtually collapsed. As one interviewee put it, 'the rats [men] were leaving the sinking ship and only women were left'. At the same time, the stakes are lower for non-competitive parties. They do not have winnable seats to allocate and do not need to worry about perpetuating national party leadership in parliament. It is telling that on the Green Party list cited above, the only slot that did not go to a woman was the top position, the only one that could remotely be considered competitive if the party had an unusually good showing.

For the competitive parties, the stakes are much higher. Few women make it into the candidate pools of these parties, and fewer still make it into the prized 'winnable' candidacies. Women in Fidesz-MPP appear to face the greatest obstacles. The number of strong female candidates has increased over time for all of the parliamentary parties *except* Fidesz and the MDF. Furthermore, looking strictly at 1998 (the election for which we have the most complete regional candidate lists), we find that Fidesz nominated a smaller proportion of female candidates than the other parties and concentrated those women more frequently in ornamental slots. The majority of list slots at any given time will be ornamental, but Fidesz placed fully 96 per cent of its female candidates and only 89 per cent of its male candidates in such positions. No other party displayed such a pronounced gender gap.

Table 6.4 shows that, if we exclude the unusual case of the Christian Democrats (KDNP) in 1998, the Free Democrats (SzDSz) and the Socialist Party (MSzP) recruited more women across all mandate categories. These same two parties were least likely among the major parliamentary parties to concentrate women in ornamental slots. Indeed, for the SzDSz, there was no gap between the per cent of male candidates and female candidates placed in ornamental slots on the regional lists.

The literature in the established democracies suggests several party characteristics can account for differences in levels of female recruitment: ideological affiliation, organization, and nomination procedures. Women are expected to have the fewest opportunities in rightist parties, particularly where recruitment is based on murky, personalized procedures, and patronage. They should fare better in parties that hold leftist, particularly 'new left', values and in parties with institutionalized and centralized nomination procedures.

Fig. 6.1 arrays each major Hungarian party according to the degree of centralization in nominating procedures and the level of institutionalization. The placement of each party attempts to capture the basic tendency of the party over the post-communist period (Ilonszki 1999).

In the early stages of transition, none of the parties employed clear bureaucratic procedures for recruiting candidates. Practices ran the gamut from parties like the MSzP, where the top two or three leaders formulated lists following undefined principles, to the newly legitimized opposition association, SzDSz, which grew so rapidly it operated on a 'first come, first seated' policy. Today the parties listed in the lower half of the figure should provide the least favourable recruitment scenario for women. In the Hungarian Justice and Life Party (MIÉP) and the Smallholders (FKgP), decision-making is centralized, and the nomination criteria emphasize the

Table 6.4. Number of female candidates nominated by major parties according to mandate type, 1990–8

Party	SMD	County[1]	National	Totals
1990				
MSzP	13	4	12	29
SzDSz	12	6	10	28
MDF	6	0	9	15
FKgP	5	2	5	12
KDNP	7	2	4	13
FIDESZ	7	7	5	19
Total	50	21	45	116
1994				
MSzP	17	7	5	29
SzDSz	16	7	9	32
MDF	12	5	7	24
FKgP	8	3	8	19
KDNP	13	7	1	21
FIDESZ	14	5	4	23
Total	80	34	34	148
1998				
MSzP	16	13	5	34
SzDSz	24	10	4	38
MDF	5	7	5	17
FKgP	15	10	4	29
KDNP	25	18	9	52
FIDESZ	8	7	1	16
MIÉP	22	14	1	37
Total	115	79	29	223

Information based on published lists that only included top 32 names for national lists.
[1] County data only include top 3–5 candidates.

patronage resources of the candidates. In MIÉP, for example, candidates often emerge by writing letters to the party leader, István Csurka, praising him on his speeches and writings. In the FKgP, the central leadership has the final right of approval over all candidates, so personal connections to the top party leaders are important. The wife of the party president, for example, was placed fourth on the party's 88-name national list in 1998; but there were only four other women in the top half of that same list.

The parties in the upper half of the figure all follow fairly explicit rules for candidate selection, emphasizing merit and records of local party service. The SzDSz and Fidesz-MPP are centralized enough that party leaders can recruit

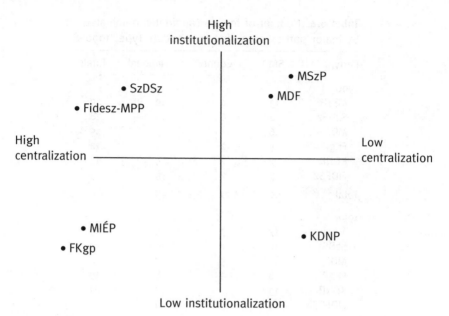

High
institutionalization

• MSzP
• SzDSz
• MDF
• Fidesz-MPP

High
centralization

Low
centralization

• MIÉP
• KDNP
• FKgp

Low institutionalization

Figure 6.1. Classification of Hungarian parties according to centralization and institutionalization of recruitment

women if that is a goal; and for the SzDSz (to a point) it is. The MDF and MSzP are also institutionalized, but unlike the SzDSz and Fidesz, they place considerable weight on the input of local party organs in drawing up party lists. Regional leaders may be more conservative than the central party, and that can hurt female recruitment, particularly where the party's grassroots supporters hold traditional social values. This has been the case in the MDF but less so in the MSzP, which has a history of women's involvement in the party.

Below, we examine each party in detail, aligning parties along a rough scale of woman friendliness in terms of recruitment. Fidesz-MPP clearly anchors the least-friendly end of the spectrum, followed by MIÉP, the FKgP, and MDF in roughly descending order. The liberal SzDSz and the leftist MSzP occupy the high end of the scale. Within the middle group, arguments could certainly be made to place one party over another, but our focus will be on the lowest and highest ends of the spectrum.

The Young Democrats-Civic Party (Fidesz-MPP) began its life as a movement of young, liberal-minded intellectuals from the Budapest law and economics faculties. Women played a significant role in founding the movement; but with the transformation into a political party, the goals and leadership of the group changed. In 1993, the 'cafe-intellectual' wing of the party was expunged.

❖ K. A. MONTGOMERY AND G. ILONSZKI

With it went several young, educated women. The party leadership became almost exclusively male, dominated by the aggressive style of the party president, Viktor Orbán. After two surprisingly sharp electoral defeats (in 1990 and 1994), the party jettisoned its liberal ideology and migrated to the right. It joined the MDF, KDNP, FKgP, and MIÉP in opposing abortion, emphasizing the role of women in preserving and passing on the national identity, and expressing concern over declining birthrates among ethnic Hungarians. The ideological transformation of the party has no doubt damaged the position of women. Kapitány and Kapitány (1999) found that Fidesz-MPP did not feature even one woman speaking in its 1998 campaign video.

All of this, however, should be viewed in terms of a broader struggle to gain and keep power in unfavourable conditions. Prior to 1998, Fidesz was a minor member of the opposition. It won just 21 seats in 1990, less than a quarter of the seats won by its fellow liberal party, the Free Democrats. In 1994, Fidesz actually lost one seat, despite leading public opinion polls in the run up to the election. The poor electoral performance of the party caused it to seek a new ideological niche and to develop a bunker mentality with regard to recruitment. With consistently low party magnitudes and few safe seats to allocate, party gatekeepers have had strong incentives to protect and perpetuate the party leadership in power. Fidesz has never had a strong grassroots movement or a large national party. The parliamentary party has been virtually synonymous with the national party. Hence, despite strong popularity heading into the 1998 election, Fidesz leaders took very few chances. On the large magnitude Budapest territorial list, for example, the top ten names belonged to leaders of the parliamentary party, all of whom happened to be men.

According to one woman we interviewed, the party's emphasis on its core of male party leaders has not diminished since its resounding success in the 1998 elections. Coalition uncertainties and the paucity of women in the party have created conditions in which women sometimes 'do not feel comfortable in the party's benches'. The party does not maintain a women's caucus; and it has never seriously entertained the notion of a gender-based quota for recruitment. Moreover, it does not appear that the party will be punished for these policies. According to a poll taken among 1000 voters in December of 1999, the potential party vote for Fidesz-MPP is slightly higher among women than men (52 and 48 per cent, respectively).

The Party of Hungarian Justice and Life (MIÉP) did not exist in 1990. It formed in 1993 from the radical populist wing of the MDF and did not cross the threshold for parliamentary representation until 1998. We therefore know comparatively little about how the party will perform as a party in power with regard to female recruitment. What we do know offers little promise. In 1994, MIÉP managed to field a national list. Among fifty names, there were only two women, placed in slots 48 and 50. In 1998, the picture improved slightly.

A woman economist was placed in the sixth slot. There were six other women on the list, but none above the thirty-fifth place.

MIÉP leadership is dominated by the personality of the party president, István Csurka. One interviewee claimed that Csurka is popular among female voters for his 'passionate and compassionate style', but the survey cited above shows much stronger party support among men (60 per cent vs. 40 per cent for women). Unsurprisingly, MIÉP did not include any speaking women in its campaign video for 1998. MIÉP does not maintain a women's caucus, and it has never considered a quota for female recruitment.

The Independent Smallholders' Party (FKgP) is the most successful of a handful of parties that seek to represent Hungary's significant peasant and agricultural interests. Resurrected from the interwar era, the Smallholders today take ideological stands similar to those of other conservative parties, but many see the party president, József Torgyán, as an extremist. With regard to women, the party presents a somewhat mixed image. It engages in many charitable activities on behalf of women and families and will expect to draw about half of its vote from women. It maintains a women's organization, the Independent Women's Association (Független Női Szövetség), which is housed in party headquarters. It boasts a membership of between 13 and 14 thousand members, and is led by the wife of the party president. The organization has successfully mobilized conservative women, but these women do not see political equality as an end. The prominence of Mrs. Torgyán should be viewed primarily as evidence of the centralized and personalistic nature of power in the party.

The party did increase its number of female candidates quite sharply in 1998, but most of those women were in lower list positions. It remains to be seen whether the token positions of today will lead to increased legitimacy for women as an intra-party interest in the future. József Torgyán, as chair of the Agriculture Committee has tended to favour male-dominated peasant and agricultural interest groups, but the party has also considered adopting a geographical quota to expand its voting base into Budapest. The party has not seriously considered a quota for female representation, because, in the words of the Vice President of the women's organization: 'Quotas raise bad memories from past times. Only individual qualities can challenge prevailing practice. Only highly qualified and able women, who might even be more professional that their male colleagues, can establish the credibility of women politicians'.

The Hungarian Democratic Forum (MDF) holds the distinction of having the only female president, Ibolya Dávid (Justice Minister in the Fidesz-led government); but the party's rightist ideology and close current association with Fidesz mitigate against a more profound commitment to women's legislative recruitment. Ideologically, the MDF has been more or less rightist over the course of the post-communist period. It led the first post-communist coalition government, which also included the FKgP and KDNP. In that first election, the MDF gained success by positioning itself as a moderate right-wing alternative to the reformed Socialist Party and the (then) more radical Fidesz and SzDSz. During the first parliament, the moderate party president, József Antall, expelled the radical right wing of the party, led by István Csurka. After a resounding electoral defeat in 1994, however, the MDF also lost its moderate conservative wing, including the prominent female politician Katalin Kutrucz (wife of the former MDF fraction leader). The MDF cooperated closely with Fidesz in the 1998 election and in 2002 sponsored all of its candidates jointly with Fidesz.

The MDF has never maintained a women's caucus within the party, though there is an unofficial grouping (Nőforum) which seeks to attract both men and women who are sympathetic to the party, but not yet ready to join. This group organizes events and lectures, but it does not seek to put pressure on the party to place women in leadership positions or winnable candidacies. The MDF does not explicitly consider gender in its recruitment strategies and has not discussed using a quota for gender representation. Like Fidesz-MPP, the MDF's proportion of strong female candidates has actually declined over time. This is perhaps a reflection of the transformation from a movement to a political party or a product of electoral disappointments that have placed a premium on survival of national party leadership in parliament.

The Alliance of Free Democrats Party (SzDSz) offers a more favourable ideological orientation for women; it recognizes there is a 'woman's issue' in parliament, that women are under-represented and face special obstacles to legislative recruitment. Moreover, the large number of women it nominated in 1998 represents more than a low rent strategy, such as we saw with the KDNP. The SzDSz believed that it would win far more seats than it ultimately did.

That said, there are limits to the party's commitment to women's equality. The SzDSz began its life as a European-style liberal party and has tended therefore to focus on the talents and capabilities of individuals. In the lead-up to the 1994 election, the SzDSz held cookouts and retreats to identify and train potential recruits. The party even put aspirants through an extensive psychological screening process. The party does not currently maintain a women's caucus and it has rejected affirmative action for women. One of the women we interviewed tried to raise the subject in the central decision-making body of the party but said that she was 'swept aside'.

After a terrible showing in the 1998 election, it appears that the SzDSz is primarily concerned with party survival. Planned modifications of party rules include a quota for balancing representation between the capital city, long the centre of SzDSz support, and the countryside.

The Hungarian Socialist Party (MSzP), more than any other major party, maintains a historical and formal ideological commitment to women's emancipation. This continuity from the past can be seen among MPs like Mrs. Jákab Robert, who has served in all three post-communist parliaments as well as the communist-era legislature.

The MSzP lags behind the more staunchly leftist Worker's Party and the new left Green Party in terms of raw numbers of female candidates. Nevertheless, the MSzP maintains a women's caucus (Nötagozat) with a membership of about a thousand. The leadership of this group meets fortnightly and sponsors four big events per year. The party featured speaking women in its 1998 campaign videos; and a recent party conference accepted a 20 per cent quota in the party leadership for women and those under the age of 35. This will not immediately affect recruitment levels, but it could be important over time. There has also been a move to introduce quotas for women's representation on the party lists. The initiative, introduced by a male MP, would have placed the quota at 50 per cent. A female interviewee said that this was either meant as a joke or intended to incite controversy, since there is strong objection to affirmative action among the membership and the local party organs. It appears likely that a 20 per cent quota will eventually be adopted at the leadership level.

Despite the move toward affirmative action, the MSzP's ticket-balancing strategies do not overtly consider women. In 1994, the secure slots on the MSzP's national party list went to the party leader, the controversial finance minister, and the leader of the largest trade union association in the country. All three candidates are male, and the latter two represented conflicting streams within the party regarding the proper pace and style of economic transition.

❖ THE INTERACTION OF ELECTORAL STRUCTURE AND PARTY CHARACTERISTICS

Given the differences among parties with regard to female recruitment, the explanation for variations in women's representation in the post-communist period appears obvious. Each post-communist election has almost completely reversed government and opposition benches, see Fig. 6.2. In 1990, the MDF, FKgP, and KDNP formed a coalition with a bare majority and women obtained only 7 per cent of legislative seats. When a Socialist-Free Democrat alliance came to power in 1994 with nearly three-quarters of the seats, women's representation rose to 11 per cent. The proportion of women in parliament fell again when Fidesz-MPP won the largest number of seats in the Assembly and formed a coalition with the Smallholders and MDF. When rightist parties win power, women's access to parliament deteriorates.

The concentration of particular parties within particular categories of mandate might also help to explain the apparent decline in significance for the

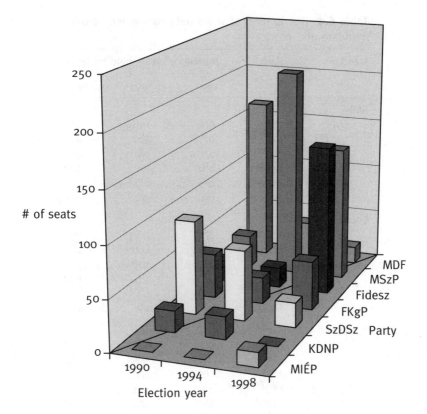

Figure 6.2. Party strength in three elections

electoral system explanation over succeeding elections. The governing party in Hungarian parliament has typically won the largest number of district seats. This was particularly true in 1990 (when the MDF won 114 of 176 district seats) and 1994 (when the MSzP went from a single district seat to 149). Due to the use of remainder votes in the national list component, success in the territorial contests typically entails a smaller number of national list seats. Hence, the shift in power between the MDF and the Socialists from 1990 to 1994 also resulted in a shift at the mandate level. When the MSzP increased its district seats, it nearly halved the number of seats it obtained through the national lists.

The impact of this on female recruitment is shown in Table 6.5. In 1990, the MSzP contributed the highest number of women through the national list portion of the system of any party. Due to its changed fortunes in 1994, the party did not contribute a single woman through the national list but was responsible for *all but one of the women* elected through single member districts. An opposite shift in fortunes for the MDF helps explain the decline

Table 6.5. Distribution of seats held by women across mandate and party

Mandate	Party	Number of seats held by women		
		1990	1994	1998
SMD				
	MSzP	0/1	15/149	5/54
	SzDSz	0/35	1/17	1/2
	MDF	4/114	0/4	0/2
	FKgP	1/11	0/1	0/12
	KDNP	0/3	0/3	0/0
	Fidesz	0/1	0/0	6/105[1]
County list				
	MSzP	0/14	7/53	6/50
	SzDSz	3/34	4/28	2/5
	MDF	4/40	1/18	—[2]
	FKgP	0/16	1/14	1/22
	KDNP	0/8	1/5	—
	Fidesz	1/8	1/7	4/48
National list				
	MSzP	5/18	0/7	3/30
	SzDSz	4/23	5/28	1/17
	MDF	1/10	5/15	—
	FKgP	2/17	1/11	3/14
	KDNP	1/10	0/14	—
	Fidesz	1/12	0/13	0/10
	MIÉP	0/0	0/3	1/11

[1] Half of these were jointly sponsored with the MDF.
[2] The MDF and KDNP did not qualify to participate in the proportional components of the system.

of women elected through national lists. Change in the party of the seatholder between 1990 and 1994 positively correlates with changes in the sex of the seatholder (tau-β coeff. = 0.48, sign. <0.01). Hence, it appears that the reversal of fortunes between rightist parties and the Socialists accounts not only for the increase in women's representation in 1994; the success of the MSzP in the districts also helps to explain the higher than expected proportion of women recruited via the districts.

These findings suggest that the effect of party magnitude may be party specific. When a more woman-friendly party like the MSzP sends large delegations to parliament, it will use the opportunity to recruit women. In order to test this, we created a new variable for the interaction of left-liberal party (MSzP and SzDSz) and party magnitude. We found a strong and significant correlation between this variable and the sex of the seatholder in the pooled data (tau-β = 0.11, p < 0.00). Over the course of post-communist elections, when the MSzP and SzDSz have been able to take advantage of large party magnitudes, they have brought women into parliament. The opposite has been true of the rightist conservative parties, particularly Fidesz-MPP. When we look solely at the interaction of Fidesz-MPP and size of party delegation, we actually find a negative correlation with sex of the seatholder. This was particularly true in 1998 (tau-β = $-$0.044, p < 0.05).

To test for the effects of ideology and electoral system we ran a logistical regression to model the dichotomous dependent variable, sex of the seatholder. Party ideology is entered as a dummy variable with left/liberal parties coded as 1 and rightist/nationalist parties coded as 0. Ballot structure distinguishes between the single member districts and the PR seats (smd seat = 0, PR seat = 1). As the equation shows the relationships with party ideology and ballot structure are strong, significant, and in the expected direction.

$$\text{Candidate sex} = -3.55 + 0.54^{**} \text{ (Party ideology)} + 0.65^{**} \text{ (Ballot structure)}$$
$$(0.21) \qquad\qquad\qquad (0.22)$$

$-$2 Log likelihood = 671.98,
Goodness of fit = 1141.17,
Model chi-square = 15.21; Sig. = 0.0005,
N = 1141.

To further test the impact of the Fidesz-MPP victory, we used the 1994 voting outcomes to simulate a hypothetical 1998 election. If the 1994 results had been precisely duplicated using the 1998 lists and district candidacies, representation of women would have been noticeably higher, 46 women would have entered parliament as opposed to 32. The greatest increase would have occurred on the national lists (from 7 to 14), with smaller increases on the regional lists (13–18) and in single member districts (12–14). In most of these cases, MSzP and SzDSz women would have won seats won by Fidesz-MPP men. The greatest impact is at the national list level. Had the SzDSz elected precisely the same number of MPs from their national list in 1998 as 1994, six more women would have entered parliament.

The success of Fidesz-MPP and its rightist allies clearly hurt women's representation in 1998. It is, however, hard to argue that greater success for the MSzP (and to a lesser extent the SzDSz) would have resulted in big gains for women. The MSzP's greatest losses in 1998 were in district contests. It went from 149 to just 54, but in the simulation, only two more women would have entered parliament from the SMDs if these seats had not shifted to Fidesz-MPP. Moreover, in the 1998 election MSzP won 30 national list seats (and the SzDSz 17), yet together they only elected four women through this component of the system. Such large party delegations gave the two most woman-friendly parties opportunities to recruit women, but by and large, they did not.

This helps to explain the failure of the electoral system variables in 1998. The very parties that increased female representation in the national list component in 1990 failed to do so in 1998. This may have been partly due to multiple ridings. MSzP candidates who won in districts and SzDSz candidates who won on regional lists in 1994 had to enter from national lists in 1998. The parties were not able to go as far down into their national lists and large magnitude regional lists, and the upper slots went to men, because even in the more woman friendly parties, women occupy lower status in the recruitment calculus of party leaders. The MSzP, like several other parties, has overtly attempted to achieve a geographical balance; but one female MP we spoke to said that according to population she should have been placed third on her list but she was only placed in the fifth position. An SzDSz woman similarly reported being placed lower on the list than her parliamentary career would have justified. Hence, while it may be true that the SzDSz and MSzP make better use of large party magnitudes over time, they used their relatively large number of national list seats in 1998 to maintain their predominately male party leaderships in power.

❖ CONCLUSIONS

Our analyses suggest that persistent female under-representation in post-communist Hungary results from a confluence of electoral, cultural, and party system factors. The built-in majoritarian bias of the electoral system means that party gatekeepers have fewer incentives and opportunities to balance the ticket than the literature might predict. All too often, the calculus in the territorial lists becomes zero-sum, and party leaders, operating in an environment of uncertainty, fall back on the surety of male candidates. Men represent more entrenched interests within the party, and, in light of popular anti-feminist sentiment, male candidates can be expected to have broader appeal.

Without a popularly supported, pro-equality women's movement and organized women's caucuses within the parties, gatekeepers face little pressure to become more pro-active about female recruitment. Even if such pressures did develop, the complexities of the Hungarian system, with its multiple ridings and remainder votes, would tend to insulate party leaders from pressure to recruit specific interests. If party leaders cannot readily predict which slots on the party lists will enter parliament, they cannot be held accountable for failure to place representatives of a particular interest in a particular slot.

The rightist parties, and Fidesz-MPP in particular, have additional ideological and structural reasons to resist placing women in competitive slots, but there is evidence that all of the parties pursue recruitment strategies aimed at perpetuating the national party leadership in power. Nothing has happened to make the major parties view female recruitment as electorally necessary. The MSzP has a formal ideological commitment to women, but it has little pressure to make good on that commitment by placing women in the most valuable candidacies. Neither the staunchly leftist Worker's Party nor the new left Green Party has ever cleared the 5 per cent threshold. The SzDSz, for its part, has the highest proportion of female support of any major party, but it has lost ground in every post-communist election. On the right, the KDNP's last gasp promotion of women failed completely. In the absence of electoral, grassroots, or intra-party pressures, the major political parties may continue to see female recruitment as an unnecessary and potentially costly strategy.

The 2002 elections seem to support these points. On the face of it, the electoral environment in 2002 should have been more favourable to women than in prior contests. Two rightist parties failed to cross the 5 per cent threshold entirely. At the same time, two large parties—the Fidesz–MDF joint list and the MSzP—together controlled more than 80 per cent of the popular vote. The size of party delegations recruited through the list components of the electoral system therefore should have been larger than in the past. Finally, the two most woman friendly parliamentary parties, the Socialists and the Free Democrats, emerged from the elections to form the new government. All of this should have been good for women; yet, the 2002 elections only produced a one per cent increase in female representation.

It appears that this puzzle may be largely accounted for by the continued strength of Fidesz, which controls just under half of the seats in the Assembly (48.7 per cent), slightly more than the Socialists (46.1 per cent). The Socialists were only able to form a bare majority cabinet with the inclusion of the Free Democrats' Party, which surmounted the threshold with just 5.56 per cent of the vote and 4.9 per cent of the parliamentary mandates. Had the Socialists and Free Democrats attained a more substantial share of the seats in the Assembly, we would likely see a higher percentage of women.

As we might expect, the Fidesz–MDF alliance was particularly unaccommodating towards women in its recruitment practices. Preliminary data released on-line by the Hungarian Central Election Commission indicate that only 8.4 per cent of Fidesz–MDF candidates were women. This stands in sharp contrast to the Socialists' candidate pool, which contained 23.4 per cent women and the Free Democrats', which contained 18.7 per cent. While women did quite poorly in being nominated by Fidesz–MDF, they did substantially worse in actually getting elected as Fidesz–MDF representatives. All of the members who entered the Assembly from the Fidesz–MDF joint national list were men. While 14 women won in the SMD component, only three were candidates of Fidesz–MDF (and one of those was the MDF President). As long as a party that has virtually no women in its top leadership continues to enjoy significant electoral success, there will be little incentive to use the limited opportunities afforded by the Hungarian electoral system to improve women's representation.

❖ NOTES

1 Women are also severely underrepresented in government (about 6% of ministers) and at the local level (13% of municipal government seats). Working Paper of the Directorate General for Research of the European Parliament, Working Document Women's Rights Series, 1997.

2 Unless otherwise indicated, all data on seatholders in the 1990 election are drawn from Az 1990-ben megválasztott Országgyülési Almanachja [Almanac of the Parliament Elected in 1990]. 1994 data can be found in Országgyülési Válastások 1994 [Parliamentary Elections 1994] an official publication of the National Election Press. 1998 data are drawn from 'Parlamenti Ki Kicsoda '98' [Parliamentary Who's Who '98] published in the Hungarian newspaper *Magyar Hirlap* on Saturday, 30 May 1998 and two publications from the Hungarian Interior Ministry: Választás '98: Az 1998 Évi Országgyülési Képviselöválasztás Hivatalos Végeredménye [Election 98: Official results of the 1998 election of parliamentary representatives] and Választási Füzetek 52.: Az 1998. Évi Országgyülési Képviselö-Választás Jelöltjei [Electoral Notebooks 52: The 1998 Candidates for Parliament]. Interviews were conducted by Gabriella Ilonszki during 1999 with representatives in each of the main parties, including Dávid Ibolya (MP and party president of MDF), Filló Katalin (MDF), Herczog Edit (MP from MSzP), Hortobágyi Krisztina (MP from Fidesz-MPP), Kiszely Katalin (MP from FKgP), Korényi Attiláné (FKgP), Kórodi Mária (three time MP from SzDSz), Mátrai Márta (MP from Fidesz-MPP), Papolczy Gizella (MIÉP), Mizsei Zsuzsanna (former MP from KDNP), and Szili Katalin (MP from MSzP).

3 That figure in Poland was only 16%. Richard Rose and Christian Haerpfer, 'Adapting to Transformation in Eastern Europe: New Democracies Barometer-II', Studies in Public Policy 212 (Centre for the Study of Public Policy, University of Strathclyde: Glasgow, 1993).

4 In 1998, the Central Statistical Office began to prepare a questionnaire for all candidates; but with reference to the protection of personal data, the Ombudsman stopped the process. They ended up with 741 respondents (657 men and 84 women) out of a possible 2182 (34.0%). We must be careful in drawing conclusions from these data, as it is not possible to determine the representativeness of the sample; however, the trends we mention concur with interview evidence and expectations from the literature.

5 Remainder votes include registered candidates' votes from the first round of district contests who did not win, as well as, surplus votes from parties that won at least 2/3 of the quota calculated in their county constituency but failed to obtain seats. These votes are summed nationally and then distributed using the D'Hondt method.

6 To code list placement in terms of guaranteed, winnable, and ornamental seats, we follow the measure used by Mark Jones (1996) in his research on Argentine local

elections. His measure takes into account both past party performance and the reliance of party leaders on polling data to make prospective calculations about delegation size. We do not include the founding election in our analysis, because practically speaking it is impossible to calculate an average party seat change. For each relevant party in each county, we determined the guaranteed positions in the following manner. We took the minimum number of seats won by the party in each election and subtracted from it the same minimum multiplied by the average percentage change in the number of county seats won or lost by the parliamentary parties in 1990–8 (i.e., 0.75). Seats the party still would hold under this 'worst case' simulation are guaranteed seats. Ornamental seats were computed by taking the maximum number of seats won in current and past elections and adding to it the same maximum multiplied by (0.75). Seats the party still did not win under this 'best case' simulation are ornamental seats. The seats that fell between were considered potentially winnable but not guaranteed. We could not analyse the national list seats in this manner, due to the difficulties posed by remainder votes and multiple ridings.

7 ❖ Women and Political Representation in Contemporary Ukraine[1]

Sarah Birch

The overall trend in female legislative recruitment in Ukraine is similar to that of most post-communist states, but even by Eastern European standards the absolute numbers have been small. There was a sharp decline in the proportion of parliamentary seats occupied by female deputies with the opening up of the electoral process to competition in the semi-competitive elections of 1989 and 1990. There has since been a gradual increase in women's representation, but following the 1998 elections women made up only 7.9 per cent of the Ukrainian parliament (see Table 7.1), well below the regional average. The reasons for Ukraine's relatively poor performance in this domain may be sought in the nature of the transition process.

The correlates of post-communist change include economic, cultural, and political factors. As is the case across Eastern Europe, women in Ukraine have suffered disproportionately from the declining levels of production and underemployment that have accompanied economic restructuring (ILO-CEET 1995: 62–3; Burmistenko 1996). They make up 70 per cent of the unemployed, and two-thirds of these women have higher education (Pavlychko 1997: 225). The state-run enterprises on which women had relied to meet many of their basic needs often ceased to be able to provide for them in situations of economic hardship. At the same time, private enterprises have been very slow to get off the ground, which has meant that women have had few alternative income options.

Developments on the cultural front have also led to changes in women's place in Ukrainian society since the end of the Soviet period. As in many former communist countries, political democratization was accompanied by a swing in cultural values back toward traditional gender roles, which focused on women as child-bearers and keepers of the private sphere. In Ukraine the

Table 7.1. Overview of the recent history of female representation in Ukraine

	Men				Women			
	Candidates		Deputies elected		Candidates		Deputies elected	
	N	%	N	%	N	%	N	%
1985 Ukrainian republican parliament	400	61.5	400	61.5	250	38.5	250	38.5
1989 All-Soviet Congress of People's Deputies	257	82.4	157	90.2	55	17.6	17	9.8
1990 Ukrainian republican parliament	2489	91.8	425	97.0	222	8.2	13	3.0
1994 Ukrainian parliament	5172[1]	92.6	381[2]	95.7	412[1]	7.4	17[2]	4.3
1998 Ukrainian parliament	5215	89.5	410	92.1	612	10.5	35	7.9
List seats	3214	89.2	204	90.7	391	10.8	21	9.3
Single-member seats	3585	90.5	206	93.6	375	9.5	14	6.4

[1] Candidates in March 1994.

[2] As of 1995 (308 men and 11 women were elected in March/April 1994).

Sources: Pravda Ukrainy 8 Feb. 1985, pp. 1–4; Potichnij, 1992, p. 200; *Khto ye khto v yukraïns'kii politytsi*, Kiev: K.I.S.: 1995; Birch, 2000; *Uryadovyi kyr"yer* 9 April 1998, p. 5; 21 April 1998, pp. 4–10; *Holos Ukraïny* 18 April 1998, pp. 3–9; 28 April 1998, p. 3; 18 August 1998, p. 2.

rejection of socialism and socialist values was linked also to the rise of nationalism in the late 1980s and early 1990s, which entailed a reconsideration of the gender egalitarianism that had been part of official Soviet ideology (Pavlychko 1996; Rubchak 1996; Wanner 1998: 112–18).[2]

Both economic and cultural imperatives thus have been instrumental in pressuring women to leave the sphere of public activity and return to the home. Under these circumstances they have been poorly represented in the upper echelons of the elite. It is estimated that in 1996 women occupied a mere five per cent of 35,000 top managerial and governmental positions in Ukraine (Burmistenko 1996: 16), and another estimate put the percentage of women in government and administration at less than one per cent (Bohachevshy-Chomiak 1995: 12). In this context it is not surprising that women's representation in legislative structures should have fallen dramatically since the Soviet days of rubber-stamp parliaments. The dire economic conditions in which women

WOMEN'S REPRESENTATION IN UKRAINE ❖

in Ukraine have found themselves in the post-Soviet years, combined with culturally induced inhibiting factors, undoubtedly explain much of their unwillingness and/or inability to become involved in politics.

It is also necessary to consider the role of political organization and political institutions in legislative recruitment. In theory, the introduction of electoral competition should have provided opportunities for women, but in practice these were limited, especially in the early years, by the lack of extensive social and political infrastructures outside the control of the Communist party that could provide support for aspirant female politicians. The workings of the electoral system interacted with political organizational structures to further reduce the chances that women would achieve electoral success.

As outlined in Chapter 2, majoritarian electoral systems are generally less conducive than proportional representation to electing women, largely because of the winner-take-all competitive scenario they establish. It may be hypothesized that this will be especially true under conditions of weak party organization, when those aiming to hold office are obliged to rely mainly on the resources they can command as individuals. Since women typically have access to fewer material resources than men, are less well linked into informal networks of power and influence, and find it more difficult to mobilize the help of their friends and peers in support of their political aspirations, they will be disadvantaged by non-partisan competitive situations or situations in which parties are weak. These factors can be expected to be especially relevant in the context of post-communist economic collapse and social dislocation.

A quick overview of the summary data on female legislative recruitment in Ukraine suggests that these hypotheses are not too wide of the mark. Since 1989 there has been a steady rise in the *absolute* numbers of women contesting elections in Ukraine, a rise that has gone in tandem with increasing civil society and political organization. There was also a marked increase in female *success rates* at the time of the 1998 elections when Ukraine abandoned its majoritarian system in favour of a semi-proportional formula. The ratio of the proportion of female winners to the proportion of female candidates gives some indication of the trends in the electoral strength of women relative to men. From a baseline of 1.0 in 1985 when all candidates, male and female, were elected, this figure fell to 0.56 in 1989, and further to 0.37 in 1990. But in 1994 it rose slightly to 0.58, and in 1998 it jumped to 0.75. Another way of interpreting these numbers is to say that the chances of a woman candidate getting elected were only two-fifths those of a man in 1990, whereas they rose to over one-half in 1994, and to three-quarters in 1998 (see Table 7.1 for full data).[3] Women in Ukraine are still not on par with men in terms of electoral competition, but their relative success rate has risen in recent years. The thesis of this chapter is that this rise has been linked to three factors: increased party organization, electoral reform, and the partisan distribution of electoral support.

As described in Chapter 2 the literature on legislative recruitment identifies three hurdles that any potential electoral contestant must cross to achieve success: self-selection, selection by nominating agent, and selection by voters. Individuals first have to make a decision to enter the electoral arena, they then have to be nominated for a seat, and finally the voters must select them from among the pool of nominees. This model provides a useful device in structuring the discussion that follows. Focusing on the first two parliamentary elections held after independence in 1991, the analysis draws on a number of different data sources including a database compiled by the author of demographic and political details of all successful and unsuccessful candidates for elections to the 1994 and 1998 parliaments, and two nation-wide sample surveys conducted by the author in 1998—a survey of citizens conducted shortly before the March 1998 parliamentary elections and a simultaneous survey of candidates.

❖ THE 1994 ELECTIONS

Ukraine held its first post-Soviet elections unusually late. During the period between the achievement of independence in 1991 and the elections of 1994 political actors had little incentive to form mass political parties. The Ukrainian system was thus severely under-developed at the time of the 1994 elections; organized politics tended to take the form of small groupings of elite individuals who projected potential mass support bases rather than attempting to mobilise concrete sectors of the electorate.[4] Thus, when it came to engaging in electoral competition, they were poorly equipped to mount organized campaigns. This left the way open to well-known local individuals and those already in power to sweep a large proportion of the seats; indeed, half those elected to the parliament in the spring of 1994 were members of no political party whatsoever (see appendix). There was a clear relationship between the gender and the occupation of candidates (see Table 7.2). A significantly larger proportion of the female candidate corpus came from the liberal professions (lawyers, architects, accountants, etc.) and the social sector, whereas those involved in business—enterprise heads and workers—tended to be almost exclusively men. This distribution undoubtedly reflects differences in the gender composition of those groups in general, differences which mean that smaller numbers of women find themselves in occupational positions that give them the wherewithal to compete for political office.

Selection by organized political groups was not particularly important in the 1994 contest. In order to be registered as a candidate, one had to obtain the signatures of only 300 voters. For parties to nominate candidates the

Table 7.2. Occupational distribution of 1994 candidates by gender[1]

Occupation	Women		Men		All	
	N	%	N	%	N	%
Liberal professions	138	33.7[2]	1131	22.2[2]	1269	23.0
Government officials	75	18.3	1089	21.3	1164	21.1
Heads of enterprises	35	8.6[2]	828	16.2[2]	863	15.7
Social sector	83	20.3[2]	710	13.9[2]	793	14.4
Workers	9	2.2[2]	388	7.6[2]	397	7.2
Other	69	16.9	956	18.7	1025	18.6
All	409	100	5102	100	5511	100

[1] Excludes 86 cases for which data were missing.
[2] Difference significant at the 0.001 level.

Source: Calculated from the Vybory-94 database constructed by the Petro Mohyla Scientific Society, Kiev.

process was much more complicated. A local party branch had to have at least 100 members to be eligible to nominate a candidate, and at least two-thirds of all the branch members had to be present at the nomination meeting. The names and addresses of all those present were then sent to the electoral commission along with details of the nominee. This arrangement provided a strong incentive for freelance politicians to try their hand at the electoral lottery. Of the more than five thousand candidates who stood, political parties nominated only 643 (11.0 per cent); the rest had their names placed on the ballot through the good graces of groups of voters (62.3 per cent) or workers' collectives (26.7 per cent). This was in part due to the fact that, as noted above, the grass-roots networks of parties were generally under-developed in Ukraine at this time, and partly due to the difficulty many parties had in fulfilling the requirements for nomination. Party membership was printed on the ballot, but because few who were labelled as party members on the ballot were actually nominated by the party in question, parties had only weak control over the use of their label and scarce opportunity to exercise constraint over the nomination process. Many candidates who were party members chose to stand as independents instead of attempting to have themselves nominated through their party, and in other cases parties supported candidates who were not formally their members. Given this discrepancy between party membership and mode of nomination, it makes sense to analyse the two separately.

Women do not appear to have been disadvantaged by the party nomination process; if anything, they benefited from it. Approximately a quarter (26.9 per cent) of all female candidates were party members, almost the same figure as for men

(27.3 per cent). For almost all parties, women were a higher percentage of the candidates who were formally nominated by the party, than they were of all candidates associated with the relevant party (i.e., both those who are formally nominated and those who are members, but running independently) (see Table 7.3). This may be due to the greater willingness of male candidates to stand for election without the formal backing of their party, but certainly there is no indication the parties discriminated against their female members in choosing nominees. Unfortunately data on the mode of nomination of Communist party members were unavailable, but among the other parties, only the far right-wing Congress of Ukrainian Nationalists had a smaller percentage of women among its nominees than among its member candidates overall.

When we aggregate up to the level of ideological party 'camps', it is evident that a larger proportion of the candidates from the leftist and centrist parties were women than their counterparts in right-wing parties.[5] More female candidates were members of the Communist party than any other; indeed, Communist party members represented nearly a third (32.4 per cent) of all female candidates who were party members. When combined with their Socialist counterparts and the eight women nominated by the Rural party, they made up almost half of all the female candidates in these elections who were associated with political parties (either through membership or through nomination). All three of the left-wing parties were successors to the Communist Party of the Soviet Union (CPSU), and the tradition of female involvement in party affairs appears to have been passed on (if in somewhat diluted form). Several of the liberal and social-democratic parties of the centre had sizeable groups of women among their parliamentary hopefuls, but the small absolute numbers represented by these candidacies meant that centrist women did not figure large in the candidate pool overall. Moreover, many of these parties had relatively narrow and geographically concentrated organizational bases, such that they were not even a potential vehicle for women in many parts of Ukraine (see Birch 1998). The parties on the right of Ukraine's ideological spectrum were mostly nationalist or what is referred to in Ukrainian parlance as 'national-democratic'—the successors to Ukraine's movement for independence in the late Soviet period. The leading organization in this camp is Rukh, whose toll of female candidates was, at 5.6 per cent, typical of right-wing parties. The social conservatism associated with traditionalist and nationalist views most likely accounts for the relative dearth of women among these parties' candidates.

Finally, it is necessary to consider the results of the elections and the impact of voters' choices. Of the successful women in the March/April rounds, only a minority (four of eleven) were party members—all members of the Communist party. This pattern contrasts sharply with that for male winners,

Table 7.3. Women in the 1994 elections: party members, party-nominated candidates, and deputies

Party	Party membership of female candidates		Nominating party of female candidates		Party membership of successful female candidates	
	N	%[1]	N	%[2]	N	%[3]
LEFT						
Communist	36	9.7	N/A	N/A	4	4.7
Socialist	12	7.1	11	11.5	0	0.0
Rural (SelPU)[4]	0	0.0	8	7.5	0	0.0
Other left	0	0.0	0	0.0	0	0.0
	48	8.0	N/A	N/A	4	3.3
CENTRE						
Greens	8	22.9	—	—	0	0.0
Liberal Party	8	7.6	5	14.3	0	0.0
Socialist Democratic Party	4	13.8	—	—	0	0.0
Civic Congress	2	8.7	—	—	0	0.0
Other centre	7	7.1	2	8.7	0	0.0
	29	9.0	7	11.5	0	0.0
RIGHT						
Rukh	13	5.6	6	6.2	0	0.0
Republicans	6	4.8			0	0.0
Congress of Ukrainian Nationalists	5	9.8	1	3.3	0	0.0
Org. of Ukrainian Nationalists	3	27.3	3	33.3	0	0.0
Democratic Party	2	2.8	1	8.3	0	0.0
Conservative Republicans	2	8.0			0	0.0
Christian Democratic Party	2	6.1	1	9.1	0	0.0
Other right	1	4.8	—	—	0	0.0
	34	5.6	12	7.0	0	0.0
Independents	301	7.4	345	7.1	7	4.2
All	412		N/A		11	

[1] The proportion of the total number of candidates in this category (male and female) who were members of the party in question.

[2] The proportion of the total number of candidates in this category (male and female) nominated by the party in question.

[3] The proportion of the total number of candidates in this category (male and female) elected from the party in question.

[4] The Rural party nominated 79 candidates who were not members of the party; eight of these were women, of which one won a seat.

Source: Calculated from the Vybory-94 database constructed by the Petro Mohyla Scientific Society, Kiev.

❖ SARAH BIRCH

half of whom were members of political parties from across the spectrum. The Communists alone provided women with an effective vehicle to power at this time.[6] Although the small and generally badly organized parties of the centre had proportionately more female members standing for election than the parties of the better-organized left and right, the poor overall showing of the centre meant that candidacies did not translate well into victory. Only 15 centrist deputies were elected total, and none of the centrist winners were women. It is less clear why no women from right-wing parties won; though candidates from the nationalist and national-democratic right were less likely to be women than those of the centre and the left, there were nevertheless enough of them that their complete failure is somewhat of a surprise. It might be thought that this phenomenon could be attributed to the growing social conservatism of right-wing voters, yet multivariate analysis of the determinants of candidate success in these elections reveals no evidence of gender bias among voters (Birch 2000, Ch. 6).

Women as a whole fared worse at the polls than men: only one in 17 female candidates was elected, as against one in 10 males (a difference significant at the 0.001 level). The tendency of women to concentrate in lower occupational categories accounts in large measure for their lower success rate. Male candidates more often come from occupational categories associated with business (workers and enterprise heads), which generally have easier access to the resources necessary to win elections. The working-class candidates tended to have the support of one of the left-wing parties behind them, and enterprise heads could command economic support, not to mention the votes of their employees. Of those women who had by the end of the 1994 by-elections been successful in winning seats, five were government officials, nine were professionals, and only two were enterprise directors. By contrast, over a fifth of male deputies were enterprise directors. In sum, whereas business interests were increasingly positions from which men could gain legislative seats, they rarely propelled women to power.

Nevertheless, the 1994 electoral contests were the first step in the involvement of women in genuine multi-party competition, and they paved the way for greater success in years to come. Two of the women deputies elected in 1994 subsequently split from the left-wing parties that had promoted them and formed new political organizations—the Progressive Socialists on the far left under the leadership of Nataliya Vitrenko, and the Agrarians in the centre under Kateryna Vashchuk. In 1997, Yaroslava Stets'ko, leader of the far-right Congress of Ukrainian Nationalists, was elected to parliament in a by-election, raising the number of women party leaders in the parliament from none in 1994 to three at the time of Ukraine's second parliamentary elections in 1998. Multiparty elections may not have been successful in promoting large numbers of women to positions of legislative power, but they

WOMEN'S REPRESENTATION IN UKRAINE ❖

did provide a mechanism whereby a small number of well-known women could get their foot in the door and establish themselves at the top of the political elite.

❖ THE 1998 ELECTIONS

After the election of 1994, there was a general consensus that a move to a semi-proportional mixed electoral system would be desirable for a number of reasons: the introduction of proportional list voting would strengthen Ukraine's weak party system, it would help to reduce the dependence of parties on regional fiefdoms, and it would give more power to party leaders. The result was an electoral law which stipulated that half (225) of Ukraine's deputies in the 1998 elections would be elected from single-member constituencies by simple majority, and half would be elected from closed national lists by the largest remainders method with a four per cent threshold. The top five names on each list were printed on the ballot, together with the occupation and place of employment of each candidate. This information was also printed next to the names of the candidates in the single-member constituency races, along with their party membership.

Although political parties did not provide women the most effective means of achieving success in 1994, the introduction of a proportional list component to the ballot represented new opportunities. One such opportunity was the explicit mobilization of female voters on the basis of their sex. Prior to the 1998 elections two specifically women's parties formed—Women of Ukraine, and Women's Initiatives—evidently in the hopes of repeating the success on the list ballot of Women of Russia in 1993, when that party won 8.1 per cent of the list vote in the Duma elections and 21 list seats. These hopes were disappointed. Of the two new Ukrainian parties, only Women's Initiatives succeeded in collecting a sufficient number of valid signatures to have its name put on the ballot at all, and on election day it received a mere 154,650 list votes, or 0.6 per cent of the total.

The other type of opportunity was increased representation of women through the agency of mainstream parties. The existing literature suggests the type of list system adopted in Ukraine is one that should favour women: the single nation-wide constituency means more potentially winnable places on each individual list, and thus more opportunities for women to be put on the lists for the purposes of gender balance. For the same reasons, women should be advantaged by the moderately high threshold, which translates into a minimum of nine seats for any party that clears it (see Chapter 2 for a review of these arguments).[7]

Eight parties managed to cross the threshold on the list ballot (see results in the appendix). The consequence was a doubling in female representation from 17 in 1994–5 to 35 in 1998. Reform of the electoral system was clearly one of the main reasons for this change. Twenty-one women were elected from party lists as opposed to fourteen from single-member constituencies. There was also a rise in the proportion of *single-member* seats filled by women— from 17 of 338 in 1994 (5.0 per cent) to 14 of 220 in 1998 (6.4 per cent).[8] It appears the electoral system contributed to the overall result both directly, through the list component of the ballot, and indirectly through its strengthening of parties. It is noteworthy that women fared far better as members of parties than as independents. Only slightly over a quarter (4 or 28.6 per cent) of women elected in single-member constituencies were elected as independents, vs. half (107 or 51.9 per cent) of the men who were so elected.[9] This contrasts sharply with the situation in 1994, when two-thirds of the successful women were not members of any party. This is probably attributable to the parties being more active in 1998 in nominating candidates, partly as a consequence of easier nomination procedures, and partly due to an increase in the grass-roots development of party organization.

Certainly the advent of lists helped women get elected, but what is interesting about the 1998 results is that almost as many women got elected from single-member constituencies as had been elected in this manner in 1994, despite the fact that the total number of such constituencies had fallen by half. How do we explain this result? Let us once again analyse selection by self, by nominating agents, and by the electorate. There was a rise in the proportion of women contesting the single-member races from 7.4 per cent in 1994 to 9.5 per cent in 1998. This is most likely the effect of three factors: (1) the development of political parties devoted specifically to women's concerns, (2) greater women's involvement in civil society organizations (see Bohachevsky-Chomiak 1995), and (3) increased economic security among certain sectors of the elite.

Social change during the 1994–8 period may well account for more women being in positions to be able to raise campaign funds in 1998 than had been the case four years previously. When we examine the occupational structure of the candidates in the single-member constituency races in 1998 (see Table 7.4), we see there are fewer significant differences between women and men than in 1994 (cf. Table 7.2). The gender differences in the categories of social sector and manual workers have declined. On the other hand, the differences that remain significant have gotten larger. A 5.5 per cent drop in the proportion of men from the liberal professions, coupled with an 8.2 per cent increase in the proportion of men who are head of enterprises means an expanding gap despite a small drop in the proportion of women from the liberal professions (3.0 per cent) and a noticeable increase (4.7 per cent) in the proportion of women who are enterprise heads. The move of several well-known female figures into positions of political authority may also have

WOMEN'S REPRESENTATION IN UKRAINE ❖

Table 7.4. Occupational distribution of 1998 candidates by gender[1]

Occupation	Women		Men		All	
	N	%	N	%	N	%
Liberal professions	115	30.7[2]	597	16.7[2]	712	18.1
Government officials	79	21.1	753	21.1	832	21.1
Heads of enterprises	50	13.3[2]	869	24.4[2]	919	23.3
Social sector	61	16.3	472	13.2	533	13.5
Workers	10	2.7	133	3.7	143	3.6
Other	60	16.0	742	20.8	802	20.4
All	375	100	3566	100	3941	100

[1] Excludes 20 cases for which data were missing.
[2] Difference significant at the 0.001 level.

Source: Calculated from *Vybory '98: Yak Ukraïna holosyvala*, Kiev: K.I.S., 1998, and the Website of the International Foundation for Electoral Systems at www.ifes.kiev.ua.

boosted women's perceptions of their own chances of rising in the political world, attracting competent women who might otherwise have shunned politics.

Lacking sufficient mass survey data with which to analyse self-selection, the next-best option is to ask people who do choose to stand for office about their motives and to trace differences among different groups. Data from a candidate survey conducted in the two weeks prior to the 1998 elections in 25 randomly selected constituencies throughout Ukraine can be used to elucidate these questions.[10] Candidates were generally disillusioned with political life in their country in early 1998. When we asked respondents 'To what extent do you think the political situation has improved since the passing of the constitution in 1996, a lot, some, not much, or not at all?', 42.7 per cent responded 'not at all'. Women overall were even less sanguine about the general political situation than men. Whereas 41.0 per cent of men gave this response, the figure for women was 57.7 per cent. If answers to this question are positioned on a scale—where 'not at all' = 0, 'not much' = 1, 'some' = 2, and 'a lot' = 3, the mean response among women who answered the question is 0.58, and for men 0.89 (difference significant at the 0.06 level).

This general gloominess about politics among female candidates renders all the more striking their relative enthusiasm about the recent electoral reforms. We asked the candidates to evaluate the new electoral system in comparison with the old.[11] Two-thirds of the 27 women who responded said the new electoral system would be more democratic. Nineteen per cent said it would be the same, while only 11 per cent thought the new system would be less democratic. Among the 229 male candidates who responded, on the other hand, there was general support for the reforms, 62 per cent said the new system was more democratic, but there was also greater scepticism, 21 per cent said the system was less democratic, while 13 per cent said it would be the same. Although the number of female respondents is too small for these findings to be conclusive, the responses are compatible with the hypothesis that women should favour a system that includes an element of proportional representation over one that does not.

In light of these results, it is worth asking the question of whether the new system encourages women to stand for office who would not previously have done so. There is actually little evidence that this is the case. The men in our candidate sample were slightly more likely than the women to say they had held elected office before (24.0 per cent vs. 18.5 per cent), but the women were more likely to admit to having stood unsuccessfully for office in the past (33.3 per cent as opposed to 32.8 per cent). The small numbers represented by these percentages caution against drawing any firm conclusions, but certainly they suggest there is little reason to suspect that female entrants in 1998 were more likely to be new to politics than male entrants.

One might think that greater approval for the semi-PR system among women would coincide with an approach to representation that stresses the role of parties as aggregative mechanisms and policy-forming agents within the structures of parliament rather than an approach that focuses on the link between the representative and the individual voter. Interestingly, however, female candidates were more likely to emphasise the importance of catering to voters' needs than were male candidates. When we asked 'Which of a deputy's roles do you think is most important, 'work in the structures of parliament' or 'dealing with voters' problems', a plurality of both genders replied that 'both are equal', and among the rest more opted for work in parliament than dealing with voters problems. But there was a decided difference between men and women. Male candidates were nearly four times as likely to choose work in parliament (40.6–11.4 per cent), whereas women were only slightly more likely to give this answer (25.9–18.5 per cent). These differences are not statistically significant due to the small N involved, but they are suggestive nonetheless. The finding may be linked to the tendency of women to view the sub-group rather than citizenry as a whole as the appropriate object of representation. In answer to the question 'Which of the following reasons comes closest to describing your own reason for standing for election?', nearly two-thirds of men (64.6 per cent) replied 'I want to help Ukraine', whereas fewer than half (48.1 per cent) of women chose this response. Conversely, less than a third of men answered 'I want to promote the interests of people like me', while 48.1 per cent of women gave this answer.[12] Although these differences again fail to reach statistical significance, it seems that women are more likely to take a particularistic view of representation, whereas men tend to favour the wider view. This may well be because men have a greater tendency to universalise their views than women, who are constantly reminded of their particularity as the 'second sex'.

Given women's more group-oriented understanding of the representative process, it is not surprising that political parties should be seen as attractive vehicles for their candidacies. Although only slightly more female than male candidates claimed to identify with a party (55.6 per cent vs. 46.7 per cent), more indicated links with party as a factor in the decisions surrounding their nomination, even among those who chose to stand in single-member constituencies. When we asked an open question about reasons for choosing a given mode of nomination, half the 18 female candidates in single-member constituencies gave answers in some way linked to political party membership: parties offered to nominate them for a constituency seat, or they had been nominated both on lists and in constituencies, or they had not obtained a high enough place on their party list, so they had opted to stand in a constituency instead. Only 19 of the 155 male constituency candidates (13 per cent) gave answers that were in any way linked to party membership. Parties clearly figured larger in the nomination prospects of female candidates than those of their male counterparts.

At the time of the first multiparty election in 1994, most candidates were, as we have seen, nominated as independents—by groups of voters or by work collectives—whether or not they were party members. As argued above, this was due to limited grass roots party organization, to popular antipathy towards parties, and to the exigencies of the electoral law then in force.

In 1998 the situation was to an extent the same in single-member constituencies, where over half of all candidates were nominated without the help of a political party and half of those elected to these seats were independents (approximately the same proportion as in 1994). Although parties failed to increase their penetration of the SMDs, the gender composition of the SMD races was rather different from what it had been four years previously. For those with limited personal resources parties represented in some senses a substitute, especially for women. Thus we find that more female candidates were party members than male candidates; 66.7 per cent as opposed to 52.7 per cent. The only major occupational category for which this discrepancy does not hold is enterprise directors, where the proportion of male party members actually slightly outnumbers that of women (52.3–50.0 per cent). It seems those women who have their own resources are no more likely than men to seek the assistance of a party in planning a political career; it is women who are in less fortunate positions who tend to do so. If party membership is an asset to women, then it is as much a matter of women choosing parties, as it is parties choosing women.

❖ SARAH BIRCH

On the party list component of the ballot the situation was obviously different.[13] It was here the parties had the power to include and to exclude, though the procedures through which the lists were drawn up varied considerably from organization to organization. Ironically, the parties with the most 'democratic' procedures generated lists containing the fewest women, while those that relied on the tried-and-tested methods of selection by a handful of elites resulted in more feminine lists.

Of the major parties, Rukh and the Popular Democratic Party (NDP) have the most formal and democratic nomination procedures; their lists contained 9.8 per cent and 10.1 per cent women candidates, respectively (see Table 7.5). The most elite-dominated and informal procedures were those of the

Table 7.5. Female candidates on lists by party, 1998

Party	Number of women on list	Women as a proportion of list candidates (%)	Number of women in the top five of list	Number of women in the top 20 of list	Number of women in the top 50 of list	(Average) place of top woman on the list	Proportion of all women on the list in the top half (%)
LEFT							
Communists	27	12.0	1	1	6	5	37.0
Soc./Rural	20	10.0	0	2	4	10	35.0
Prog. Soc.	20	24.1	1	5	11	1	40.0
All left	87	11.5	3 (10.0%)	12 (10.0%)	30 (10.0%)	9.0	39.5
Left >4%	67	13.2	2 (13.3%)	8 (13.3%)	21 (14.0%)	5.3	36.5
CENTRE							
Popular Democrats	19	10.1	0	0	3	30	31.6
Social Democrats	17	9.2	0	0	0	54	17.7
Greens	9	11.7	0	2	5	14	44.4
Hromada	15	6.7	0	2	4	6	46.7
All centre	211	11.6	9 (10.6%)	36 (11.3%)	75 (10.3%)	13.7	32.5
Centre >4%	60	8.9	0 (0.0%)	4 (5.0%)	12 (6.0%)	26.0	34.3
RIGHT							
Rukh	22	9.8	0	3	4	8	50.0
All right	93	9.0	3 (8.6%)	8 (5.0%)	25 (6.3%)	10.3	36.7
Right >4%	22	9.8	0 (0.0%)	3 (15.0%)	4 (8.00%)	8	50.0
All	391	10.8	15 (10.0%)	56 (9.3%)	130 (9.1%)	12.0	35.2
All > 4%	149	10.6	2 (5.0%)	15 (9.4%)	37 (9.3%)	16.0	37.6

Sources: *Vybory '98: politychnyi kompas vybortsya*, Kiev: K.I.S., 1998; *Politychnyi kalendar 6* (February 1998), *Vybory 98: yak holosyvala Ukraïna*, Kiev: K.I.S, 1998.

Hromada party, which gave only 6.7 per cent of its places to women. The lists with the largest proportion of women were the Communist and Progressive Socialist parties—12.0 per cent in the first instance and 24.1 per cent in the second. The nomination procedures of these parties were in theory highly democratic, but evidence suggests that they were in practice orchestrated from the top in much the same way as candidate-selection had been conducted during the Communist period.[14] As can be seen from these data, it is parties with top-down decision-making procedures that allowed the most women a chance to compete.

These are interesting findings, in as much as they challenge the literature on candidate selection, which suggests that more formalized procedures ought to favour the selection of female candidates. Though the party with the least formalized procedure did indeed nominate the smallest proportion of women, the converse was not true. There are two possible reasons for this. First, pressure has to be put on institutional mechanisms in order for them to favour women. In the absence of sufficient impetus from below, even the most democratic mechanisms will be of little avail. Second, it may well be that women were chosen with greater frequency by the left-wing parties because women tend to adapt well to the organizational style of these parties: the tight discipline exercised over parliamentary deputies affords the individual legislator relatively little autonomy, and it may well be that women have proved easier to discipline than men. Party ideology could thus be a key intervening variable here.

But the 'ideology' that makes left-wing parties in Ukraine more favourably disposed to promoting female candidates is a matter of organizational ethos rather than policy position. None of Ukraine's parties seriously engaged with the discrimination against women which is rampant in Ukrainian society, and virtually all viewed women first and foremost as procreators. The Communist party programme claims that '[if the Communists come to power] women will stop being afraid of having children, and will be able to bring them up in peace, sure of their future'. The programme of the Socialist/Rural bloc, for its part, contented itself with aiming 'to guarantee women a worthy place in society'. The Progressive Socialists, who were led by a woman and who had, of all the major parties, the largest proportion of women candidates on their list, made no mention of women in their programme at all. Nor did the Agrarian party, the other main political organization in Ukraine to be headed at that time by a woman.

Of the centrist parties, Hromada and the NDP also omitted mention of women from their campaign platform, while the SDP(u) alluded briefly to 'state care for the family, motherhood, and childhood'. Most depressingly of all, even the Party of Women's Initiatives saw women mainly as mothers; the opening lines of its programme were: 'Responsibility for the future of the human species naturally lies with women. Bearing and rearing children is the highest goal and content of their lives'. The text goes on to argue that responsibility for children can be equated with responsibility for society, and for this reason women have an obligation to play an active role in politics. Apart from calling for higher levels of female representation at all levels and in all branches of government, however, the programme does not address any issues faced by women as a social group. The right-wing Rukh was arguably less sexist when it asserted that 'woman is the basis of the family. The family is the basis of society', but also vowed to 'promote the activity of women in civil society organizations and the participation of women in [commercial] enterprises'. It was left to the Green party, which of all the main parties had the smallest absolute number of women on its list, to take up the female cause directly. It devoted the largest amount of text to women's issues and though it described women as 'mothers of society', it also called for them to 'have the same rights as men to work in leadership positions' and supported the idea that time spent bringing up children should be considered work which would entitle women to pension benefits.[15] It was clearly not parties' position on women's issues that accounted for differences among them in their promotion of female candidates. Women's issues did not play a prominent role in the electoral campaign, policy differences among the parties were meagre, and none took a strong stand against the gender stereotyping that in all likelihood accounts for the paucity of women active in Ukrainian politics.

Nevertheless, the advent of list voting did provide moderately greater opportunities for women to be elected to parliament in Ukraine. The question arises as to whether they were able to take as great an advantage of these opportunities as men. The discrepancy between the proportion of women among those who obtained list slots (10.8 per cent) and the proportion of those elected through this means (9.3 per cent) suggests either that women were either not always on the right lists, or that they were less likely to be placed in winnable positions. Upon inspection, the latter explanation appears to be the correct one. On most measures, the parties that won representation represented women as well as those that were failed to win seats (see Table 7.5). The lists that crossed the threshold had 10.6 per cent women among them vs. 10.8 per cent among all parties; 9.3 per cent of the top 50 places on the winning lists were occupied by women, compared with 9.1 per cent of the top 50 positions on all 30 lists, and 37.6 per cent of all the women from winning parties were in the top half of their respective lists, as against 35.2 per cent of all women on lists generally.

This last measure gives some indication as to why women on lists performed worse overall than men: more of them were clustered in the lower reaches. There were two groups of slots that were of key importance in these elections: the top five names which appeared on the ballot alongside the name of the party/bloc, and the top twenty 'mandate' or 'fighting' slots whose holders would be well positioned to get a place in parliament if the list cleared the four per cent mark. Eleven lists had women in the top five places. The Women's Initiatives party was the leader with three women in the top five, including the number one place. Four other lists from across the political spectrum were also headed by women: the Progressive Socialists on the far left, the Agrarians and the Union party in the centre, and Fewer Words on the far right. Most of the eleven were minor parties, however, and only two parties with women in the top five crossed the threshold—the Communists and the Progressive Socialists. Almost all the lists had women among the top 20 candidates. The only major exceptions were two of the main centrist parties, the National Democratic Party, whose top female candidate was in the thirtieth position and the Social Democratic (united) party, whose highest-placed woman was to be found at number 54.

When we analyse these data in terms of Ukraine's main party camps, some interesting patterns emerge. The centre slightly outperforms the left in terms of both number of candidates and number of women in top positions, but this is due almost exclusively to the strong showing of the Women's Initiatives list. Among the centrist parties that won list seats, the picture is quite different. The winning centrist lists had only 8.9 per cent female representation, and women filled only five per cent of their top positions. Only one had a woman among its top ten, and none had a female name showing on the ballot. These parties have strong links with various branches of Ukraine's emerging business community, and their failure to include significant numbers of women on their lists corresponds to the tendency in evidence since 1990 of candidates from the business sector to be almost exclusively male. It is clear the parties on the left of the political spectrum offered the greatest opportunity to women in terms of winnable placements. Women filled approximately one in eight of their list slots, and the same share of the key winning places.

The choices made by the different parties are reflected in electoral outcomes (see Table 7.6). We observe relative consistency in the pooled results of the parties of the left. The proportion of left-wing list seats won by women was, at 12.6 per cent, only slightly higher than the proportion of female list candidates on the left (11.5 per cent), and not much higher than the proportion of seats won by left-wing women in single-member constituencies (8.9 per cent). The advent of party list voting benefited left-wing women candidates partly because it benefited the parties of which they were members. A total of 16 women of the left entered parliament through the list ballot, whereas only four were elected in single-member constituencies. The figures for other party camps vary considerably more. As might be guessed from the tendency of the major centrist parties to place few women in top positions on their lists, the female portion of the centrist list take is the lowest of any of the three party camps (three winners, or 4.5 per cent of all successful centrists). Centrists did

Table 7.6. Female winners by party, 1998

Party[1]	List		Single-member seats		All	
	N	%[2]	N	%[2]	N	%
LEFT						
Communists	9	10.7	3	7.8	12	9.8
Socialist/Rural	3	10.3	0	0.0	3	8.8
Progressive Socialists	4	21.4	1	50.0	5	31.3
Other	0	0.0	0	0.0	0	0.0
	16	12.6	4	8.9	20	11.6
CENTRE						
Popular Democratic Party (NDP)	0	0.0	0	0.0	0	0.0
Social Democrats (united)	0	0.0	0	0.0	0	0.0
Hromada	1	6.3	2	28.6	3	13.0
Greens	2	10.5	—	—	2	10.5
Agrarian Party	0	0.0	3	37.5	3	37.5
Women's Initiatives	0	0.0	0	0.0	0	0.0
Other	0	0.0	0	0.0	0	0.0
	3	4.5	5	13.9	8	7.8
RIGHT						
Rukh	2	6.3	0	0.0	2	4.4
Reforms and Order	0	0.0	1	33.3	1	33.3
National Front	0	0.0	1	20.0	1	20.0
Other	0	0.0	0	0.0	0	0.0
	2	6.3	2	7.4	4	6.8
Independent (elected from a single-member constituency and not a party member)	—	—	3	2.7	3	2.7

[1] Parties in italics are those that cleared the four per cent threshold on the list vote.
[2] The proportion of the total number of candidates in this category (male and female) elected from the party in question.

Sources: *Politychnyi kalendar* 6 (February 1998), *Vybory 98: yak holosyvala Ukraïna*, Kiev: K.I.S, 1998.

better in single-member constituencies, but the three seats won by Kateryna Vashchuk's Agrarian party largely explain this. On the right of the party spectrum, the one successful list contained two women among its winners (6.3 per cent), and two right-wing female deputies were elected in the single-member constituencies. All in all the parties of the centre and the right promoted only 12 women to parliamentary seats, whereas the left-wing parties secured seats for 20 women, partly because they won more seats as parties, but also because they placed more female candidates in winnable slots.

What role did the electorate play in generating these outcomes? Did they hold gender against female candidates? Because the PR component of the ballot operated on the basis of closed lists, this question is of greatest relevance to the single-member constituency races. When asked what qualities influenced their choice of candidate in single-member seats, voters were extremely reluctant to admit that gender was a major consideration. Only eight (four men and four women) of 1741 citizens surveyed in Ukraine in the last two weeks before the 1998 elections listed the sex of the candidate as the principal factor influencing their choice.[16] But these findings do not exclude the possibility that gender indirectly affected the way candidates' other qualities were evaluated by voters. Over half of all voters (62.4 per cent of women and 55.4 per cent of men) listed 'honesty' as the most important quality for a candidate to possess, and a further third (28.8 per cent of women and 33.2 per cent of men) listed 'professionalism'. It may be that perceptions of these two attributes were coloured by gender stereotypes. Yet a regression (not shown) of candidate vote share on candidate characteristics—gender, age, occupation, incumbency, and party membership—for all 3961 candidates who stood in the single-member constituencies in 1998 demonstrates that gender had no significant effect on candidates' ability to win votes, once other factors are taken into consideration. It appears that the role of gender in influencing electoral outcomes has more to do with its effect on a person's chances of attaining desirable occupational and party political positions than its impact on voter perceptions and choices. Once women have gained access to the economic and political resources that favour electoral success, they are at no disadvantage with respect to men.

❖ CONCLUSIONS

During the heady years surrounding the movement for independence, the political rhetoric that set the tone in Ukraine was one that was politically radical but socially conservative. This, combined with the collapse of organized politics, led to a virtual eclipse of women from the structures of national representation. The subsequent construction of a competitive party system in independent Ukraine brought with it new opportunities for women, and as the party system has gained in strength, women have found increased potential to compete for and be elected to parliamentary seats. The change from a single-member to a semi-proportional electoral system enhanced the political role of parties and prompted their organizational expansion, leading to a larger number of women being elected to parliament than at any time since the introduction of electoral competition.

The revival of the organized left starting in 1994 was especially helpful in this regard, as left-wing parties have been most diligent in promoting the candidacies of women. There is some irony in the fact that it was the parties least supportive of radical political reform and least reformed in terms of their own party organization that have gone furthest in propelling women to positions of legislative power. At the same time, there is evidence that the profile of women is becoming more prominent across the political spectrum. A small handful of women from all three of Ukraine's main party camps have risen to positions of influence, often by breaking with established political organizations and forging new structures. These include Nataliya Vitrenko of the Progressive Socialist Party, Kateryna Vashchuk of the Agrarian Party, and more recently, Yulia Tymoshenko, head of the Fatherland party. It is also noteworthy that women have *not* been most successful in rising to positions of leadership when they have championed explicitly female causes. None of the women's parties that has formed has met with electoral success, and none of the female party leaders has made a point of championing women's issues. Female politicians in Ukraine are clearly using the institution of the political party to their advantage; the question remains as to whether they are using it to the advantage of Ukrainian women. But that is a question for another study.

This chapter has concentrated on the quantitative dimension of representation. It has shown that, though the number of women who have attained positions of legislative power in Ukraine is relatively low, it is on the rise. This rise can be attributed to three interlocking factors: a gradual increase in the institutionalisation of political parties since 1990, the move toward a more proportional electoral system in the 1998 elections, and the improving political fortunes of left-wing parties. The last of these factors is conjunctural and may thus be subject to change, but current trends suggest that the first two factors will remain prominent and may even become more so. The rigours of electoral competition are prompting parties to develop their infrastructures, and many members of the Ukrainian parliament support a move to an even more proportional electoral system. Thus, we can expect to see a slow but steady rise in the number of women in representative roles. We can also expect to see an increase in gender-related differences among the parties as their internal organizational structures become more clearly defined.

The next logical step for researchers is an analysis of the quality of representation offered to women in Ukraine by both male and female legislators. What do Ukrainian women want? How well does the Ukrainian parliament serve their interests, and which sectors of the parliament are most effective in catering to the needs of women? Much work remains to be conducted in this field, and such research has an important role to play in helping Ukraine's 27 million women to make the institution of political representation work for them.

Appendix: Parliamentary Elections: 27 March–10 April 1994; 29 March 1998

Party	1994		1998							
	Seats[1]	%	List votes	List seats	% List seats	% SM votes	SM seats[2]	% SM seats	Total	% Total
Communist	86	25.4	24.7	84	37.3	14.7	37	16.9	121	27.2
Socialist/Rural	33	9.8	8.6	29	12.9	4.5	5	2.3	34	7.6
Progressive Socialists			4.1	14	6.2	1.0	2	0.9	16	3.6
Working Ukraine	2	0.6	3.1	—	—	0.5	1	0.5	1	0.2
Other left			1.1	—	—	0.3	—	—	—	—
Total left	121	35.8	40.6	127	56.4	21.0	46	20.9	173	38.9
Greens			5.4	19	8.4	0.8	—	—	19	4.3
Popular Democrats			5.0	17	7.6	4.2	11	5.0	28	6.3
Hromada			4.7	16	7.1	3.7	8	3.6	24	5.4
Social Democrats (united)			4.0	14	6.2	1.9	3	1.4	17	3.8
Agrarians			3.7	—	—	3.3	9	4.1	9	2.0
Together	4	1.2	1.9	—	—	1.3	1	0.5	1	0.2
NEP	2	0.6	1.2	—	—	1.2	1	0.5	1	0.2
Social Liberal Union (SLOn)			0.9	—	—	0.5	1	0.5	1	0.2
Party of Reg. Revival			0.9	—	—	0.9	2	0.9	2	0.4
Union			0.7	—	—	0.2	1	0.5	1	0.2
Other centre	6	1.8	2.4	—	—	0.9	—	—	—	—
Total centre	12	3.6	30.9	66	29.3	16.9	41	18.6	98	22.0
Rukh	20	5.9	9.4	32	14.2	6.3	14	6.4	46	10.3
Reforms and Order			3.1	—	—	1.9	3	1.4	3	0.7
National Front	15	4.4	2.7	—	—	2.7	5	2.3	5	1.1
Forward Ukraine			1.7	—	—	0.6	2	0.9	2	0.4
Christian Democrats			1.3	—	—	0.8	2	0.9	2	0.4
Fewer words			0.8	—	—	0.3	1	0.5	1	0.2
Other right	2	0.6	0.9	—	—	0.7	—	—	—	—
Total Right	37	11.0	19.4	32	14.2	13.3	27	12.3	59	13.3
Independents	168	49.7	—	—	—	46.9	111	50.5	111	24.9
All	338	100	100	225	100	100	220	100	445	100

[1] A total of 112 seats remained vacant following the March/April rounds of voting.
[2] A total of five single-member seats remained vacant following the elections.

Source: Database of Central and Eastern European Elections at www.essex.ac.uk/elections.

❖ SARAH BIRCH

❖ NOTES

1 Research for this chapter was funded by Economic and Social Research Council Grants No. R000222380 and L213252021.

2 For comparative Eastern European perspectives, see Funk and Mueller (1993), Rueschemeyer (1998a), Marsh (1996), and Buckley (1997).

3 These findings are not the result of incumbency bias (a factor which generates apparent gender effects in some other countries). The proportion of incumbents in the candidate pools for these elections was small, and though incumbency helped candidates, the over-representation of men in the 1990 and 1994 parliaments is not in either case a significant direct cause of the gender imbalance of subsequent parliaments: when re-calculated for non-incumbents alone, the figures cited above were nearly identical.

4 See Wilson and Bilous (1993), Bilous (1993), Bojcun (1995), Birch (1998).

5 The tendency of right-wing parties to select women in fewer numbers than their counterparts in other segments of the political spectrum is consonant with the findings of cross-national studies (Rule 1981, 1987; Norris 1985; Caul 1999).

6 Of the six female deputies elected in by-elections later in 1994, one was a Socialist and the remainders were independents at the time of their election.

7 In practice the minimum was bound to be higher for two reasons. First, in as much as not all parties cross the threshold, the list seats are distributed to parties that collectively represent less than the total number of list votes (65.8% in Ukraine in 1998), which will lead to the magnification of each party's seat share relative to its vote share. Second, individual candidates were allowed to stand both on lists and in single-member constituencies in these elections. If elected in a single-member constituency, they would be removed from the list and their place allocated to the next name down. Most parties had candidates removed from their lists in this way. The net result was that even the Social Democrats and the Progressive Socialists, who barely scraped past the threshold with 4.01 and 4.05% of the vote, respectively, each saw the top 17 names on their list enter parliament.

8 Of the 14 women elected from single-member districts in 1998, six were incumbents, of whom three were party leaders, and a fourth (Yulia Tymoshenko) was a well-known member of the leadership of the Hromada party. The remaining women were mostly either enterprise directors (4) or academics/teachers (3). The three successful independent candidates were all enterprise directors.

9 Turning the figures round, we find that 10.1% of those who won in the constituencies as party nominees were women—an even greater proportion than among those who won party list seats (9.3%).

10 The constituencies were selected through stratified random sampling from among Ukraine's 225 single-member seats. The aim was to interview all 483 candidates standing in these constituencies, as well as 326 candidates randomly selected from among the top 100 candidates on each of the 30 party lists. Interviews were carried out in the two weeks prior to the election, but unfortunately the interviewers experienced

considerable difficulties contacting the respondents. Of the 483 candidates in the constituencies only 172 were successfully interviewed (63.2% of those contacted, and 35.6% of the target sample). Of the 326 candidates in the list sample, 81 were successfully interviewed (45.3% of those contacted and 24.9% of the target sample). A total of 256 interviews were therefore conducted with 255 candidates (one respondent was selected as part of both the constituency and the list sample and was interviewed twice), an overall response rate of 32.8%, or 56.8% of those contacted. The response rate was disappointing, and there are reasons to believe that the candidates interviewed might not be in all respects representative of the total candidate corpus. But there is little grounds for suspecting that the sample would not be representative as far as gender differences are concerned. Further details of survey design and of the gender composition of the achieved sample are available from the author upon request.

11 The precise wording of the question was 'As you know, a new system of voting is going to be used in the elections this March. Each voter will have two votes, one for a candidate in your constituency, and one for a party list. Half of the deputies will be elected from the candidate ballots, and half from the party list ballots. Do you think this electoral system will be more or less democratic than the old one?'

12 The third option was 'I want to establish contacts'. This may have been a plausible motivation for standing, but only two candidates in our sample (both men) were willing to admit to it.

13 Of the 1738 candidates who stood both in single-member seats and on lists, 8.9% were women, as against 9.5% of single-member constituency candidates overall and 10.8% of the list candidates. Women thus had slightly fewer opportunities than men to contest both types of seat, but the difference is not great.

14 For an overview of the nomination practices of Ukraine's parties, see Wilson and Birch, n.d.

15 The descriptions of party programmes contained in this paragraph refer to the one-page programmes that were printed and distributed by the state free of charge at the time of the election and posted in polling stations. Although most of the parties also had longer programmes, these abridged versions are the texts that voters are most likely to have been familiar.

16 The survey referred to here employed a multi-stage clustered probability sample design. The population sampled consisted of adults eighteen years or older on 29 March 1998 (the day of the elections). The primary sampling units were the 25 constituencies employed in the candidate survey described above. For the total sample size of 2050, the response rate was 1741 or 85.0%. The data were weighted to compensate for under-representation of the western region in the achieved sample. Further details of the survey design and execution are available from the author upon request.

❖ SARAH BIRCH

8 ❖ Electoral Systems and Women's Representation: The Strange Case of Russia

Robert G. Moser

This chapter examines the representation of women in Russia's mixed electoral system. In Russian national elections, voters cast two votes. The first is for a party in a closed party-list proportional representation (PR) race in one single nationwide district with a five per cent legal threshold and another for a candidate in a plurality election. Each tier elects half of the 450 deputies to the lower house, the State Duma. The system is non-compensatory, meaning the proportion of seats awarded on the PR side does not take into consideration the results in the single member district side of the election, as it does in Germany or Hungary. Such a system allows for the examination of electoral system effects holding all other socioeconomic, political, and cultural factors constant. I use this approach to examine the effects of electoral systems on women's representation in Russia.

Women's representation in Russia after the collapse of communism has followed a familiar trajectory. The proportion of female deputies has been significantly lower than during the Soviet period or the levels of female representation in the West. The likely reasons underlying this phenomenon include the cultural, social, and institutional factors affecting the supply of and demand for female candidates cited in Chapter 2.

Despite these common threads, female representation in Russia is an unusual and theoretically significant exception to the conventional wisdom regarding the inter-relationship between electoral systems and women's representation. Contrary to international experience, proportional representation has not consistently promoted the election of Russian women to office. In fact, the relationship between PR and female representation in Russia has tended to be negative: significantly more women have been elected under the plurality half of Russia's mixed electoral system. No other post-communist state examined in this volume shows a similar pattern. While Matland and Montgomery note in Chapter 2 that women in post-communist states might not be effectively organized to take advantage of the opportunities for representation offered by PR, they do not expect to find an inverse relationship between PR rules and representation. This chapter examines this anomaly and in the process sheds light on how the legacies of communism interact with institutional forms to produce an unexpected political outcome.

❖ THE COMMUNIST LEGACY AND WOMEN IN RUSSIA

The anomaly of Russian female representation highlights the multifaceted impact of the country's communist legacy. On the one hand, this legacy has produced a set of social, cultural, and economic conditions that have undermined women's ability to pursue elected office. On the other hand, the Soviet legacy also produced a female population that was well educated and employed outside the home. This created a pool of female political entrepreneurs who could muster the resources necessary for success in single-member districts.

Nevertheless, upon democratization, women's representation in new legislatures dropped precipitously across the Soviet Union. Official quotas had kept the levels of female representation in Soviet political institutions relatively high, even though women were kept out of the highest positions within the Communist party and thus denied real political power (Nechemias 1996: 23–4). Once quotas were removed completely in the 1990 election to the Russian Congress of People's Deputies, women won only five per cent of the seats. As noted in earlier chapters, the type of egalitarianism introduced by the Soviet regime actually presented women with the double burden of a profession and a domestic role as caretaker of the family and home. This left very little time or energy for other enterprises such as public service. It also corrupted feminism as a label and equality as a mobilizing ideal. Consequently, sexist attitudes regarding the proper place of women in society emerged. State officials openly declared that men should be first to occupy scarce jobs, because women should be at home raising children. This was manifested most overtly in an unofficial 'return to the kitchen' campaign that began under Gorbachev and sought to channel women out of the workforce and back into domestic roles, which were seen as their natural roles in society. On the opposite side of the spectrum, increased freedoms produced a burgeoning trade in pornography and the sexual objectification of women's bodies in popular culture (Sperling 1999: 64–78).

These cultural attitudes have surely had a negative impact on both the supply of and demand for female legislators. On the supply side, the women's movement could not mobilize effectively around an ideology of equality.

❖ ROBERT G. MOSER

The Soviet experience denied women the vocabulary that counterparts in the West so effectively utilized to challenge injustice. On the demand side, there is evidence of overt discrimination by voters against female candidates, but it is rather thin. Early survey research suggested a bias against women candidates. A 1990 survey of Moscow voters showed that only a slight majority of voters (54 per cent) claimed that gender was not important in their voting decision. Those who did factor in gender overwhelmingly preferred a male to a female candidate (Nechemias 1994: 96). A survey in 1993 showed that 64 per cent of respondents in Moscow, St. Petersburg, and Yaroslavl preferred a male candidate (White, Rose, and McAllister 1997: 118). Yet, the fact that women tended to gain more success as individual candidates in SMD races than as anonymous members of party lists undermines the assertion that Russian voters have been the primary obstacle to women's representation. Rather, the explanation requires one to examine how culture, the women's movement, and institutional rules have interacted with political parties' gatekeeping role in the nomination process.

❖ Russia's Emerging Party System

Parties have been weak throughout post-communist states, but Russia's parties are markedly fragile. The emergent party system has been extremely volatile. Party identification, although growing, remains rudimentary. Party organizations are fragile and rarely penetrate society. Most importantly, parties do not control ballot access in single-member district contests, making nonpartisanship a common and viable option (Moser 2001). Independents have remained a dominant force in SMD elections and are even more prevalent in regional and local elections where national parties are virtually nonexistent (Nowacki, this volume, Moser 1999; Solnick 1998). Yet, despite this fluidity, one can identify certain families of parties that offer some order to this chaotic picture and allow for the classification of individual parties in Russia.

The Russian ideological spectrum comprises four major categories: reformists, centrists, leftists, and nationalists (Oates 1998). Reformists generally support the move to a free market (but not necessarily the policies followed by the Yeltsin government) and individual freedoms. Russia's Choice (and its successor parties, Democratic Russia's Choice and the Union of Right Forces) have been the most stable members of this camp. Yabloko offers a similar set of political ideals but has cast itself as the democratic opposition against the more authoritarian practices of the Yeltsin (and now Putin) regime. Centrists occupy a vague middle ground. They tend to support a market economy, but place greater emphasis on state intervention in the market, support for industrial production, and protection of social welfare. Many special interest parties, including the Women of Russia, adopted this type of political position. Leftist parties have been the strongest critics of market reforms. Until 1999, they offered programs for substantial reversals of the privatization program and other reforms of the Yeltsin era. The Communist Party of the Russian Federation (KPRF) and Agrarian Party of Russia have been the most prominent members of this ideological niche. Nationalist parties have concentrated on populist appeals concerning the need to reestablish domestic law and order as well as international prestige as a great power. Vladimir Zhirinovsky's Liberal Democratic Party of Russia (LDPR) epitomized this part of the political spectrum, although nationalism was a favorite theme for many parties after the surprising success of the LDPR in 1993.

The more important issue in terms of the party system in Russia is the weakness of the emergent party system, a factor that affects women's representation in several ways. First, endemic party fragmentation has tended to hinder female representation in the PR tier by lowering party magnitude. Men led the rush to form new parties to contest elections and, as leaders, typically occupy the top slots on party lists. In both 1993 and 1999 the relatively high number of parties surpassing the threshold meant that parties were not able to elect candidates from lower positions on party lists, where women were more frequently located. At the same time, party weakness may have actually *increased* the opportunities for women to be elected in single-member districts. Candidate proliferation lowered the effective threshold of representation in single-member districts, possibly encouraging more women to run in plurality elections. Finally, as gatekeepers in the nomination process, Russian parties have tended to constrain female candidates. Under Russian conditions, however, parties control access to the party lists used in the PR portion of the electoral system, but they do not serve a similar gatekeeping role in SMD contests. Since parties were relatively underdeveloped at the grass-roots level, well-known local candidates could shop around for a party label or run a competitive campaign as an independent. The professionalization and higher education of women produced during the Soviet period created favourable conditions for ambitious female politicians to be more successful in such an environment than in the competition for prize slots on major parties' PR lists.

❖ NOMINATION PROCEDURES

As noted in Chapter 2, well defined, uniform laws governing party nomination procedures tend to promote women's representation by establishing clear access points for women's groups to influence the process. Several features of the nomination procedures of Russian parties and the electoral law may affect the opportunities for women to enter elected office.

❖ ROBERT G. MOSER

In Russia's mixed electoral system, the effective district magnitude of the PR tier is actually determined by each individual party because the electoral law requires that parties are divided into regional sublists of their own choosing. Officially, the PR half of the election is held in a single large (225 seat) nationwide district with a five per cent legal threshold. The five per cent legal threshold should constrain the number of parties and thus produce relatively large party magnitudes. Beginning in 1995, however, parties were required to divide their lists into a national list, comprising up to the top 12 slots (18 in 1999), and a series of regional lists defined by the parties. In 1993, parties were given the option of dividing their PR lists into regional sublists. Of the seven parties that won PR seats, Russia's Choice, Yabloko, and PRES divided their parties this way. However, Yabloko listed 34 candidates on its national list, which accounted for all of the party's 20 deputies sent to the Duma. PRES listed 16 candidates on its national list, accounting for all but two of its PR deputies. Only Russia's Choice, which elected 21 out of its 40 deputies from its regional sublists, was significantly affected by organizing its list by region.

Parties overcoming the five per cent barrier first sent the candidates on their national list. Any further deputies were chosen from regional lists, depending upon the proportion of the vote received in the designated regions. Lists from regions with higher proportion of the vote sent more deputies than regions with lower proportion of the vote. Some regions did not send any deputies. Since parties were given control over how their regional sublists were defined, this presented candidates with very different effective thresholds between parties and within a single party. One could find herself as the sole candidate in a rather obscure region or just one in a long list of candidates vying for a seat in Moscow. In general, this provision dramatically lowered the effective threshold for representation in the PR tier for most candidates on regional sublists to something equal to or even less than the single-member district races. Moreover, this produced a complicated strategic environment in which a PR candidate's chances of gaining election depended not only on her rank within a regional list, but also on the performance of the party in that region. For example, Fatherland-All Russia sent seven candidates from its Moscow sublist but zero candidates from 21 out of the remaining 35 other regional sublists.

The electoral law also provides for simultaneous candidacy on a PR list and in a single-member district. Candidates who win election in both the PR race and a single-member district can accept the single-member district seat and allow their party to give the PR seat to the next eligible candidate on the list. By allowing parties that find success in single-member districts to go farther down on their party lists where more women may be located, this should encourage women's representation by increasing party magnitude. This is particularly important given the effect of regional sublists just discussed. For example, the Communist Party was able to send candidates from fourth and fifth places on regional sublists in 1995 partly because the candidates ahead of them declined their PR seats.

Candidates in single-member districts composed of roughly 500,000 voters each can be nominated by parties or by groups of voters. Essentially, the only hurdle to nomination is the signature requirement, equal to one per cent of voters or roughly 5000 voters' signatures. This has severely weakened the control parties have wielded over access to office in the plurality half of the election. This weakened role for political parties (combined with the proliferation of candidates in plurality elections) may have increased opportunities for women by effectively removing the filter of party nomination that may have kept women off the ballot in PR elections.

Finally, the internal organization and rules of Russian parties may have negative effects on women's representation. If bureaucratically organized parties that formalize rules of nomination and faithfully follow these rules promote women's representation, then Russian parties themselves may serve as an impediment to women gaining elected office. With few exceptions, notably the Communist Party, Russian parties have tended to be dominated by charismatic leaders. Candidate recruitment, particularly to the PR list which parties fully control, are often levers of patronage doled out to leaders' clients (and in the case of the nationalist LDPR, Zhirinovsky's family members and criminal elements willing to pay for a top slot). Since parties tended to be formed by men, it is not surprising that most have become a 'boy's club' that seem closed to aspiring female politicians.

❖ THE CONTOURS OF WOMEN'S REPRESENTATION, 1993–9

Women's representation experienced dramatic swings over the first three elections in Russia. After an auspicious beginning in 1993, in which women won 13 per cent of the seats, female representation dropped dramatically to just less than eight per cent by 1999. However, a closer examination shows that this dramatic decline was driven mostly by the fate of Women of Russia. Patterns of female nomination and election among all other parties have maintained a rather stable pattern throughout the post-communist period. These patterns became clear once Women of Russia failed to overcome the five per cent legal threshold necessary to win PR seats, but are evident even at the height of women's representation in 1993. Table 8.1 shows the number of women nominated and elected for all parties winning representation in the PR tier from 1993 to 1999.

❖ ROBERT G. MOSER

Table 8.1. Number of women nominated and elected, 1993–9

Party	Total number (%) of women elected	Number (%) of women nominated in PR tier	Number (%) of women elected in PR tier	Number (%) of women nominated in SMD tier	Number (%) of women elected in SMD tier
1993					
VR	4 (8.2)	17 (8.1)	2 (5.0)	10 (8.4)	2 (8.0)
KPRF	7 (17.5)	16 (10.6)	3 (9.4)	5 (8.6)	4 (36.4)
LDPR	5 (7.9)	9 (6.1)	5 (8.5)	4 (6.6)	0 (0)
Yabloko	3 (13.0)	23 (13.4)	2 (9.5)	8 (8.7)	1 (14.3)
WOR	23 (100)	36 (100)	21 (100)	7 (100)	2 (100)
PRES	0 (0)	6 (3.1)	0 (0)	2 (2.6)	(0)
Agrarians	2 (5.3)	7 (4.8)	0 (0)	4 (5.6)	2 (13.3)
DPR	1 (6.7)	11 (6.6)	1 (7.1)	4 (6.3)	0 (0)
Inds.	15 (11.9)	N/A	N/A	57 (7.1)	15 (10.9)
Total	60 (13.7)	164 (9.3)	34 (15.0)	116 (6.4)	26 (11.6)
1995					
KPRF	17 (9.7)	26 (11.2)	9 (9.1)	14 (11.0)	8 (13.8)
NDR	5 (7.5)	34 (13.0)	3 (6.7)	21 (20.6)	2 (20.0)
Yabloko	6 (14.0)	30 (13.0)	2 (6.5)	9 (14.1)	4 (28.6)
LDPR	1 (2.0)	17 (6.3)	1 (2.0)	9 (4.9)	0 (0)
Inds.	10 (13.2)	N/A	N/A	90 (8.7)	9 (12.3)
Total	46 (10.1)	N/A	15 (6.7)	285 (12.5)	31 (13.8)
1999					
KPRF	11 (9.7)	30 (11.1)	3 (4.5)	18 (14.1)	8 (17.4)
Unity	7 (11.1)	19 (10.8)	3 (5.6)	5 (16.7)	4 (44.4)
OVR	8 (11.8)	32 (12.3)	5 (13.5)	13 (14.8)	3 (9.7)
SPS	4 (13.8)	33 (17.2)	2 (8.3)	14 (21.2)	2 (40.0)
Yabloko	2 (10.0)	30 (13.0)	2 (12.5)	18 (15.9)	0 (0)
LDPR	0 (0)	2 (2.4)	0 (0)	11 (12.4)	0 (0)
Inds.	3 (2.9)	N/A	N/A	102 (9.4)	3 (2.9)
Total	35 (7.8)	N/A	15 (6.7)	263 (13.4)	20 (8.9)

❖ *Nomination of women*

Several patterns deserve attention. First, in terms of raw numbers of nominations, the PR tier has produced proportionately far more female candidates
than the plurality tier in every post-communist election. Parties from across
the political spectrum ran more women candidates on their PR lists than in
SMDs at a rate of approximately 2:1. Even if one eliminates the Women of
Russia bloc, there were still more women nominated in the PR half of the 1993
election (128) than in the SMD tier (109).

What does this tell us about the supply of female candidates? The relatively low numbers of women running in both halves of the election may suggest that, contrary to my claims of a vibrant pool of qualified female candidates, there is actually a dearth of women willing and able to run for the national legislature. Unfortunately, I do not have the gender makeup of every party that ran in 1995 and 1999 to determine the overall numbers of female candidates in the PR election in these two elections (there were 43 parties in 1995 and 26 in 1999). Extrapolating from the levels of female nominations on major party lists, it is clear that female nominations rose substantially after 1993, but quickly leveled off at around 15 per cent of candidates for both PR and plurality halves of the election. Such stagnant levels of nomination are not likely to produce growing numbers of female legislators.

❖ Election of women

When examining the proportion of women winning legislative seats, the picture becomes more ambiguous. In 1993, more women were elected in the PR tier than the plurality tier, but only on the strength of the Women of Russia bloc. If one removes the Women of Russia bloc from the calculation, more women were actually elected in the SMDs than under PR. Of course, such a comparison is unfair since one of the main reasons PR is more conducive to women's representation is precisely because it encourages smaller parties like the Women of Russia to contest elections. However, it does highlight the fact that PR does not necessarily promote women's representation across the political spectrum. In subsequent elections, Russian voters and the five per cent threshold removed Women of Russia from the scene, laying bare how little PR actually promoted women's representation outside the parameters of a women's party.

In 1995, the gap in women's representation between the two tiers was greatest—over twice as many women entered the legislature from the SMDs as the PR race. This is particularly striking because party magnitude in the PR tier was greatest in 1995. The 1995 election saw the peak of fractionalization of the Russian party system. Forty-three parties ran on the PR ballot and divided the electorate to such an extent that a full 50 per cent of the votes were used on parties that did not overcome the legal threshold and thus were denied seats. This led to a windfall of seats for the four parties that did manage to win representation in the PR tier. This allowed parties to go further down their party lists where more women should have been found. This should have offset the loss of women's seats suffered when Women of Russia narrowly missed the legal barrier.

The shift to regional lists may have dampened the positive effects that increased party magnitude offered in this election, as the case of the Communist

Party suggests. The Communist Party won 99 PR seats in 1995, nine of which were occupied by women, a threefold increase over 1993. Had the Communists won that many seats in 1993, when it did not divide its list into regional sublists, it would have sent 14 women to the legislature, all but two of the women on its list. The same phenomenon holds true for the nationalist LDPR. In 1995, only one woman made it to parliament from the LDPR PR list, down from five women in 1993, despite the fact that the party won nearly as many PR seats (50 in 1995 vs. 59 in 1993). In 1993, 50 slots on the LDPR list not distributed among regional sublists would have included four women. This explanation does not work as well for Yabloko though. Yabloko split its list into regional sublists in 1993 but retained a large national list (34 slots) that elected all its deputies. Had Yabloko won the number of seats that it did in 1995 in 1993 (31 rather than 20), the party would have still sent only two women to the legislature, all from the national list. This suggests that parties put women so far down on their lists that district magnitude and party magnitude only make a difference at very high levels.

In 1999 women still were elected in higher numbers in plurality elections, but the gap narrowed. This narrowing was driven by a significant decline in the number of women elected in the single-member districts. The level of women coming from the PR tier remained constant. The source of the sharp drop-off of female plurality winners is not difficult to discern. Partisan female candidates retained their relatively high success rates. Women candidates from the Communist Party performed exceptionally well and the new party of power, Unity, did better than both previous pro-government parties. Female independents and minor party candidates, however, saw their fortunes drop sharply. One Russian feminist journalist suggests this is due to the changing nature of Russian SMD elections. These elections are costing more money and are increasingly dominated by local authorities, or even criminal elements, both of which have few women members.[1]

If one defines success as the proportion of women nominees who win election, then female candidates also tended to find more success in the SMDs than the PR contest. The 1993 election is the only one in which I have complete data on all candidates running in both tiers. Women running in single-member districts won 23 per cent of the time, while women running in the PR race won 19.5 per cent of the time. If one excludes Women of Russia, then women only won 10.2 per cent of the time in the PR tier. In other words, outside the experience of the women's party, female candidates in plurality elections were more than twice as likely to win election than women nominated on PR party lists. A similar trend is found when one examines the success rates of women in particular parties throughout the post-communist period. Female SMD candidates have experienced remarkable success compared to their PR counterparts for virtually all parties except the women's party and nationalist LDPR (see Table 8.2).

ELECTORAL SYSTEMS AND WOMEN'S REPRESENTATION ❖

Table 8.2. Position of women on PR lists, 1995–9

Party	Number of women on national list	Average position of women on regional lists	Number of women in top position on regional lists	Number of women in positions 2–4 on regional lists	Number of women in positions 5 or lower on regional lists	Average number of candidates elected from each regional list
1995						
KPRF	1	6.40	5	5	15	4.83
LDPR	1	2.50	5	10	1	0.29
NDR	2	2.94	5	22	5	0.43
Yabloko	2	3.18	5	18	5	0.38
1999						
KPRF	1	8.21	4	3	22	2.55
Unity	0	6.37	3	5	11	2.46
OVR	3	7.79	2	9	18	0.64
SPS	1	7.91	3	4	25	0.81
Yabloko	1	6.68	3	1	15	0.26
LDPR	0	3.00	0	2	0	0.00

The disparity between the success rates of women in the plurality and PR tiers suggests a couple of important developments. First, the success of individual female candidates may be a relic of the difficulties that women must overcome to be nominated in a single-member district. The fact that so many of the women who do run end up winning may be due to a pernicious winnowing out process that excludes all but the most qualified women from running in the first place. While this may produce high rates of success, the low numbers of nominees may be a sign that viable candidates are not competing. Ironically, a lower winning percentage for women in single-member districts may be the first sign of an increase in overall female representation.

Second, this disparity is a telling sign of the discrimination women face from parties when they assemble their PR lists. Left to their own devices as individual candidates in SMDs, women perform remarkably well. Because PR tier nominations are party-controlled, however, and parties routinely place most of their women in unwinnable spots on the PR list, women usually do not do well in PR elections.

The 1993 election is the only election in which some parties (KPRF, LDPR, DPR) did not divide their lists regionally. Therefore, rank was a straightforward measure of one's chances to gain election. This election shows a clear pattern among parties across the political spectrum of concentrating women in the bottom parts of PR lists. The KPRF had only one woman among its top

30 positions, the DPR had three, and the LDPR had zero. Women were some-what better represented in the next 30 positions (KPRF had eight, LDPR had five, and DPR had two), but women were most often found below the sixtieth position (KPRF had seven, LDPR had four, and DPR had six). Looking across all lists 62 per cent of women were placed below sixtieth and 90 per cent were below thirtieth place on the lists. When we then juxtapose these placements with the election results, where *no* party won as many as 60 PR seats (LDPR had 59 PR seats, which was the most won by a party), and only three of the eight parties winning PR seats had more than 30 seats, we see how very dif-ficult access was via the PR system. Obviously, under such circumstances, very high party magnitude was the only means toward substantial women's representation outside the women's party.

The 1995 and 1999 elections are more difficult to interpret. Regional lists were not uniform in length across or within parties. Therefore, even the aver-age rank within regional sublists does not fully capture the chances for elec-tion. The best proxy for rank in these circumstances is a comparison of the distribution of women within regional sublists with the average number of candidates elected from each region as seen in Table 8.2. The latter measure captures the effective district magnitude faced by candidates trying to navig-ate not only the rank order within regions, but also the chances that no candidates would be elected from a particular region. Most parties actually averaged less than one candidate per regional list because so many regions did not send a single member to the parliament. From this comparison one can see how women did relatively well on the Communist PR list in 1995 but worse in 1999, and why so few women made it from regional lists of most parties.

❖ EXPLAINING WOMEN'S REPRESENTATION IN RUSSIA

Accounting for the patterns of women's representation in Russia requires the examination of two questions: (1) What accounts for the general level of women's representation? and (2) What accounts for the surprising success of women in plurality elections compared with PR elections? I answer each of these questions in turn and show that the same factors can be seen as having very different effects depending on the type of question one asks.

❖ *General patterns of women's representation*

The interactive effects of culture, political parties, and the women's movement best explain the general contours of women's representation. At its deepest level, the generally low level of women's representation is due to the fact that society has not placed a priority on gender equality. Consequently, the women's movement has been ineffective in mobilizing demand for female candidates, and parties have little incentive, strategically or normatively, to nominate women in favorable PR slots or safe plurality districts.

The role of Women of Russia deserves special attention in this regard. While Women of Russia clearly contributed to the cause of women's representation in many ways, the existence of a women's party in Russia was actually a sign of weakness of the women's movement for several reasons. First, Women of Russia was born out of the inability of the women's movement to effectively pressure major parties to address women's issues. Women of Russia was hastily assembled during the shortened campaign of the 1993 election by three women's organizations, the Union of Russia's Women (URW), the Union of Navy Women, and the Association of Women Entrepreneurs. These organizations all had roots in the Soviet era and ties to the Communist Party, most notably the largest, the URW, which was formed out of the defunct Soviet Women's Council, the Communist Party's subordinate organization for women (Sperling 1999: 119–20). The URW initially sought to lend its support to parties proclaiming a women-friendly policy agenda. Only after the lack of response from major parties (only three responded to the organizations inquiries on their position regarding women's rights) did the URW decide to form its own electoral bloc (Sperling 1999: 118–19).

Second, while one might expect the success of Women of Russia in 1993 would spur other parties to take up the cause of women's rights and nominate more women, the most that could be claimed was that other parties provided a few token spots for women at the top of the party list at the next parliamentary election in 1995. Moreover, a women's party might actually restrain parties from actively soliciting the women's vote, thinking that no efforts could match the appeal of a women's party.

Finally, once Women of Russia failed to cross the five per cent electoral threshold in 1995 it was a detriment to the cause of women's representation because it demonstrated that an appeal of gender equality did not have much resonance with voters. The causes of the collapse of Women of Russia as a viable electoral bloc are multifaceted, but the ramifications are clear enough. In the Russian case, a women's party has been a fragile and rather ineffective basis for women's representation.

The role of political parties and ideology in the general lack of female legislators is also complex. On the one hand, the evidence on women's positions in PR lists suggests that parties have been a uniform constraint on women's representation. Yet, two caveats mitigate this judgment. First, over time, ideology has apparently emerged as a significant factor influencing how well a party will represent women. As the literature would predict, the nationalist LDPR has been male-dominated. Thus, women's representation has been furthered by the relative decline of this party since 1993. Although patchy, the Communist Party's record on women's representation suggests that leftist parties tend to favor women, at least relative to the other ideological alternatives. The reformist parties seem to be a more neutral presence, better than the nationalists, but not as consistently pro-women as the Communists.

Secondly, while the behavior of parties in the PR tier suggests a detrimental role in women's representation, the role of parties in single-member districts offers a more complex picture. Independent female candidates did not perform significantly better than partisan women in the first two elections. They also performed dramatically worse than party candidates in 1999. At the very least, one must admit that parties have not been the overt obstacle to female nomination and election in plurality elections that they seem to be in the PR tier. One could imagine that parties are willing to nominate women in safe districts in plurality elections even though they place them at the bottom of PR lists. Female candidates may provide assets, such as name recognition, service in local politics, or ties to local social organizations, that make them attractive candidates in a local SMD contest but do not carry over to the PR race. The legacy of the Soviet experience, allowing women some access to the political and economic systems but keeping them out of the higher echelons of power, may have reinforced this 'localization' of power. On the other hand, it is difficult to imagine why these same assets do not help women get better positions on the PR list, if not on the national list, at least on regional sublists of parties. Thus, it seems the weakness of party control itself is a major factor explaining this disjuncture between the PR and plurality tiers. Russian SMD candidates often pick parties rather than the other way around, allowing strong local candidates to assert their own candidacies with or without a partisan label. Under such circumstances parties become the rather neutral force in the SMDs that the evidence suggests (Moser 1998).

❖ The electoral system puzzle

Possible explanations for the relationship between electoral systems and women's representation in Russia include institutional rules, party ideology, electoral fragmentation, and the legacies of communism. The role of institutional rules has already been discussed. The introduction of mandatory regional sublists changed the environment facing candidates, effectively reducing district magnitude and detracting from the positive effects of higher party magnitude. Essentially, regional sublists have made the district magnitude of the PR tier comparable to or even lower than that of SMDs in cases where many regional lists send no representatives to the Duma (see Table 8.2). This explanation, however, is not the whole story.

Another potential explanation is that the intervening effect of individual political parties may account for the proportion of women elected in PR and SMD tiers. If parties that are more favorable to women are more successful in

SMD elections, this may account for the higher level of success for women in this tier compared to the PR tier. Such a scenario is more likely in mixed electoral systems with linked tiers, which use the seats gained in the PR tier to compensate for disproportionality in the SMD tier by either subtracting the seats won in the SMD tier from a party's PR total or adding a tertiary level of elections that adds seats to party totals in proportion to their national vote. Russia's mixed system mitigates against this phenomenon because no system of compensatory seats is used.

Nevertheless, the fate of individual parties may still affect the relationship between PR and SMD elections and women's representation in mixed systems. Except for Women of Russia in 1993, however, no party that won PR seats was overly concerned with promoting the election of women. Moreover, those parties that did have a better record of women's representation, particularly the Communist Party, actually saw as many or more of its female deputies come out of the plurality races as the PR contest. This interrelationship between electoral system effects and parties can be analysed through multiple regression analysis.

Logistic regression was used to test the relative importance of the electoral system and party affiliation in Russia's three post-communist elections. The dependent variable was the gender of the representative (0—male, 1—female). The independent variables were the electoral system (0—SMD, 1—PR) and dummy variables for all significant parties (parties that won five seats or more). Controlling for party with logistic regression resulted in a meaningful difference in the behavior of the electoral system variable in only one election—1993. In the 1995 and 1999 elections, the electoral system continued to be negatively correlated with women's representation (that is, women were more likely to be elected in the SMD rather than the PR tier), even when controlling for party. No party variable was statistically significant.

Table 8.3 shows the results of the logistic regression analysis for the 1993 Russian election. This confirms the point made earlier that the party that drove women's representation in the PR tier in 1993 was a women's party. Although the p-value for Women of Russia is not statistically significant, its odds ratio is so astronomically high that there was clearly an effect. After controlling for this effect, the electoral system variable became statistically significant and changed signs. It was then negatively correlated with the election of women. The logistic regression model was statistically significant at the $p < 0.001$ level and correctly predicted 92 per cent of the observations. This negative relationship between PR and women's representation matches the relationship found in 1995 and 1999 when, upon the failure of Women of Russia to overcome the five per cent legal threshold in the PR tier, a substantially greater proportion of women were elected from the SMD tier of the system. The logistic regression analysis suggests that the same general tendency

Table 8.3. Logistic regression of electoral system and party affiliation on gender of elected representative in 1993 Russian election

1993 Russian election

Variable	B (std. error)	Odds ratio
Electoral system	−0.967* (0.500)	0.38
APR	−0.145 (1.16)	0.86
DPR	0.460 (1.16)	1.58
KPRF	1.247* (0.587)	3.48
LDPR	0.616 (0.687)	1.85
PRES	−6.25 (21.01)	0.002
RC	−0.003 (0.621)	0.997
WOR	12.33 (20.71)	227,227
YAB	0.758 (0.737)	2.13
Constant	−2.226 (0.272)	—

$N = 450$.
−2 Log likelihood = 239.971.
Goodness of fit = 404.891.
Model chi-square = 113.436, Sig. = 0.0000.
% Correctly predicted 91.78.
$+ p \leq 0.1$, $* p \leq 0.05$, $** p < 0.01$, $*** p < 0.001$.

existed in 1993 but was masked by the success of Women of Russia in the PR tier.

A third factor potentially intervening in the relationship between electoral systems and women's representation is party fractionalization and weakness. The weak and fractured party system can help explain the two developments that are responsible for the electoral system puzzle: the relatively low number of women elected under PR (save the Women of Russia) and the relative success of Russian women in winning election in single-member districts. It has already been shown how party fragmentation hurts women's representation in PR elections. By lowering party magnitude, fragmentation did not allow parties to go down their party lists to where female candidates were concentrated.

ELECTORAL SYSTEMS AND WOMEN'S REPRESENTATION ❖

The fact that parties were forced to divide into regional sublists beginning in 1995 exacerbated this problem. While a factor, however, this effect should not be exaggerated. There were no more women elected in 1995 when only four parties overcame the five per cent barrier than when six did in 1999. The deeper problem is that the women's movement and society did not provide enough pressure on parties to make it strategically advantageous to nominate women in winnable positions on their party lists, leaving parties able to place women so far down on their party lists that only an extremely high party magnitude would allow their election.

What makes party fragmentation a particularly interesting factor in the electoral system puzzle is that it potentially has had the opposite effect in single-member district races. The literature suggests that a primary obstacle to women's representation in single-member districts is the high electoral threshold necessary for victory, usually a majority or near majority. The two major parties that usually dominate such elections take a risk in nominating any type of candidate that diverges from the accepted stereotype of a 'typical' representative who is usually deemed male and of the ethnic, racial, and religious majority. In competitive districts in which the margins for victory are small, the risk of turning away even a small proportion of voters with a woman or minority candidate tends to hinder major parties from nominating these types of candidates (Taagepera 1994: 238).

In Russia, party fragmentation may have lowered these obstacles in the single-member districts. Since the single-member districts were not two candidate races, the threshold for victory was much lower, increasing the chances for women to win election (Rule and Shvedova 1996: 56). A female candidate did not have to win a majority or near majority to capture a seat. Instead, the victorious candidate in Russia's single-member districts averaged 31 per cent of the district's vote in 1993 and only 29 per cent in 1995 (Belin and Orttung 1997: 128). This may have changed the calculus for parties nominating women and for ambitious women running as independents. Unlike in a two-candidate race where parties take a risk-averse strategy, which usually includes nominating a man, being a woman may have been an advantage that set one apart from the dozen candidates that often crowd Russian single-member districts. One can test this hypothesis by analysing the correlation between the electoral threshold of a district (defined here as the proportion of the vote for the winner) and the nomination and election of a woman. This assertion gains some support in a simple comparison of electoral thresholds of those districts with at least one female candidate and those districts without a single woman running. In those districts that had at least one female candidate, the candidate elected averaged only 28 per cent of the vote while all-male districts had winners gaining 31 per cent on average. I also conducted a multiple regression analysis using district-level data from 1995 to examine the influence of electoral threshold, incumbency, and environmental factors such as urbanization and ethnic diversity on the number of female candidates running in a single-member district. The results are found in Table 8.4.

The results suggest that a lower electoral threshold is associated with a higher incidence of female candidates. The winner's percentage of the vote was negatively correlated with the number of women nominated and statistically significant at the $p < 0.01$ level. No other factor—not incumbency, urbanization, or non-Russian regional status—had a statistically significant relationship with the number of women candidates.

Finally, the Communist legacy of relatively high socioeconomic status of women in Russia may help to account for their greater success in single-member district elections. Legacies of Communist policies may have produced a critical mass of well-educated, politically active women who are more competitive in the local milieu of SMD elections than the national stage at which competition for the choice spots on PR party lists takes place. While the fragmentation of Russia's party system may have opened up greater opportunities for women in SMD elections, it did not guarantee greater success. Women still needed to marshal the resources necessary to conduct a winning campaign to take advantage of these opportunities. Women were at a great

Table 8.4. Multiple regression on number of female nominations in 1995 single-member district races

Independent variables	Coefficient estimates (std. error)	p-value
INCUM	0.058 (0.159)	0.717
REGION	0.299 (0.198)	0.132
URBAN	0.240 (0.167)	0.152
THRESHOLD	−2.08** (0.773)	0.008
Constant	1.71 (0.284)	0.000
Adjusted R^2	0.033	0.023

$+ p < 0.10$, $* p < 0.05$, $** p < 0.01$, $*** p < 0.001$.
$N = 2569$
Variables:
INCUM—Incumbent running (0 = no, 1 = yes).
REGION—Ethnicity of region (0 = Russian, 1 = Non-Russian).
URBAN—Urban/rural (0 = < 500,000, 1 = > 500,000).
THRESHOLD—Vote proportion of winning candidate.

ELECTORAL SYSTEMS AND WOMEN'S REPRESENTATION ❖

disadvantage in Russia, a country with a long-standing patriarchal power structure and cultural biases against women practicing politics. A look at the occupational backgrounds of successful female candidates shows that women who won election in the SMDs overcame these obstacles by matching their male counterparts in terms of political experience and social standing.

Table 8.5 shows the occupational background of male and female deputies elected in 1995. Social status and political experience in particular seemed to be key factors in the election of women in single-member districts in Russia. Similarities rather than differences stand out when comparing successful female and male candidates in the single-member districts. For both women and men, previous experience in political office was a great benefit to gaining election to the State Duma. Quite predictably, incumbents made up the largest contingent of winning candidates. However, since incumbents made up much

Table 8.5. Occupational background of women and men deputies in 1995

Occupation	PR women ($n = 14$)	SMD women ($n = 29$)	PR men ($n = 206$)	SMD men ($n = 192$)
SMD incumbent	0 (0)	9 (31%)	11 (5.3%)	67 (34.9%)
PR incumbent	4 (28.6%)	4 (13.8%)	48 (23.3%)	19 (9.9%)
Federation council	0 (0)	1 (3.4%)	0 (0)	5 (2.6%)
National executive branch	0 (0)	0 (0)	2 (1.0%)	2 (1.0%)
Regional head of administration	0 (0)	0 (0)	6 (2.9%)	2 (1.0%)
City/Raion head of administration	0 (0)	1 (3.4)	3 (1.5%)	4 (2.1%)
Regional executive branch	0 (0)	1 (3.4)	6 (2.9%)	5 (2.6%)
Regional legislature	1 (7.1%)	2 (6.9)	3 (1.5%)	11 (5.7%)
City/Raion legislature	1 (7.1%)	1 (3.4%)	1 (0.5%)	1 (0.5%)
Legislative aide	1 (7.1%)	2 (6.9%)	15 (7.3%)	3 (1.6%)
Professional intelligentsia[1]	1 (7.1%)	3 (10.3)	17 (8.3%)	2 (1.0%)
Academic/Artist	4 (28.6%)	1 (3.4)	26 (12.6%)	6 (3.1%)
Party activist	1 (7.1%)	0 (0)	9 (4.4%)	9 (4.7%)
Social movement	0 (0)	1 (3.4)	8 (3.9%)	5 (2.6%)
Trade union	0 (0)	0 (0)	5 (2.4%)	2 (1.0%)
Agricultural manager	0 (0)	1 (3.4)	5 (2.4%)	6 (3.1%)
Industrial manager	0 (0)	1 (3.4)	11 (5.3%)	19 (9.9%)
Entrepreneur/banker	0 (0)	0 (0)	19 (9.2%)	13 (6.8%)
Military	0 (0)	0 (0)	3 (1.5%)	4 (2.1)
Other[2]	0 (0)	0 (0)	6 (2.9%)	3 (1.6%)

[1] Includes doctors, lawyers, procurators, economists, school teachers/administrators, and engineers.
[2] Includes workers and pensioners.

❖ ROBERT G. MOSER

less than half of the deputies for both men and women, incumbency was not the obstacle to legislative turnover that it is in established democracies with single-member district elections like the United States. Over half of both female and male deputies had some experience in national, regional, or local political office, with a greater proportion of women (65 per cent) than men (59 per cent) holding some type of executive or legislative office.

The greatest difference between women and men was the proportion of winning candidates from among the economic elite. In the single-member districts, 20 per cent of male winners were industrial managers, collective farm chairmen, entrepreneurs, or bankers, while only seven per cent of women winning seats in single-member districts were from the economic elite of Russia. Such patterns point to political service at the regional and local levels as the primary route for women to election to the State Duma in the single-member districts.

Female and male PR deputies also had similar backgrounds. Incumbents and regional politicians made up a smaller share of the PR contingent in favor of academics for both women and men. Like the SMD deputies, the economic elite made up a significant portion of the men elected from PR party lists, but was completely absent among women.

A comparison across electoral systems shows that electoral rules not only affected the number of women elected, but the type of women elected as well. Political experience was much more important for election in the single-member districts than in the PR election. Incumbents made up the bulk of single-member district female deputies (45 per cent), but academics and artists were as numerous as incumbents among the PR female deputies, each accounting for roughly 29 per cent of the total. Regional political experience was also more pervasive among women elected in the SMDs than women elected on a party list. This is not surprising given that name recognition was so decisive to electoral success in the SMDs, and a certain anonymity existed for members of party lists ranked lower than the top three candidates who appeared on the ballot. The regional character of the SMD elections made political service, particularly at the regional level, the best route to gaining that essential name recognition and reputation as a politician interested in protecting her constituency's interests in Moscow.

❖ CONCLUSIONS

On a general level, low women's representation in Russia is relatively easy to explain. Cultural attitudes and weak demand for female candidates have resulted in Russian parties having little incentive to nominate women in winnable positions. Ironically, the presence of a women's party has been indicative of this weak demand and may have even perpetuated it.

By concentrating on the unusual phenomenon that women tended to win more seats in the plurality rather than PR half of the mixed electoral system, I have shown that a multitude of factors come into play when canvassing the whole experience of the representation of Russian women. Institutional rules, party fragmentation, and communist legacies have had complex, interactive effects that closed certain doors to representation in the PR contest but offered other opportunities in single-member districts for women.

What are the implications of this study? Unfortunately, there is little evidence to lead one to be optimistic about the near-term future prospects for women's representation. The relatively high rate of women elected in the single-member districts in 1993 and 1995 suggested that a critical mass of highly educated, politically active women capable of building a political career beginning at the local level and remaining in office through incumbency was emerging. However, the decline of female victories in the plurality elections of 1999 calls this into question, suggesting that even this avenue to the legislature may be closing for women. The future electoral fortunes of women in the PR tier are even more disheartening. The dismal two per cent showing for Women of Russia in the 1999 election virtually foreclosed the option of a women's party providing a stable foundation for women's representation over the long term. If President Putin's plan for more stringent party registration rules designed to reduce fragmentation are adopted as expected, then it is unlikely that there will be a women's party on the ballot at all in the next election. Only if the women's movement can reorient itself to pressuring the remaining parties to nominate more women in winnable seats will progress be made. The fact that parties most supportive of women, like the Communist Party, actually had a worse record on PR nominations of women in 1999 does not bode well for the future.

❖ NOTES

1 Author interview with Nadezhda Azhgikhina, December 1999.

❖ ROBERT G. MOSER

9 ❖ Women in Russian Regional Assemblies: Losing Ground[1]

Dawn Nowacki

At the beginning of the new millennium, across all regions and republics, women constituted around nine per cent of the elected deputies in regional parliaments. This figure represents a steep decline from the Communist period, when at least one-third of the deputies to republic and oblast (provincial) soviets were women. The proportion of women in Russian regional assemblies now varies from 0 to 35 per cent (see Table 9.1).[2] This chapter proposes and tests several hypotheses expected to explain variations in the level of women's representation in Russian regional assemblies. Despite the lack of stable party systems in the Russian regions, political institutions such as the electoral system and district size, along with the level of support for political reform, play important roles in explaining the variation in female election rates. Political culture, measured indirectly using dominant religion, also plays a significant role in women's access to regional parliaments.

❖ Why Examine the Regions?

Western research on women's representation at Russia's national level is only in its beginning stages (Hesli and Miller 1993; Nachemias 1994; Racioppi and See 1995, 1997; Rule and Shvedova 1996; Buckley 1997; Moser, this volume). Published studies at the regional level are virtually nonexistent. Why, then, focus on regional assemblies? An examination of women's representation at the regional level is valuable for several reasons. First, assemblies have important representational and regime-legitimizing functions in the development of local democratic processes (Hahn 1996). Moreover, during the time period studied, regions as territorial units became more important politically because of the general devolution of power from Moscow to the provinces (Shlapentokh, Levita, and Loiberg 1997; Solnick 1998; Stoner-Weiss 1999).[3]

Table 9.1. Type of region, size of legislature, number and percentage of women deputies in the legislatures

Region Type	McFaul and Petrov categorizaton	Legislature size	Number of women	Percentage of women
REPUBLIC				
Ingushetia	Controlled	27	0	0.00
North Osetia-Alania	Controlled	75	2	2.67
Mari-El	Conservative	66	2	3.03
Kalmykia	Controlled	27	1	3.70
Karachai-Cherkessia	Controlled	73	3	4.11
Tatarstan	Controlled	139	6	4.31
Buriatia	Protest	65	3	4.61
Dagestan	Controlled	122	6	4.92
Bashkortostan	Controlled	185	10	5.41
Chuvashia	Conservative	87	6	6.90
Udmurtia	Moderate reform	100	8	8.00
Mordovia	Controlled	74	6	8.10
Altai Republic	Conservative	49	4	8.16
Kabardino-Balkaria	Controlled	72	6	8.33
Komi	Moderate reform	50	6	12.00
Adygeia	Conservative	45	5	11.11
Sakha (Yakutia)	Controlled	70	10	14.29
Karelia	Strong reform	63	9	14.29
Khakassiia	Protest	75	12	16.00
Tyva	Controlled	62	13	20.97
Chechnia-Ichkeria	Controlled	No data		
OBLAST				
Kursk	Conservative	44	0	0.00
Novosibirsk	Protest	49	0	0.00
Tyumen	Protest	25	0	0.00
Leningrad	Moderate reform	49	1	2.04
Rostov	Protest	45	1	2.22
Lipetsk	Conservative	38	1	2.63
Nizhnyi Novgorod	Moderate reform	70	2	2.86
Astrakhan	Conservative	29	1	3.45
Penza	Conservative	45	2	4.44
Perm	Strong reform	40	2	5.00
Vladimir	Moderate reform	37	2	5.41
Belgorod	Conservative	35	2	5.71
Saratov	Protest	35	2	5.71
Orenburg	Conservative	47	3	6.38
Voronezh	Conservative	45	3	6.67
Tomsk	Moderate reform	42	3	7.14
Cheliabinsk	Moderate reform	41	3	7.32
Kaluga	Protest	40	3	7.50

❖ DAWN NOWACKI

Table 9.1. continued

Republic	McFaul and Petrov categorizaton	Legislature size	Number of women	Percentage of women
Ryazan	Conservative	26	2	7.69
Orel	Conservative	50	4	8.00
Samara	Moderate reform	25	2	8.00
Tambov	Conservative	49	4	8.16
Murmansk	Strong reform	24	2	8.33
Tula	Protest	48	4	8.33
Irkutsk	Moderate reform	45	4	8.89
Tver	Protest	33	3	9.09
Pskov	Protest	22	2	9.10
Kirov	Protest	52	5	9.62
Smolensk	Conservative	30	3	10.00
Vologda	Moderate reform	30	3	10.00
Kostroma	Protest	19	2	10.53
Novgorod	Moderate reform	26	3	11.54
Moscow	Strong reform	50	6	12.00
Briansk	Conservative	49	6	12.24
Kamchatka	Strong reform	49	6	12.25
Kaliningrad	Moderate reform	32	4	12.50
Volgograd	Conservative	32	4	12.50
Amur	Conservative	30	4	13.33
Omsk	Protest	30	4	13.33
Ulyanovsk	Conservative	25	4	16.00
Yaroslavl	Moderate reform	50	8	16.00
Sverdlovsk	Strong reform	48	8	16.67
Ivanovo	Moderate reform	35	6	17.14
Magadan	Moderate reform	17	3	17.65
Sakhalin	Protest	27	5	18.52
Arkhangelsk	Strong reform	36	7	19.44
Kemerovo	Conservative	35	7	20.00
Chita	Conservative	39	8	20.51
Kurgan	Conservative	29	7	24.14
KRAIS				
Stavropol	Conservative	25	1	4.00
Khabarovsk	Moderate reform	25	1	4.00
Krasnoyarsk	Protest	42	4	9.52
Primorye	Protest	39	4	10.26
Krasnodar	Conservative	50	6	12.00
Altai	Conservative	41	9	21.95
AUTONOMOUS OKRUGS				
Komi-Permiak	Controlled	15	0	0.00
Aga-Buriatia	Controlled	15	1	6.67
Khanty-Mansi	Strong reform	23	3	13.04

Table 9.1. continued

Republic	McFaul and Petrov categorizaton	Legislature size	Number of women	Percentage of women
Yamal-Nenets	Strong reform	21	3	14.29
Nenets	Moderate reform	15	3	20.00
Ust-Orda Buriat	Controlled	19	4	21.05
Koriak	Strong reform	9	2	22.22
Yevrei	Protest	15	4	26.67
Taymyr (Dolgan-Nenets)	Strong reform	11	3	27.27
Chukchi	Strong reform	13	4	30.77
Evenki	Moderate reform	23	8	34.78
CITIES				
St. Petersburg	Strong reform	50	1	2.00
Moscow	Strong reform	35	7	20.00

A second reason for looking at the regions is theoretical. The efforts of authors in this volume are contributions toward building a *general* model of women's legislative recruitment in post-communist cases. A useful general model should be able to explain outcomes at the provincial level as well as at the national level.

Finally, while the regions and republics differ greatly from each other along many dimensions, they possess important contextual commonalities. Similar cultural, institutional, and historical influences from 70 years of communist rule shape their current political situations. This provides a modicum of control not available to researchers engaged in cross-national analyses.

This chapter considers the regional effect of three sets of factors that the literature shows affect women's legislative recruitment: level of economic development, culture, and political institutions. Evidence from two datasets is used to test hypotheses about the relative importance of economic, cultural, and political factors in explaining differences in electoral outcomes for women. One dataset utilizes the 89 regions and republics as the unit of analysis, while the other focuses upon the characteristics of individual deputies to the assemblies.[4] Information was coded for 3496 deputies in 85 regions who were in office as of summer 2000.[5] Of these, 334, or 9.5 per cent, were women. In addition, personal interviews with 10 of the 16 female deputies to the regional assemblies in the Republic of Karelia and Arkhangelsk Oblast were conducted in spring 2001.

There are several types of subunits in the existing federation inherited from the Soviet territorial division. The Soviet division recognized ethicity as an organizing principle. The territorial divisions were hierarchical, with those of higher status receiving certain privileges for their non-Russian ethnic inhabitants (such as native language schools and publications). Union republics were at the top of the hierarchy, followed by autonomous republics, autonomous provinces (oblasts), and autonomous districts (okrugs). All were located within union republics, and the specific designation depended mainly upon the size of the ethnic group.[6] Since all of the union republics became separate nation states in 1991, the republic currently has the highest status within the Russian Federation.[7]

Republics were the first to conclude bilateral treaties with the central government, which spelled out areas of jurisdiction separate from the Russian Constitution and the Union Treaty of 1992. Oblasts and Krais are administrative units inhabited by ethnic Russian majorities. Since 1994, they, along with other territorial units, also made separate treaties with Moscow. This treaty making has resulted in 'asymmetrical federalism', a situation in which some regions and republics have more rights and privileges than others. Asymmetrical federalism is one cause of the chaotic relations between centre and periphery throughout the 1990s. It allowed the subunits to become the loci of real power in the federation before Putin's election in 2000. One important consequence was the leeway to adopt different kinds of electoral rules.

❖ A MULTIVARIATE ANALYSIS OF WOMEN'S REPRESENTATION IN THE REGIONS

I use multivariate analyses to test for the effects of a set of independent variables that I expect should influence women's representation in the regions. Before presenting the regressions, I present a short description and justification for the variables that are included in the model. These include economic and social conditions, a set of political institutions, and support for political reform.

❖ *Economic and social conditions*

Matland (1998*b*) has argued that changes brought about by socioeconomic modernization—decreased fertility, increased urbanization, and greater education and labour force participation by women—changes attitudes towards women's place in the public sphere. These changes provide an expanded pool of female aspirants with the kinds of resources and qualifications that party gatekeepers and voters find attractive. Such women, in turn, are able to organize effectively to demand greater access to power. Therefore, I expect a positive correlation between a region's level of socioeconomic development and the proportion of seats held by women in the legislature. The regions vary widely on easily measurable characteristics such as average income, level of urbanization, and the percentage of the population engaged primarily in agriculture.

It is somewhat more difficult to operationalize the impact of modernization on cultural values regarding the appropriate role of women in society. Matland (1998b) suggests that where we find gender equality across a range of variables, including the ratio of women to men in university education and the paid labour force, we can conclude that the prevailing gender attitudes are egalitarian. Unfortunately, it is not possible to gather detailed regional data on all of these factors. Moreover, widespread access to higher education stands as one of the few positive legacies of the Soviet gender regime. I expect little meaningful variation on these measures. Fertility (births/1000 women), on the other hand, provides a more reliable indicator of both economic development and traditional culture. In general, regions and republics characterized by values that are more traditional have higher fertility rates.

Another available indicator of political culture is the traditional religious heritage of the predominant ethnic group in a region. The main religious identifications in Russia are Christianity (primarily eastern Orthodox, with small minorities belonging to other Christian denominations), Islam, Buddhism, and Shamanism. Eighty per cent of the population of the Russian Federation is made up of ethnic Russians, most of whom are Orthodox Christians. Recent research has documented a resurgence of religious belief in the non-Russian ethnic areas, however, especially in the Muslim regions (Lehmann 1998). Lehmann found that '[t]he lowest levels of religiosity are to be found in the shamanistic republics, followed by increasing levels in the Russian oblasts, Christian republics, Buddhist republics, and Muslim republics, in that order' (p. 474). I have coded each region to reflect the predominant religion of the titular nationality. I expect Muslim regions to have relatively lower proportions of women. This is both true because of the relatively strong disapproval of women participating in public affairs in conservative Islamic circles and because these regions are expected to have the highest levels of religious activism. Conversely, higher proportions of women are expected to be elected to the assemblies where shamanism is dominant. This is not necessarily because of the religion's progressive view of women, but because I expect to see a more secular society that will be more open to female participation.

❖ Political institutions

Electoral systems and women candidates. As noted in Chapter 2, electoral systems are expected to differ in their ability to benefit female candidates. Specifically, multimember districts with closed party-list proportional representation should help women gain parliamentary seats. An important intervening variable, however, is strong and effective political parties that place women in high ballot positions in order to 'balance the ticket'. In the absence of such parties in Russia, and given that most candidates run as independents, should larger district magnitudes favour women's election? I believe so. In multimember districts with magnitudes of three or four, female candidates only have to come in third or fourth in order to win a seat, rather than having to win the majority of votes in a district. Having some portion of the population that is biased against women is likely to be less crucial when the threshold of representation, i.e., the per cent of vote needed to win election, is lower.

It is possible to test this hypothesis across regions because many have adopted multimember district systems since the mid-1990s devolution of power from the centre. The majority of regional assemblies (65, or 73.1 per cent) still use single member districts (SMD), but the remaining 24 have adopted a variety of systems. Four regions use mixed single and dual member districts, 14 have mixed single member and multimember districts, three regions use dual mandates, and three regions have multimember districts. Table 9.2 shows a preliminary test of the effect of district magnitude, as the table presents the configuration of the remaining 24 districts and the proportion of women elected in regions and republics with district magnitudes greater than one. With the exception of the three regions with party list systems (Koryak A. O. Krasnoyarsk Krai and Ust-Orda Buryat A. O.), all use plurality-based voting systems in multimember districts.

In three of the four cases in which a region has both single member and dual member districts, there are a higher proportion of women elected in the single member districts. In the 14 regions where the comparative multimember district had a magnitude greater than two, however, there is a clear tendency towards more women getting elected in multimember districts. In four regions, women do better in the SMD, while in two, the results are equivalent, and in eight districts, women do better in the multimember districts. Finally, women do better than the national average in four of the six districts that are exclusively multimember, equal to the national average in one, and only slightly worse than the average in a single district. Based on this admittedly mixed picture, I would cautiously assert that, even in the absence of strong parties and in the presence of plurality rules, female candidates generally benefit from larger district magnitudes.

I also expect there to be a negative correlation between the number of constituents per deputy and the proportion of women elected. In smaller places with a relatively modest number of constituents per representative, women are more likely to be able to run successfully as local notables. When the number of constituents one represents is relatively low, it is likely that both prestige and pay will be lower. Furthermore, when the constituent-to-representative ratio is low, the individual voters are more likely to know the representative and

Table 9.2. Women deputies elected in non-SMD regions

	SMD plurality % women	Multimember % women (district magnitude in parens.)
MIXED SMD/DUAL MANDATE		
Karelia Republic	40.0	6.0 (2)
Bashkortostan Republic	20.0	1.4 (2)
Adygei Republic	14.8	11.0 (2)
Koryak A. O.	0	25.0 (2)
MIXED SMD/MMD		
Kurgan Oblast	42.9	5.3 (2.4)
Kaliningrad Oblast	14.8	0 (5)
Khanty-Mansi A.O.	18.2	8.3 (4)
Orenburg Oblast	8.3	4.3 (2.6)
Ingush Republic	0	0 (5)
Nenets A. O.	20.0	20.0 (5)
Krasnoyarsk Krai	9.5	10.0 (20)
Kalmyk Republic	0	8.3 (4)
Murmansk Oblast	0	9.0 (2.3)
Sverdlovsk Oblast	10.0	20.7 (29)
Yevreiskaia A. Oblast	22.2	33.3 (6)
North Ossetia A. O.	1.4	20.0 (5)
Yamalo-Nenets A. O.	11.1	33.3 (3)
Ust-Orda Buryat A. O.	6.7	50.0 (4)
DUAL MANDATE		
Amur Oblast		13.3 (2)
Kirov Oblast		9.3 (2)
Tomsk Oblast		7.1 (2)
MULTIMEMBER DISTRICTS		
Kamchatka Oblast		13.3 (3)
Krasnodar Krai		13.0 (4)
Sakhalin Oblast		14.8 (3)

campaigns are much more likely to require relatively modest resources. Both factors should allow women to compete on more even footing. To deal with the significant differences in size across districts, we take the logarithm of constituents per representative in each region.

❖ *Political reformism*

A final factor considered is a geographically based estimation of the level of support for political reform. It is plausible that support for reform and the election of women are correlated. Women often campaign as reformers, and electorates that are willing to support reform also may be willing to support non-traditional candidates (i.e., women). Based on voting patterns in the 1995 parliamentary elections and the 1996 presidential elections, as well as some general regional criteria (industrialization and urbanization), McFaul and Petrov (1997) divide the 89 regions and republics into five groups: strong reformist, moderate reformist, protest, conservative, and controlled. The values for each of the 89 regions and republics are presented in Table 9.1. McFaul and Petrov were able to successfully predict the kinds of regional governors elected after 1997 on the basis of these categories.

Characteristics common to the strong reformist regions included the highest relative percentage of population living in urban areas (79 per cent) and high levels of industrialization. Furthermore, these districts were the ones that had the highest percentages of their votes going to reform candidates in the 1995 and 1996 elections (Yeltsin and Yabloko's Yavlinsky for president, and reform party candidates to the Duma). Equal proportions of voters for reformist/centrist candidates on the one hand, and communist/nationalist candidates on the other, were found in the moderate reformist regions. These regions were also relatively highly industrialized and urbanized (on average 73 per cent). Protest regions resemble moderate reform regions. However, they have some additional characteristics, including ethnic tension and/or hostility towards the centre that made electoral preferences unstable. Many voters supported third-party (non-communist and non-democrat) candidates. Conservative regions' voters tended to vote Communist and are much less urbanized (62 per cent). Controlled regions are those in which electoral politics are constrained by strong leaders, chiefly in the ethnic republics, oblasts, and autonomous districts.[8] These regions are described as having 'a mix of Soviet and ethnic political culture... [which allows] local leaders... to limit competition, exaggerate turnout, and falsify election results to maintain their hold on power' (p. 517). Such regions support whomever is in power in Moscow, and are only 45 per cent urban. I have coded regions and republics according to McFaul and Petrov's categorization, from one (controlled) to five (strong reformist).

Finally, I included a dummy variable for the city of Moscow. Moscow's politics are highly correlated with those of the national level and its values for several of the independent variables are so extreme that it can completely dominate the regression analysis.

Table 9.3 presents a multivariate regression model of the discussed variables. The first column shows the complete model, the second column shows the reduced model. The political variables in both models consistently work as predicted and are significant, while most of the economic and cultural variables are weak and insignificant. To see if this was because the various measures were

WOMEN IN RUSSIA'S REGIONS: LOSING GROUND ❖

Table 9.3. Multivariate regression model of development, cultural, and political predictors of the percentage of women deputies in the regions[1]

	Complete model	Reduced model
Constant	20.71*	28.8***
	(14.89)	(10.4)
Average income	−0.008	
	(0.023)	
% Urbanization	0.068	
	(0.075)	
% of population in agriculture	−0.05	
	(0.18)	
Fertility (births/1000)	0.601**	0.54*
	(0.358)	(31)
Ratio of females to males with higher education	4.81	
	(5.10)	
Muslim (dummy)	−4.73**	−5.07**
	(2.68)	(2.32)
Shamanist (dummy)	2.34	
	(3.57)	
District magnitude	2.43**	2.10**
	(1.30)	(1.23)
Log of constituents/member	−7.08***	−7.05***
	(2.32)	(1.82)
McFaul & Petrov's reform typology	1.49**	1.87***
	(0.77)	(0.56)
Moscow Dummy	14.67**	13.74**
	(7.55)	(6.24)
N	87	87
Adjusted R-squared	0.30	0.32
S.E.E.	6.02	5.94

[1] Unstandardized coefficients reported with standard errors in parantheses under.
Sig level, * = .10, ** = .05, *** = .01.

tapping into the same construct and diluting their individual effects, the variables were standardized and a development factor was created. The factor consisted of income, per cent urbanization, per cent in agriculture, and fertility (Cronbach's Alpha = 0.77). Replacing the three economic variables with this single development factor showed an even weaker effect than that of the individual variables. The only development variable that shows anything approaching significance was the fertility rate, and its value goes in the opposite direction from what was predicted. Representation appears to increase with fertility rates. While only weakly significant, the effect is quite surprising. I strongly suspect this is a spurious result due to greater fertility in the periphery, where women tend to do better in getting elected for other reasons.

When we look at the cultural variables, we see that both Shamanism and the ratio of females to males with higher education work in the expected directions, but are insignificant. The cultural variable of religion is significant in Islamic regions. As expected, having a region where Islam is the majority religion negatively affects women's representation.

Looking at the political institutions, we find a series of significant effects in the predicted directions. As average district magnitude increases, women's representation increases, consistent with the international literature. We also find a strong effect for district size: women do much better in districts with fewer constituents. Political culture also appears to matter, as regions that are most supportive of reform are also those where women tend to do best. Finally, there is a large positive coefficient for Moscow. Women do much better in the capital than elsewhere. This single variable has greater predictive capacity than several others in the model. I will have more to say about the regression results in the conclusion.

❖ POLITICAL PARTIES AND THE ELECTION OF WOMEN

In most contexts a central part of evaluating women's chances of being elected would consider the recruitment processes in the political parties. That is not true in the Russian regions because political parties played a limited role in candidate recruitment in the 1990s. This is chiefly due to the party system's fragmented and chaotic nature (Remington 1997; Rose, Munro, and White 2001), which is underpinned by institutional arrangements that fail to link voter identities and interests with policy making in the executive (Urban and Gel'man 1997). One could easily say there is no such thing as a party system in the Western sense operating in Russia's regions. National parties have little impact (Stoner-Weiss 1999: 97–8), and local parties tend to be 'notable' rather than 'programmatic' parties (Ishiyama 1996). They are formed to elect regional governors. Slider concludes, '. . . rarely do regional elections represent a distinct choice between different ideologically based parties that favour socialist or liberal—or any other coherent—alternatives' (Slider 1996: 257–8).

While there is a consensus on what the picture for most of the 1990s looks like, there is some disagreement as to how this picture should be interpreted. One group of scholars look at the lack of coherent programmatic based party competition and voices a concern that democracy is not developing in the Russian regions. Another group of scholars argue this is merely a natural pattern. A coherent party system tends to start in the centre and then moves to the periphery. These scholars argue that coherent institutions, both party systems and legislatures will develop over time.

One characteristic of institutionalized legislatures is relatively modest turnover rates. We do not have complete information on turnover, but, looking at a sample of six regions, we see turnover is quite high.[9] These regions all had new parliamentary elections in 1999. Overall, 37.7 per cent of the new legislators were returning members. The proportion of returning parliamentarians ranged from 48.7 per cent in Bashkortostan to only 8.9 per cent in Kemorovo Oblast. We do not know if these low return rates are because of voluntary exits or electoral defeats. These rates are so low, however, that we can assert two central facts. First, these legislatures are still a long way from being institutionalized. Second, the lack of legislative turnover is not a serious barrier to women's access to political office unlike the United States, where the lack of turnover is a crucial element in explaining low levels of women's representation (Darcy, Welch, and Clark 1994; Seltzer *et al.* 1997).

❖ Nominating organizations and the election of women

In the absence of effective parties, how do candidates qualify to get on electoral ballots? Most are nominated by anywhere from 50 to 2500 voters, depending on regional electoral rules. This group may range from the candidate's extended family and friends to a more organized interest group. Table 9.4 displays the nominating organization of the individual deputies.

We have nominating organization data for 3109 of 3468 deputies in the dataset. The overall patterns for men and women are quite similar. Of the 2810 male deputies for whom we have data, 78.6 per cent were 'nominated by a group of voters', 3.3 per cent were independent,[10] and the rest had some kind of official party or organizational support. Of these, the greatest number, 10.2 per cent, was affiliated with the Communist Party or its allied parties (such as the Agrarians). In the case of the 299 female deputies, 67.9 per cent were 'nominated by a group of voters', 4.7 per cent were independent, and 14.7 per cent were affiliated with the Communist Party. Thus, *the vast majority of deputies were elected without formal party or organizational affiliation.* Note that candidates may receive support from political parties and organizations, even though candidates do not want to be, or due to electoral laws cannot be, publicly affiliated with these parties (Politicheskii almanakh Rossii 1997; McFaul, Petrov and Ryabov 1999). At this stage, no systematic data are available on the covert or informal affiliations. Thus, it is not possible to know how many ran as true independents. Moreover, many newly elected deputies join party or deputy factions within the assemblies after the elections. Nevertheless, the data here provide important evidence that there has been little movement in the direction of coherent party systems in the Russian regions.

Although only 27 per cent of the women elected are affiliated with some kind of organization, the figure for men is significantly lower ($p < 0.01$) at 18 per cent. Women are more likely than men to be nominated by the Communist Party or by interest groups (if one includes women's interest groups).

❖ DAWN NOWACKI

Table 9.4. Nominating organization by gender[1] (Numbers and percentages)

	Men	Women	Total
Generic 'Group of voters'	2210	203	2412**
	78.6%	67.9%	77.6%
Communists/allies	288	44	332*
	10.2%	14.7%	10.7%
Independent	94	14	108
	3.3%	4.7%	3.5%
Nationalists/patriots (Russian)	90	10	100
	3.2%	3.3%	3.2%
Interest Groups/orgs.	47	7	54
	1.7%	2.3%	1.7%
Democrats	27	4	30
	1.0%	1.3%	1.0%
Regional autonomy/ interests	26	2	26
	0.9%	0.7%	0.9%
Centrists	19	3	22
	0.7%	1.0%	0.7%
Women's groups		12	12**
		4.0%	0.4%
Minority nationalists	9		9
	0.3%		0.3%
Total known	2810	299	3109
	(100%)	(100%)	(100%)
Unknown	324	35	359
	(10.4%)	(10.5%)	(10.4%)
Grand total	3134	334	3468

* Difference between male and female deputies significant at 0.05 level.
** Difference between male and female deputies significant at 0.01 level.
[1] Based on individual deputy dataset from 84 regions. Figures for the five additional regions were from aggregate level data provided by the Russian Central Electoral Commission.

The comparative literature suggests that active women's organizations participating in politics are likely to have a positive impact on women's election to regional assemblies. In a system characterized by a lack of effective political parties, such organizations may take on even greater importance in providing financial and other resources to support electoral campaigns. While political parties foundered in the 1990s, interest groups developed as a potential resource for female candidates throughout the 1990s (Lipovskaia 1997: 197). These organizations cover a broad range, from groups that promote women's retraining and employment to those encouraging women business entrepreneurs, to those supporting the mothers of war victims, and victims of domestic abuse (Racciopi and See 1997; Liborakina 1998).

WOMEN IN RUSSIA'S REGIONS: LOSING GROUND ❖

While this possible resource has been growing, it is rarely present in the political sphere. Sperling (1999) studied women's organizations in half a dozen regions. She found very few links between women's organizations and female candidates. Most women's organizations showed little interest in promoting female candidates. Sperling's finding is largely confirmed by the data I have collected. Despite the virtual irrelevance of parties, women's groups have only stepped in to promote candidates in a very limited manner. Of the 3109 representatives, only 12 (0.4 per cent of all elected representatives) have been nominated directly by a women's organization. Even limiting the sam-ple to only women elected, a mere 4.0 per cent of all women elected were nominated by women's organizations. The few organizations that specifically nominated female deputies have their roots in the traditional Soviet women's councils and committees and appear to be the heirs of greater organizational and other resources than independent post-Soviet women's groups. Yet, this sort of action was very rare in the regions.

❖ Political party ideology and the recruitment of women

While political parties are much weaker at the regional level of Russian politics than in many other polities, they are relevant. Almost one-fifth of the deputies have some kind of party affiliation when they run and the proportions are higher within the regional assemblies. Furthermore, if the optimists are correct, as democratic competition is established the role of parties will continue to expand in the regions. What types of parties are likely to nominate successful women candidates?

In the mid- to late 1990s, the Russian ideological spectrum at the national level was reflected in political parties that represented four large political identities: democratic and market reformist, reformed communist, nationalist, and centrist (Oates 1998). Such political tendencies could also be found in greater or lesser degrees at the regional level. Branches of the larger national parties could be found in the regions beside local parties which pressed for more autonomy relative to the centre, for example, or which supported local interests and personalities.

The Communist Party of the Russian Federation (KPRF) is the Soviet Communist Party's successor. Branches of the KPRF exist in all of Russia's regions and republics. It advocates a much larger economic role for the state than either the federal government or pro-market reform parties. It also calls for a stronger social safety net, which would benefit many women who were harmed in the economic transition. The KPRF has maintained the old Communist Party's official desire for gender equality as party policy. How deep these attitudes stick is another matter, however, as their leaders are quite capable of evincing very traditional Soviet attitudes toward women.[11] The party has benefited from the organizational resources of the old Communist Party of the Soviet Union, and is arguably Russia's closest approximation of an effective political party. Thus, to the extent that women are attracted to the KPRF's promise of increased social welfare and can strategically count on the party's organizational strength, the KPRF would appear to be the best affiliation for women office seekers.

Several political parties represent the national-patriotic force in Russian politics; the strongest of these at the national level in the 1990s was Vladimir Zhirinovsky's Liberal Democratic Party of Russia (LDPR). In general, the national-patriots support a return to traditional Russian values, such as Orthodoxy and the strengthening of Russian culture. Since traditional Russian values included an essentialist view of women's place in society and the nationalists view women as 'mothers of the nation', it is no surprise that parties and organizations representing the national-patriotic tendency take a dim view of women in the public arena. Ethno-nationalist parties in Muslim regions, particularly in the Caucasus region, have similar views about women in politics. Overall, it is expected that successful female candidates will be less likely to be affiliated with nationalist parties or parties representing a specific ethnic group.

A few relatively small liberal democratic parties exist. The most enduring democratic party is Yabloko (headed by Grigory Yavlinsky, and firmly in opposition to the central government). On the one hand, the democrats' more liberal wing supports a less traditional view of women and seems willing to place women on party lists based on merit. On the other hand, the parties' more market-oriented wings are indifferent to women's interests. Such parties are unlikely to nominate women more often than the KPRF, but should nominate them more often than the Russian nationalists.

Finally, a somewhat ambiguous political centre is occupied by non-ideological parties and groups whose main purposes seem to be to either launch particular candidates into office, or to maintain office for those who already have it. Most important is the 'party of power', which has presented itself under different names at different times and is organized by the supporters of the president and his administration. In the 1995–6 elections, this party was called 'Our Home is Russia', while in the 1999 Duma elections it was called 'Unity'. Having no ideological reasons to support or oppose women, I would expect the federal centrist category to occupy a middle ground in terms of women's representation. In addition, the centre contains numerous parties indigenous to various regions. These are difficult to categorize by ideology, but as they are usually built around prominent local actors whose support structure is heavily male, it is likely that relatively few women would be elected.

Table 9.5 shows the results for various party blocs. We find some support for the hypotheses presented. Women did worst among the parties that have an

Table 9.5. Women's proportion among MRPs for various political parties

	MRPs	Female (%)
COMMUNIST & ALLIES		
Communist Party of the Russian Fed. (KPRF)	241	14.1
Other Communist Parties (non-KPRF)	41	17.1
Russian Communist Workers Party (RKRP)	7	14.3
Agrarians	28	0
COMMUNIST–NATIONALIST		
Narodovlastie 'A.M. Tuleev'	11	27.3
NATIONALIST/PATRIOTIC		
Russian Nationalist/Patriotic	32	18.7
LDPR	9	0
Parties supporting A. Lebed	16	0
REFORMIST/DEMOCRATIC OPPOSITION		
'Yabloko'	23	17.4
Constitutional Democrats of RF	1	0
CENTRIST—FEDERAL[1]		
Fatherland (Otechestvo)	38	10.5
'For Social Justice'	28	3.6
People's Party of Free Russia (NPSR)	18	5.6
'Our Home is Russia'	8	37.5
Democratic Choice—Russia	2	0
Interregional Association of Deputies	1	0
'Luzhkov'	2	0
CENTRIST—REGIONAL		
Nash Dom Nash Gorod	5	0
Soyuz dela i poriadka	10	0
'Transformation Ural'	14	14.3
ETHNIC AND INDEPENDENCE PARTIES		
Regional independence parties	2	0
Titular ethnic party	5	0
SUBTOTAL PARTIES	**542**	**12.5**
Trade Union/business organizations	28	14.3
Women's organizations	10	100.0
Total	**580**	**14.1**

[1] Either of national prominence or popular in many regions/republics.

ethnic or regional base (zero per cent and 6.9 per cent, respectively). The centrist parties that have a federal base and the nationalist parties with a federal base fall into a middle category (9.4 per cent and 11 per cent). The Communist party, despite inheriting and continuing the old Soviet platform of gender equality, has not lived up to its commitment to equality in practice and lies

✧ DAWN NOWACKI

just slightly above 14 per cent in terms of women's representation across regional legislatures. Women's rates of representation in the Communist parties are nevertheless greater than in most of the other party blocs. For the Communists' allies, the Agrarians, however, the picture is dismal. There are no women among their 28 members in regional parliaments. On the high end, the governmental party of power, 'Our Home is Russia', Narodovlastie-Aman Tuleev and the Yabloko party elected relatively more women proportionally than the other parties. The first two parties' numbers, however, are too small to generalize about their suitability as vehicles for female candidates. Moreover, these parties are ephemeral, and will no doubt have disappeared by the next round of elections. Relatively speaking, the best bet for women appears to be the reformist Yabloko or the Communist party.

❖ Individual characteristics of regional representatives

We know from studies of candidate recruitment that viable candidates tend to come disproportionately from higher SES professions. In the Soviet period, women achieved levels of higher education and representation in many professions (in particular, the scientific-technical and cultural intelligentsia) almost equivalent to those of men. If all individuals with higher education defined the complete pool of aspirants, there would be little reason to expect that pool to be biased towards men. Regional legislators are not, however, evenly pulled from all high SES areas. There is a clear bias towards the areas in which women have the least representation. Most importantly, women are underrepresented among the ranks of enterprise directors and managers and the political executives at all territorial levels. As it turns out, political representatives are disproportionately chosen from these sectors.

Hughes found those who were elected to regional assemblies from 1995 to 1996 came mainly from two occupation categories: political-administrative leaders and economic leaders (1997: 1031). Based on 1995 data, Slider (1996) has also found that the majority of deputies to the regions and republics' assemblies were 'executive officials' and 'enterprise/farm managers' (p. 245). He notes,

> Local elites who won in most regions had considerable electoral advantages. [They] . . . were typically well-known in their regions, an enormous advantage given the short time-frame for campaigning and the expense of advertising . . . [They] were also able to use the resources of their institutions for gathering the necessary signatures to register candidates and for campaigning . . . The local media were often under the de facto control of local administrators who could use this power to restrict access by political outsiders. (pp. 247–8)

Table 9.6 presents a breakdown of occupations for 3283 deputies from the 85 regions for which we have data for 2000. These overall patterns generally corroborate Slider's findings. Most male deputies are either economic leaders

Table 9.6. Occupational breakdown by gender of regional deputies (Numbers and percentages)[1]

Occupation	Male	Female	Total
Economic leaders	1210	46	1256**
	40.6%	15.2%	38.3%
Political leaders	631	55	686
	21.2%	18.2%	20.9%
Head professionals	399	96	495**
	13.4%	31.7%	15.1%
Administrators	208	24	232
	7.0%	7.9%	7.1%
Interest group	164	28	192**
representatives	5.5%	9.2%	5.8%
Professionals	144	43	187**
	4.8%	14.2%	5.7%
Managers	139	3	142%
	4.7%	1.0%	4.3%
Marginals	33	5	38
	1.1%	1.7%	1.2%
Military/police	35	1	36
	1.2%	0.3%	1.1%
Employee/workers	17	2	19
	0.6%	0.7%	0.6%
Total	2980	302	3283
	100.0%	100.0%	100.0%

** The difference in proportions meets tests of statistical significance at the $p < 0.01$ level.
[1] Occupational codes and definitions are from Slider (1996).

or political leaders. Using a difference of proportions test, we find recruitment patterns for female deputies are significantly different from those of male deputies. By far the most important occupation among women is head professional (heads of schools, hospitals, etc.). Women are significantly less likely to be economic managers or leaders ($p < 0.01$), and thus cannot take advantage of financial and other resources these positions confer on would-be candidates. Women are significantly ($p < 0.01$) more likely to be head professionals, professionals, or interest group representatives. Thus, it appears that women who are well known in their regions can turn their visibility into an electoral advantage. This finding reinforces the regression model's finding that constituents per deputy is an important factor, with women doing better in smaller places.

Information from personal interviews with female deputies to the Karelian Republic and Arkhangelsk Oblast assemblies provides additional evidence supporting this finding. Eight of ten women interviewed were school directors at some point in their careers and identified support from parents and students as crucial to their electoral success. Informants also noted that it was becoming progressively more difficult for women, who rely on their local name recognition and personal constituent work as electoral resources, to be competitive in urban races. Male candidates with either personal or special interest financial backing increasingly dominate such races. These women also observed that electoral campaigns were becoming increasingly 'dirty', with devious tricks and corruption playing a more prominent role.

When looking at the individual characteristics of legislators, a common question in the Western literature is whether the need to raise a family delays the start of a woman's political career and diminishes the age at which women are politically active. To examine this question in the Russian regions, we looked at the age distribution of male and female deputies. In general, women legislators in other countries tend to be older, because women pursue politics after their children are grown.

We find a similar pattern in the Russian regions. Among female regional deputies, 5.7 per cent were under 40 (none were under 30), 43.1 per cent were between 40 and 50, 45.8 per cent were between 51 and 60, and 5.4 per cent were over 60. Among male regional deputies, 10.9 per cent were under 40 (1.2 per cent of those were under 30), 40.0 per cent were between 40 and 50, 36.7 per cent were between 50 and 60, and 12.4 per cent were over 60. Two things stand out in the data. As predicted there are few female deputies in their twenties and thirties. Only 5.7 per cent of female deputies as opposed to 10.9 per cent of male deputies, are younger than 40 (sig. of difference of proportions, $p < 0.01$). This is as expected and is consistent with our suspicion that women tend to start political careers later than men. More surprisingly, we also see a significant difference among elderly politicians. While 12.4 per cent of male deputies are over 60 years of age, only 5.4 per cent of the women are this age ($p < 0.01$). This is especially striking when one considers that the Russian population over the age of 60 is overwhelmingly female.

Interviews with female deputies in Karelia and Arkhangelsk provide corroborating evidence on the issue of age and political careers; the majority of women were married and had children, but most were in their fifties and their children were already grown. A few were in their forties and had children at home. Informants noted that female deputies generally had help from female relatives at home. Husbands were generally supportive of wives' political careers, although several of the deputies were divorced.

When we consider the role and power in regional legislatures, it is reasonable to conclude that people do not serve in these assemblies primarily for pay and power. First, the assemblies are 'amateur'. A small number of deputies meet on a continual basis, but the majority are part-timers. Therefore, relative to high administrators and other government executives, and relative to their professional occupations, representatives receive low pay. Second, real policy and decision-making power generally lies with the executives. A legislative position could be valued because service in the regional legislature can be a springboard to positions in the national legislature or executive positions at the national and regional levels (McFaul, Petrov, and Ryabov 1999). Furthermore, my interviews suggest that some of the businessmen in the legislature were there to promote their business interests. It is most likely, however, that people decide to run for legislative office for the prestige involved and the opportunity to serve constituents.

In interviews with representatives in Karelia and Arkhangelsk, all ten female deputies cited the opportunity to make a real difference in people's lives, to 'do something for people', as the main reason they ran for office. Many of them regarded politics as a 'dirty business', but said that if women were not responsible for their own well-being and the well-being of children, pensioners, invalids, and other marginal groups, society would be worse off. The female deputies did not regard themselves as feminists, but they did believe they were strong and extremely capable. They reported having good working relationships with their male colleagues, and most did not feel disadvantaged or discriminated against in their work.

❖ Conclusions

The Russian regions present a picture of great diversity in terms of women's access to political power. Political geographers often define areas of a country in terms of centre, semi-periphery, and periphery. These labels refer both to the physical proximity to the centres of political power and the level of influence a region has over the course of political events in the country as a whole. Table 9.7 presents the representation levels according to economic regions and in terms of centre, semi-periphery, and periphery, classified roughly by their distance from the Moscow–St. Petersburg axis. As the table clearly shows, women have done much better in peripheral regions than in the central regions. This was unexpected. I had initially predicted that the economic factors often associated with being in the centre would lead to there being a larger pool of elite women with the resources and interest necessary to compete for political office. The economic variables, however, had very little effect on women's representation. The political factors dominated the model, and while many work individually in ways similar to what has been found in other countries, the overall pattern is uniquely Russian.

To search for an explanation as to why the peripheries in the East and North should prove to have more fertile ground for women, we can examine the results of our previous analyses. In terms of economic development, such regions do not depend upon agriculture, and the types of industrialization

Table 9.7. Representation by economic region

Economic region	Centre/periphery	Number of regions included	Av. % women
Eastern Siberia	Periphery	10	17.02
Far Eastern	Periphery	10	16.47
Northern	Semi-periphery	6	14.01
Central	Centre	13	11.07
Western Siberia	Periphery	9	10.88
Urals	Semi-periphery	8	9.11
Northwestern	Centre	5	7.43
Volga	Centre	8	7.27
Volga-Vlatka	Semi-periphery	5	6.10
North Caucasus	Semi-periphery	9	5.48
Central-Black Earth	Centre	5	4.64

and urbanization[12] that characterize them are conducive to less conservative politics and less traditional attitudes toward women than those of the 'red belt' regions of central and southern Russia. Furthermore, the statistically significant variables all work in favour of women in these peripheral regions. Culturally, northern and eastern regions have lower proportions of Muslims than those in the mid-section and southern regions. Therefore, they have a less aggressively anti-woman political culture. On McFaul and Petrov's support for reform scale, the peripheries score higher than either the centre or semi-periphery. In addition, the political institutions are arranged in the peripheries in the manner that works best for women. Multimember districts that benefit women are more common in the peripheries. Perhaps most important is that representatives come from relatively small population districts. As noted when we looked at the legislators' individual characteristics, men were much more likely to be economic leaders or managers. Women, on the other hand, were far more likely to be head professionals or professionals.

I believe women who are highly educated and prominently placed professionals are already known among voters as local notables. In smaller districts where the costs of running a campaign are modest and it is possible to meet a significant number of the voters, women are able to compensate for their economic disadvantages through personal contacts. In larger districts, however, it becomes necessary to have effective economic backing. This means it is harder for women and easier for men, especially those who serve as economic leaders, to gain access.[13] Both of these are important factors benefiting women in the periphery.

On the negative side, in terms of women's future electoral prospects, there is a downward trend in the proportions of women getting elected over time. Several developments give grounds for pessimism that this downward slide will not soon change. These include the Federal Duma's passage of a new law on electoral systems that requires candidates for single member district seats to be nominated by formally recognized political parties (and the concurrent readings of similar laws in regional assemblies). Moreover, there is evidence that shows that increasingly more money is needed by candidates to get elected, especially in urban constituencies. Women candidates do not have the same resources as men, as our occupational and party data attest. Women could be viable candidates given their qualifications and experience. Over the short- to medium-term, however, the barriers to future party selection and access to the kinds of resources necessary to get elected may be too formidable for most women to overcome.

❖ NOTES

1 The author wishes to thank the Fulbright Scholar Program and Linfield College for providing travel and research support for this work. Larisa P. Shvets and Valentina Rusanova of the Karelian State Pedagogical University, Elena V. Kudriashova of the Pomor State University (Arkhangelsk), and Vladimir A. Lavrov at the Russian Central Electoral Commission were instrumental in providing access to data and most helpful in providing their insights. Zach Bowen provided excellent research assistance help.

2 The McFaul and Petrov scale regarding level of support for political reform is also presented in Table 9.1, and will be described in detail later in the chapter.

3 After his election as Russian president in March 2000, Vladimir Putin pursued a policy of recentralization. See Brown (2001) and Petrov (2001).

4 Data have been collected from several sources including the Russian Central Electoral Commission, the Russian Federation State Statistical Commission (Goskomstat), the Panorama website (http://www.panorama.ru:8100/works/regs. html), The Women's Information Network website (http://www.owl.ru/win/winet/ Russian/Organiz/Contents/Area/main.html), and from the Norwegian Institute of International Affairs, Centre for Russian Studies website(http://www.nupi.no/ RUSSLAND/DATABASE/start.htm). The most useful source of information on the individual characteristics of deputies was the Panorama website. Panorama is a non-profit organization specializing in political analysis, funded by the National Endowment for Democracy.

5 Individual deputy data were available for 85 of the 89 regions. The missing regions were Chechnya, the Buryat Republic, Kabardino-Balkaria, and Nizhegorod Oblast. Data on some variables, such as age and occupation, were also missing for a few additional regions.

6 An additional criterion for union republics was a border with a foreign country.

7 Soon after the Russian Federation became a nation-state, the 'Autonomous Republics' assemblies dropped the 'autonomous' from their names.

8 Two exceptions are Khanty-Mansi A. O. and Yamal-Nenets A. O., both in Tyumen Oblast. Their elections are not 'controlled', and more closely resemble those of strong reformist regions. Their ethnic populations are small, relatively urban, and have large oil and natural gas reserves. They are coded as strong reformist.

9 The six regions on which we have information are skewed, as five are ethnic republics (Bshkortostan, Komi, Dagestan, North Osetia-Alania, Udmurtia) and the sixth is an oblast located in Western Siberia (Kemerovo).

10 The difference between 'nominated by a group of voters' and 'independent' has to do with who is responsible for gathering the signatures needed to place the name on the ballot. In the first instance, someone other than the candidate is responsible. In the second, the candidate is responsible.

11 Indicative of this are the words of Gennadi Zyuganov, who finished second to Boris Yeltsin in the 1996 presidential election. In an interview with ITAR-TASS on International Women's Day in 1998, he said he preferred women 'who do not ask too many questions and, after offering advice, do not come back the next day to see whether it has been acted on. In general, women should not argue about critical issues'. Calling women who are both clever and pretty 'frightful', he nevertheless complimented the 18 female Communists in Parliament for being 'charming and attractive' and said that he would include them in his proposed 'government of national trust'.

12 Industrialization in these regions is based on extraction of metals, logging, etc. People who would have flocked to the cities in the Soviet period could not have made their living from farming to the same degree as in the more central regions.

13 As a very preliminary test of this, the correlation between log of population per district and having a former economic leader as the representative is positive (albeit small) and statistically significant ($r = 0.08$, $p < 0.01$).

10 ❖ Establishing a Machocracy: Women and Elections in Macedonia (1990–8)

Karolina Ristova

In 1991, Macedonia declared not only its independence from the former Yugoslav federation, but also its transition to a market economy and representative political democracy. As in the other former socialist countries, one of the most interesting and least examined features of the democratic transition is the decrease in women's political representation. The first three post-communist elections through 1998 produced between three and seven per cent female representation. Those figures placed the Macedonian *Sobranie* among the least equitable of the European parliaments. Rather than establishing the 'rule of the people', democratization in Macedonia seemed to have ratified a 'machocracy', rule by men. This chapter will show that machocracy has deep roots. Macedonia is marked by a traditionalist political culture that emerges from and is reinforced by the socio-demographic and economic structure of the nation. This prevailing culture has been enshrined in the legal and party frameworks adopted in the transition. Taken together, these factors help us to explain both the low supply of and the low demand for female candidates.

❖ BACKGROUND

Women did not achieve the franchise in Macedonia until 1944, and there was never a forceful female suffrage movement. Furthermore, unlike several other Eastern European states, women were never well represented in the Macedonian parliament in the socialist period, but they were present. Even these modest levels of representation appear to have been lost with the advent of democracy (see Table 10.1).

In part, the decrease in women's parliamentary representation can be explained by the differences between the old and the new political system.

Table 10.1. Gender structure of the Macedonian *Sobranie*, election results 1974–98[1]

Election year	1974	1978	1982	1986	1990	1994	1998
Total number of MPs	237	250	250	247	120	120	120
Men	200	219	222	204	115	116	111
Women	37	31	28	43	5	4	9
Per cent women	15.6	12.4	11.2	17.4	4.2	3.3	7.5

[1] Data taken from the Statistical Yearbook of the Republic of Macedonia 1998, Statistical office of Macedonia, Skopje, December 1998, pp. 52–61.

During the socialist period Macedonia was a member state of the Yugoslavian federation. Macedonia and the other member states of the federation had powers that were specified in the federal and state constitutions. These powers included the establishment of their own political institutions, including a state parliament, and representation in the federal parliament. The electoral procedure for the tri-cameral Macedonian parliament was complicated and bureaucratized. Its main aim was to provide corporate representation of different socioeconomic organizations and institutions of the 'working people'. The recruitment and selection process was guided by the principle of 'representation by key', an informal quota system aimed at maximizing descriptive representation. In this way, women were guaranteed a presence in the legislature, but for reasons outlined in the opening chapters of this volume, this was only token representation.

The first multi-party and democratic elections in 1990 produced a new approach to women's representation. Representation 'by key' was strongly rejected by all newly formed political parties as an artificial criterion for selection and nomination of candidates, something that belonged to the communist past.

In November 1991, the Macedonian parliament adopted the first constitution of Macedonia as an independent state. This constitution envisioned Macedonia as a parliamentary democracy and was an important step in the direction of political democratization. The election results from 1994, however, did not reflect a democratization of the process in terms of women's representation in the parliament. The aversion toward affirmative action continued to dominate the electoral process and only four members in the 120-seat legislature were women.

At the level of government, women continued a pattern of underrepresentation that existed even during the communist era. In the 1990–2 'expert government' not a single woman held a government portfolio. Since then, the number has gone as high as three (around 11 per cent). It is interesting to note that none of the female ministers in the period between 1990 and 1998 were candidates in popular elections. For the most part, they were members of the party leaderships who were promised a government position if they did not run in the elections.[1] What this suggests is, that while there are avenues for women to access power, electoral politics is not yet a particularly amenable path. Several factors conspire to discourage women from becoming aspirants and to prevent party gatekeepers from widely nominating women. We begin with the institutional framework of democratic politics.

❖ ELECTORAL RULES

Initially, democratic elections for parliament were conducted under a two-round majoritarian system. According to the 1990 Electoral Law,[2] the 120 seats in the parliament were distributed based on the votes in the 120 single member districts. In order to be elected, a candidate needed to win 51 per cent of the ballots cast, provided this represented at least one-third of the total number of registered voters in the district. Failing that, a second round of elections was to be held 14 days later, at which time only the candidates who won at least seven per cent of the votes in the first round could compete. In the second round, the candidate who received 51 per cent of the votes from all the ballots cast won the seat. For reasons described in Chapter 2, this system—a small legislature apportioned entirely on the basis of winner-take-all districts—should have been very unfriendly toward female candidates. As Table 10.2 shows, it was. Women won only three to four per cent of the legislative seats. With the introduction of a mixed majoritarian system in 1998,[3] the number of women elected nearly doubled.

Under the 1998 rules, 35 seats were distributed according to the percentage of votes that the parties won in a single nationwide constituency, using the D'Hondt formula and a five per cent electoral threshold. Party lists were closed and the system was not compensatory. The remaining 85 seats were determined according to the old two-round majoritarian system. As the table clearly shows, the new PR element (albeit small) had noticeable ramifications for women's recruitment. In addition to nearly doubling the number of female MPs, PR also had a positive effect on the *nomination* of women. The number of female candidates was almost twice as high on the party lists as in the single member districts. If one has in mind that between 1994 and 1998 there were no significant changes in the other factors that influence women's representation, it becomes clear that the electoral system itself had a direct influence on this increase. It may have encouraged more women to come forward as aspirants by lowering the costs of running. It certainly affected party strategies about whether or not to nominate women.

❖ KAROLINA RISTOVA

Table 10.2. Number of female candidates and elected MPs according to the electoral system, parliamentary elections of 1990, 1994, and 1998[1]

	1990		1994		1998	
	Majoritarian electoral system		Majoritarian electoral system		Combined electoral system	
Female candidates	59/1157	5.1%	126/1775	7.1%	152/1401	10.8%
Female candidates on party lists	—	—	—	—	99/785	12.6%
Female candidates in single member districts	59/1157	5.1%	126/1775	7.1%	53/616	8.6%
Total number of female MPs	5/120	4.2%	4/120	3.3%	9/120	7.5%
Female MPs from party lists	—	—	—	—	4/35	11.4%
Female MPs from single member districts	5/120	4.2%	4/120	3.3%	5/85	5.9%

[1] Data taken from: Statistical Yearbook of Republic of Macedonia 1994, Statistical Office of Macedonia, Skopje, 1994; Parlamentarni izbori 98-Konecni rezultati, Drzavna izborna komisija, Skopje, 1999.

In Macedonia, as a legacy of authoritarianism, nominations have always been centralized in all political parties. The experience from the 1998 election, however, confirms that the party leaderships have somewhat different considerations when nominating candidates for the party lists and for the single member districts. Having the support of the local party branch is an important factor for a district candidate, and local party leaderships tend to be conservative. The composition of the party lists, on the other hand, depends primarily on national party leaders. Party programmes and leadership take centre stage in the campaign, and individual candidates become secondary players. This enables party gatekeepers (if they are so inclined) to show more sensitivity toward demands for higher women's representation without frustrating any local party figures or intraparty demands. Due to the fragmented nature of the nascent party system, most parties have been forced to make electoral pacts in the majoritarian contests and therefore to appease the (mostly male) leaders of more than one party. On the other hand, under the PR rule, the larger parties can field lists on their own, and that gives women in the parties more chances to become candidates. Woman of the Albanian minority exemplify this point. In 1998, not one woman received a nomination from the Albanian parties in a single member district, all of the Albanian female candidates appeared on the party lists.

The 1998 elections also suggest that mixed rules may help women in a couple of less obvious ways. First, the electoral system did not allow for a candidate to run both in a single member district and on a party list. This created additional 'space' for female candidates. When local party (male) leaders secure their placement on the party list, they become more willing to let women run in the single member districts. In the 1998 elections, three out of five women candidates in single member districts were elected in 'safe districts' reserved for local party leaders that had moved to become candidates on the party lists. In the second place, since parties shifted their resources to the party lists, the individual electoral campaigns in the single member districts became marginalized, and consequently, less expensive. Women, who have access to fewer personal economic resources than men, may benefit from the shift. Finally, the constitutional ban on concurrent membership in parliament and government could help women to enter parliament through the 'back door'. Though women in the 1998 elections were generally placed in lower positions than men on the party lists,[4] women who made it to the list still sometimes had realistic chances to become members of parliament. The government is typically composed of prominent party leaders, those placed in top-10 positions on party lists. If a party participates in the formation of a new government, which in Macedonia is quite sizeable, most of these leaders move to the government and have to be replaced by candidates lower on the closed party lists. This does not help to explain the increased success of women in the 1998 elections,[5] but this 'mechanism' could benefit women's representation in future elections.

The obvious benefit of the PR element in the 1998 election begs the question: Would the implementation of a pure proportional electoral system drastically improve women's representation in Macedonia? In considering this question, the experience of PR on the level of local elections is suggestive.[6] In Macedonia, the local self-government has narrow communal competencies, local council members are paid significantly less than the members of parliament, and the political parties tend to nominate less influential and younger party members to run in the local elections. These factors, coupled with PR electoral rules, ought to produce the ideal conditions for female recruitment. However, the data presented in Table 10.3 show that, although the percentage of female candidates and municipal council members is higher than on the national level, it is not drastically higher. Even with woman-friendly electoral rules, there are still significant obstacles to women's access to political decision-making.

❖ PARTIES AS GATEKEEPERS

The literature suggests that one barrier to female recruitment may be the parties themselves. The Macedonian party system is still fluid in many respects.

❖ KAROLINA RISTOVA

Table 10.3. Female candidates and elected members on municipal councils, local election results for 1996[1]

Political party	Female candidates		Female members in the municipal councils	
Social-Democratic Alliance	136/1596	8.5%	39/503	7.8%
Socialist Party	122/1323	9.2%	11/155	7.1%
VMRO—DPMNE	68/1365	5.0%	22/350	6.3%
Liberal Party	112/1099	10.2%	12/105	11.4%
Democratic Party	90/1227	7.3%	8/119	6.7%
Party for Democratic Prosperity	13/624	2.1%	1/158	0.6%
Party for Democratic Prosperity of Albanians	15/551	2.7%	3/117	2.6%
Party for Emancipation of Gypsy	15/228	6.6%	0/3	0
Democratic Party of Turks	9/296	3.04%	0/35	0
Democratic Party of Serbs	18/168	10.7%	0/7	0
Total (including other minor political parties)	1230/12724	9.7%	105/1720	6.1%

[1] Data taken from: Statistical Yearbook of the Republic of Macedonia 1997, Statistical Office of Macedonia, Skopje, December 1997.

Party pluralism was introduced with the 1990 constitutional amendments, both to the Yugoslavian and Macedonian Constitutions, which ended the political monopoly of the Communist Party (Communist Alliance of Macedonia). Its timing echoed the revolutionary changes in the political land-scape throughout Eastern Europe and it was viewed as an inevitable historic turn even among certain groups in the party leadership of the Communist Party. The party renamed itself the 'Party for Democratic Transformation' (SKM-PDP) and embarked on internal reforms. These reforms, however, did not prevent the internal disintegration process. Many previous members of the party and the party leadership formed or joined other political parties. By the first multi-party elections held in October 1990, there were 20 regis-tered political parties in Macedonia; 18 took part in the elections.[7] The orienta-tion towards developing a multi-party system was confirmed with the Constitution of 1991. Ever since, the development of the Macedonian party system has been a highly dynamic process of party formation, unification, and division.[8] Only a few of these parties, however, have a significant impact on the political and election processes.

In their party programs, all of the Macedonian parties use liberal rhetoric: All parties stand for market economy, privatization, individual rights, and establishing a democratic political system. In political practice, however, when in opposition, political parties use a more leftist and populist rhetoric to attack the very same liberal policies, arguing then that the processes of privatization and marketization must not be carried out at the expense of the social rights of citizens and the social and economic functions of the state.

Although cleavages and ideology prove problematic in the characterization of post-communist parties, it can be said that the main Macedonian political parties include a centre-left Social-Democratic Alliance (SDSM), a more populist-nationalist VMRO—DPMNE, and a set of primordial cleavage parties representing the substantial (23 per cent) Albanian minority.

Social-Democratic Alliance of Macedonia (SDSM) has a legal continuity with the transformed communist party (SKM-PDP), which renamed itself in 1991. The party subscribes to the 'positive legacy' of the old regime and the partisan Communist movement that led to recognition of Macedonian statehood in the Yugoslav federation after Second World War. However, the party denies any exclusive personal, political or ideological legacy to the Communist Party; the Communist legacy, it believes, is an equal inheritance of all the newly formed political parties. The SDSM was a leading party in the government coalitions in the periods of 1992–4, 1994–6, and 1996–8. In the economic sphere, the party has pushed for a model of paid privatization and wide liberalization of the economy, which resulted in huge social stresses and widespread political and economic corruption. After losing the elections in 1998, this party has been attempting to adopt a more traditional social-democratic political agenda.

International Macedonian Revolutionary Organization—Democratic Party for Macedonian National Unity (VMRO—DPMNE)[9] was formed in 1990 and until 1998 it was the main opposition party in national politics and the dominant party at the local level. Its rhetoric had been strongly nationalist and populist. It pushed aggressively for independence from the Yugoslav federation and adoption of a 'nation-state' constitution. It attacked the government for cooperation with the Albanian parties and for providing 'extremely wide minority rights'. It considered the Albanian minority as a separatist ethnic group because of the rhetoric and the acts of some illegal Albanian separatist groups. In the period of 1997–8, however, VMRO—DPMNE changed its policy towards the national minorities and focused only on the economic failures and corruption of the government. In 1998, the coalition of VMRO—DPMNE and Democratic Alternative formed a coalition government, which was then joined by the Party for Democratic Prosperity of the Albanians.

The third group of major players on the Macedonian political scene is the political parties of the Albanian minority: *The Party for Democratic Prosperity* (PDP) and *the Party for Democratic Prosperity of the Albanians* (PDPA). PDP was formed in 1990 and is considered a 'moderate' Albanian party, which seeks higher representation of the Albanian minority in state institutions. It was part of the coalition government with the coalition 'Alliance for

Macedonia' in the period of 1992–4, 1994–6, and 1996–8. PDPA was formed in 1996 from a fraction of the PDP. It opposes the minority status and rights of the Albanians and seeks recognition as a 'constitutive nation' of Macedonia.[10] Its declared political aim is eventual confederalization of Macedonia. Most of the other political parties view this as an extremist demand, yet after 1998 the VMRO—DPMNE, one of its main critics, invited it to help form a government. Apart from questions concerning the status of the Albanians in Macedonia, the PDP and PDPA do not differ in their political agenda from the other political parties. In addition, the maximalist rhetoric of both parties seems to shift depending on whether the party is participating in the government or in the opposition.

There are political parties of the other national minorities such as the *Party for Emancipation of Gypsies, Democratic Party of Serbs,* and the *Democratic Party of Turks,* but they are far less vocal or influential than the political parties of the Albanian minority. Also, these minorities are much more open to join the political parties dominated by the Macedonian majority. Several other parties, such as the *Liberal-Democratic Party*[11] and *Democratic Alternative*[12] claim the centre between SDSM and VMRO-DPMNE and have played the role of kingmaker in the formation of governments.

❖ The attitudes of the political parties towards the 'women's question'

When we look at party programs, membership structures, and parties' records on nominations, the lack of concern for women as a constituency across the parties is evident. There is some evidence that the liberal and socialist left, and some of the less relevant political parties, are more amenable to women. But the overwhelming picture is that of male-oriented parties.

In their everyday rhetoric, all parties represented in the parliament declare their dedication to gender equality. The electoral programs, however, are much better indicators of the importance that these political parties give to the 'women's question'. It is notable that, with each subsequent election, the interest of the political parties in women's issues has been growing, at least at a declaratory level. In 1990, the major political parties only mentioned women in the context of family relations. In 1994 and 1998, the electoral programs covered a much broader range of issues concerning gender relations and the status of women (e.g., improving women's political representation, and protection of employment rights). This was true across parties. There are no significant ideological differences among the political parties in their views on women's role in society, though there are some differences of approach depending on the ethnic structure of the party. Parties dominated by the Macedonian majority address issues of concern to women in general. Political parties of the national minorities show preference for issues and matters of concern to women belonging to the respective national minorities (e.g., women's education and emancipation from traditional family roles). A common characteristic of all political parties' programs is they approach the women's question on a declaratory level. There is a noticeable absence of concrete measures to back the declared policies.

Although there are no data about the gender structure of the membership of the political parties, it is commonly recognized that fewer women join political parties than men, especially in the political parties of the Albanian and Gypsy minorities. The gender structure is more balanced in the youth organizations of the parties, which very often have female leaders, especially the Social-Democratic Youth and the Liberal-Democratic Youth.

The data in Table 10.4 show that the smaller parliamentary political parties of the centre have much better women's representation in their party organs than the two major political parties; the Albanian parties lag even further behind. In comparing the smaller centre parties with the two major parties, there are two plausible explanations for this internal representation gap. First, smaller parties have fewer chances to win seats in the parliament and, consequently, the power struggle is far lower than in the bigger parties. Second, these parties have to struggle much harder for political support and one way to attract voters, especially among the youth, is to present themselves as 'modern' and 'European', which also means delivering on better women's representation.

When we look at the actual record of parties with regard to nominating women, we can see the affirmative rhetoric of the Macedonian political parties on women's participation is drastically different from their nomination

Table 10.4. Women's representation in the highest party bodies and functions in the parliamentary political parties after the 1998 elections

Political parties	Democratic Alternative (%)	Liberal-Democratic party (%)	Social-Democratic Alliance (%)	VMRO—DPMNE (%)	Party for Democratic Prosperity of Albanians (%)	Party for Democratic Prosperity (%)
President	0	0	0	0	0	0
Vice-President(s)	100 (2/2)	50 (1/2)	33.3 (1/3)	100 (1/1)	0	0
Secretary General	100 (1/1)	0	0	0	0	0
Central party organ	40.3	22.2	14.7	2.8	3	2.3
Executive organ	31.6	14.3	26.7	7.1	1	0

❖ KAROLINA RISTOVA

practices. Tables 10.5 and 10.6 do show that the Socialists, the Liberals, and the Democratic Alternative post a better record on female recruitment than the more right-wing parties and the ethnic minority parties.

If political parties have a commitment to gender equity they have the capacity to recruit female candidates due to the centralization of the nomination procedure in all parties. The nomination of candidates is regulated by party statutes and *ad hoc* election rules, which mostly concentrate on the nomination criteria. The nomination procedure is almost identical in all political parties (Mojanovski 1996). The local party branches give proposals for potential candidates, especially in regard to the single member districts, to a Nomination Commission, which is selected by the executive organ of the party and affirmed by the highest party body between two party conferences/congresses. This commission, in regular consultation with the party leadership, nominates the candidates, both for single member districts and the party lists. The nominated candidates are formally confirmed by the party conference/congress. Although theoretically the nominated candidates can be challenged by the conference/congress, experience shows the confirmation process is mostly of ceremonial character. Any challenge to nominations occurs during the drawing up of lists, both in formal ways (party meetings,

Table 10.5. Female party/party coalition candidates in the single member districts in the 1994 parliamentary elections[1]

Party/party coalition	Total number of candidates	Female candidates	Percentage of female candidates
Social-Democratic Alliance	7	0	0
Liberal Party	8	0	0
Socialist Party	3	0	0
Social-Democratic Alliance/Liberal Party/Socialist Party	108	4	3.7
VMRO—DPMNE	119	12	10.1
Democratic Party	115	6	5.2
Party of Democratic Prosperity	55	1	1.8
Party for Emancipation of Gypsies	24	1	4.2
Democratic Party of Serbs	13	0	0
Democratic Party of Turks	54	2	3.7

[1] This table contains data for only the most significant parties that took part in the 1994 parliamentary elections. Data taken from: Statistical Yearbook of Republic of Macedonia 1994, Statistical Office of Macedonia, Skopje, December 1994; data from 1990 parliamentary elections were not available.

ESTABLISHING A MACHOCRACY IN MACEDONIA ❖

Table 10.6. Female party/party coalition candidates in the 1998 parliamentary elections: single member and proportional list[1]

Party/party coalition	Single member districts			Proportional representation lists		
	Total number of candidates	Female candidates	Percentage of female candidates	Total number of candidates	Female candidates	Percentage of female candidates
Social-Democratic Alliance	75	2	2.7	35	6	17.1
Liberal-Democratic Party/ Democratic Party of Macedonia	84	4	4.8	35	8	22.9
Socialist Party[2]	56	8	14.3	35	5	14.3
Socialist Party/Party for Emancipation of Gypsies/ Democratic Party of Turks[2]	11	0	0	–	–	–
VMRO—DPMNE/ Democratic Alternative	69	6	8.7	35	4	11.4
Democratic Alternative	9	1	11.1	35	9	25.7
Party for Democratic Prosperity[3]	26	0	0	35	4	11.4
Party for Democratic Prosperity of Albanians/People's Democratic Party[3]	13	0	0	–	–	–
Democratic Party of Serbs	9	1	11.1	35	5	14.3

[1] Data taken from: Parlamentarni izbori 1998—konecni rezultati, Drzavna izborna komisija, Skopje, February 1999.
[2] The Socialist party ran a joint list for the proportional section of the electoral system with the Party for Emancipation of Gypsies, Democratic Party, Democratic Progressive Party of Gypsies, and the Democratic Party of Turks.
[3] The PDP and PDPA along with the People's Democratic Party ran a joint list for the proportional section of the electoral system.

communications to the nomination commission) and informal ways. Thus, if the party leadership is convinced that more women as candidates would bring more votes, the number of women candidates can be increased with no special effort. The question then is, what makes women attractive candidates for party gatekeepers?

❖ WOMEN AND FACTORS THAT MAKE AN 'IDEAL CANDIDATE'

Mojanovski (1996) finds there are several criteria that all major political parties use to identify 'ideal candidates', such as, university education, respected professions, successful businesses, financial contributions to the party and the public profile of the candidate. In the Macedonian political culture, politics is generally viewed as an activity reserved for those who have a university education. This is a legacy of the countries' past struggle with illiteracy[13] and the communist party's ideology that proclaimed that the communist state could be reached only by mass education and leadership by an educated political elite. This view has become even stronger in the transition. As a result, and as Table 10.7 shows, parties nominate and voters elect well-educated candidates. In 1998, 29.9 per cent of the candidates had a high school education or less, but only 2.5 per cent of the elected MPs had this level of education. Consequently, quite 'educated parliaments' were established in the recent years. The same conclusion can be drawn for all the Macedonian governments in this period.[14]

Education appears to be particularly important for women: in all three elections, all of the nominated women candidates held a university degree.[15] Women without university education appear to have no chance of being nominated or elected. Men with lower education have fewer chances than men with university education, but there are some cases of men with only high school education who become party candidates and get elected to the parliament. The situation is exactly the same at the level of local elections. Statistical data show that all the candidates and elected members in municipal councils held in 1990 and 1996 who only had elementary or high school education were men, all the women had university degrees. The same bias exists at the national cabinet level also; all the female members in the governments in the past eight years held a doctoral degree, and that was certainly not the case with their male counterparts.

Since the mid-1970s, women have constituted at least 50 per cent of university students, sometimes even surpassing the men's share. This tendency remains unchanged after the transition. The number of female post-graduate students, however, has always been lower, especially at the level of doctoral studies where in the period from 1990 to 1998 the average per cent of women

Table 10.7. Education level of candidates and elected members in the *Sobranie*, 1990–8[1]

| | Candidates | | | | | | Elected MPs | | | | | |
| | 1990 | | 1994 | | 1998 | | 1990 | | 1994 | | 1998 | |
	N	%	N	%	N	%	N	%	N	%	N	%
Elementary school	29	2.6	130	7.1	37	3.1	0	0	0	0	0	0
High school	163	14.5	338	18.4	324	26.8	9	7.5	6	5	3	2.5
Bachelor's degree	770	68.3	1215	66.1	674	55.8	84	70	79	65.8	89	74.2
Master's degree	110	9.8	113	6.1	113	9.3	21	17.5	24	20	9	7.5
Doctorate (Ph.D.)	54	4.8	43	2.3	61	5.0	6	5	11	9.2	19	15.8
Total	1126	100	1839	100	1209	100	120	100	120	100	120	100

[1] Data taken from: Statistical Yearbook of the Republic of Macedonia 1991, Statistical Office of Macedonia, Skopje, December 1991, p. 65; Statistical Yearbook of the Republic of Macedonia 1994, Statistical Office of Macedonia, Skopje, December 1994, p. 62; Parlamentarni izbori 1998—Konecni rezultati, Drzavna izborna komisija, Skopje, February 1999.

among doctoral students was 30.9 per cent.[16] In most cases, students finance their own postgraduate studies, and women can afford such studies less than men. In addition, these studies are usually undertaken when students already have families, which creates more problems for women than for men due to traditional gender roles in family life. If women must be more educated than their male counterparts, then this probably diminishes the pool of attractive female candidates.

Due to women's weaker positions in the economy and a traditional political culture, women possess fewer economic resources than men. Political parties are very interested in candidates with a strong economic base and the attached economic and social leverage, influence and connections. While the central party pays for a national campaign, local candidates who wish to run a visible and active campaign usually have to generate most of the funds for the local campaign themselves. When the party is considering candidates, someone who is known to have significant financial resources, or is known to be capable of generating such resources, is likely to be preferred to an equally qualified, but relatively poor potential nominee. This sort of consideration clearly hurts women when the party chooses its candidates.[17]

Given these concerns it is no surprise that parties have drawn candidates rather heavily from businessmen and company managers. In the 1990 elections, 21.8 per cent of the candidates were company managers and businessmen (246 out of 1126 candidates); in the 1994 elections, this number increased to 35.3 per cent (650 out of 1839 candidates), while, in 1998 elections, the number dropped to 16.6 per cent (201 out of 1209 candidates). Unfortunately, it was not possible to break these data down by gender; but the economic position of women in Macedonia has always been and continues to be weaker than that of men. While women made up 38.7 per cent of the overall workforce in 1997, they were only 17.8 per cent of the employers and managers, and only 25.9 per cent of the entrepreneurs.[18]

Female labour force participation is largely a product of the so-called 'shortage economy'. Whatever paid labour might bring in terms of emancipation from traditional social and family roles, it is fundamentally connected to the necessity of female income for family survival. Yet, the evidence suggests that women are less fully integrated in the economy than men; two comprehensive surveys on the labour force conducted in 1996 and 1997 indicated there are almost twice as many women outside the labour force as men.[19]

Women are forced not only to face an extremely difficult unemployment situation, but they also face gender discrimination in the employment sphere. First, many employers take advantage of the high unemployment rate in the country[20] and fail to register new employees in order to avoid paying health care and retirement benefits. Women are more reluctant than men to accept such 'gray employment', because it makes it harder for them to combine work, motherhood, and family obligations without the employment rights and bene-fits. Second, privatization has had an adverse effect on women's employment. There are indications that women face employment discrimination in the newly forming private sector of the economy. Although there are no precise data on the extent of this discrimination, the job announcements in the daily newspapers are quite revealing. In many of these announcements, private employers, alongside other qualifications (e.g. education, age, driver's license, etc.) explicitly state they are looking for male candidates. Imposing such an employment condition is unconstitutional, but there is no record of any legal action for gender discrimination and there are no adequate legal mechanisms that would address such discrimination. In addition, interestingly, there is not much public awareness that the private ownership of a company does not entitle the employer to set any condition that he sees fit. Another indicator of the existence of discrimination in the private sector is that, in 1998, only 30 per cent of the employees in the private sector were women. To many private employers, women employees are more expensive because, in addition to the other employment benefits, all employers are obliged to pay for maternity leave for female employees. It is no coincidence that the unemployment rates are highest among women within the age group of 20–30 years old.

To some extent, these conditions have been inherited from the past; how-ever, the transition to a competitive market economy reinforces machocracy in critical ways. The decreasing demand for women in the labour force, combined with the overall deterioration of the living standard of families caused by unemployment and weakening of the welfare state, are reviving the traditional role of women in rearing children and sustaining the household. Further, women's weakening economic position not only makes them less able to con-tribute direct material resources to party coffers, it also reduces their ability to form and run influential political organizations or to organize campaigns that would channel their interests and promote eligible women candidates (M. Najcevska, T. Arifii, and N. Gaber 1997). As a result, women's chances to become party candidates are significantly crippled. Even when women work, they rarely reach positions that provide public visibility, influence, and con-nections, factors that appeal to party gatekeepers and make an 'ideal candidate'.

The existence of a highly educated female population and substantial female participation in the paid labour force fails to undermine machocracy, girded as it is by attitudes toward gender roles that have been simultane-ously influenced by patriarchy and socialism. Patriarchy promotes a view of a woman as part of and subsumed to her family. Socialism promoted a vision of society where women had the same rights as men and were to be socially and politically engaged. The interaction of these two traditions lead to three paradigms of women's involvement in politics, ranging from attitudes of open disapproval (the model of patriarchal woman), to attitudes of limited acceptance for involvement that does not hinder a woman's role in family life (the model of humanitarian woman), and, finally, to the belief that it does not necessarily harm women to combine career and family life (the model of the 'superwoman'). These three models are reflected through the legal framework regarding women, women's access to political power, and the development of a women's movement.

The democratic transition did not bring any drastic changes in the emancipatory legislation enacted by the former communist regime, and when the International Monetary Fund (IMF) pressured the Macedonian government to shorten the maternity leave, there was energetic public resistance.[21] The model of patriarchal woman has not yet found its way into the legislation. The dual political and (particularly) economic transition, however, is generating new issues of concern to women. The old legislation does not respond well to novel problems like abuses of maternity leave by private employers or the growing incidences of sexual harassment in the workplace. At the same time, existing labour laws fail to provide for effective legal protection against gender-based employment discrimination.

All three cultural models recognize the crucial role of women in the family. This creates concerns among party gatekeepers that women (particularly young women) will lack the time and dedication to politics that men can afford. Potential female aspirants may eschew high profile political involvement for the same reasons. The combination of patriarchal and socialist cultural patterns means that women may be welcomed in parties, but only declaratively and without adequate political support. Interestingly, when voters were asked in a national public opinion poll, after the 1996 local elections, 'What was the most decisive factor in your decision concerning who you will vote for?', characteristics of the individual candidates (specifically personality of the candidate) was of only minor importance. It was mentioned by only 11.8 per cent of the respondents. Voters tended to focus on party programs (34.8 per cent) and party leadership (29.0 per cent).[22] Furthermore, the experience from three elections indicates that women fare about as well as men when placed in winnable constituencies, yet, party gatekeepers still express concern that female candidates will lose votes.

It is true that parties have yet to receive much organized pressure to change this view. The dual legacies of patriarchy and socialism have slowed the development of effective women's pressure groups. In the period of 1990–4, the sharp decline in women's political representation failed to provoke any negative reactions among women and women's organizations. Macedonia was struggling to maintain peace and stability, which were seriously challenged by the war on the territory of former Yugoslavia and by its own diplomatic battle for international recognition as an independent state. Women were more concerned with the safety of their children and families than with their political representation.[23] In addition, the major influence of the socialist egalitarian ideology in the formation of women's political culture has entrenched the belief that women already have equal rights with men and that there are no obstacles to women's political involvement. Significantly, most of the women's organizations that existed prior to 1994 did not deal with the women's political representation and were somewhat confused about their role in a situation of political pluralism. The NGOs in this period understood independence from politics as the total absence of contact with politics and political issues. The 'politics free' attitude of NGOs was also strengthened by their financial dependence on the state budget, which rendered them largely compliant. Finally, women did not feel threatened in a substantial way by their absence from politics, because the process of privatization did not effectively start until late 1993.

The 1994–8 period was marked by increased women's mobilization on the issue of political representation. The issues of peace and stability were less pressing and privatization started to show its side effects. Nine women's organizations were formed in this period and most of them addressed women's status in politics.[24] Women within the parties started to adjust their tune, too. In the aftermath of the 1998 elections, separate women's organizations were formed within three political parties: Liberal-Democratic Party, Democratic Alternative and VMRO—DPMNE.[25] Women of the national minorities, following the trend in the party organizations, formed their own women's organizations. Despite the controversies, this approach proved to be positive because the problems of the Albanian and Gypsy women, for example, are quite distinct from those of the Macedonian women and the women of some of the other national minorities (Vlachs, Turks, Serbs). Women from these two minorities have not even reached the level of elementary emancipation (Kasapi 1994). Their first problem is not political representation, but education, employment, reproductive and marriage rights.

In this recent period, women's organization developed a more aggressive approach in addressing specific women's problems by organizing seminars, conferences, and media campaigns. With the growth of their activities, they have started to realize that without women's political representation and party involvement, nothing serious can be done. As a result, after the local elections in 1996, women's organizations had begun to show much greater interest in the issue of women's representation. Prior to the 1998 parliamentary elections women's organizations were very vocal about the electoral model, pressing for a proportional electoral system, and several organizations launched a joint campaign titled '51 per cent of women in the parliament' as a reminder of the percentage of women's population in Macedonia.

All of these activities represent a symbolic change in women's political culture. Women started to be more aware that 'the rules' have been changed in the transition and that they need to reassess their own position. In the past years of transition, machocracy has benefited from the lack of women's political mobilization and lack of demand for women's representation. However, the new growing demand for higher women's representation should benefit women's representation in future elections, especially because of the new PR component and the centralized nomination procedures of the parties.

❖ PERSPECTIVES

In 1993, the well-known Croatian feminist writer, Slavenka Drakulic, published a book titled '*How We Survived Communism and Even Laughed*', in which she described and criticized the status of women under communism. Now that the transition has swept all over Eastern Europe, women realize that they have survived communism to end up, in many cases, with something worse. Macedonia is just part of the whole picture. Machocracy is only the most vivid example of the overall deterioration of women's status in Macedonian political and economic life. After 10 years of 'transition to democracy', it is high time to ask how women will survive machocracy and even laugh.

Unfortunately, in the short term, not much can be done with respect to the bad economic situation, a crucial factor that enables machocracy to thrive. Furthermore, the increased ethnic tensions within the country and the threats of violent conflict in bordering countries or even within Macedonia itself have made it difficult for issues of gender equality, both in representation and otherwise, to find a prominent place on the political agenda. Still, there is promising evidence that when women mobilize, there is something they can do, especially through the PR component of the electoral system and within certain parties. Organized pressure to recruit more women can help us to increase both the supply of female candidates and the demand of party leaders for such candidates. Finally, the initial experience with the mixed electoral system implemented in the 1998 elections also indicates the wider introduction of PR can help women's representation in Macedonia.

❖ POSTSCRIPT

In fact, the electoral system was changed just prior to the fall 2002 parliamentary elections. All single member district seats were eliminated and the country established six multimember districts. With the significant increase in district magnitude and the establishment of a pure PR system, representation jumped dramatically. Women won 22 of the 120 (18.3%) seats in the Macedonian parliament. Women were also aided by a resurgence in the fortunes of the Social Democratic Alliance of Macedonia which elected a significant number of women. It is worth noting the changes in the electoral system did not occur because of a concern for women's representation, but women were able to take advantage of the improved institutional structure. Women have started learning how to organize and place pressure on the State and the parties. It will be interesting to follow Macedonian politics to see how these newly elected women may be able to influence public policy to the betterment of women in their country.

❖ NOTES

1 Article 9(2) of the Constitution of the Republic of Macedonia from 1991 stipulates: ' The Prime Minster and the ministers cannot be Representatives in the Assembly'.

2 See, Zakon za izbor i otpovikuvanje na pratenici i odbornici, Sluzben vesnik na SRM, br. 28/1990.

3 See, Zakon za izbori na pratenici vo Sobranieto na Republika Makedonija, Sluzben vesnik na RM, br. 24/1998.

4 For example, VMRO—DPMNE, the Social-Democratic Alliance and the coalition of the parties of the Albanian minority (Party for Democratic Prosperity, Party for Democratic Prosperity of Albanians, and People's Democratic Party) had realistic chance to win at least 10 seats in the parliament on the proportional lists. However, the number of female candidates that were placed among the first 10 on the party lists was low: 10% for VMRO—DPMNE, 20% for the Social-Democratic Alliance, and 0% for the coalition of the parties of the Albanian minority. Data taken from: Parlamentarni izbori-konecni rezultati, Drzavna izborna komisija, Skopje, 1999.

5 In 1998, nine women were originally elected to parliament. Two of the elected female MPs became Vice Prime Ministers when the government was formed. Only one of the candidates that moved up to replace MPs that served in the government was a woman. So for the 1998–2002 time period there were only eight women serving in the Sobranie.

6 According to the 1996 Law for Local Elections, the municipal council members are elected from closed party lists in 123 electoral districts, which coincide with the number of municipalities. The seats are distributed by the D'Hondt formula and without an electoral threshold. See, Zakon za lokalni izbori, Sluzben vesnik na RM, br. 46/1996.

7 Data taken from: Janusz Bugajski, *Ethnic Politics in Eastern Europe: A Guide to Nationality Policies, Organizations, and Parties*, The Centre for Strategic and International Studies, Washington, DC, 1994, p. 102.

8 This process can best be illustrated with the changes in the number of the political parties that participated in the elections. In 1990, 18 parties took part in the parliamentary elections. In the 1994 parliamentary elections, that number grew to 38 and then fell to 29 in the 1998 parliamentary elections (Statistical Yearbook of the Republic of Macedonia, Statistical Office of Macedonia, December 1998).

9 The first part of the name (VMRO) is taken from the name of a Macedonian revolutionary organization, which fought for Macedonian independence from the Turkish Empire and Serb and Bulgarian influence in the 19th century.

❖ KAROLINA RISTOVA

10 For example, PDPA wants Albanian to be an official language in Macedonia, not only on the level of local self-government and the state elementary and high school education system, as it is at present, but also on the national level. Also, it has lobbied for a state-financed university for the Albanian minority.

11 The Liberal-Democratic Party was formed in 1996 by uniting the Liberal Party and the Democratic Party. Its first leader, Petar Gosev, was the last president of the Communist Party (SKM-PDP). The current leader is Risto Prenov, the major of Skopje, the capital of Macedonia.

12 Democratic Alternative was formed in 1998. As a result of the charisma of its leader, Vasil Tupurkovski, a well-known law professor and Macedonian politician (president of the Communist Youth of Yugoslavia, last Macedonian member in the Federal presidency, special envoy of the Macedonian President with respect to the recognition of Macedonia by the United States and UN), the party managed to win 13 seats in the Macedonian parliament in the 1998 elections.

13 According to the census of 1948, 29.9% of the population of Macedonia was illiterate. The socialist state invested much in education and placed a great emphasis on education. All levels of education, with almost no restrictions, were accessible to everybody. This policy was a success; according to the census of 1994, the number of illiterate people was reduced to 5.8%. Data taken from: *Polozbata na zenata vo sovremenite opstestveni tekovi*, Organizacijata na zenite na Makedonija, Skopje, 1994, p. 99.

14 In all the transition governments, the percentage of members with university education is 100%. The most 'educated governments' were the expert government (1990–2) in which out of 23 members, 12 were university professors, and the first political government in which out of 22 members, 11 were university professors. Data taken: L.Kitanovski, *Podelba na vlasta*, Aniskop, Skopje, 1996, p. 229.

15 In 1990 elections, out of 1126 candidates, 57 (5.1%) were women; in 1994, out of 1839 candidates, 126 (6.8%) were women; and, in 1998 elections, out of 1209 candidates, 152 (12.5%) were women.

16 Statistical Yearbook of the Republic of Macedonia 1998, Statistical Office of Macedonia, p. 622.

17 Interestingly, this may be part of the explanation for why more women end up on the PR lists than in single member districts. The expectation that a candidate will help fund some of his or her own campaign materials is especially true for candidates in the single member districts. PR candidates are seen more as part of the overall party team and their campaign expenses are part of the total party effort in the country and therefore they are less likely to be expected to contribute funds themselves.

18 Data taken from: Women in Macedonia Through Figures, Statistical Office of Macedonia, Skopje, 1994.

19 Data taken from: Statistical Yearbook of Republic of Macedonia 1998, Statistical Office of Macedonia, Skopje, November 1998, p. 199; National Report for the Fourth World Conference on women, The Government of Republic of Macedonia, April 1995, pp. 15–8.

20 For example, in 1998 the official unemployment rate was 36%.

21 Under Macedonian Law, the mother has a right to nine months paid maternity leave. The IMF wanted Macedonia to cut maternity leave to three months. The only change that was accepted was to give the mother the choice to go back to work after the sixth month of maternity leave, without losing the maternity leave pay.

22 Community problems where I live was mentioned by 9.5% of the respondents, while 14.3% stated they did not vote. See, Natasa Gaber, Aneta Jovevska, *Neophodnost od kombiniranje na izborniot model*, Forum analitika, Skopje, 1997.

23 It comes as no surprise that according to one survey from that period women rated peace much higher than gender equality. Namely, the value system of Macedonian women was as follows: 1. Peace; 2. Honesty; 3. Just financial compensation for one's work; 4. Solidarity; 5. Gender equality; 6. Living standard; 7. Political pluralism. Data taken from: C. Mojanovski, *Socijalniot i politickiot profil na politickite partii vo Makedonija*, Liber, Skopje, 1996.

24 Data taken from: Mirjana Najcevska, Teuta Arifi, Natasa Gaber, *Ucestvoto na zenite vo sovremenite trendovi vo Republika Makedonija*, Fondacija Fridrih Ebert, 1997, pp. 69–102.

25 In the Social-Democratic Alliance, there is only a 'sector for women issues' on the level of the Social-Democratic Youth of Macedonia (SDYM), which is the first and only political organization that since 1995 has introduced mandatory 30% for women's representation for all its organs and functions. See, Karolina Ristova, *Sedum godini SDMM*, Sociajdemokratska mladina na Makedonija, Skopje, 1999, pp. 346–9.

11 ❖ Women in the Polish Sejm: Political Culture and Party Politics versus Electoral Rules

Renata Siemieńska

Duverger in his classic work, *The Political Role of Women* (1955), sought an explanation for women's under-representation in the sexism of voters, in the unwillingness of male cadres to permit women positions traditionally reserved for men, and in the election system itself, which may limit access, to a greater or lesser extent, for women. In post-communist Poland, there is both evidence of a complex interaction of these factors and of their effects changing over time.

The first election of the new millennium represented a dramatic change in the fortunes of women in the Polish parliament (the Sejm). Women's representation in the lower chamber of parliament never exceeded 13 per cent in the decade following the break with the old regime, despite women playing an important role in subverting the communist regime and despite the brief ascendancy of one woman, Hanna Suchocka, to the Prime Ministership in 1992–3. In the 2001 general elections, however, there was a dramatic jump as women gained 20.2 per cent of the seats in the Polish parliament.

What explains the inability of Polish women to gain greater access to power in democratic politics during the 1990s, but a significant increase in access after the turn of the century? At least initially, the prevalence of traditional social values were effective barriers discouraging women from mobilizing pro-equality feminist organizations. Furthermore, these traditional values encouraged party leaders to view women as 'risky' candidates (regardless of whether women actually 'lose votes'). The general absence of a strong women's movement and women in party leadership positions meant that parties did not face substantial pressure to place women in competitive positions on the electoral lists; and top list placement is the one sure predictor of candidate success.

❖ Women's Representation in Polish Parliaments

As elsewhere in the region, the Communist parliament in Poland served a primarily decorative role. The membership composition was set at the top according to a more or less rigorously respected principle that parliament was to be a reflection of society. The presence of female faces was thus ensured, but these women did not represent the best and brightest of Polish society. They had fewer economic, cultural, and social resources at their disposal than male MPs (Bourdieu 1984) and fewer resources than might have been expected, given the educational and occupational attainment of women in Polish society as a whole (Siemieńska 1990, 1996a). Female parliamentarians were younger and less educated than men. The presence of women in the Sejm was accompanied by prejudice and sexism, much of which was expressed by female deputies themselves (Siemieńska 1990). There were changes with the advent of multi-party elections. Although the overall representation of women declined, and women remained largely outside the top leadership circles. The women who did make it were well qualified, genuine representatives of their constituents.

The long-term deliquescence of the Polish United Worker's Party (PUWP) and the rising power of the Solidarity movement led in 1989 to Roundtable Negotiations that established the rules for partly free elections. The PUWP believed it could ensure its control over the contract parliament through the reservation of seats for itself and its auxiliary organizations. The Roundtable established a bicameral Parliament, in which the opposition would be permitted to compete for 35 per cent of the seats in the Sejm (lower chamber), and all the seats in the newly created Senate (upper chamber). Elections were conducted using first-past-the-post electoral rules that the PUWP believed would reinforce its preordained majority. In the end, however, candidates from the Citizens' Committee created by Solidarity leader Lech Walesa, swept the contested seats in the Sejm and won 99 of 100 seats in the Senate.

Women did not fare so well. The majoritarian electoral system used for the lower house was certainly unfavourable. Moreover it is fair to say that none of the major actors in transition viewed women's issues as particularly relevant compared to the exigencies of a dual political and economic transition. Women constituted a decided minority of candidates in both the PUWP and the opposition groupings. Among 2500 candidates, there were approximately only 200 women. Among the 460 persons elected to the Sejm, there were 62 women (13 per cent).

The first fully free elections took place in October 1991. Parties were free to draw up lists according to their own principles, and voters had genuine choices in all constituencies. Women's representation declined again in the Sejm, the lower and more powerful chamber of parliament. Only 42 women were elected (nine per cent). Women's legislative recruitment improved in 1993 to 13 per cent and that level was replicated in the 1997 elections. The 2001 elections resulted in a jump to 20 per cent women.

❖ LEGISLATIVE RECRUITMENT IN POLISH PARTIES

When we look at the obstacles facing women in the recruitment process, one of the first factors that stands out is the socio-demographic characteristics of candidates. Women who make it through the funnel of recruitment tend to have more of the qualities that bestow legitimacy in the eyes of the party gate-keepers and that voters find attractive than do their male counterparts. More women hold university level degrees than do men. They also tend to have longer records of party and trade union service. In 1993, for example, 73 per cent of women who made it into Parliament had been members of Solidarity in 1980, 34 per cent had been members of the ruling Polish United Workers' Party (PUWP) or one of its branch unions or alliance parties (some were members of both Solidarity and the PUWP). The figures for male MPs were 49 and 23 per cent, respectively.

These data suggest that women must be hyper-qualified to be selected by party gatekeepers and voters. Why is the price of entry higher for women than it is for men? We begin by examining the structure of opportunities that female aspirants face. On the face of it, the Polish legislature ought to be rich in opportunities for women. It is large (460 seats), and the rate of party seat change has been high in every election. These factors ought to help members of marginalized groups gain access to power by creating multiple points of access; but, clearly, women's access had been quite limited prior to the 2001 election.

Three additional aspects of the opportunity structure must therefore receive attention: the characteristics of the parties and the party system, the electoral system, and the political culture. These all play important roles in determining the degree to which women have access to the halls of parliament. These factors affect the supply of female aspirants and the demands of party gatekeepers and voters. The inspection focuses on the 1997 elections because of the availability of detailed data on individual candidates and party structures and the availability of public opinion data from the 1997 election period. However, the 2001 election results are also considered and discussed.

❖ *Characteristics of the parties and party system*

In 1991, approximately 200 parties emerged on the political scene. In place of the previously unified 'Solidarity' movement there appeared an array of political parties representing a wide spectrum of political orientations.

Post-communist forces mainly gathered around the new Social Democracy of the Republic of Poland (SdRP) and trade unions of similar background. Parties that did not bear any connection to the forces in conflict prior to 1989 also appeared. The channel of party or union selection was the only instrument of nomination to the Sejm or Senate. Women of different political orientations tried to become candidates on behalf of various political parties. They also created their own lists of candidates: the Election Committee of the Coalition of Women's Groups 'Family and Woman', which registered in four districts, and a small women's group, 'The Women's Alliance Against Life Difficulties', that contested and won a single seat.

Table 11.1 shows how seats were distributed among the various parties in the Sejm for the 1991, 1993, and 1997 elections. The Polish elections of the 1990s saw a consistent cycle of rejecting the sitting government. The first fully free elections in 1991 saw an unruly coalition of independent, Solidarity affiliated, right-wing parties form the first government, with a post-communist Democratic Left Alliance (SLD) as the primary opposition. In 1993, the right-wing parties faced a disappointed electorate and their own failure to organize effectively under the new electoral rules. They paid at the polls as the Democratic Left Alliance (SLD) and the Polish Peasant Party (PSL) coalition became the ruling parties. In 1997, reorganized as a broad coalition under the banner of 'Electoral Action Solidarity' (AWS), the right-wing parties returned to power and banished the SLD and PSL to the opposition. In 2001, the SLD in coalition with the Labour Union (UP) won a clear plurality as the 'Electoral Action Solidarity' (AWS) failed to win a single seat in parliament. Furthermore, Electoral Action Solidarity's erstwhile partner in government, the Freedom Union, also failed to win sufficient votes to return to parliament (see Table 11.2).

Table 11.1 shows the women who entered parliament were mainly candidates of the biggest parties or election coalitions. Half of all women deputies in 1991 were from two parties, either the Democratic Union (UD) or the Democratic Left Alliance (SLD), even though these parties only won slightly more than 25 per cent of the seats. In the 1993 elections, once again the UD and SLD contributed the overwhelming percentage of female MPs. Between them, they had slightly more than 50 per cent of the MPs in parliament, while they had 75 per cent of the women deputies. In 1997, the largest parties also produced a more than proportionate sector of the women MPs. These results make sense. Election of women depends both upon getting nominated by parties and getting nominated in a prominent position on the party list. When the party delegation is larger, the party can go deeper into its lists, down to the slots where women and other 'non-leaders' are most likely to be slated.

As in many Western European countries, however, not all parties are equally likely to place women on their lists, let alone in competitive slots.

❖ RENATA SIEMIEŃSKA

Table 11.1. Party representation and women's representation among deputies to the Sejm, 1991–7

Name of party or electoral coalition	1991[1]				1993				1997			
	Total	% Total	Women	% Women	Total	% Total	Women	% Women	Total	% Total	Women	% Women
Total	460		42	9.1	460		60	13.0	460		60	13.0
Democratic Left Alliance (SLD)	60	13.0	9	15.0	171	37.2	28	16.4	164	35.7	31	18.9
Labour Union (UP)	4	0.9	–		41	8.9	7	17.1				
Polish Peasant Party (PSL)	50	10.9	1	2	132	28.7	8	6.1	27	5.9	–	–
Democratic Union (UD)[2]	62	13.5	12	19.4	74	16.1	16	21.6				
Liberal-Democratic Congress (KLD)[2]	37	8.0	–									
Freedom Union (UW)									60	13.0	9	15
Confederation of Independent Poland (KPN)[3]	51	11.1	5	9.8	22	4.8	1	4.5				
Electoral Catholic Action (WAK)[3]	50	10.9	6	12.0								
Civic Centre Alliance (PC)[3]	44	9.6	1	2.3								
Polish Peasant Party–Popular Agreement (PSL–PL)[3]	28	6.1	1	3.6			–	–				
Solidarity[3]	27	5.9	3	11.1								
Polish Party of Beer-Lovers[3]	16	3.5	–									

Table 11.1. continued

Name of party or electoral coalition	1991[1]				1993				1997			
	Total	% Total	Women	% Women	Total	% Total	Women	% Women	Total	% Total	Women	% Women
Party of Christian Democrats (PChD)[3]	4	0.9	1	25								
Non-party block in support of reforms (BBWR)[3]					16	3.5						
Electoral action 'Solidarity' (AWS)									201	43.7	20	10
Social and cultural society of the German minority in Silesia (MN)	7	1.5			3	0.7	—	—	2	0.4	—	
Social and cultural society of Germans in Katowice					1	0.2	—	—				
Polish Western Union	4	0.9	2	50								
For Wielkopolska region and Poland	1		1	100								
Women's alliance against life difficulties	1		1	100								
Movement for the Reconstruction of Poland (ROP)									6	1.3	—	

[1] Parties listed are only those with the highest number of seats or those that have women among their deputies. Twenty-nine parties or groups of various types had representatives in the 1991 Sejm.

[2] The UD and KLD formed the Freedom Union (UW) in 1997.

[3] The set of parties, trade unions, etc., which constitute the Electoral Action Solidarity (AWS) in 1991.

Sources: Announcement of the State Election Commission, 31 October 1991, published in *Rzeczpospolita*, 4 November 1991; *Kronika Sejmowa* (Sejm chronicle) 124 (4 October 1993); Data of the State Election Commission 1997, and author's calculations.

Post-communist elections in Poland show that leftist parties are more willing to nominate women as their representatives. Furthermore, there has been a steady growth in the proportion of women who have been elected in the major leftist alliance—the SLD. As the SLD has become more Europeanized and shed its ties to the formerly ruling PUWP, the number of women among its MPs has increased. From a modest 15 per cent of MPs in 1991 (nine out of 60), after the 2001 elections, women in the SLD now hold 25 per cent of the SLD (50 of the 200) seats in the parliament. The other leftist party, Labour Union (UP), has shown an even greater commitment to equality for women, as 31 per cent of its 2001 delegation is female (5 of 16).

A highly significant agreement to institutionalize women's representation was reached in the leftist SLD shortly before the 2001 elections. The SLD agreed to establish a principle that a minimum of 30 per cent of their list positions must be held by each gender. This policy was developed in response to a variety of internal and external pressures, including efforts by the Parliamentary Group of Women, the influence of Polish MPs' contacts with parliamentarians from different countries, and the desire to increase support from the female electorate.[1]

While the left has gradually, but consistently, increased representation of women, among the parties in the centre and right, there have been much broader variances and idiosyncratic patterns. For example, in the Democratic Union (UD), a party that evolved from Solidarity and groups of the intellectual elites of that movement, women constituted a significant internal group in the 1980s, as activists in the underground opposition structures. Their position within 'Solidarity' and then the Citizens' Committee allied with Lech Walesa, was the basis for their involvement in political activity during the transition period. In both the 1991 and 1993 elections, among all of the significant parties, women had their highest proportion of seats in the UD delegation. In 1997, the UD was the dominant partner in the newly organized Freedom Union (UW), which continued to elect above average numbers of women to parliament. In 2001, UW maintained its pattern of being strongly supportive of women by establishing a 30 per cent quota and honoring it by having women fill 31 per cent of its list positions. The UW, however, failed to win sufficient votes to be eligible for seats in the 2001 parliament.

Not all Solidarity successors have been as woman-friendly as the UD/UW. The Solidarity Election Action (AWS), for example, was a right-wing opposition bloc of 36 parties founded in 1996. AWS had a similar economic and foreign affairs platform as the leftist SLD, but it put a greater emphasis on traditional, Christian values and, among other things, opposed abortion. The AWS gained 201 seats in 1997, more than any other single party, but it brought only 20 women into parliament. This could be explained in terms of the traditional-conservative AWS electorate rejecting women; but the AWS party gatekeepers, perhaps anticipating voter rejection of women in politics, nominated relatively few women.

This phenomenon is not unique to the AWS. Women deputies are convinced that introducing women on candidate lists is difficult, because men largely compose the party commissions that decide list composition. These men may or may not be opposed to women in politics, but they are primarily interested in candidates that have economic and social capital—that is, persons well placed in the local or national economic and political structures, who may be useful in building support for the parties and its politicians. Women belong to this type of network much less frequently than do men. The resources at their disposal include professional qualifications, although often in areas considered as 'feminine', and possibly a relatively long period of work in the party or trade unions, though rarely in leadership positions. To the degree that party bosses have not valued these attributes, it has been difficult for women to get nominations.

In 1992–3, I conducted an elite survey of all seated female MPs and senators (48) and a random selection of 96 male MPs and senators. I asked: 'Why do you think your party put you on the list'? The female respondents were more likely than the male respondents to conclude they were attractive to the party due to 'efficiency' resources, their professional or social work, and their work in the party or their legislative experience. They were far less likely to note individual resources, such as personality traits (being intelligent, knowledgeable, and honest). Eighteen per cent of male deputies cited these factors, compared to only 10 per cent for women. Twenty-six per cent of male deputies believed they brought popularity, sympathy, and confidence among voters to the party ticket, whereas only about 19 per cent of women cited these characteristics as factors in their recruitment. These data may reflect differences in the objective characteristics that parties are looking for in male and female aspirants, as well as gendered differences in levels of candidate assertiveness (Siemieńska 1996b).

Statements made by male and female deputies at conferences and in individual interviews carried out following the elections in 1997 highlight the murkiness of the candidate selection process ('Women in politics: post-election reflection', 3 November 1997). One member we interviewed noted that the composition and order of the lists are determined by the party selectorate's 'own sweet will'. Others confirmed there are rarely any clearly defined recruitment criteria. The situation is particularly complicated when broad coalitions, such as SLD and AWS are formed. These large umbrella coalitions consist of many smaller and larger political parties and groups, whose representatives must be considered when constructing the candidate lists of the entire coalition. Each 'partylet' may have the chance to place only a single representative of the party on a given list. In that circumstance, they promote party leaders who tend to be male, at the cost of possible female nominees.

The 2001 election produced substantial upheaval and some surprising results, both in terms of the party system and in terms of women's representation (Table 11.2). Unlike the SLD, which had been able to maintain a significant presence in parliament, even when the voters turned it out of government, the Solidarity based coalition, which had been the core of the right wing of Polish politics in the 1990s was effectively wiped out. Neither of the parties forming the governing coalition, that is the Solitary Election Action (AWS) or the Freedom Union (UW), received sufficient votes to receive any representation in parliament. While the major victors were the parties on the Left (SLD/UP), there were substantial changes in other parts of the political landscape.

Two parties with radical populist messages voicing serious skepticism to the proposed entry into the European Union, the Self-Defense of the Polish Republic (SO) and the League of Polish Families (LPR), had strong showings

Table 11.2. Party representation and women's representation among deputies to the Sejm, 2001

Name of party or electoral coalition	2001			
	Total[1]	% Total	Women	% Women
TOTAL	460		93	20.2
Democratic Left Alliance (SLD)[1]	*200*	*43.5*	*50*	*25.0*
Union of Labour (UP)[1]	*16*	*3.4*	*5*	*31.3*
Polish Peasant Party (PSL)	42	9.1	0	0.0
Civic Platform (PO)	65	14.1	13	20.0
Self Defense of Polish Republic (SO)	53	11.5	9	17.0
Law and Justice (PiS)	44	9.6	6	13.6
League of Polish Families (LPR)	38	8.3	10	26.3
Social and Cultural Society of the German Minority in Silesia (MN)	2	0.4	—	—
Electoral Action 'Solidarity' (AWS)	—	—	—	—
Freedom Union (UW)	—	—	—	—

[1] SLD and UP (in italics) ran in an electoral coalition the Democratic Left Alliance.

Source: www.ipu.org.

capturing 11.5 and 8.3 per cent of the seats, respectively. It was especially striking that women captured 26.3 per cent of the seats won by the LPR. The women who have been elected from the LPR expound a very traditionalist and nationalist message. Their relatively significant numbers can be attributed to several factors. First, as a new party, the LPR had few established old guard politicians who had the right to demand nominations. Second, being female was an advantage in emphasizing a tie to traditional Polish values. Third, the LPR voters were overwhelmingly women.[2] Radio 'Maryja', a media outlet with strong nationalist tones, whose listeners are primarily women, was an important source of support for the LPR during the campaign. Emphasizing the need to protect Polish values of language, family, and home was the crux of the LPR program. This was a message that was especially attractive to elderly women, who have felt the societal changes of the last decade have produced few advantages for them.

We also see in the more centrist Civic Platform (PO) that it may be easier for strategic women to make significant advances in relatively new parties rather than established parties. The Civic Platform, like the LPR, had never run before the 2001 elections (although there were some previous AWS/UW MPs who moved to PO). The PO ended up being the largest opposition party with 14.1 per cent of the MPs and with fully 20 per cent of their delegation being women. Juxtapose this with the Polish Peasant Party (PSL), the only party outside of SLD (and a very small ethnic minority party for Germans) that has been represented in every parliament since 1991. Despite winning 42 seats in the 2001 elections, not a single PSL MP is a woman.

❖ Electoral system

Following the 1989 election, the Polish President and the Sejm rejected the first-past-the-post system that had been preferred by the communist side in the Roundtable Negotiations. The new system was designed to maximize the representation of small and newer parties and it achieved this aim in part through the adoption of a highly proportional system. The 460 seats in the Sejm were divided between 391 seats elected in 37 multimember constituencies ranging in magnitude from 7 to 17 (mean 10.5), and 69 seats apportioned through nationwide party lists. Any party or alliance of parties could receive seats through the national list, provided that they had either won seats in five or more constituencies or polled 5 per cent of the national vote. Significantly, there was no threshold for the provincial constituencies. Given the size of several constituencies, a party with as little as 3 per cent of the vote in a district could win representation in parliament.

The result was a highly fragmented Sejm with some 29 parties or groupings represented. The instability of governing coalitions that ensued led to a

❖ Renata Siemieńska

consensus for electoral reforms aimed at reducing the number of parliamentary parties. A new electoral law was established in May 1993 that reduced average district magnitude (the number of constituencies was increased to 52 with magnitude ranging from 3 to 17, an average of 7.5). Only parties achieving five per cent of the total national vote would be entitled to participate in the proportional allocation in the districts, with an exception for ethnic parties. Electoral alliances would be subject to an eight per cent threshold. In addition, the mechanism by which seats were distributed was changed from the St. Lague to the somewhat less proportional d'Hondt method.

On one level, the permissive proportionality of the system used in 1991 might have been expected to aid women by allowing the entrance to parliament of narrowly based parties and New Left parties that tend to promote women. The relatively large district magnitudes in 1991 also might have been expected to provide opportunities for parties to balance their tickets with women. Women fared worse, however, in 1991 than in either the majoritarian and partly free election of 1989, or the subsequent elections held under less proportionate rules. This is consistent with research that suggests that high levels of party fragmentation decrease party magnitude (the size of the delegation that a party sends from a given district), and therefore reduces the ticket balancing incentives for party gatekeepers.

When the 1993 rules were redesigned, the goal was to reduce fragmentation by becoming less proportional. This goal was dramatically met. Fragmentation among the 'rightist' Solidarity successors that had gone unpunished in the 1991 election was severely penalized in 1993. Several parties on the right failed to clear the threshold. This, in turn, gave a disproportionate victory (in terms of legislative seats) to the parties of the left, the post-communist Democratic Left Alliance (SLD) and its partner in the coalition government, the Polish Peasant's Party (PSL). The electoral system, by itself, should have been less friendly to women, with smaller district magnitudes and a less amenable method of seat allocation. The proportion of women in parliament increased, however, partly because the system reduced fragmentation (increased party magnitudes), and partly because it helped parties of the left.

The 1997 electoral system was the same, but the political parties had learned the lesson that excessive fragmentation would have significant negative effects. The right reorganized under the rubric of the Solidarity Electoral Action (AWS) and won slight over-representation in the Sejm, while the Polish Peasant's Party (PSL) saw a dramatic drop in representation from 29 per cent to 6 per cent of the parliament. This change did very little to affect women's representation, however, as it declined by less than one percentage point to 13 per cent.

The electoral rules were changed only slightly in 2001 as the number of multimember districts was reduced to 41 (average district magnitude 11.2).

Importantly, under all of these various systems used for national elections in Poland, voters have had the ability to influence which candidates on a party's list are elected. The preferential voting system allows the voters to determine which party candidates will represent them. This reduces the power of party leaders to control recruitment. The preferential voting system also was important in providing a signal to party leaders that women were viable candidates. In both the 1993 and 1997 elections, preferential voting led to more women being elected than would have been elected had seats been allocated strictly according to the order determined by the party in putting together their party lists (Gibson 1999). Seeing that women were able to attract votes possibly made it easier for party leaders to consider increasing the number of women on their party lists, as occurred in the 2001 elections.

❖ Polish political culture and social context

Popular attitudes about the appropriate role of women in society affect women's legislative recruitment in ways already outlined in Chapters 1 and 2. In post-communist Poland, a number of factors contributed to a traditionalist political culture regarding women in the 1990s. One factor was a reemergent nationalist rhetoric, associated with the Catholic church, encouraging women to assume their 'proper' place in the home as the reproducers of Polish culture and identity. Data suggest, however, that over time the legitimacy of the Catholic Church as a social institution is declining, and there has been a small but steady increase in those who disagree with the statement: 'Women should look after the home, and governing the country should be left up to the men'. In 1992, only 39 per cent of survey respondents disagreed with that statement. By 1997, roughly half disagreed.

A gender gap is emerging in Poland with regard to traditional gender roles. In research carried out by the author, survey respondents were asked to react to the statement: 'Some believe that women should play the same role in business, industry, and politics as men. Others believe that a woman's place is in the home'.[3] Figure 11.1 shows that the mean response is fairly traditional, around four on a seven-point scale in which seven indicates that women ought to stay in the home. In later years, however, male respondents have become slightly more likely to take a traditional approach, while women have become slightly less traditional.

Figure 11.2 displays a similar gap when the question is limited to the area of politics. Women are far more likely than men to disagree with the statement: 'Men are better suited to politics than women'. Over 60 per cent of female respondents disagreed with that statement in 1993 and 2001, while never more than about 40 per cent of male respondents have disagreed (Siemienska 1994, 1998, 2002). The short-term increase in non-traditional attitudes toward

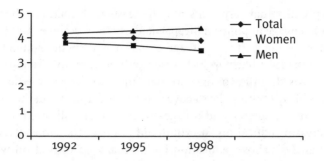

Figure 11.1. Public opinion concerning equal rights for women in business, industry, and politics*

* The graph shows the mean scores for men and women to the question *'Some believe that women should play the same role in business, industry and politics as men. Others believe that the woman's place is at home'*. Respondents identified their position on a 7-point scale, where '1' means that women should play the same role in business, industry and politics as men, and '7' means that women's place is at home.

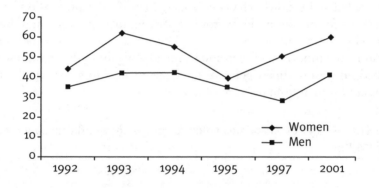

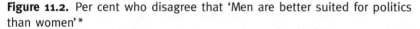

Figure 11.2. Per cent who disagree that 'Men are better suited for politics than women'*

* The graph shows the per cent of men and women who *do not* agree with the statement that 'Men are better suited for politics than women'.

women in politics around 1992–3 is probably tied to the Prime Ministership of Hanna Suchocka. The popular acceptance of her in that role led to a significant, albeit temporary, growth in the acceptance of women in the role of politician. While Suchocka may have briefly influenced the perception of female political competence, she was not a champion of gender equality in society. She even favoured a restrictive anti-abortion act when about 80 per cent of society preferred a more liberal version of the law (Cichomski, Morawski 1996; Siemieńska 1994, 1996). The increase from 1997 to 2001, however, may indicate a more permanent shift in the direction of accepting women in the political sphere.

WOMEN IN THE POLISH SEJM ❖

The supply of female aspirants may increase as women see themselves as competent to engage in political life, particularly since younger and better educated women are the least likely to agree that men are better suited to politics; and they are the least likely to have voted only for men in the 1997 elections. Table 11.3 shows that the younger women are, and the more education they have, the less likely they are the to have voted only for men. On the other hand, the majority of young men and college-educated men still voted only for men in 1997. Increasing education and youth did not have the same effect for men. Additional analysis shows education has virtually no impact on whether or not men see women as suited for politics. Party gatekeepers tend to be men, and these men are likely to have a traditional perspective that suggests men are better at all phases of politics. Perhaps just as importantly, even if they do not believe this themselves, party gatekeepers may believe that voters have this perspective and therefore, they may see nominating female candidates as being risky among a significant proportion of the electorate. These attitudes served as a significant brake on the promotion of women in politics in the 1990s, but may be slowly changing today. In 2001, the proportion of men voting only for men went down from 57 per cent to 46 per cent, and the proportion of women voting only for men fell from 43 per cent to 31 per cent. In addition, the proportion of men and women voting for both men and women climbed noticeably (up 11 per cent for female voters to 55 per cent, and up 6 per cent for men to 39 per cent of male voters).

Table 11.3. Gender of candidates voted for in the 1997 parliamentary elections (%)

	Women voted for				Men voted for			
	Only men	Men and women	Only women	I don't remember	Only men	Men and women	Only women	I don't remember
Total	43	44	1	12	57	33	1	9
AGE								
< 29	31	58	—	10	53	32	4	11
30–39	52	41	1	6	60	33	—	7
40–49	44	41	—	14	53	34	—	13
50–59	45	46	—	9	62	32	—	7
60 +	44	36	4	16	60	34	—	6
EDUCATION								
Primary	43	39	2	16	64	30	—	7
Vocational	56	35	—	9	54	30	3	13
Secondary	40	52	1	8	54	36	—	9
College	39	46	3	12	56	41	—	3

❖ RENATA SIEMIEŃSKA

The most detrimental effect of cultural traditionalism may be the barriers it put up against the formation of an organized pro-equality women's movement. The lack of a women's lobby is at least partly an inheritance from a communist system that did not tolerate grassroots initiatives. Male-dominated interests have recovered and found a place in the democratic political landscape more quickly than women's groups. In 2001, however, the first signs of a nascent, but possibly influential women's movement were seen.

❖ THE WOMEN'S MOVEMENT IN POST-COMMUNIST POLAND

Students at the University of Warsaw created the first feminist group in the early 1980s. This organization eventually attracted some interest outside of academic circles, but it never gained a successful foothold among women workers, who believed the newly created trade union Solidarity would solve their problems, ultimately allowing them to escape the dual burden imposed by directive emancipation. At the same time, women who were professionally successful believed that anyone talented and motivated had opportunities to pursue a career. Many did not believe that women faced different or more significant barriers than men.

Several feminist groups emerged after martial law was lifted in the mid-1980s. Small as a rule (from several to a couple of hundred members), these associations were active in urban centres and in student and intelligentsia communities. Four groups survived the transition from communist authoritarian rule and organized alongside approximately a dozen new groups to oppose a restrictive anti-abortion law put forth by the new democratic government. This helped put feminism on the map in Poland, but since several of the currently existing feminist organizations are clearly left-wing, connected with the Polish Socialist Party, the Social Democracy of the Polish Republic (Profemina, the Democratic Union of Women), many associate feminism with a discredited communist past.

In recent years, professional organizations have been created for female managers and business owners. These organizations have sprung up spontaneously in different parts of the country, and led to networking on a national level. Many of them assume at the start that they will be highly selective in their membership to maintain their elitist character, promoting women in high positions in enterprise and state administration.

Both the feminist and women's professional associations that started to appear in the 1990s had a general lack of interest in promoting gender equity in politics. Feminist groups, which emerged from academic circles, typically promoted studies of women's status according to feminist theoretical approaches, while the general associations focused on making it easier for women to attain qualifications needed in the market. Furthermore, the women who did reach competitive slots on candidate lists usually did not act on behalf of, or call on the support of, these organizations. The only groups that specifically focused on increasing women's political influence were those directly connected with given political parties (e.g. Women Also of the Freedom Union, Democratic Union of Women of the Democratic Left Alliance, or the Women's League of the Labour Union). These organizations conducted training with candidates and conducted publicity campaigns for women candidates during elections. They had not, however, widely campaigned to place direct pressure on party gatekeepers to put more women on the lists prior to the 2001 campaign.

Before the 2001 campaign, however, women's organizations became more active, exerting more influence on political parties and public opinion. Fifty organizations joined the Pre-Electoral Coalition of Women, an open agreement between women's organizations and groups created a few months before the elections. The objectives of the coalition were clearly defined. They included the struggle against gender discrimination, demonstrated by unequal access to power and the labour market. The Electoral Coalition's slogans during the election campaign fully reflected its program: 'I've had enough of this. I support election of women', 'Enough adoration—we want representation'. At the same time, the members emphasized the broad based character of the coalition, and that it was not associated with any specific political party.

The women who were already in parliament also supported the actions of the Pre-Electoral Coalition of Women. Within parliament, there is a women's caucus, the Women's Parliamentary Group (WPG). The original intention of the WPG, when it was established in the beginning of the 1990s, was to provide a forum where women parliamentarians from different parties could unite. Over time, however, as tensions between political parties escalated, the WPG gradually began to consist almost exclusively of members of the Democratic Left Alliance (SLD). This had the disadvantage of the WPG not being able to speak for all women in parliament, but this structure did enable the Women's Parliamentary Group to organize a forum of women's organizations, thus creating some space for the exchange of opinions and the articulation of issues of interest to women.

Despite the splits in the WPG, an important pre-electoral agreement, organized by female members of the Parliament from all parliamentary groups, resulted in a united 'women run, women vote' initiative. The aim of this initiative was to convince voters that it made sense to vote for women. Furthermore, because the electoral system allows for preference voting, voters were urged to exercise this right to vote for women within their individual parties.

All of these actions were conducted under the banner of ensuring equal status for women. The high level of women's qualifications associated with their unique experience, resulting from their roles in the sphere of public life as well as their private life was emphasized. It was also repeatedly pointed out that greater representation was needed to comply with recommendations of international organizations. One of the reasons this movement had a greater impact than others in the 1990s, was that this was one of the first times that politically active women had been effective in mobilizing women who were not members of a specific political party to participate in a call for greater representation.

To understand fully the representation of women in post-communist Polish legislatures, we must study the interplay of cultural, electoral, and partisan factors. Poland failed to make strides in female representation in the 1990s, at least partly because there was a lack of pressure to place more women in winnable positions on party lists. A closer examination of the 1997 election elaborates this point and can be juxtaposed with the 2001 election, where noticeable gains were made.

❖ THE 1997 ELECTION

Data from the 1997 election clearly demonstrate the bottleneck women faced at the nomination stage. Women constituted 15.7 per cent of the candidates to the Sejm and, as a result of the elections, women were 13 per cent of deputies of the Sejm. Women fared well in elections relative to their share in the candidate pool. Before voters can select women, however, parties must nominate them, and there were obstacles to nominations. In several districts, a voter who desired to support a specific party, but also had a strong desire to vote for a woman, would not have been able to do so. The only party that included women on its list in all 52 electoral districts was the Labour Union (UP), a party that in 1997 ultimately failed to clear the 5 per cent threshold for representation. Women were entirely absent from the lists of the Freedom Union in five districts, AWS in 11, SLD in 8, PSL in 12, and ROP in 9. Women were on all the lists of parties and coalitions in only 25 per cent of the districts (13).

When women did make it into the candidate pool, they were far less frequently placed in top list positions. Only the unsuccessful Labour Union and Pensioners' Party placed large numbers of women in top list positions. This is important because list placement largely determines candidate success. Those candidates placed at the top of party lists are far more likely to get into the Sejm, even though party lists are open and voters may express preference. Voters, who do not have a candidate preference and have only decided to vote for a particular party or coalition, often mark the top candidate from the party's list (Raciborski 1997).

Table 11.4 shows that as the number of women in the top three positions on a list increased, so did the number (and per cent) of women elected to

Table 11.4. Impact of key economic, cultural, and political variables on women's presence among candidates and elected, 1997 (Pearson's correlation coefficients)

	Candidates				Elected	
	Number of lists without women	Number of women on the lists	Per cent of women on the lists	Number of women in the top three positions on the lists	Number of women	Per cent women
Number of telephones per 1000 inhabitants in a district (1)	− 0.27*	0.55***	0.11	0.21	0.53***	0.25
Magnitude of a district (2)	0.30*	0.94***	− 0.02	0.41**	0.78***	0.23
Per cent of urban population in a district (1)	− 0.05	0.61***	0.06	0.22	0.58***	0.32*
Per cent of unemployed people (3)	0.01	− 0.49	− 0.03	0.05	− 0.34**	− 0.01
Voted for women and men (4)	− 0.16	0.20*	0.062	0.05	0.30*	0.27*
'Men are better suited to politics than women' (4)	0.09	0.08	− 0.22	0.13	0.24	− 0.32*
Number of lists without women (2)	—	0.12	− 0.45***	0.03	0.03	− 0.14
Number of women on the lists of candidates (2)	0.12	—	0.23	0.51***	0.80***	0.2
Per cent of women on the lists of candidates (2)	− 0.45***	0.23	—	0.44***	0.11	− 0.04
Number of women in the top three positions on the lists	0.03	0.51***	0.44***	—	0.54***	0.27*

❖ RENATA SIEMIEŃSKA

Table 11.4. continued

	Candidates				Elected	
	Number of lists without women	Number of women on the lists	Per cent of women on the lists	Number of women on the top three positions on the lists	Number of women	Per cent women
Number of elected women (2)	0.03	0.80***	0.11	0.54***	—	0.68***
Per cent of elected women (2)	−0.14	0.19	−0.04	0.27*	0.68***	—

Level of significance: ***$p < 0.001$, **$p < 0.01$, *$p < 0.05$.

Sources: (1) Statistical Yearbook 1998 (1998) Warsaw: GUS (Main Statistical Office); (2) Data of the State Electoral Commission and authors' calculations; (3) Statistical Yearbook of Voivodeships 1998; (4) Post-election study in 1997 conducted for R. Siemieńska by 'Pentor'—Institute for Opinion and Market Research.

parliament. It is, perhaps, an obvious point, but a candidate's position on the list does matter. *Ceteris paribus*, women have the fewest chances in very small magnitude districts, where women are less likely to be present on party lists. In larger magnitude (often urban and more economically developed) districts, the lists contain more names and therefore (unsurprisingly), they contain more women. District magnitude has a positive, but not a statistically significant effect on the percentage of women elected to parliament. Hence, the hypothesis set forth in the literature, that higher district magnitudes encourage parties to increase the *proportion* of women they nominate (in order to balance their tickets), is not confirmed. Higher district magnitudes, however, did correlate with higher numbers of women placed in the top three list positions, a factor that was strongly related to the number and percentage of women elected to the Sejm.

When we look at the factors that measure cultural traditionalism, the picture becomes clearer. The only consistent factors influencing the number and per cent of women elected to the Sejm were the per cent urban population in the district, the per cent of voters in the constituency who cast votes for both women and men, and the per cent of voters in the constituency who agreed with the statement that men are better suited for politics than women. This suggests that women have the greatest chance of being elected in those constituencies where the traditionalist culture is most attenuated.

Those same factors, however, do not seem to have strikingly altered the calculations of party gatekeepers regarding the *nomination* of female candidates.

WOMEN IN THE POLISH SEJM ❖

The percentage of urban population does not affect the percentage of women nominated or the presence of women in the top three slots. The same was true for the more direct measures of political culture. One might have expected that party gatekeepers assessed the riskiness of female candidates in terms of the relative traditionalism of voters in a given constituency. This has been a common hypothesis: parties eschew female candidates because there has been a post-communist voter backlash against female politicians. If party gatekeepers were anticipating the hostility of voters, then this was solely based on party leaders' perceptions of what voters want and not on empirical data about the willingness of voters to choose women in given constituencies. In the absence of organized pressure to recruit more women, the 'facts' of voter preferences may go unnoticed or be subordinated to the party gatekeeper's expectations. Under these conditions, other interests will receive priority in their ticket-building strategies.

The data in Table 11.5 show that in 1997 women fared better as candidates among parties of the left and centre, among parties that have an ideological commitment to gender equality in politics, and among parties that have women in their leadership ranks. Women held more than 25 per cent of the nominations for one of the Pensioners parties and for the leftist Labour Union (UP). The Freedom Union (UW) had a respectable 18.6 per cent of women among their nominees, their total number of women listed among the top three candidates on their district lists, 21, was the highest of all parties. The leftist SLD had a modest 15.1 per cent women among its candidates, with a large number of parties falling in the 10–15 per cent range, including the ultimate election winner, the Electoral Action Solidarity (AWS). Women were only 10.9 per cent of the AWS's candidates and only 10 of 156, or 6.4 per cent, of the candidates with a top three nomination on its lists.

The absence of women on many lists and in many districts clearly affected the results of the elections. Obviously, on the party lists that did not include women, it was impossible for voters to select female candidates. The number of women who, despite this, found themselves among the deputies, further demonstrates the bottleneck for women is at the nomination stage.

In Fig. 11.3 we compare the total per cent of female candidates for each party with the per cent of votes cast for women (via preference votes) on each party's lists. We find an interesting set of patterns. The overall pattern is that women get roughly the same number of votes as they get nominations, although in general women fared better among the voters. This was particularly true among parties of the left and centre. Those parties had more viable female candidates placed on their lists than the other parties. Furthermore their voters were more likely to vote for women. In those parties where there were fewer women candidates, the electorates were also less likely to vote for women. The more traditionalist electorates of parties, like the National

Table 11.5. Women candidates by party in the 1997 parliamentary elections

Name of party, coalition	Number of districts in which women were on the list (max. = 52)	Number of candidates	Number of women	Per cent of women in total number of candidates	Number of women on first positions on the list	Number of women on second positions on the list	Number of women on third positions on the list	Total number of women on 1–3 positions on the list[2]	Per cent of votes for women	Number (and per cent) of women who received more than mean number of votes[1]
National agreement of retirees & pensioners (Por. Em. i Ren.)	50	593	164	27.7	8	10	0	18	29.6 / 30.7[1]	72 (43.9%)
Labour Union (UP)	52	604	151	25.0	9	8	2	19	28.8 / 28.8[1]	53 (34.9%)
Freedom Union (UW)	47	722	134	18.6	8	12	1	21	19.8 / 21.1[1]	39 (29.1%)
National–Christian Bloc for Poland (BdP)	41	559	86	15.4	4	8	1	13	12.2 / 14.3[1]	30 (34.9%)
Alliance of Democratic Left (SLD)	44	548	83	15.1	6	8	1	15	22.4 / 24.3[1]	38 (45.8%)

Table 11.5. Continued

Name of party, coalition	Number of districts in which women were on the list (max. = 52)	Number of candidates	Number of women	Per cent of women in total number of candidates	Number of women on first positions on the list	Number of women on second positions on the list	Number of women on third positions on the list	Total number of women on 1–3 positions on the list[2]	Per cent of votes for women	Number (and per cent) of women who received more than mean number of votes[1]
National party of retirees & pensioners (Partia Em. i Rent.)	31	389	53	13.6	2	7	2	11	13.1 / 19.7[1]	26 (49.1%)
Movement for Rebuilding of Poland (ROP)	44	651	84	12.9	1	5	0	6	9.4 / 10.7[1]	21 (25.0%)
Polish Peasant Party (PSL)	40	659	84	12.7	2	8	1	11	8.4 / 10.6[1]	24 (28.6%)
Electoral Action Solidarity (AWS)	41	773	84	10.9	3	6	1	10	10.9 / 12.6[1]	51 (60.7%)
Union of the Republic Right (UPR)	34	652	63	9.7	3	9	0	12	9.4 / 12.1[1]	26 (41.3%)

[1] Per cent of votes for women calculated only for districts where women were on the lists of candidates.

[2] Data of the group 'Women Also'.

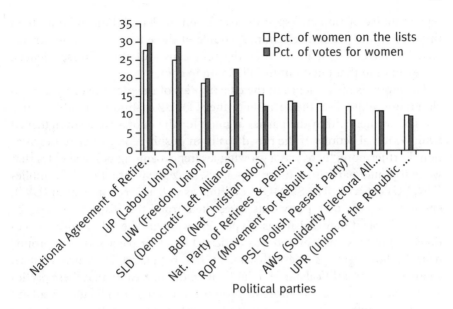

Figure 11.3. Women's percentage of list names and votes, 1997

Christian Bloc and the Polish Peasants' Party (PSL), were less woman-friendly than the party selectors. The survey data indicate that men tended to support the PSL more frequently, while women supported SLD and UW. This may explain the greater tendency to support female candidates in those parties, particularly in light of the data presented in Table 11.3, showing that large portions of men only voted for men.

❖ THE 2001 ELECTION

Women did substantially better in the 2001 election than in any election up to that point. A number of factors combined to lead to this result. There was an electoral law change that increased the average district magnitude, as the number of districts was dropped from 51 to 42. In addition, public attitudes towards women in politics appear to be changing in a positive direction. As noted in Fig. 11.2, there has been a noticeable increase in the number of women and men who disagree with the opinion that 'men are better suited to politics than women'.[4] Politics is now seen as a more legitimate field in which women can aspire. Perhaps the most important factor was that women arguing for greater representation were much better organized and mobilized than they had been in the past. Finally, the parties that tend to be more representative of women, especially parties on the left, did much better than they had in the previous election. A couple of these factors must be considered in greater depth to uncover the root causes of the increased female representation that burst out in full bloom in 2001.

The most visible evidence of the effectiveness of the pressure campaigns to elect more women was the decision by the SLD–UP coalition to establish quotas. The women within the parties arguing for the quotas were strengthened by the external actions of the broad coalition pushing for greater representation. Furthermore, there was a growing awareness among political elites that women should participate more in politics, since the international assemblies (UN, EU) expect it. The SLD–UP coalition, as well as Freedom Union (UW), endorsed a rule that party lists, presented from the districts, would be approved only if they had at least 30 per cent women. The rule aroused objections within these parties and was criticized by other parties and by prominent Catholic groups. Nevertheless, as has happened in many Western countries, other political parties could not ignore the reality that these parties were making a concerted effort to promote women as candidates (Matland and Studlar 1996). If they failed to do likewise, there was a danger that some part of their electorate could turn away from them. Thus, the parties on the right of the political scene were indirectly pressured to put a greater emphasis on nominating women in 2001, even if they did not adopt quotas.

The changes in electoral preferences of the society also played a role. The move from the right to the left in voting behaviour this time, as opposed to the shift in 1993, coincided with a substantial jump in women's representation. This is true because in 2001 women played a much more prominent role in the composition of the SLD–UP coalition's ticket than they had eight years earlier. The gains, however, were not exclusively on the left.

Comparing Table 11.5 with Table 11.6, the number of women on party lists was substantially higher in 2001. While in 1997 there were several parties, including the election winner the AWS, that had no women on their party lists in up to 20 and even 30 per cent of the districts, in 2001 the eight major parties together had women on their lists in 312 of the 328 district lists, more than 95 per cent of all lists. In 2001, the major party with the lowest proportion of female candidates was the Electoral Action Solidarity (AWS) with 14.9 per cent of its candidates being women. At 14.9 per cent, however, Electoral Action Solidarity was higher than a majority of the party lists from 1997. In short, in 2001 women made significant gains across the board.

One factor holding down the number of women nominated has been the presumption that women would not be as effective at winning votes for the party as men. The 2001 election provides considerable evidence that this is not the case. There was some concern that introducing quotas and explicitly

Table 11.6. Women candidates by party in the 2001 parliamentary elections

Name of party, coalition	Number of districts where women were on the list (max. = 41)	Number of candidates	Number of women	Per cent of women in total number of candidates	Number of women on first positions on the list	Number of women on second positions on the list	Number of women on third positions on the list	Total number of women on 1–3 positions on the list[2]
Alliance of Democratic Left/Labour Union (SLD–UP)[1]	41	907	325	35.8	7	5	11	23
Freedom Union (UW)	41	800	251	31.4	1	11	14	26
Polish Peasant Party (PSL)	39	882	163	18.5	1	4	3	8
Civic Platform (PO)	37	761	117	15.4	6	6	5	17
Electoral Action Solidarity (AWS)	36	726	108	14.9	2	2	7	11
Self-Defense of Polish Republic (SO)	38	664	131	19.7	7	5	3	15
Law and Justice (PiS)	40	750	137	18.3	3	7	6	16
League of Polish Families (LPR)	40	719	177	24.6	7	15	8	30
Social and Cultural Society of the German Minority in Silesia (MN)	2	36	5	13.9	1	–	–	1

[1] SLD and UP ran in an electoral coalition, the Democratic Left Alliance. The candidate numbers are for the combined slate.
[2] Author's calculations.

Source: www.sejm.gov.pl.

promoting women as candidates might discourage voters from voting for specific parties, which could be perceived as feminist. Survey data show that a great majority (95 per cent of men and 85 per cent of women) of voters said that parties adopting a rule that women were to make up at least 30 per cent of their candidates was of no significance to them. For seven per cent of the women and two per cent of the men, adopting the rule made them more likely to vote for a party. For only one per cent of the respondents were the rule adoptions something that made them less likely to vote for this party. In general, for more than 60 per cent of male and 80 per cent of female respondents, the gender of the candidate was of no importance. However, 36 per cent of men and two per cent of women stated they preferred to vote for men, and two per cent of the men and 14 per cent of the women said they would rather vote for women. These results show that gender, to some extent, is taken into consideration by some voters when using their preferential votes to select candidates of the party they identify with, but the introduction of quotas does not discourage voting for the party as such.

❖ Prospects for the Future

The 2001 elections provided a significant boost to women in Polish politics, catapulting Poland from being a laggard to a leader. It is difficult to predict if it will continue to be a leader. The electoral system is relatively woman friendly. The rules adopted to reduce party fragmentation in 1993 successfully helped increase party magnitudes, and nowhere do women need to fight a battle to be the exclusive nominee of their party.

Women are most successful when the parties of the left do well. With the development of formal procedures to guarantee representation of women among the candidates of the SLD and UP, it is probably going to continue to be true that as long as the left does well, women will tend to do reasonably well. It is well worth noting, however, that in several of the parties of the centre and right, women did surprisingly well also. Whether this is simply a blip caused by unusual election results and the rise of previously miniscule or nonexistent parties, will be determined in the future.

In the end, much depends on the will of party gatekeepers. Until the last election, there had been little pressure on these gatekeepers to promote female recruitment. The Polish electorate is still traditional in its conception of appropriate gender roles. This may discourage women from entering the funnel of recruitment and may prevent the formation of an organized, explicitly pro-equality women's movement that could place pressure on parties to get women into competitive slots or adopt quotas. One positive result of the

2001 elections across all parties is the strong showing of women in the 2001 elections, which may start to change the way party leaders assess the 'riskiness' of nominating female candidates. Dispelling the myth that women 'lose votes' may make it easier for party leaders to select women. Furthermore, the polling evidence that some voters reacted positively to the slating of more women, while very few voters reacted negatively, will make it easier for women in other parties to argue for representation that is more equal. It is most realistic, however, to assume that party leaders will only begin to emphasize female recruitment if they believe that they must do so in a competitive electoral environment.

At the same time, an age-gender gap similar to what scholars have found in Western Europe seems to be materializing in Poland. Younger and better-educated women hold less traditional gender role conceptions and are less likely to see politics as the domain of men. Women with a college education and women under 29 years of age were the least likely of any age or educational group to vote only for men in the 1997 elections. Men of all age cohorts and education levels continue to hold inegalitarian values and prefer male candidates; and men still hold the gatekeeper positions. Nevertheless, we may see the ingredients of a pro-equality women's movement emerging within a younger generation of educated women. If these women mobilize, they may be able to press the parties to take fuller advantage of opportunities provided by the electoral rules, particularly if the party system becomes less fragmented and umbrella parties settle into single unified party organizations.

❖ NOTES

1 Information from interview with Grazyna Kopinska—leader of the group Women Also connected with Freedom Union (UW) party.

2 All survey results reported are from national representative samples of 1000 respondents and are from surveys carried out by the Institute of Research of Opinion and Market 'Pentor'. Since 1995, these polls have been conducted in cooperation with the Interdisciplinary Research Division on Gender of the Institute of Social Studies, University of Warsaw and F. Ebert Foundation (Warsaw office). This 2001 Pentor poll asked the respondents how they voted. Among those who did vote, the party with the greatest inequality in terms of where they got their votes was the LPR. 67% of their votes came from women.

3 These results are based on public opinion survey of a representative random national sample of 1000 voters taken by Pentor in conjunction with the national elections held in October 1997.

4 These results are based on a public opinion survey of a representative random national sample of 1000 voters taken by Pentor in October 2001. It is worth noting these are respondents who actively disagree with the statement. The remaining 40% of women and 60% of men include both those who agree with the statement and those who are neutral, i.e., they neither agree nor disagree with the statement.

❖ RENATA SIEMIEŃSKA

12 ❖ Czech Political Parties Prefer Male Candidates to Female Votes

Steven Saxonberg

More than a decade after the fall of Communism, Czech women have made limited headway in society's political sphere. The current number of female parliamentarians, at 17 per cent, after the 2002 elections, is slightly more than half the number serving during the last Communist parliament (30 per cent). The first two parliamentary elections immediately after the democratic transitions in 1990 and 1992 produced parliaments where women had 10 per cent of the parliamentary seats. In 1996 representation advanced to 15 per cent, where it remained after the 1998 election. In terms of governmental portfolios, there were no female ministers in the government from 1992 to 1996 and in the Zeman government that served from 1998 to 2002. In the two governments between 1996 and 1998, there was only one female minister. This chapter examines the causes of low female representation in the Czech Parliament. Three commonly cited factors, electoral systems, party ideology, and level of modernization, will be examined first. After showing these factors do not go far in explaining the modest level of female representation in the Czech parliament, I investigate the candidate recruitment process.

❖ Do electoral systems matter?

Studies of Western democracies conclude that proportional electoral systems are more conducive to getting women elected than majoritarian systems. In proportional systems, parties have an incentive to distribute the winnable places on the ballot list among different interest groups, including women. In majoritarian systems, however, parties support only a single prominent candidate, most often a man, in each district. Matland (1993: 742) further suggests that not all PR systems are equally preferred. Systems producing many small parties with few representatives are expected to elect fewer women than systems with fewer and larger parties. Finally, the district-magnitude hypothesis states that women's representation should increase in proportion to a district's size.

The Czech Republic finds itself in a good position on all three accounts. First, it has an electoral system based entirely on proportional representation with a system that gets close to being closed lists;[1] second, there is a five per cent barrier that keeps smaller parties out; third, there have been relatively large districts, in which every party represented in Parliament will gain several seats. Until now, the number of seats per district ranged from 12 to 39.[2] In the 1996 elections, the two largest parties (the social democratic, ČSSD, and market liberal, ODS) gained at least five seats in every district. In the 1998 elections, they received at least four seats in every district.

The electoral system has, in other words, a high district magnitude and a relatively low number of parties, leading to high party magnitude, which is a condition that should be favourable to female representation. Matland (1993) posits that as the number of seats a party wins in a district increases the proportion of women elected increases. In the Czech Republic, party magnitude does seem to matter to some extent. Table 12.1 presents a test of the party magnitude hypothesis. In 1996, the tau-β coefficient is nearly significant at the 0.05 level, using a one-tailed test. Moreover, if the two extremist parties are excluded (the communist KSČM and the populist-nationalist Republicans, SPR-RSČ), then tau-β is significant at the 0.01 level. The relationship is no longer significant in the 1998 elections, but approaches significance ($p = 0.085$) if extremist parties are eliminated. Party magnitude seems to matter more for the broad range of parties, but not for outlier parties. The two extremist parties, the KSČM and SPR-RSČ, sent significant numbers of women to Parliament even when they won only two or three seats in a district. Note, however, that *none* of the parties sent women to Parliament from districts with party magnitudes of one. Nevertheless, the fact that the two largest parties have won at least four seats in every district and averaged more than eight seats per district in the last two elections, but elected only a few women, indicates that party magnitude has not been the biggest obstacle to electing more women.

One way to examine the electoral-system hypothesis is to compare the results of different institutional arrangements within one country. This method holds cultural and historical factors constant, eliminating them as possible explanations for differences in outcomes. A majoritarian Senate based on single-member districts was added in 1996. We must be cautious, however, in comparing different institutions. The Senate has little prestige and power, minimizing competition and making it easier for women to gain seats.[3] There is a small, but consistent, difference between the two institutions. In both 1996 and 1998, women won 15 per cent of the seats in the Chamber of Deputies, while winning only 11.1 per cent (nine of 81) of the Senate seats. These differences are in the direction predicted by the electoral systems variable and run counter to

❖ STEVEN SAXONBERG

Table 12.1. Party magnitude and representation (number of women elected/number of districts with that party magnitude)

Party magnitude	KSČM 1996	KSČM 1998	ČSSD 1996	ČSSD 1998	KDU–ČSL 1996	KDU–ČSL 1998	ODA 1996	US 1998	ODS 1996	ODS 1998	SPR-RSČ 1996	Female % of all elected 1996	Female % of all elected 1998
1	–	–	–	–	0/4	0/3	0/5	0/1	–	–	0/2	0.0	0.0
2	3/5	1/4	–	–	0/1	1/2	0/1	1/4	–	–	1/2	22.2	15.0
3	–	1/1	–	–	1/2	0/1	0/2	1/2	–	–	4/4	41.7	16.7
4	0/1	3/2	–	–	–	1/1	–	1/1	–	0/1	–	0.0	25.0
5	1/1	1/1	4/3	1/1	–	–	–	–	0/1	0/1	–	25.0	13.3
6	–	–	0/1	3/2	0/1	1/1	–	–	1/2	0/1	–	0.4	16.7
7	3/2	–	–	–	–	–	–	–	–	–	–	21.4	–
8	–	–	–	3/2	–	–	–	–	–	1/1	–	–	16.7
9	–	–	–	0/1	–	–	–	–	3/2	3/1	–	16.7	16.7
10	–	–	–	–	–	–	–	–	–	2/2	–	–	10.0
11	–	–	–	–	–	–	–	–	3/3	1/1	–	9.1	9.1
12	–	–	2/2	–	–	–	–	–	–	–	–	8.3	–
14	–	–	2/2	–	–	–	–	–	–	–	–	7.1	–
>14	–	–	–	2/2	–	–	–	–	–	–	–	–	12.5

1996: $\chi^2 = 180.66$ ($p < 0.001$, $n = 48$); tau-$\beta = 0.18$ ($p = 0.06$, one-tailed test); if SPR-RSČ and KČSM are excluded: $\chi^2 = 101.46$ ($p = 0.002$, $n = 32$); tau-$\beta = 0.36$ ($p = 0.007$, one tailed test).

1998: $\chi^2 = 269.48$ ($p < 0.001$, $n = 40$); tau-$\beta = 0.14$ ($p = 0.001$, one-tailed test); If KSČM is excluded: $\chi^2 = 211.24$ ($p < 0.001$, $n = 32$); tau-$\beta = 0.19$ ($p = 0.085$, one tailed test).

predictions based on the level of prestige of the institutions, where we would expect to see more women in the less prestigious Senate.

❖ Does party ideology matter?

In Western countries, left-leaning parties have been more interested in promoting gender equality than the right-leaning parties that support conservative, traditional values. Social democratic parties are especially likely to increase female representation in their parliamentary groups if faced with the pressure of smaller leftist parties' quota systems (there is a 'contagion effect'—see Matland and Studlar 1996). To the left of the Czech Social Democratic Party (ČSSD) are the Communists (KSČM), who have greater female representation than the ČSSD and the liberal and conservative parties. However, citizens of the Czech Republic largely frown upon communism. Therefore, policies promoted by the Communists may be less likely to be adopted by other parties.

Table 12.2 lists the parties in approximately ideological order from left to right and shows their representation levels. In 1996, the Social Democrats (ČSSD) had less female representation than the Communists (KSČM), but had greater female representation than the liberal and conservative parties. Although the distribution of female seats seems to follow a left-right scale, the pattern is broken up by the right-wing populist Republicans (SPR-RSČ), who had greater female representation than any other party. In the 1998 parliamentary elections, the left-right scale effect weakened even further, as both the Christian Democrats (KDU-ČSL) and the new liberal-conservative party, Freedom Union (US), surpassed the ČSSD in female representation. The χ^2 and Kendal tau-β scores for both 1996 and 1998 are not even close to being statistically significant. There is no strong correlation in the Czech case between political ideology and female representation.

❖ Modernization

As Matland (1998*b*) points out, female representation in parliament is usually higher in more 'modernized' countries. When women are highly educated and participate more in the work force, they are more likely to be politically active. If women stay at home and raise their children full time, however, they are unlikely to play an active role in, or even join, political parties. Moreover, if women are poorly educated, they are unlikely to be chosen either by voters or parties over better-educated male candidates.

These minimal conditions for female participation in politics are easily met in the Czech Republic. Czech women are well educated and almost all have work experience. During the Communist era, most women worked when they were not on parental leave. The level of female labour market participation

❖ STEVEN SAXONBERG

Table 12.2. Female candidates and elected MPs, 1996 and 1998 parliamentary elections (chamber of deputies)

Party	Female MPs		Number of female candidates		Total seats		% of MPs who are women		% of candidates who are women	
	1996	1998	1996	1998	1996	1998	1996	1998	1996	1998
KSČM	5	6	49	60	22	24	22.7	25.0	16.4	20.1
ČSSD	11	11	42	43	61	74	18.0	14.9	14.1	14.4
KDU–ČSL	2	3	38	41	18	20	11.1	15.0	12.8	13.8
ODS	7	7	67	52	68	63	10.3	11.1	22.5	17.4
US	—	3	—	51	—	19	—	15.8	—	17.1
ODA	0	—	46	—	13	—	0	—	15.4	—
SPR–RSČ	5	—	44	—	18	—	27.8	—	15.7	—
Total	30	30		247	200	200	15.0	15.0		16.6

Relationship between ideology and female representation.
For 1996 ($n = 6$, coded so extreme Left $= 1$ and extreme Right $= 5$): $\chi^2 = 24$ ($p = 0.24$); Tau-β for 1996 $= -0.14$ ($p = 0.35$, one-tailed test).
For 1998 ($n = 5$, coded so extreme Left $= 1$ and extreme Right $= 5$): $\chi^2 = 15$ ($p = 0.24$); Tau-β for 1998 $= -0.32$ ($p = 0.22$, one-tailed test).
For the χ^2 tests, the parties were coded as follows: KSČM $= 1$, ČSSD $= 2$, KDU–ČSL $= 3$, ODS, ODA, and US $= 4$, SPR-RSČ $= 5$.

Sources: The number of female MPs for 1998 was calculated based on the list of newly elected MPs from the ČTK on the Internet http://www.ctknews.com/archiv/volby.htm; for 1996, the statistics are calculated from the list of parliamentary members printed in *Parlament zpravodaj* (06/96–7), pp. 229–31. The lists of candidates comes from the Internet address: http://www.volby.cz.

has declined somewhat, but it is still among the highest in the world. Women are also well-represented in institutions of higher learning. Czech women make up about one-third of all university employees (8594 of 25,304) and about 40 per cent of those employed by scientific research institutes (411 of 1004) (Český statistický úřad 1997: 25). Women also comprise 38 per cent of people with university educations (Čermáková 1997*a*: 9).

❖ NOMINATING AND RECRUITING

None of the broad factors suggested above give us a good explanation for the representation levels found. Therefore, let us take a more detailed look at the recruitment process. In Chapter 2 (see Fig. 2.1), the recruitment process is broken up into several steps, from eligibles to aspirants to candidates to MPs. These steps are discussed below, although in a slightly different order. The issue of voters will be discussed first, because the view of voters could obviously affect both the desire of women to become candidates and the desire of parties to nominate women.

❖ The voters

One reason why parties might discriminate against women in the nominating process is the belief that voters are less supportive of women than men. Chapter 2 posits several reasons for this: (1) differences in political experience, (2) males have more attractive qualities (such as higher education), and (3) cultural hindrances (politics is considered a male field).

The first two factors were not important in the Czech Republic. Except for the Communist Party and the ČSL portion of the KDU–ČSL coalition, virtually all candidates in the first free elections were people without any previous political experience. Even these two Post-Communist parties purged their most prominent pre-1989 leaders before the first free elections. Since the new party activists had little political experience, women did not have to fight against any incumbents in the 1990 elections. In the ensuing elections, they did not have to compete against anyone with more than a few years of political experience. Turnover was also comparatively high in the earliest parliaments.

A more relevant obstacle may be political culture. Surveys show that Czech society has a conservative attitude towards gender roles (Čermaková 1995). For this reason, political parties could legitimately fear that female candidates would do worse than males. Some evidence, however, points in the opposite direction. In the late 1990s, female social democratic politician Petra Buzková was the most popular politician in the country, surpassing even President Havel. In addition, Senate President Libuše Benešová, of the ODS, was the second most popular politician of her party after the 1998 elections. She was only a few percentage points behind the party's charismatic leader, former Prime Minister Václav Klaus.[4] The few women who were nominated did quite well in the 1998 Senate elections. In general the evidence indicates that voters do *not* provide a substantial obstacle to increased female representation in parliament. Women do as well as men with voters. Rather, the problem is to get women nominated in the first place.

❖ Women's desire to become candidates

Most authors writing about gender issues in post-Communist Eastern Europe emphasize the region's anti-feminist atmosphere. The lack of pro-feminist attitudes and strong women's groups to support female candidates could discourage women from becoming politically active. Women entering politics are disadvantaged by the prevailing traditional gender roles giving them full responsibility for the household and child-raising duties (Čermáková 1997*b*: 391). Even female activists have a tendency to avoid direct involvement in party politics. For example, the founder of the Gender Studies Centre, Jiřina Šiklová (1998: 10), advocates a continuation of the 'anti-politics' tradition from the Communist era, during which dissidents aimed to build up a civil society in opposition to the regime rather than directly confront it.

Nevertheless, the available evidence shows that women are much more willing to enter politics than is suggested by their low representation in Parliament. For example, the Department of Sociology at Charles University conducted a survey showing that 40 per cent of Czech men and 27 per cent of Czech women were 'interested in being involved in public affairs' (cited in Potůček 1996). Although the percentage of men interested in being involved in public affairs is greater than the percentage of women, the difference between the two groups in interest, is much smaller than the differences in actual political representation. Forty per cent of those interested in getting involved in public affairs were women, while only 17 per cent of parliamentarians that year were women.

Similarly, a survey conducted by the Czech Academy of Science's Institute of Sociology in 1996 shows that women comprised 35 per cent of those who were very interested in politics.[5] However, women are less visible when it comes to party membership. The survey shows only 29 per cent of those belonging to a political party were women. Nevertheless, this is still twice the percentage of female parliamentarians. Furthermore, as can be seen in Figure 12.1, there is no relationship between the percentage of membership that is female and the percentage of female MPs for each party. We see in the KDU–ČSL, women make up more than 50 per cent of the membership (52.3), but the parliamentary delegation is only 15 per cent.

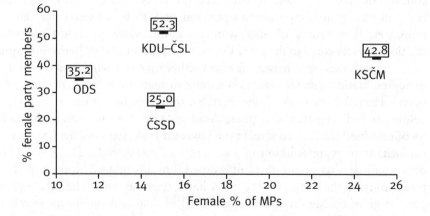

Figure 12.1. Female party membership and female per cent of MPs

Moreover, the rates of female party membership in the Czech Republic do not look dramatically different from those in the Scandinavian countries. Women comprise 30–40 per cent of party members in most Swedish parties (Sundberg 1995: 94). Yet, the Scandinavian countries have substantially higher rates of female representation in parliament. Female representation in the Swedish parliament is usually at the same level as the percentage of female party members or higher.

Women who are interested and involved in politics may not receive parliamentary nominations because they already have the double burden of paid and household work. It is also very possible, however, that parties discriminate against women in the nominating process. At the very least, it is likely the parties are not taking any measures to encourage women to become candidates. If interest in politics or party-membership rates determined what proportion of parliament was female, then we would expect there to be fewer women than men in parliament, but there would still be considerably more female MPs than there are today.

❖ The nominating process

The most significant obstacle in front of women seeking parliamentary positions is the parties' internal nominating process. It involves two issues: (1) nominating women for a place on the ballot, and (2) placing these women in 'winnable' positions on the ballot. Women's position on the ballot is extremely important. Table 12.2 shows that for most parties, the number of women nominated exceeded the total number of seats the party won. If all the women on the ballot were placed at the top of the list, 100 per cent of the MPs for the KSČM, KDU–ČSL, and US in the 1998 elections would be women. In addition, 58 per cent of the ČSSD MPs and 83 per cent of ODS MPs would be women.

Table 12.3 indicates there are big differences across the parties in willingness to place women in good positions on the ballot. In the fourth and ninth columns of Table 12.3 I present coefficients of representation. This coefficient is calculated by dividing women's per cent of MPs by women's per cent of nominees. It measures whether women's nominations provide them with election chances equal to the party's men. A coefficient of representation equal to 1.00 means that nominations favour neither men nor women; a coefficient of representation greater than 1.00 means women are a larger portion of a party's elected MPs than of the party's candidates for office; a coefficient below 1.00 indicates that women are disadvantaged *vis-à-vis* men in the quality of nominations they receive. In the 1996 and 1998 elections, the KSČM had coefficients of representation of 1.40 and 1.25, respectively. The KSČM not only nominated large numbers of women, but advantaged women in their positioning on the ballot. On the other hand, the ODS, which had the highest percentage of female candidates nominated in 1996 and significant numbers of female candidates in 1998, had very low coefficients of representation (0.44 and 0.63). Women make it onto the ODS ballots in large numbers, but

❖ STEVEN SAXONBERG

Table 12.3. Discrimination in allocating spots on the ballot

Year	1996					1998				
Party	Per cent female candidates	Per cent female elected	Coefficient of representation	Winnable* seats +10%	Winnable seats +20%	Per cent female candidates	Per cent female elected	Coefficient of representation	Winnable* seats +10%	Winnable seats +20%
KSČM	16.4	22.7	1.40	16.7	23.7	20.1	25.0	1.24	25.0	27.5
ČSSD	14.4	18.0	1.25	15.9	16.6	14.4	14.9	1.03	17.1	16.1
KDU–ČSL	12.8	11.1	0.87	8.0	6.1	13.8	15.0	1.09	10.7	11.1
ODS	22.5	10.3	0.46	10.5	10.7	17.4	11.1	0.64	15.5	15.0

Calculations based on the Czech Statistical Office's information on the Internet at http://www.volby.cz.

* 'Winnable Seats +10% is defined as an electoral result in which the party would gain 10% more seats in each district. For example, if a party actually won 20 seats in a district, then the number of winnable seats would be 22. If a party only won 3 seats, then the number of winnable seats would be 4. In cases in which a party won 15 seats a 10% increase in votes would have meant a gain of 1.5 seats. In these cases, I rounded off upwards giving the party 2 extra seats. Similarly, I added a minimum two-seat gain at 20%.

are much more likely to be placed at the bottom of the ballot, where they are unlikely to get elected. The KDU–ČSL gave women nominations that qualitatively are equivalent to those given to men. Meanwhile, the ČSSD elected a significantly larger percentage of women than it nominated in 1996. This difference disappeared, however, in 1998.

Another way to analyse this is to look at the percentage of women given 'winnable seats'. If, for example, a small party only wins one or two seats per district, then these top spots usually go to local male notables. If the party merely increased representation by one seat per district, however, they may radically increase the percentage of female MPs. To check for this possibility, I have calculated the change in female representation for each party given the party won 10 per cent more seats or at least one more seat per district, and then for the case in which the party would win 20 per cent more seats or at least two more seats per district.

In 1996, increasing the number of seats a party would have won causes results similar to those of the election. In several cases, however, an increase in seats won would have actually led to a decrease in the percentage of female MPs. This category includes the KSČM (for a 10 per cent increase), the ČSSD, and the KDU–ČSL. In 1998, the results show that a moderate increase in the number of seats won would have impacted only the ODS' female representation. In this case, the ODS would have increased female representation by about four per cent if it had won 10 per cent or 20 per cent more seats. The KDU–ČSL's case in 1998 is special. It appears that an increase in seats won would have caused a decline in the percentage of women elected. However, preferential voting was not included in calculating winnable seats. In the 1998 election, Vlasta Parkanová won a seat because of preferential votes. If there had been no preferential vote, only 10 per cent of ODS representatives would have been female.

The calculations of winnable seats show that, for the most part, parties cannot blame the low female representation on poorer than expected electoral results. There would not have been big jumps in representation if the parties had done slightly better. On the other hand, the range of coefficients of representation indicate that, outside of the ODS, the quality of women's nominations are at least as good as those received by men. The problem, in other words, is that so few women are being nominated.

Czech parties use one of the two basic types of nominating processes. One is a system of direct democracy while the other comprises what I term a 'pyramid' model. In the direct democracy model, the party holds primary elections at the regional level, in which all party members vote directly for the candidates. In the pyramid model, there is a caucus held by local party organizations, in which each member presents votes for delegates to the district conference and usually on candidate nominations for the parliamentary elections. Delegates are elected to attend the district conference, and the list of candidate nominees is sent to the district executive committee that plans the district conference. The pyramid model, shown in Fig. 12.2, is by far most common in the Czech Republic.

If female politicians are more popular than male politicians, but due to sexism the party leadership is not interested in recruiting women to top positions, then we would expect direct elections to be more favourable to women than the pyramid model. The fact that members have more than one vote may benefit women. In a sense, party members could play the role that party leaders have in balancing the ticket in Western parliamentary systems, in which there are large electoral districts and centralized nominating procedures.

In contrast, in the absence of a strong women's movement to pressure the party leadership into increasing female representation, the pyramid system might make it more difficult for women to get nominated to winnable seats. This is because this system strengthens territorial politics, allowing nominations based on territorial affiliation. Moreover, even if there is a strong women's organization within the party, the pyramid model forces women to keep up the pressure at many different points. It is easier to mobilize members for one round of internal party elections than it is for several rounds. On the other hand, if party leaders insist on including high female representation in their efforts to balance the ticket, then the pyramid model, which gives more power to leaders, might actually help women.

Finally, studies of Western democracies have shown that women tend to do better when parties have clear and transparent rules in their nominating process. In such cases, women can more easily organize and lobby to get more candidates nominated. If the rules are not transparent and institutionalized, patronage systems usually emerge that allow 'old-boy' networks to prevent women from advancing.[6] Let us now turn to the nominating processes of each of the major parties.[7]

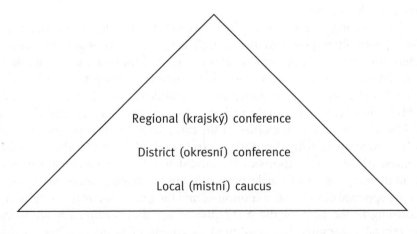

Regional (krajský) conference

District (okresní) conference

Local (místní) caucus

Figure 12.2. Pyramid form of candidate selection

❖ *KSČM*

The Communist Party uses the pyramid model, the first step of which is the local membership conference recommending candidates to the district conference. In addition, the district party organization and other executive bodies make district-level recommendations (KSČM 1995a).

According to Naděžda Machů, Secretary of the KSČM Club of MPs, the district executive committee normally makes candidate recommendations to the local organization. This means the head of the committee usually has the greatest influence on candidate selection. Only five of the 86 district heads were women at the time of the interview. However, about 50 per cent of the district's executive committee members were women. Machů adds that although the district executive committee makes recommendations, the local organizations need not support them. She noted that her local organization usually adds some of its own suggestions. Theoretically, this opens up the possibility of mobilizing women around female candidates; however, she said they have not been very successful on that front because the discussions on ticket balancing do not prominently consider sex. Instead, they focus on the perceived greater need of finding young candidates.

Moreover, she notes, the Club of Leftist Women has close ties to the party, but its influence is limited because it is not an official party organization and not all of its members belong to a party. The organization cannot make demands on the party or mobilize all its members to attend local caucuses. Another problem is that many women who are not in the Club do not actively support female candidates. Therefore, even successful attempts to get women to attend local meetings do not ensure female nominations. Nevertheless, the Club meets before the caucuses and tries to mobilize women. This may be a partial explanation for the *KSČM* having a higher percentage of female MPs than the other parties.

After receiving proposals from the local districts and other party bodies, the district committee puts together a draft list of candidates for the caucus. Before the caucus, the regional electoral staff decides how many candidates each district may nominate. At the district conference, delegates vote by secret ballot to determine the popularity of the candidates. The district conference sends its list of candidates to the regional electoral staff. The regional electoral staff in turn decides on the order of the candidates, but it is supposed to do so 'in cooperation with the district executive body'. Finally, the statewide congress of the KSČM approves the candidate lists of the regional electoral committees. Delegates can make proposals, but no changes can be made without the approval of the central committee and the general secretary of the party. According to the head of the party club of deputies, Vědunka Stuchlíková, the central committee has only made a couple of cosmetic changes that concern unwinnable seats in order to increase the number of candidates from youth and similar groups.

Since the Central Committee normally only makes symbolic changes, it does not seriously utilize its ability to push for greater female representation. Several factors might account for the relatively high number of female representatives in the KSČM. First, organizations other than the local party conferences are allowed to propose candidates, giving greater incentive to consider factors other than territorial representation. While the Club of Leftist Women perceives itself as having only limited success, its attempts to mobilize female members separate the Communists from all of the centre-right parties. Furthermore, in contrast to the other parties, it is official policy to encourage higher female candidacy rates. For example, the party's Central Operative Electoral Staff in 1995 suggested that 'nearly 50 per cent of the candidates should be women, especially in the "leading positions"' (KSČM 1995b). The party does not, however, have an official quota system. Finally, the party has had the same nominating practices for at least the last two elections and the rules are clearly written in party documents. This stability is enhanced because many of the members have known each other since the Communist era, which gives them an advantage over the newly founded parties. Consequently, the KSČM has more institutionalized nominating procedures, which could make it easier for women to penetrate the system.

❖ ČSSD

In contrast to the KSČM, the Social Democrats have had little stability in their nominating procedures. In the 1996 elections, each regional organization decided for itself how to choose candidates. Some regions used the pyramid model. Others chose variations of direct elections. Each member had seven votes for the direct elections in 1996, and could choose among 60–80 candidates in the regional primary. Candidates were then placed on the ballot in order of the votes received, meaning the least popular candidates failed to make the ballot.[8]

In the Prague region, according to Světlana Navarová, the party opted for the direct democracy model. However, since party leaders were aware that the primary election results were unpredictable and they wanted their most popular politicians in Parliament, the regional organ reserved the top spot on the ballot for Petra Buzková. The party was dissatisfied with the results of the direct elections. In Prague, for example, a popular singer gained a high spot on the ballot despite the fact that party leadership did not consider him politically knowledgeable. Furthermore, the head of a security company also gained a high spot because he persuaded his firm's employees to join the party and vote for him.

A pyramid model was formalized for the entire party for the 1998 elections since the party leadership was dissatisfied with the 1996 results in regions using direct elections.[9] Nomination procedures under this system had four steps:

1. Local branches suggested candidates for parliament (6–8) to the district executive committee and elected delegates to the district conference. The district executive committee also had the right to propose candidates as well, as did internal party organizations, including the Social Democratic Women.
2. Delegates at the district conference voted on the proposed candidates and each district proposed four candidates to the regional executive committee. District conference members included members of the district executive committee, the head of each local branch organization, and additional delegates chosen by the local organizations.
3. The regional executive committee puts together a list of candidates based on the district nominations and proposes the ballot's candidate order.
4. A regional conference is held. Delegates include the members of the regional executive committee, the heads of each district executive committee, and further delegates chosen at the district conference (which, in practice, appear to be the district conference's most successful parliamentary candidates). The regional conference decides whether or not to approve the list. The number of votes each delegate has corresponds to 10 per cent of the candidates. Thus, if there are 40 candidates, each delegate has four votes. Any candidate who receives more than 50 per cent of the votes moves to the top of the ballot list in order of the votes received.

In contrast to the party conferences, district and regional executive committee members are not chosen during the nominating process. However, these party organs clearly have great influence on the nominating process. They have the right to propose candidates at the district level and to propose the order of candidates to the perspective conferences at both levels. Even though all members have a vote at the local level, in practice, the decision is made by the district executive committee. The local caucus merely confirms these decisions. As Jan Korf, head of the organizational branch of the Secretariat of the ČSSD, said, 'usually, the candidates for parliament are discussed and negotiated at the level of the district executive committee; then it goes back to the local organization and they implement that already-negotiated proposal'. Thus, despite the local organization's formal rights, the district executive committee becomes the true centre of nominating power rather than the local caucuses.

Executive committee members have added influence because they also attend party conferences. For example, Anna Čurdová recalls that at the regional conference in central Bohemia, seven members from the regional executive committee, the heads of the district executive committees, and parliamentary candidates with the highest number of votes from each of the 12 districts served as delegates. Since women rarely top the local or district conference lists, relatively few women attend the district and regional conferences.

❖ STEVEN SAXONBERG

The ČSSD is the only party to have a quota system, and 25 per cent of all delegates, unlike candidates, must be women (ČSSD 1997*b*). Therefore, organized women somewhat influence conferences. A problem occurred, however, because the local party organizations were not required to ensure 25 per cent of their conference and top party nominees were women (Social Democratic Women 1997). If they nominated less than 25 per cent women—which they often did—the Social Democratic Women's organization (SDŽ) had the formal power to nominate extra women. Both former International Secretary Světlana Navarová and Anna Čurdová, general secretary of the SDŽ, claim that party officials used the quota system to discriminate against women. Rather than nominate females, local party officials claimed that women could get elected anyway because of the quota system. Thus, the quota became a difficult-to-surpass *maximum* level. Moreover, local organizations were not responsible for recruiting more women to top positions. Another disadvantage is that the SDŽ's female delegates did not have strong party support.

Lack of rule institutionalization between the 1996 and 1998 elections increased the difficulty in mobilizing support for female candidacies. Without clear knowledge of rules and procedures, it becomes difficult for female groups to lobby for increased representation. Navarová gives the following example of females' difficulties in the many rounds of candidate selection: In the Prague region in 1998, the regional conference voted to reject the regional executive committee's proposal. Although it was against the official rules, the conference voted to change the candidates' ballot order. Afterwards, it submitted the candidate list for the approval of the regional executive committee. Navarová notes that women had higher positions on the regional executive committee's original list.

Delegates at the regional conference represent their districts. Because they represent territorial rather than group interests, they do not try to balance the ballot in the same way as the regional executive committee. Navarová claims that delegates bargain at the conference to gain support for a candidate from their own district. Men have an advantage because local male constituency leaders are usually promoted.

In addition to regional balance, Jan Korf claims that the ČSSD takes the candidates' professions into account. It will try, for example, to recruit experts from a region's largest industrial or agricultural sectors. Gender is not a major factor in the ticket-balancing process.

It is particularly interesting that while all the other parties increased their percentage of women in their parliamentary delegation from 1996 to 1998, the ČSSD's proportion dropped. It seems reasonable to speculate that the decline came from the shift from primary elections to the pyramid system. In the primary elections, women benefited from being more popular than their male competitors between the populace and party members at large. In the pyramid system, the ticket balancers have not taken gender issues into account and the dominance of territorial issues gives an advantage to men.

❖ KDU–ČSL

In 1998, the Christian Democrats revamped their system of nominations, without affecting female representation. This could have occurred for two reasons. First, new procedures resulted in opaque rules that obstructed women's ability to organize and get their own candidates elected. Second, as members of a conservative Catholic party, females have not been particularly interested in representation. Both Nad'a Vitásko (Chair of the Club of Christian Women) and Luděk Kudláček (International Secretary of the KDU–ČSL) noted in interviews that there has been no discussion within the party about women's role or the need to increase female representation.[10]

The nominating process was very centralized in 1996. Delegates negotiated a preliminary list and candidate ballot order for eight regions at the statewide conference. Then, the statewide executive committee decided on the final lists and candidate order (KDU–ČSL 1996). In contrast, in the direct elections two years later, all party members could vote on the list of candidates in their region. It was put together by the Regional Nominating Commission, but the commission did not suggest any candidate order. Instead, they were listed alphabetically (KDU–ČSL 1998).

According to the official statutes, the party had an extremely complicated, difficult-to-understand nominating procedure. According to the rules, candidates with the most and the least votes were to be eliminated from the party lists.[11] If these rules were truly followed, then the party leader and other ministers would probably not have been nominated. It is clear, however, that these rules made it difficult for female 'outsiders' to organize support. Even though there was some devolvement, the central organizations in the party maintained their central role.

❖ ODS

The ODS practices a pyramid model.[12] Petr Plecitý, ODS' Foreign Office secretary and First Deputy Chair of the fourth district of Prague, admits members at the local caucus do not have much influence on the nominating process. Although the local organizations have the right to nominate candidates to parliament, they rarely do so. They formally select delegates to the district conference. Access to the district conference is relatively easy to attain as up to one-third of the total membership may participate. Thus, there is not much politicking at the local level. At the district level, candidates are nominated for parliament and delegates are chosen for the regional congress.

❖ STEVEN SAXONBERG

Most of the decision-making at the regional congress is based on secret agreements between districts. Consequently, the process is not very open and there is little possibility for women to mobilize around female candidates. Finally, the statewide party's executive counsel has the right to change the lists. According to Zahradil, the executive counsel only exercised this right once or twice in 1998.

Zahradil also notes that the party did *not* change its nominating procedures during the last two elections, becoming more institutionalized than in either the KDU–ČSL or the ČSSD. This should theoretically make it easier for women to organize and push for more female candidates. However, women made no such attempts. Furthermore, the party never discussed quotas or other measures of increasing female representation. The party leadership holds considerable power, but has felt little need to use it to promote women.

❖ *Conclusion*

So far, it does not appear that differences in nominating processes have a systematic impact on the percentage of women elected to Parliament. The ČSSD sent more women to Parliament when it allowed for direct elections. For the KDU–ČSL, however, the change in the nominating process made little difference. While many of the parties with the lowest levels of representation used a pyramid structure, the KČSM's pyramid system resulted in the highest percentage of female MPs. The difference probably lies in two factors: the KČSM leadership's greater commitment to elect women to Parliament, and more transparent, institutionalized nominating rules that make it easier for women to utilize the system. The ČSSD is committed to greater female representation. Nevertheless, Social Democratic women experienced the delegate quotas as a maximum limit rather than a minimum requirement. Finally, although both parties used pyramid systems in the 1998 election, the ODS has consistently had lower female representation than the ČSSD. The difference between the two parties probably lies in the fact that the ODS does not have any women's organizations, nor does it have any debate on female representation. Let us now turn to women's organizations' attempts to influence party nominations.

❖ **WOMEN'S ORGANIZATIONS' ATTEMPTS TO INFLUENCE THE NOMINATING PROCESS**

Rightist and Centre-Rightist Organizations. The Democratic Alternative is the best-known liberally oriented women's organization. Its president, Hana Vosečková, admits that it has not had much influence on the right-wing parties. The ODS and ODA are conservative in family issues and thus not interested in discussing the need for more female politicians. Quotas are taboo for both the ODA and ODS, and since neither have formal women's factions, the Democratic Alternative could not do much to influence them. Thus, the Democratic Alternative has basically limited its electoral activities to encouraging women to become candidates within their parties and supporting female candidates in the elections. Moreover, the organization has few resources. Therefore, it has limited its help to personal campaigning for Social Democratic and similar candidates.

The most important Christian Democratic women's organization is the Club of Christian Women, which is affiliated with the KDU–ČSL. Its chair, Naďa Vitásko, said the organization has made no attempt to influence the number of female candidates or press women's issues because it sees itself as a self-help organization. Consequently, other than the fact that highly placed functionaries in the Club of Christian Women gain organizing experience and often come in contact with politicians from the KDU–ČSL, it has not had any influence on the number of women nominated to Parliament.

Leftist organizations. The most important women's organization to the left of the Social Democrats is the Club of Leftist Women, which cooperates closely with the KSČM. Although it is not officially affiliated with the party, about 70 per cent of its members are also party members.[13] The party originally had its own women's organization. However, from 1992 to 1996 the KSČM had an electoral alliance with a reform Communist group and formed a 'Left Bloc'. In conjunction with this alliance, most of the local Communist women's organizations dissolved to join the newly formed Club of Leftist Women.[14]

According to Stuchlíková, the organization has tried to press the party to increase female representation. It has even suggested introducing a quota system, but it is doubtful that the party congress will accept this proposal. Club member Machů also claims the organization has had limited success in influencing the party. It normally has meetings aimed at mobilizing its members around female candidates before the local party caucuses, but as already mentioned, not all its members attend the caucuses. Furthermore, Machů complains that it has been difficult to get other women within the party to support their candidates. It should be noted that while these women feel their efforts have not been particularly successful, their success rate is higher than other parties.

The organization of Social Democratic Women (SDŽ) is officially affiliated with its mother party (the ČSSD), although not all its members are party members. General secretary of the SDŽ, Anna Čurdová, said that the organization would like to increase the number of female MPs, but does not openly lobby on this issue because it meets much resistance. Nonetheless, the SDŽ is aware the party discriminates against female politicians in its selection process. In Čurdová's words, 'There is no problem in getting female candidates; we have very good, highly educated and well-qualified women. The problem is the nominating

❖ STEVEN SAXONBERG

process'. Čurdová also notes that female politicians within the party are more popular than male politicians, so there is no rational reason for the party to continue favouring male candidates. It is striking that she sees no problem finding well-qualified women despite the ČSSD's having the lowest percentage of female members among the four main parties (see Fig. 12.1).

The SDŽ is trying to educate party members about this problem. It suggested using quotas in nominating candidates for parliamentary elections, but there is not much support in the party for such steps. Čurdová feels that rather than try the Scandinavian method of directly demanding higher positions and greater representation, her organization must try the more indirect Dutch method. In the Netherlands, Social Democratic women have succeeded in increasing their parliamentary representation to about one-third of the party's MPs. However, rather than have their own women's organization, they built informal contact networks. Moreover, they do not have any formal quotas.

Finally, the organization is involved in educating the party's female politicians. They are trained to get more publicity and taught about women in politics in EU countries. So, although the SDŽ has failed to increase female representation within Parliament and the organization conflicts with the party, the organization is very active in trying to influence the party.

Despite these efforts to influence the party, it appears that the SDŽ is on the wane. A proposal was passed at the party's 1999 Congress to take away the SDŽ's right to appoint women to positions in order to fill the party organs' 25 per cent quota. However, the proposal is so vaguely worded that it is still not clear how and if it will be implemented. There are also fears that, if implemented, this proposal will weaken the SDŽ. It became clear in private talks with party members that there are tensions between the Social Democratic Party and its women's organization. In a symbolically significant move, indicative of the SDŽ's fall from grace, the organization was moved out of the party headquarters during a renovation and into the national trade union building. They have not moved back in.

Other party members confirm that the SDŽ is becoming increasingly isolated from the party (interviews with Profant, Hamáček, and Dolínek). This isolation stems from the SDŽ decision to strongly support Miloš Zeman for Prime Minister rather than work out its own platform. The SDŽ broke with him when he failed to appoint any female ministers, but had nobody else to turn to. Their positions also alienated them from the party's 'modernizing' faction. It remains to be seen, whether these strategic mistakes will have permanent negative consequences.

❖ Neutral organizations

The largest non-party women's organization that actively tries to increase female representation in Parliament is the Czech Union of Women (ČSŽ).

It has historical ties to the official women's organization from the communist era, causing other organizations to be skeptical of it, but is now independent. Nevertheless, the communist past also gives it a big advantage over other women's organizations. It has the best infrastructure and largest membership reservoir. Since the organization is politically independent, it offers to help all parties' female candidates, although the right-wing parties are generally disinterested in cooperating.[15] In the 1996 parliamentary election, for example, it was very active in promoting female candidates for the Small Pensioner's Party, which failed to make Parliament. Despite its independence, the organization appears to be particularly influential within the Social Democratic Party. For example, the organization's chair, Zdeňka Hajná, claims that the ČSŽ mobilized its members within the Social Democratic Party in some regions at the nominating meetings to encourage more women to become senatorial candidates. The organization was particularly successful in northern Bohemia. In addition to mobilizing members for nominating conferences, the ČSŽ also provided female candidates with campaign assistance in order to increase their number of preferential votes in the parliamentary elections. Again, since the right-wing parties are generally not interested in getting help from the ČSŽ, such activities tend to help Social Democrats (as well as the smaller parties, such as the Pensioner's Party and perhaps the Communists). Despite theČSŽ and SDŽ's efforts, the percentage of female Social Democratic MPs decreased from the 1996 to 1998 parliamentary election, showing that these organizations' influence on the party is still fairly limited.

❖ *Organizations' influence on party nomination procedures*

Although the women's organizations in the ČSSD and the KSČM do not appear to have a great deal of power, their mere existence might explain why these parties have had slightly greater female representation than centre-right parties in Parliament. Democratic Alternative, a liberal-conservative organization, has not been able to gain any influence within the centre-right parties. Meanwhile, although it has not yet increased the number of female MPs, the Czech Union of Women has actively tried to promote female candidates within all parties. Since the Union is the only non-party women's organization with the resources to mobilize large numbers successfully, they could perhaps 'pack' future meetings. Before the Union can hope to become successful in these endeavours, however, it will probably have to overcome party skepticism of its communist past.

❖ CONCLUSION: FEMALES AND THE FUTURE

According to the usual indicators, the Czech Republic should have a higher rate of female representation in its Parliament. Most women have entered the workforce and women are nearly as well educated as men. Until now, the country has had a proportional electoral system with large districts to allow the party to balance group interests, including the need for more women. Furthermore, the percentage of female party members is significant in all parties. Female politicians in the Czech Republic also appear to be more popular than their male counterparts. Their biggest obstacle is the nominating process. In the absence of a strong women's movement, the parties deciding how to balance the tickets appear to give regional balance top priority. This tendency strengthens when the pyramid model is used. A second obstacle is the nomination process' apparent lack of transparency. Since both the ČSSD and KDU–ČSL changed their nominating processes between elections, the rules of the game were not clear for everyone. This tends to hurt female, minority, and other groups outside of the power structure.

To some extent, the Communist KSČM provides an exception to these generalizations. Although it follows the pyramid model, its statutes strongly encourage the party to nominate women to all positions. It also has significant numbers of women in local party leadership positions and the highest rate of female representation in Parliament. In addition, the party has not changed its procedures for nominating candidates, which means that it probably has the most institutionalized rules.

The social democratic party shows that quotas are complicated. It is not merely a question of whether a party should have quotas, but also how quotas are implemented. Women's representation would increase if the quotas were used at all party levels rather than just for executive levels and the statewide conference. Allowing the women's organization to nominate delegates to fill the gap removed the responsibility of ensuring gender equality from the lower level organizations. It also ensured the quota would be a maximum level of female representation, as local party organizations otherwise refused to support qualified women on the grounds that they could get appointed by the women's organization. Women would do better if party organizations at all levels were conscious of the need to have more women in top positions. Of course, it would also make a big difference if the quotas were extended from party delegates to actual candidates.

The Western experience shows that women do best in parliamentary systems when the party leadership realizes that having more female candidates increases votes. It is already clear to many female politicians and political activists that women are effective vote-getters. So far, however, the women's organizations have been much more successful in helping female candidates than in lobbying party leaders. Both the party women's organizations (such as the Club of Democratic Women) and the independent organizations (such as the Union of Czech Women and Democratic Alternative) actively campaign for and train female candidates. They have, however, continued to struggle with increasing their influence in the party.

❖ Notes

1 Voters are allowed to give 4 preferential votes to candidates of one party; if a candidate gets preferential votes equaling 10 per cent or more of the party's total votes, he or she moves to the top of the list. In practice this barrier is so high that it has been extremely rare for anyone to gain a seat due to preferential voting. It has affected Parliament's gender composition only once in 1996 and 1998, and it was in favour of women. In 1998, Christian Democrat Vlasta Parková, gained a seat due to preferential votes.

2 The government has proposed increasing the number of districts from 8 to 35, thus limiting the number of seats per district from 4 to 8.

3 The Senate has limited formal powers. As a consequence, there has been low voter interest in Senate elections. In 1996, only 30.5 % of all eligible voters turned out for the second round of voting (about 5% less than in the first round; Lidove noviny, 25 November 1996). In comparison, 76.4% voted in the lower house elections to the Chamber of Deputies. Turnout in the 1998 Senate elections was even lower as only 20.4% voted in the second round of elections (Lidove noviny, 23 November 1998).

4 The polls were conducted by the Institute for Public Opinion Research and reprinted on the Social Democrats' website: http://www.cssd.cz/aktuality/a-113.htm.

5 The Czech title of the data base collection is 'Role vlády—1996', it was created in conjunction with the international ISSP survey entitled 'The Role of Goverment III'.

6 See Marila Guadagnini (1993: 180–2) and Miki Caul (1999).

7 The information presented here comes from interviews with members of the four parties (KSČM, ČSSD, KDU–ČSL, and ODS) and internal party documents.

8 Personal interview with Světlana Navarová.

9 Personal interviews with Navarová, Anna Čurdová, Jan Korf, Jan Hamáček, and Petr Dolínek and internal ČSSD documents (1997).

10 Personal interview with Naďa Vitásko and Luděk Kudláček.

11 KDU–ČSL 'Nominační řád KDU–ČSL', internal party document (1998).

12 Personal interviews with Jan Zahradil and Petr Plecitý.

13 Personal Interview with Vědunka Stuchlíková.

14 Much of this information can be found in the descriptions of women's organizations in the Gender Studies Centre's handbook (1995).

15 Zdeňka Hajná noted in the interview that the ČSŽ sent letters to all of the political parties before the 1998 elections and offered their help, but the ODS and ODA did not answer them. The KDU–ČSL was also not very interested, since it cooperates with the Christian Women's Clubs.

13 ❖ Factors Influencing Women's Presence in Slovene Parliament

Milica G. Antić

In 1991, Slovenia declared independence from the federal socialist state of Yugoslavia and after a brief armed clash, Slovenian independence was established. Slovenia is a post-socialist state and shares many of the policy legacies of the socialist project of directive emancipation. Developmentally and socially, however, it is comparable to Western Europe. Excluding East Germany, Slovenia stands alone as the only 'high income' economy among some twenty-six socialist successor states. It is a member of the Council of Europe and is among the frontrunner candidates applying for membership in the European Union and NATO.

Its policy problems, too, converge with those of the post-industrial democracies. It has an aging population, low birthrates, relatively high unemployment, and immigration and minority rights issues. Reminiscent of the long-standing Western democracies, women in Slovenia have been vocal and organized on issues like abortion. Given the close comparison with Western Europe, we might expect Slovenia to produce the highest levels of female representation in the post-socialist region. Its National Assembly, however, has a lower percentage of women than the average in Eastern Europe and there has been absolutely no growth in the number of women in parliament over the past decade. The question for this research is: Why aren't there more women in Slovene national politics?

❖ THE ADVENT OF REPRESENTATIVE DEMOCRACY

By the end of the eighties, civil society had begun to solidify in Slovenia. This process reached a zenith with the formation of representative political parties. The highlight of 1990 was the first democratic and multiparty election. At that time, Slovenia was still a part of former Yugoslavia and still a socialist state with a three-chamber assembly: the Chamber of Communes, the Socio-Political Chamber, and the Chamber for Associated Labour (Grad 1997: 174). The Assembly of Associated Labour, a vestige of the Communist past, stood alongside new competitive leagues (proto-parties). For the first time in decades, the electorate was able to choose among different political orientations. These included: the Party of Democratic Renewal (now United List of Social Democrats—ZLSD), the Liberal Democratic Party (now Liberal Democracy of Slovenia—LDS), the Slovenian Christian Democrats (SKD), the Slovenian Farmers Party (now Slovenian People's Party—SLS + SKD), the Slovenian Democratic Alliance (SDZ), the Greens of Slovenia (ZS), the Social Democratic Party of Slovenia (now Social Democratic Party—SDS), the Socialist Alliance of Slovenia (SZS), the Liberal Party (LS), and the Slovenian National Party (SNS).

Some of the parties were transformed socio-political organizations (such as the ZLSD which is largely a 'reformed Communist party' or the Alliance of Socialist Youth, which has developed into the LDS). Some of them arose from oppositional movements. Others were organized from new social movements (e.g., the Greens). Nine parties ultimately won seats at the first 'multiparty' election to the three-chamber assembly. A broad coalition of anti-Communist forces, called DEMOS, formed a government that would last two years.

Each chamber employed a different electoral system, yet female representation declined in all three. Each chamber had 80 seats: 12 women were elected to the Chamber of Associated Labour (15 per cent) under a simple plurality system; the Chamber of Communes had three women MPs (3.75 per cent) elected via a two-round majority system; and the Socio-Political Chamber recruited 12 women (15 per cent) through party list proportional representation (PR). Overall, out of the 240 seats, women won 27 (11.25 per cent), decreasing women's representation by more than half from the Communist era norm for the Slovene Assembly of between 24 and 28 per cent.

Subsequent elections have been carried out under a new set of complicated PR rules for a 90 member National Assembly. This system allowed eight parties to enter the legislature in 1992 (of 28 that competed), seven parties in 1996, and eight in 2000 (including the newly formed Party of Young People). After the first post-independence elections in 1992, female representation was 13.3 per cent. That figure fell to only 7.8 per cent in 1996, but rebounded to 13.3 per cent in 2000 with the strong return of centre-left parties to government (see Table 13.1).

Women are similarly underrepresented in government. There has never been a female Prime Minister. In 1992 the government had only one woman among 14 ministers. In 1996 there were no women at the beginning, and only after three years in power did the Prime Minister nominate a female minister

❖ Milica G. Antić

Table 13.1. Parliamentary deputies by party and sex after the 1992, 1996, and 2000 elections

Political party	1992			1996			2000		
	M	F	Total	M	F	Total	M	F	Total
United List of Social Democrats (ZLSD)	12	2	14	9	0	9	8	3	11
Liberal Democracy of Slovenia (LDS)	20	2	22	24	1	25	29	5	34
Democrats of Slovenia (DS)	5	1	6						
Greens of Slovenia (ZS)	5	0	5						
Party of Young People (SMS)							4	0	4
Democratic Pensioners Party of Slovenia (DeSUS)				4	1	5	4	0	4
Slovene People's Party (SLS)	8	2	10	18	1	19			
Slovene Christian Democrats (SKD)	13	2	15	9	1	10			
SLS-SKD Slovene People's Party (SLS + SKD)							9	0	9
Social Democratic Party of Slovenia (SDS)	4	0	4	15	1	16	14	0	14
New Slovenia Christian People's Party (Nsi)							6	2	8
Slovenian National Party (SNS)	10	2	12	3	1	4	3	1	4
Ethnic minorities	1	1	2	1	1	2	1	1	2
Total	78	12	90	83	7	90	78	12	90

Source: Milica G. Antić, Ženske v parlamentu (Women in Parliament), Ljubljana: Znanstveno in publicistično središče, 1998 and author's later calculation.

for economic affairs and Secretary General of the Government. In 2000 there were three female ministers: for Education, Research, and Sport; for Culture; and for Economy.

Why did female representation decline with the advent of competitive elections, and why have women remained marginal players in official politics? The answer to these questions is complex and multi-causal, but we can begin by examining some of the commonly cited barriers in the literature.

❖ BARRIERS TO FEMALE RECRUITMENT

❖ Socioeconomic and cultural

It has frequently been asserted that after the fall of Socialism, women had had enough of forced emancipation and therefore willingly withdrew from political life. *The Inter-Parliamentary Union* concludes that women worldwide may eschew political competition because they lack necessary resources and qualifications, have overwhelming family demands, and/or fear hostility in the electorate. On the face of it, Slovenian women are quite successful in the present system of education and employment. Women form a higher share of students enrolled in higher education institutions than do men–around 60 per cent in 1995–6 and 56 per cent in 1997–8 (*Women in Slovenia in the 1990s*, 23–40). The share of women among Master's students and professional studies is consistently around half. Only at the highest levels are women underrepresented. The share of women doctoral students hovers around 30–35 per cent.

The situation is similar with regard to employment. Women in Slovenia have long considered their paid employment a source of economic and social independence. The share of women among paid employees was consistently high during the socialist years. Additionally, unlike in many other postcommunist countries, women did not lose their jobs at a significantly higher rate than did men during the transition. Their share in paid employment varies from 46.8 per cent in 1990 to 48.3 per cent in 1995 (*Women in Slovenia* 43). Nevertheless, there remains a gender-wage gap. In 1996, women made, on average, 85 per cent of men's monthly wages. This may be related to the fact that women only make up about 7 per cent of directors of large companies and 14 per cent of directors of small companies.

From these data we may conclude that Slovene women lack some of the resources that men possess. Men continue to dominate the highest positions in the economy and the educational hierarchy, but this is not much different than what we see in the post-industrial countries. In Slovenia, as elsewhere, there are qualified and resourceful women in the pool of eligibles, but these women may not be willing to step forward as candidates for other reasons. According to interviews with party officials responsible for identifying new and promising candidates, economically successful and highly educated women are approached to run for office, but these women often decline, saying they prefer to continue working in their companies or they cannot just leave their posts. To the extent that women have to work harder than men to achieve top positions in companies, they may be loathe to leave those positions for comparatively uncompensated political work. Leading managers in Slovenia make considerably more money and command greater social prestige than do career politicians.

❖ MILICA G. ANTIĆ

These anecdotes receive some support from public opinion data gathered through telephone interviews by the daily newspaper, DELO (2 March 1996). Female respondents described politics as 'too time consuming', 'too dirty', or 'too boring' to merit their involvement. Some 40 per cent of all respondents said that they believe there are so few women in politics because women have too many responsibilities with family and the activities of everyday life. Nearly a third claimed that 'parties do not place enough women on their electoral lists'. This was the second most frequent response. Only 14.5 per cent believed that women simply lack interest in politics. When we break those responses down by gender, men are more likely than women to believe that women are under-represented due to a lack of interest in politics. Women attribute it to family obligations. Perhaps the most notable survey finding is that some 90 per cent of respondents supported the idea of a law demanding a higher share of women in politics (i.e., affirmative action or quotas). When asked: 'At which posts would women be equally responsible and successful as men'? over half of the survey respondents chose 'all positions' (i.e., MP, minister, highest posts in science and culture, managing big companies, etc.). More than 11 per cent in addition to that specifically answered 'in parliament and as ministers' (DELO, 2 March 1996).

Taken together, these responses suggest that Slovenian society, in contrast to much of the rest of Central and Eastern Europe, is not especially anti-feminist in terms of gender role norms, but women do have reasons to enter the candidate pool less frequently than do men. They have more complicated family-work roles, and they tend to view politics as a less prestigious and lucrative use of their talents, particularly since party nomination practices are seen as blocking women's chances for political advancement.

❖ *The nomination bottleneck*

Electoral data tend to confirm this suspicion. In 1992 there were 1475 candidates for 90 seats in the National Assembly. Among those, only 219 (14.8 per cent) were women. In 1996, there were 1311 candidates, among them 246 women (18.8 per cent).[1] In 2000, there were 234 women among 1001 candidates (23.4 per cent). Despite a general upward trajectory over time, voters have had far fewer opportunities to vote for women than to vote for men.

If we look at the data for each election broken down by party in Table 13.2, then we can see that women did as well or better than their share in the pool of candidates (by party) would have predicted. A major bottleneck for women appears to occur at the point of receiving the party nod. When Liberal Democracy (LDS) increased its share of female candidates to 25 per cent in 2000, up from 14 per cent in the prior election, it managed to elect five women, a figure that accounted for almost half of all the women elected to parliament.

Table 13.2. Women's share of candidates and elected MPs in Slovenian parliamentary election by party 1992, 1996, and 2000

Party	Election 1992				Election 1996				Election 2000			
	Candidates		MPs		Candidates		MPs		Candidates		MPs	
	Number	Share	Number	Share	Number	Share	Number	Share	Number	Share	Number	Share
ZLSD	14	15.5	2	14.2	36	40.2	0	0	29	33.3	3	27.2
LDS	7	9.3	2	9.1	11	13.6	1	4.0	21	25.3	5	14.7
DS	12	13.9	1	16.6	20	24.4	0	0	–	–	–	–
ZS	12	14.9	0	0	12	23.1	0	0	–	–	–	–
DeSUS	–	–	–	–	17	21.8	1	20.0	15	17.0	0	0
SLS	7	8.7	2	20.0	11	13.6	1	5.2	–	–	–	–
SKD	10	11.2	2	13.2	8	9.5	1	10.0	–	–	–	–
SLS + SKD	–	–	0	0	–	–	–	–	11	22.7	0	0
SDS(S)	6	7.9	0	0	10	11.9	1	6.2	11	12.7	0	0
Nsi	–	–	–	–	–	–	–	–	14	16.0	2	25.0
SNS	4	7.0	2	16.6	6	10.7	1	25.0	12	20.3	1	25.0
Other	–	–	1	–	–	–	1	–	–	–	1	–
Total	72	14.8	12	13.3	131	19.0	7	7.8	113	23.5	12	13.3

Source: Milica G. Antić, Ženske v parlamentu (Women in Parliament), Ljubljana: Znanstveno in publicistično središče, 1998 and author's calculations.

So, the question arises that: Why don't the parties nominate more women? The point is frequently made that there is no women's movement to speak of in Central and Eastern Europe. In addition, when women do organize, they do not problematize their concerns as 'women's issues' or see gender equity in politics as a means to achieve their demands. As a result, they do not place pressure on party gatekeepers to recruit more women. In Slovenia, however, this is only partly true.

According to the Women's Policy office, 'there are more than 50 non-governmental women's groups in Slovenia, which can further be divided into five major groups organized on the basis of profession, politically engaged women's groups, independent women's groups, women's groups in the border regions and groups for assisting women who are victims of violence'.[2] Non-governmental women's groups are less numerous and tend to be small and single-issue based. Frequently these groups consider themselves non-political, since they deal with social issues, such as aid to the victims of violence, self-help groups, legal aid, and cultural development.

From the end of the 1980s through the early 1990s, however, there was a small feminist group, *Women for Politics*, which played a visible public role in the field of women's politics. This group explicitly demanded more women in politics. The group published proclamations in daily newspapers addressed to important politicians. They emphasized the importance of gender equity in politics, demanded special governmental bodies to deal with women's questions, and, together with other groups, successfully defended a constitutional guarantee of reproductive rights. Although most explicitly mobilized on the issue of protecting abortion on demand, the activities of *Women for Politics* managed to raise consciousness of gender issues in at least some strata of society, particularly active party women, and encouraged the formation of women's caucuses within parties, which remain highly masculine.

Statistics show that female membership in parliamentary parties ranges from 61 per cent in the Slovenian Christian Democrats (SKD), which is high, but a not atypical percentage for Christian Democratic parties elsewhere in Europe, to a number of parties where women represent a third of the membership (SLS—33 per cent; ZLSD—37 per cent; LDS—28 per cent), to some parties which only have 20 per cent or less of women members (SDS—20 per cent; SNS—18 per cent).[3]

Party councils and executive boards, which are given the responsibility of setting party policy and running the organization, are even less representative of women (Table 13.3). There is only one party where the participation of women in the highest bodies of the party approaches one third (27 per cent in the centre-left LDS). In other parties the percentage varies from 23 per cent (SLS) to 11 per cent (SDS). At the highest level, however, there is no female party leader; only three parties have a female vice president and only one party

Table 13.3. Share of women in membership and important party bodies

Party	Year	Percentage of party women members	Percentage of women in party bodies	Women in party leadership	Percentage of women in party parliamentary group
SLS	1993	33.3	22.7 (Executive Committee)		20.0
	1997	35.0	18.4 (Executive Committee)	1 Vice President out of 5	5.2
SDS	1993	20.3	10.5 (Presidency)	NA	0
	1996	28.0	NA	NA	6.3
ZLSD	1993	37.3	17.5 (Presidency) 16.7 (Party Council)	1 Vice President out of 3	14.3
	1997	35.6	18.3 (Presidency) 16.7 (Party Council)	1 Vice President out of 3	0
LDS	1993	28.3	27.2 (Executive Committee) 26.6 (Party Council)	1 Vice President out of 3	9.1
	1997	30.1	27.2 (Executive Committee) 27.0 (Party Council)	1 Vice President out of 3	4.0
SNS	1993	18.0	12.0 (Presidency)	NA	8.3
	1997	NA	NA	NA	33.3
SKD	1993	61.7	18.6 (Presidency)	1 Vice President	20.0
	1997	60.0	23.0 (Executive Committee)	1 Secretary General	10.0
(DeSus)	1997	31.0	13.3 (Presidency)		20.00

NA: No data available.

Source: Milica G. Antić, Ženske v parlamentu (Women in Parliament), Ljubljana: Znanstveno in publicistično središče, 1998, reproduced by kind permission.

has a female secretary-general. In short, women are poorly represented in the forums where parties make their decisions.

Women within the various parties have felt a need to organize. In 1990, women in United List of Social Democrats (ZLSD) organized their women's section, and in 1993 this was transformed into Women's Forum. In 1992, women in Liberal Democracy (LDS) organized their club Minerva, which functioned as a think tank. In 1995 Minerva was reorganized into a wider Women's Net. That group disbanded in March 1999 as a protest against the lack of party activity in support of gender equity in politics. In 1992, women in three right-of-centre parties (People's Party, Christian Democrats, and Social Democrats) organized their own women's groups. Ideologically, the

❖ MILICA G. ANTIĆ

aims of these groups are quite different, but they all underline the need for more female participation in politics.

When asked about the power of women's groups,[4] all group leaders replied either that they are powerful or it depends on the issue. The leader of the Women's Alliance at SLS says that their group is active at the early stage in selecting female candidates. Leaders of women's groups in SDS and SKD are particularly proud that they got their parties to accept the rule that the leader of the women's group becomes a member of all important party bodies.

Only two parties, however, have been pushed by their women's organizations to incorporate quotas in their party bodies: LDS and ZLSD. These groups argued for quotas both in terms of them being justified as fair and legitimate policy, but also as a manner in which their parties could fall more in line with their European sister parties. Many of the Western European parties that the LDS and ZLSD felt it was natural to compare themselves to have electoral quotas. ZLSD alone incorporated a quota for candidate selection and managed to put forth 40 per cent female candidates at the 1996 election. The sincerity of the party's efforts can be questioned, however, when one finds that despite electing nine MPs, the ZLSD did not elect a single female MP. LDS accepted quotas for the stage of candidate recruitment, but in the final round of selection put forth only 11 women (13.6 per cent of its candidates) at the 1996 election. Furthermore, the LDS only elected one female MP out of 25 total.

For the 2000 election, ZLSD did not have obligatory quotas but did follow a party line that at least one third of the candidates would be women. In 2000, without a formal quota, but with a clear goal of 1/3 when they won 11 seats, three of the elected MPs were women (27.3 per cent). The LDS, on the other hand, lowered its quota in 2000 to 25 per cent. The LDS met their quota in terms of candidates (25.3 per cent), but only 14.7 per cent of their elected MPs (5 out of 34) were women. Slovenia provides evidence that quotas, *when they are taken seriously*, improve women's legislative access.

In terms of party organization and recruitment procedures, a few general conclusions may be drawn: (1) most parties are centralized with strong leadership structures (the ZLSD provides a partial exception); (2) the most democratic procedure for drawing up and approving lists of candidates has been established by the ZLSD (internal party election determines party candidates); (3) all the parties have internal party rules for candidate selection and nomination, but these rules are more or less *de jure*; and (4) as a rule, lists of candidates are determined and/or approved by the principal bodies of the party. In these, as it was already demonstrated, women are poorly represented and have little power. This is one of the main reasons why they have failed to be included in their parties' lists in any significant numbers. Even in those parties where women form a large part of the membership and/or form intra-party factions, they play little or no role in candidate selection.

In terms of legal constraints the law only stipulates that candidate lists shall be determined by parties in a secret ballot in accordance with their internal rules.[5] The law stipulates neither the method of candidate selection of candidates by the parties nor the method of drawing up their lists of candidates and the principles by which certain candidates are favoured over others. In practice, the electoral headquarters of individual parties usually operate in strict secrecy and a few selected individuals make the final decisions.

In the year preceding an election, parties commission various opinion polls and predictions of the prospects of would-be candidates and follow the opinion polls on party popularity published by the mass media. Analyses of data on nominees and their list placements indicate there are four concentric circles in the recruitment process.

In the first circle are the highest-profile party individuals: MPs, ministers, deputy ministers, mayors, and individuals from the highest echelons of the party apparatus. These candidates are overwhelmingly male and almost invariably placed in winnable units or top slots on national lists.

The second circle consists of candidates coming from regional and local centres. They are identified by party committees from their own members or from party sympathizers and consist of prominent local individuals (especially attractive are doctors, company managers, lawyers, and headmasters). The committee's task is to persuade these candidates to stand on the party's list. Since these candidates are often drawn from the highest managerial levels, women are also poorly represented here.

The third circle, perhaps unique to a fledgling democracy, involves well-known and high-profile individuals with a positive 'image' likely to attract voters. There are always some 'well-known faces' from cultural circles, the media, and some important state institutions, whom the electorate have never before associated with the party. Membership in the party does not pose a significant obstacle in the third circle; and women are present together with other well-known public figures.

The fourth circle consists of members in local committees with many years of service to the party, who could make—either in their own opinion or in that of the local committee—a good party candidate. This circle is the largest one and there are substantial numbers of women in this circle. The chief qualification is party service. The problem women face is that the recruitment circles they are most prominent in are the ones that are unlikely to provide sufficiently good positions to lead to election to the parliament.

With seven or eight parties represented in each parliament, Slovenian parties cover a broad ideological spectrum. The conservative government that was felled in the 2000 elections was built around a spread from the traditional corporate and Christian values advocated by the Slovenian Christian Democracy (SKD) and the Slovenian People's Party (SLS) to the right-leaning

Social-Democratic Party (SDS), and the relatively new New Slovenia/Christian Democrats (NSi). On the centre-left is the Liberal Democracy of Slovenia (LDS), with strong elements of social liberalism and emphasis on individual constitutional rights. To the left of the LDS, the reformed communists have formed the United List of Social Democrats (ZLSD). They advocate a so-called Third Way, which continues to emphasize a strong collectivist orientation. In addition to this fairly traditional alignment, there are a number of unique parties that have been able to win favour with the Slovenian voters. They vary from the nationalist Slovenian National Party (SNS) to the Democratic Party of Pensioners (DeSuS)[6] and now a youth party that gained representation in parliament in 2000 (Party of Young People SMS).

When we look at the party programmes, however, we can see they reflect the prevalence of male interests. All of the parties focus on the so-called 'big issues', to the detriment of issues like gender equality. During transition, women's interests were duly recognized as a legitimate interest of one social group, but issues associated with nation state building were in the forefront and subsumed all others, including the issue of the social status of women.[7] Instead of the old all-embracing subject, the 'working class', there emerged a new one—the 'Slovenian nation'.[8] A decade later, big issues still dominate the discourse, but now the parties all focus on consolidation of the economy and integration into Western economic and security organizations.

In a competitive electoral environment, all of the parties recognize that women form a relatively significant part of the electorate whose support must be enlisted at election time. The way that parties talk about women and attempt to appeal to female voters varies across the ideological spectrum. They range from programmes for right-wing parties, such as SNS and SDS, that do not mention women at all, to the SLS party programme that expresses the equality of men and women, to the SKD programme that equates the status of a woman as a mother and a housewife with that of an employed woman, and finally to the LDS programme, which declares it is the duty of the state to enable women to pass from the private to the public sphere on equal terms as men. The only party that uses male and female grammatical forms in its rhetoric is the LDS. Parties like the SDS and SKD use both male and female expressions inconsistently or male grammatical forms only.

Based on existing literature, we expect there to be a linkage between parties of the left (and particularly the 'new left') and the representation of women and 'women's issues'. In aggregate terms, at least, this would seem to be true in Slovenia. Women have fared best in elections where centre-left parties have fared best (1992 and 2000).

In 1996, the electorate shifted in the direction of traditionalism. The second largest party in parliament, the SLS, called in its platform for a family policy that would include 'a tax policy which will undoubtedly favour families with several children, a solution to pension legislation that will take motherhood into account, a gradual extension of maternity leave, and a mass media that will encourage the values of parenthood, marriage, and family' (SLS Programme, 16). The right-of-centre SLS, SDS, and SKD party grouping won 45 seats combined in 1996, a significant jump from the 29 seats they had in the 1992 election. The left party groupings (LDS, ZLSD, DS) lost voter support and went from 42 seats to 34 seats. The leftist ZLSD fell from 14 to nine MPs, none of whom were women. While the SLS, SDS, and SKD gained 16 MPs, their number of female MPs actually dropped from four to only three. Furthermore, two parties of the centre (by European standards)—the Democrats of Slovenia (with 24 per cent women in their lists) and the Greens (Greens of Slovenia with 23 per cent and the Green Alternative 29 per cent) did not succeed in getting any members into parliament. The story in 1996 is that when parties of the left and centre fare well, women's representation increases. The 2000 election seems to confirm this, but also provides a clear message that there are still significant limits.

The two major leftist parties (ZLSD and LDS) saw a jump in 2000 back up to 45 seats and a large jump from only one woman to eight women in their combined ranks. The defeated parties of the right returned 31 MPs; significantly down from the 45 they had had in the previous parliament, with only two female MPs included among their MPs. The minor parties have also predominately elected men, with only one of the remaining 12 MPs being female.

❖ THE ELECTORAL SYSTEM AS POLITICAL BARRIER

A key problem for women in contemporary Slovene politics is one of too many parties chasing too few seats. With seven to eight parties consistently competing for only 88 seats (two additional seats are reserved constitutionally for ethnic minorities), there are relatively few opportunities for entrance to parliament, and those opportunities go to the most entrenched interests in the parties, interests that are overwhelmingly male.

The Slovene electoral system is a version of proportional representation and therefore, should be favourable to women. PR using simple quotients is used to allocate seats in eight geographically, historically, and socially determined constituencies. For each full electoral quota a party wins (100 per cent/11 seats = 9.09 per cent of the votes = one full electoral quota), the party receives one seat from that constituency. The seats unfilled when all full quota seats have been awarded are distributed in a second tier, using the d'Hondt method.

In the 2000 election, a four per cent electoral threshold was introduced. This should have reduced the number of parties entering parliament, but while the list of parties that entered parliament changed somewhat, a relatively large number of parties still remained viable. In 2000, three parties (SNS, SMS, DeSUS) were just barely able to squeeze in above the threshold. As a result, *party magnitudes* have remained consistently low, which hurts women. If parties know they will only have a few seats from each constituency, they will reserve those positions for the top leadership of the party, which tend to be men.

The system, while in theory proportional, has significant built-in majoritarian elements. As mentioned earlier, two seats are reserved for recognized minorities (one for Hungarians and one for Italians). These seats are allocated according to a first-past-the-post principle. There are also a couple of less obvious, but even more important, features that cause the Slovene electoral system to behave like a majoritarian one: the use of geographically defined electoral sub-units (voting units) and the demise of the second-tier national lists are particularly important. The electoral sub-units emerged from compromise and negotiation among transitional actors. In the negotiations among the ruling government in 1990 and the newly established parties, the former supported a majoritarian system. The latter favoured some form of PR (Grad 1997: 174). Since no party had a clear majority, the 1990 elections were held with three different systems for three chambers. In the aftermath, most of the numerous small parties preferred a clear PR system; others favoured some sort of mixed system that would preserve elements of direct MP-voter linkage and overcome perceived weaknesses of PR. Because the final rules required a special two-thirds majority, the electoral system that emerged was a complex version of PR with elements of majoritarianism mixed in.

In each electoral constituency, the parties present 11 candidates, but they are not presented as a party list as in most PR systems. Rather, constituencies are divided into 11 electoral districts. Voters do not see the entire party list, but choose a party through the choice of a single candidate put forth by the party in their electoral district. The votes given to candidates in each electoral district are aggregated in order to determine how many seats the list/party is entitled to receive in the given constituency. This practice was designed with the goal to limit 'partitocracy' and to assure an MP-voter linkage, but it has negative implications for women.

Candidates can run in one or two electoral districts. After the total number of electoral quota seats is determined for a party, the party candidates are ranked in terms of the percentage of votes received in their districts (for those running in two units the average percentage counts). If the party has only one electoral quotient seat, the candidate with the highest percentage of votes in his or her district is elected; if there are two electoral quotient seats, the two candidates with the highest percentages are elected, and so forth. In effect, a candidate in an electoral district competes directly with the candidates from other parties, but she also competes indirectly with colleagues from her own party in terms of how well each does comparatively.

Remainder votes in the eight constituencies, that is those votes remaining after the electoral quotient votes are subtracted from the parties total votes in the constituency, are summed nationally and the remaining seats are allocated to parties using the d'Hondt method. The initial electoral law provided two ways these seats could be allocated by the parties to candidates. The first was that after determining how many seats each party was to receive at the national level, electoral officials would go back to the district level results to identify candidates who were effectively the 'best losers' for the party and these candidates are elected in the second round. For example, if it was determined the SLS was to receive four additional seats based on the national distribution, electoral officials would take the vote percentages for all of the unelected SLS candidates from the electoral district levels and order them in terms of the percentage of the votes they won in their constituency. Those four previously unelected candidates with the highest percentages would then be declared elected. Under these conditions, the candidates are local level candidates and representatives, but they win their seats based on the national level distribution of votes. The second manner in which candidates could be selected in the second tier was that up to half of the seats that a party won at the national level could be allocated according to an ordering of candidates by the party determined on a national party list.

The complicated provisions to ensure MP-voter linkage and reduce wasted votes have concrete and largely negative consequences for women. Party gatekeepers must choose one candidate for each of 88 electoral units. This fundamentally alters (and undermines) the logic of ticket balancing in a PR system. If the party chooses a woman, she will be the only name to represent the party in that voting unit, rather than being part of a party list. This makes party gatekeepers more hesitant to nominate women.

In these circumstances, party gatekeepers largely behave as they would in a majoritarian system. Analysis of the elections from 1992 on shows that parties learned quickly. They learned the strategic importance of the electoral district and discovered where they must put a candidate they would like to see elected. For example, if the party has a successful mayor in the district, they would almost always choose him to run for a party there. The need to think of a single candidate in each voting unit is another factor pushing parties to emphasize the upper circles of possible candidates when considering nominations. This again leads to a male-dominated selection process. It is also clear that parties have learned where to place a candidate they only wish to use to gather votes for the party and for symbolic purposes. To the extent that parties view women as a less important interest within the party, we might expect gatekeepers to concentrate women in unwinnable voting units.

The national party lists opened up the possibility of being able to balance out the majoritarian and personalistic elements of the system, but it has not worked out this way in practice. Initially, national lists could be used for the allocation of remainder seats in the second tier. The Law on Elections stated that: 'up to half of the mandates which lists get in the allocation of seats at the national level are allocated to the candidates in the order from the lists, determined by proponent'.[9] Alternatively, seats at the national level could be allocated based on the vote totals in the district elections, electing candidates who had run at the local level, as described above.

On the national lists, a party would list candidates in the order it would like to see them sent to parliament. Realistically, most parties would use the top slots as a means of protecting the party leadership in parliament. Candidates could appear, however, in both an electoral unit and on the national list. If a candidate was elected in the electoral unit, his/her name was automatically skipped and the next name from the national list was elected. If a candidate is not elected in the unit, then the national list becomes a backdoor entrance to the parliament, primarily for party leaders, provided the candidate is placed high enough on the list. If the party does well enough so that the party leaders win their constituencies, however, then names that are a good deal farther down on the list can get elected at the national tier. The national tier is the only place where the party can really think in terms of trying to balance a complete ticket.

The consequences of the national lists in the first election where they were used (1992) were highly favourable to women. While women won only seven of 69 seats decided by the district vote (10.1 per cent), they won five of the 19 seats selected based on national lists (26.3 per cent). Had the use of the national list process been expanded and used even more extensively, it is plausible this would have been a conduit through which at least a modicum of representation for women was guaranteed in later years. This, however, did not occur. In 1996 there were only six seats awarded off the national lists, and none of these MPs were women. In 2000 the option of using national lists for the second tier allocation was eliminated.

The reasons for the elimination of national lists are instructive. As just noted, national lists can be used to provide protection for party leaders. While this may have made their use attractive to party leaders, in fact the negative publicity around the ability of party leaders to shield themselves from the voters led many parties to not use national lists. Even when they could, parties declined to establish party lists, or made them so short that they were entirely symbolic. In 1996, only three parliamentary parties made national lists (SLS, SKD, and SNS); the LDS made a list, but only put the party leader on it—a man who would undoubtedly win a seat in his electoral district. In 1996, the parties that did establish national lists did not use them as a means of achieving descriptive balance. The rule was: start with the party leader, and follow with well-known party candidates (MPs or powerful party figures). The SLS, for example, put only three candidates on the national list and all were male.

SLOVENIA: WOMEN'S PRESENCE IN PARLIAMENT ❖

The SNS put ten candidates on the list, including only one female (second position). The SKD put 15 candidates on this list, four of whom were women but none were above the fifth position. The perception of the lists as a way for politicians to avoid accountability ultimately doomed this system. In 2000 the election laws were changed so that the possibility of having national lists was eliminated. Instead, allocating seats from the remainder votes using the alternative mechanism of selecting the 'best loser', that is, the party candidate with the highest vote percentage that failed to win his seat at the local level in the initial round, is now the law.

There have been strong criticisms of the existing system (not having to do with the effects on women's representation), but a popular referendum failed to choose between three alternative proposals (2-round majority, mixed system, or party list PR). Furthermore, a governmental proposal in 2000 to move towards a more explicitly majoritarian system failed to win sufficient support in the parliament. The two-tier PR system was therefore used in the 2000 election, with the modification of the second tier allocation system eliminating national lists. In terms of practical effect, the loss of national lists is likely to be limited. This is because so many parties responded to the negative public opinion about national lists by boycotting their use. Even if national lists had been legal in 2000, it is highly unlikely they would have been used to ensure greater representation of women.

Would a simple party-list PR system be better for women? The answer is probably, but much also depends on political parties. Parties are the actors that develop strategies within the set of existing rules. Party politics, internal organization, and ideological orientation either can have supportive effects or can create obstacles to greater involvement of women in politics.

❖ A Case of Unfavourable Political Conditions

Analyses presented in this chapter suggest the primary obstacles for greater female representation in the Slovene National Assembly are political. We may therefore conclude that a prescription for increasing female representation would include at least the following: (1) increase the size of the legislature to increase the opportunities for female entrance, (2) eliminate the territorial sub-units (voting units) and adopt a straightforward party-list PR system, (3) eliminate the second tier, either by using territorial constituencies exclusively or by collapsing geographical constituencies into a single nationwide unit, and (4) adopt affirmative action or quotas in recruitment.

A great deal of 'guilt' for the very low share of women in parliament can be placed at the feet of the Slovene parties. But, it must be said these parties have behaved rationally within the given electoral constraints. Party leaders have learned to identify the electoral units where the party has the best prospects.

❖ Milica G. Antić

They use those seats to make sure the members of the party with the most influence and power will stay in the parliament. Newcomers and more marginal interests, including women's interests, are at a 'natural' disadvantage, particularly in the most ideologically traditional parties. We might expect that more women-friendly parties would do more to balance their tickets with women if they had opportunities and incentives to do so.

Those incentives, however, may never be presented. Despite much debate and a national referendum, Slovenia has failed to change its electoral system significantly. To the extent that such institutions develop inertia, it may be that women's groups within the parties will have to find ways to improve female representation within a difficult set of electoral rules. If women's caucuses within the parties genuinely want to increase female representation, then there are some key 'pressure points'. In the first place, they must press for women in the top leadership of the parties. Those are the individuals who get recruited most 'safely' and consistently. Women must move from being backstage supporters of their parties to leaders, and that may require the adoption of affirmative action within the party. They must also put pressure on their parties to adopt meaningful forms of positive discrimination.

Outside the parties, at the national level, there have been three unsuccessful attempts to increase women's representation: the 1994 discussion of the *Law on Political Parties*, a 1995 proposal to amend Article 1 of the party law, and a 1996 proposal to make the provisions of the law on parties binding. The most radical of these was the proposed 1995 amendment which stated: 'for the 1996 election to the National Assembly and for the following local elections, a party shall in its lists of candidates ensure a minimum one-third representation of one sex. This share shall be increased each subsequent year by 5 per cent until equal representation of both sexes is ensured.'[10] Parties that increased the share of female candidates by 10 per cent would receive an additional financial reward. This proposal ultimately failed, as did a more modest attempt to make parties specify how they plan to achieve the gender equality broadly encouraged in Article 19 of the *Law on Political Parties*.[11]

Although the National Assembly has clearly taken a stand against mandating positive discrimination, experience from the Western democracies suggests that, if some parties adopt quotas for female candidates and experience electoral success, other parties will follow via a contagion effect (Matland and Studlar 1996). This could happen in Slovenia at some point, particularly if women become better organized and specifically demand such quotas. Quota provisions, however, can only be successful if certain related conditions are also met. The basic condition necessary for quotas to be effective is a political atmosphere favourably inclined towards the equality of men and women (both within the parties and in the society as a whole). Above all, quotas can only exert an influence on the opportunities of women in the conditions of proportional representation with a party list of candidates, that is, when their participation in the election is collective and not individual.

❖ Notes

1 See The Official Gazette of the Republic of Slovenia, Ljubljana 93/1997.

2 Women in Slovenia in the 1990s, Ljubljana: Women's Policy Office, 1999, p. 19.

3 All the data about parties and their women's activities have been taken from the research done by the Governmental Office for Women's Politics: Women in the Political Parties, Ljubljana 1994. Data for the parties' share of women's membership and their share in bodies are their own estimates.

4 This survey was carried out by the Women's office as a part of a project enhancing the position of women in politics. For more information see Jasna Jeram 'Women and parliamentary election 1996: Attitudes of Slovene political parties' in *Women–Politics–Democracy*, ed. by M. Antić and J. Jeram (1999).

5 Article 19 of the *Law on Political Parties* stipulates that a party shall lay down in its statutes 'a procedure and a body determining candidates for elections to Parliament and for the President of the Republic, as well as candidates for elections to local community bodies' (cf. the Official Gazette of the Republic of Slovenia, 7 October 1994). Article 43 of the *Law on Elections* stipulates, 'A political party shall determine the candidates in accordance with a procedure laid down by internal rules. A list of candidates shall be determined in a secret ballot' (*Election Regulations*, The Official Gazette of the Republic of Slovenia, Ljubljana 1992, p. 17). See Statistical Yearbook for 1992 and 1996.

6 For more about Slovene political parties see D. F. Hafner (1996), 'Political Parties in Slovenia', *The New Democratic Parliaments: The First Years*, Ljubljana and Portorož and more about their influence on women see M. G. Antić (1999), 'Slovene Political Parties and Their Influence on the Electoral Prospects of Women', *Special Issue of Communist Studies and Traditional Politics*, ed. C. Corrin, Vol. 15. No. 1, March 1999.

7 See also M. G. Antić (1991), 'Democracy Between Tyranny and Liberty: The situation of women in the Post-"socialist" nation state', in: *Shifting Territories: Feminism, Socialism, Europe*, Feminist Review 39.

8 See Carole Pateman: *The Disorder of Women*, Polity Press, Cambridge, 1989, p. 214.

9 Regulations on elections, p. 31.

10 Cf. *Parliamentary Reports* no. 55/1995, p. 22.

11 Cf. *Parliamentary Reports*, no. 22/1996, p. 55, and the report on the activities of the Commission for Women's Politics for the period 1992–1996, Ljubljana, September 1996, p. 13.

❖ Milica G. Antić

14 ❖ Croatia's Leap towards Political Equality: Rules and Players[1]

Josip Glaurdic

Croatia's socio-political development in the years after the fall of communism differed very little from the socio-political developments in other East European countries. The introductory chapters of this volume outline a few dynamics that have had significant impacts on the position of East European women in politics and society in general—particularly the re-traditionalization of popular attitudes regarding gender roles and the backlash against 'directive emancipation'. All of those dynamics were at play in Croatia and were arguably even more intense than elsewhere due to the war for independence, which began in the spring of 1991 and ended in 1995.

Franjo Tuđman's nationalist Croatian Democratic Union (HDZ), which was in power during the 1990s, used the imagery of women as the protectors of the nation very efficiently, not only in its election campaigns, but also in everyday life. Women were to stay at home and cooperate in improving Croatia's devastating demographic situation (negative population growth since 1990). As HDZ MP, Vice Vukojević, said to one of his female colleagues in the Croatian Parliament (Sabor), what was wanted of women was 'less talk, more births!' In such an environment, women's sphere of public activity was effectively limited to the anti-war movement and refugees' and POW mothers' organizations.

It therefore comes as no surprise that the level of women's parliamentary representation in Croatia throughout the 1990s was one of the lowest in Eastern Europe. In 1992 only about five per cent of members of the Lower House of the Croatian Sabor were women; in 1995 that figure rose slightly to about eight per cent. The 2000 election, however, brought significant change. Not only was HDZ ousted from power by a six-party opposition coalition, but there was also a significant improvement in the proportion of women in parliament (20.5 per cent of those elected in 2000 were women, a figure that now stands at 23.2 per cent due to personnel changes). That improvement made Croatia the first East European country to surpass its pre-transition level of women's parliamentary representation[2] and at the time, Croatia had the highest level of women's representation in Eastern Europe. What could account for such a dramatic increase?

The literature identifies cultural, socioeconomic, and political explanations for the level of female parliamentary representation. In Croatia, there is little doubt that negative gender stereotypes, like those expressed by MP Vukojević, have adversely affected the supply of and demand for female candidates. Political culture, however, is generally defined as a relatively stable set of attitudes and core values. The end of the war in 1995 may have precipitated a shift in political priorities away from national survival and martial concerns; but there is little to indicate that Croatian society became significantly less sexist in the lead up to the 2000 elections.

There is equally little reason to believe that changes in socioeconomic conditions account for women's improved access to power. Croatian women in the 1990s did not gain greater access to higher education or to the legal and business strata of the workforce. In fact, Croatia's economic depression has been much more detrimental for women. Women's unemployment levels have grown more than men's have, and the income gap between genders has been widening. Based on the literature, we would expect women's declining socioeconomic position to decrease the supply of female aspirants with the resources that party gatekeepers and voters find attractive. Yet the proportion of women elected to seats in the parliament more than doubled in a single election. This leaves us with political explanations.

The remainder of this chapter will primarily concentrate on three political factors that can potentially have a decisive effect on the level of women's parliamentary representation: the electoral system, ideology of the party in power, and institutionalization of women's intra-party positions. It is possible that the increase in women's representation was caused by the adoption of a pure proportional representation electoral system for 2000 or by the fall from power of the rightist-nationalist HDZ. It is also possible that women's organizations managed to exact deeper changes in the structural position of women within parties. To test these propositions, this study employs simulations, along with statistical analyses of candidate data, personal interviews with prominent party women, and an examination of parties' statutes, leadership compositions, and electoral programs.

✣ TESTING THE EFFECTS OF ELECTORAL SYSTEM CHANGE

While cultural attitudes may have remained relatively stable in the post-communist period, the ruling HDZ party was more than willing to tinker with

✣ JOSIP GLAURDIC

the electoral institutions of the country. As a result, all three post-communist elections have been conducted under different rules, each of which, hypothetically, should have offered a different mix of incentives and opportunities for party gatekeepers to recruit women. See Table 14.1 for a summary of the three electoral rules. Details on the Croatian parties are provided in Table 14.2.

In 1992, Croatia used a hybrid electoral system for electing 120 members to the Sabor's Lower House. One-half of the MPs were elected from 60 single-member districts; the other half was elected from a second ballot featuring closed party lists for a nationwide constituency. The electoral law set the threshold for participation in the proportional allocation of seats at a mere three per cent. The small size of the legislature, the high proportion of seats allocated via winner-take-all district contests, and the low threshold would all be expected to discourage female recruitment.

A hybrid electoral system was used again in 1995, but there were a couple of woman friendly changes. This time, only 28 out of 108 MPs were elected from single-member districts; the remaining 80 were elected from a second ballot for party national lists. In addition, a three-level threshold system was instituted: the barrier for single parties was five per cent, for two-party coalitions eight per cent, and for 'three and more'-party coalitions 11 per cent. The smaller chamber size reduced recruitment opportunities, but the higher threshold and larger number of seats allocated via party lists should have provided greater opportunities to balance party tickets with women, if party leaders were so inclined.

Those opportunities should have increased again in 2000, when Croatia adopted a pure multi-member party list PR system. The country was divided

Table 14.1. Basic features of Croatia's three post-communist electoral systems[1]

'60 + 60' (1992) System	• Size of the Lower House: 120 • 60 MPs elected from single-member districts • 60 MPs elected from national, non-compensatory party lists • 3% threshold for national lists
'80 + 28' (1995) System	• Size of the Lower House: 108 • 28 MPs elected from single-member districts • 80 MPs elected from national, non-compensatory party lists • Three-level threshold system: 5% for single-party lists, 8% for two-party coalitions, 11% for 'three and more'-party coalitions
'10 × 14' (2000) System	• Size of the Lower House: 140 • All MPs elected from 10 multi-member districts with 14 seats each • 5% threshold

[1] In order to avoid confusion, the electoral system used for the 1992 election will be labelled as '60 + 60'; the electoral system used for the 1995 election will be labelled as '80 + 28'; and the electoral system used for the 2000 election will be labelled '10 × 14'. For all three elections minority and diaspora votes are not considered.

Table 14.2. Major Croatian parties and coalitions, 1992–2002

HDS	*Hrvatska demokratska stranka—Croatian Democratic Party* Centre–right party which ran in the 1992 elections. Later merged with other small parties to form HKDU
HDZ	*Hrvatska demokratska zajednica—Croatian Democratic Union* Party in power 1990–9. Was led by late Franjo Tuđman. Self-proclaimed centre-right, although more right than centre
HKDU	*Hrvatska kršćansko-demokratska unija—Croatian Christian Democratic Union* Rightist, conservative party. Joined HSP for the 2000 elections
HNS	*Hrvatska narodna stranka—Croatian People's Party* Party of the current president Stjepan Mesić. Joined the opposition coalition for the 1995 and the 2000 elections. Saw extreme decline in popularity 1992–9, but has recently gained in power. Centre party
HND	*Hrvatski nezavisni demokrati—Croatian Independent Democrats* Party made up of former HDZ members who left the party in 1994. Founded by current president Stjepan Mesić. Centre party
HSS	*Hrvatska seljačka stranka—Croatian Peasants' Party* Participated in 1995 and 2000 opposition coalitions. Conservative party
HSLS	*Hrvatska socijalno—liberalna stranka–Croatian Social Liberal Party* Major opposition party 1990–9. Won the 2000 election in coalition with SDP. Was led by Dražen Budiša who lost the 2000 presidential election to Stjepan Mesić of HNS. Prior to 2001-centre party, now centre-right.
HSP	*Hrvatska stranka prava—Croatian Rights Party* Far-right party
SDP	*Socijaldemokratska partija—Social Democratic Party* Direct successor of the former Croatian League of Communists. Saw extreme decline in popularity 1990–6. Won the 2000 election together with HSLS. Currently the leader of the ruling coalition. Leftist party
SDU	*Socijalno demokratska unija—Social Democratic Union* Leftist party

1992 Regional Coalition	Coalition of regional parties formed for the 1992 election. Made up of:
	    DA—Dalmatinska akcija—Dalmation Action
	    IDS—Istarski demokratski sabor—Democratic Union of Istria
	    RDS—Riječki demokratski savez—Democratic Union of Rijeka
	Coalition leader IDS which joined the opposition coalitions for the 1995 and 2000 elections Centre-left orientation

1995 Coalition	Centrist coalition formed for the 1995 election. Made up of: HSS, HNS, IDS, HKDU, and SBHS (local party from Slavonia). Major coalition partner HSS
2000 Coalition	Centrist coalition formed for the 2000 election. Made up of: HSS, HNS, IDS, and LS (Liberal Party formed by former members of HSLS). Participates in the government together with SDP and HSLS. Major coalition partner HSS

into 10 electoral districts, which elected 14 MPs each.[3] This '10 × 14' system increased the size of the chamber, eliminated the winner-take-all element entirely, introduced a five per cent threshold, and provided moderately high district magnitudes. Those features should have been favourable for women, but the question is whether party list PR is responsible for the dramatic increase in female representation in 2000.

Simulations provide a means of testing the effects of electoral system change by modeling what might be the outcome of the same voting patterns if different electoral rules had been in place. In other words: 'What would have been the level of women's parliamentary representation as a result of the—(1992, 1995, or 2000) election if the—(1992, 1995, or 2000) electoral system had been in use?'

The problem with conducting electoral simulations in Croatia is that each election produced widely divergent conditions (different chamber sizes and different numbers of seats allocated according to particular rules). In order to reduce those very different electoral environments to a single metric, it was necessary to make three fundamental assumptions. The first assumption is that party gatekeepers always have full control of the candidate nomination process. If this were not the case, it would be impossible to apply different rules across elections, because the balance of nominating power might shift between regional and central bodies in response to rules changes.[4]

The second assumption is that parties are good at estimating their electoral prospects. Most of the parties employ a number of independent resources to track voters' preferences throughout the pre-election period and make their nomination decisions accordingly. While this information is not perfect, party leaders have a good idea of which seats are winnable (and which are not), and hence they are aware of the value of the nominations they are bestowing.

The third and final assumption is that Croatian voters are primarily voting for parties and party coalitions, rather than individuals. It is true that voters often identify parties by their leaders, but even in the district contests we may assume that voters cast their ballots on the basis of identification with a party label rather than on the merits of individual candidates.

Armed with these assumptions, the first stage of each simulation involved classifying all of the nominations for all of the parties according to level of competitiveness. We considered a nomination 'mandate' if it was for a seat that the party was sure to win; 'fighting' if the party might win with a particularly good showing or lose with a bad showing.[5] All other nominations were considered purely 'ornamental' or unwinnable. Using the results of the election in question, 'party centre preference lists' were formed by ranking all of the nominees according to the competitiveness of their nominations within their parties.[6]

The next step was to apply the 'simulated' electoral rules to the votes of the electorate; basically in order to answer the question of what would have been the electoral results if the electoral rules had been different. This step enabled us to create new ranking lists of nominations based on their levels of competitiveness under the 'simulated' electoral results.[7] The final step of every simulation was to apply the new ranking lists of nominations to the old 'party centre preference lists' to determine which candidates would have been elected if the electoral rules were changed.

The chief drawback of this approach is that it assumes that the party centre preference rankings remain fixed regardless of the electoral rules. This becomes, effectively, a fourth assumption in the model. Differences in the number of women recruited in the various simulations are therefore produced primarily by differences in how far parties were actually able to dip down into their preference rankings—a condition determined in part by the chamber size and in part by changes in the magnitude of the various party delegations. What this design cannot do is test for hypothesized changes in the *behaviour* of party leaders that would lead to greater recruitment of women. Party list PR is supposed to create incentives for party leaders to nominate women for ticket-balancing purposes, in other words to *elevate* women in their preference rankings. The larger a party can expect its delegation to be in a given constituency, the less risky and more attractive female candidates will seem. This should lead to more nominations for women overall and to a greater willingness by party leaders to offer women nominations for 'fighting' seats. The results reported below, therefore, tell us only one part of the story about electoral rules changes—how far parties were actually able to dip into their preference rankings—and not how those rankings might have changed with the expectation of larger delegations and the removal of zero-sum electoral contests. The results are suggestive nevertheless of the role played by electoral system change.

❖ Simulations for the 1992 election

The party scene for the 1992 election was extremely fragmented. In total, members of nine parties and one independent candidate were represented in the Lower House of the Sabor as a result of the 1992 election. However, the great majority of the seats were reserved for only one party: Franjo Tuđman's Croatian Democratic Union (HDZ). HDZ won 31 out of 60 national list seats with 44.71 per cent of the popular vote. It also won 54 out of 60 SMD seats, bringing its parliamentary majority to a formidable 85 out of 120 seats or 70.8 per cent. Next in line was the Croatian Social Liberal Party (HSLS), whose 17.7 per cent of the popular vote won it 12 out of 60 national list seats. HSLS also won one of 60 SMD seats, bringing its total to 13 out of 120 seats or 10.8 per cent. All other parties attained representation through their national lists, barely crossing the three per cent threshold barrier, with one notable exception, the coalition of regional parties. This coalition won four SMD seats in the Istria region.

As we can see from Table 14.3, although there is no *extreme* variation between the impacts of electoral systems on the level of women's representation, having a '10 × 14' electoral system in place for the 1992 election would have yielded the highest proportion of female representatives to the Lower House of the Sabor, most likely because of increased proportionality resulting from a relatively large district magnitude. An '80 + 28' electoral system would have most likely yielded the lowest proportion of female representatives—lower

Table 14.3. Simulation results

Party	'60 + 60' (1992) Electoral System			'80 + 28' (1995) Electoral System			'10 × 14' (2000) Electoral System		
	Seats	%	Women	Seats	%	Women	Seats	%	Women
SIMULATION RESULTS FOR THE 1992 ELECTION BY PARTY									
HDZ	85	70.83	3	70	64.81	1	77	55.00	2
HSLS	13	10.83	0	17	15.74	0	32	22.86	3
HSP	5	4.17	0	7	6.48	0	8	5.71	0
HNS	4	3.33	1	6	5.56	1	9	6.43	1
SDP	3	2.50	0	6	5.56	1	5	3.57	1
HSS	3	2.50	0	0	0.00	0	2	1.43	0
Regional	6	5.00	1	2	1.85	0	6	4.29	0
Ind.	1	0.83	0	0	0.00	0	0	0.00	0
Total	120	100	5 (4.17%)	108	100	3 (2.78%)	140	100	7 (5.00%)
SIMULATION RESULTS FOR THE 1995 ELECTION BY PARTY									
HDZ	60	50.00	3	63	58.33	3	79	56.43	5
Coalition	25	20.83	0	18	16.67	0	31	22.14	0
HSLS	17	14.17	1	12	11.11	1	14	10.00	1
SDP	9	7.50	2	10	9.26	3	12	8.57	4
HSP	3	2.50	0	4	3.70	0	4	2.86	0
SDU	2	1.67	1	0	0.00	0	0	0.00	0
HND	4	3.33	0	1	0.93	0	0	0.00	0
Total	120	100	7 (5.83%)	108	100	7 (6.48%)	140	100	10 (7.14%)
SIMULATION RESULTS FOR THE 2000 ELECTION BY PARTY									
SDP/HSLS	72	60.00	18	58	53.70	15	71	50.71	18
HDZ	29	24.17	3	27	25.00	3	40	28.57	7
Coalition	16	13.33	2	18	16.67	2	24	17.14	2
HSP/HKDU	3	2.50	0	5	4.63	0	5	3.57	0
Total	120	100	23 (19.17%)	108	100	20 (18.52%)	140	100	27 (19.29%)

even than the more majoritarian 1992 system—perhaps because of the smaller number of seats in the chamber.

❖ Simulations for the 1995 election

As in 1992, the party scene for the 1995 election was extremely fragmented. Members of 10 parties were represented in the Lower House of the Sabor. However, five of those 10 parties participated in the election as a coalition, thereby lowering the number of effective 'electoral players' to six. Furthermore, all opposition parties, apart from HSP, joined forces in slating SMD candidates. That attempt to jointly overthrow HDZ resulted in some opposition SMD candidates being backed by bizarre groupings of parties, ranging from extreme left to extreme right. In spite of the collective opposition effort, however, HDZ once again emerged as the winner with 63 out of 108 seats or 58.33 per cent. Forty-two (out of 80 possible) of those seats were won through the national list, whereas the remaining 21 (out of 28 possible) were won through SMDs. The five-party opposition coalition was next in line with 18 seats, two of which were won through SMDs. HSLS won 12 seats, two of which were won through SMDs. The 1995 election saw a moderate improvement for SDP, which won 10 seats (two through SMDs) or 9.26 per cent— a significant improvement over the 2.5 per cent the party had in 1992.

The simulation results for 1995 show that, as in 1992, having the 2000 electoral system in place for the 1995 election would have probably yielded the highest number of female representatives to the Lower House of Sabor. It appears, however, that keeping the less female friendly 1992 electoral system for the 1995 election would have made little difference for the number of female representatives.

❖ Simulations for the 2000 election

The 2000 election marked the end of HDZ's decade. An opposition coalition of six parties formed prior to the election with the intent of dethroning HDZ from power. A few months prior to the election, however, major coalition partners SDP and HSLS decided to run together, separate from the other four coalition members. The new SDP/HSLS alliance won 71 out of 140 seats or 50.71 per cent. Roughly two-thirds of those seats belonged to SDP and one-third to HSLS, in accordance with their pre-election agreement. The other opposition coalition won 24 out of 140 seats or 17.14 per cent. HDZ, for the first time since it came to power in 1990, became an opposition party, winning 40 seats or 28.57 per cent. The remaining five seats went to the rightist coalition of HSP and HKDU.

The 2000 simulation suggests that, while the '10 × 14' system used in 2000 produced the best results overall, women also would have fared better under the old sets of rules, given the new balance of electoral forces. These estimates for the impact of the switch to pure party-list PR are conservative for the reasons outlined earlier. Nevertheless, it is interesting to note how close the simulated results are to the actual outcome of the 2000 election.

❖ Electoral rules matter but they do not stand alone

Several points are clear from the simulations. First, the HDZ responded to changes in the balance of power among political forces with electoral rules that served its interests. Table 14.3 clearly shows that in each election the HDZ fared best under precisely the rules it engineered for that election. This lends support to the earlier assumption that parties are good predictors of electoral outcomes. The then-dominant HDZ knew that its power was deteriorating *vis-à-vis* opposition forces and crafted electoral rules to offset that decay.

Furthermore, for each election the purely proportional system produced the largest number of women MPs. If we were able to estimate changes in the preference rankings of party leaders, we would likely see an even more pronounced effect. We do know that more women were nominated across parties in 2000. That would seem to indicate that party preferences regarding female candidates did indeed change with the introduction of a pure proportional system.

We should not, however, exaggerate the impact of the '10 × 14' electoral system. Women also may have fared better in 2000 due to a combination of factors, including the demise of the rightist-nationalist HDZ and the larger chamber size, which provided richer opportunities for access. It is worth noting that party list PR has not always been unambiguously good for female recruitment in post-communist Croatia. If we look at female nomination and election rates in the two mixed electoral systems (1992 and 1995) by party and path of recruitment, we find that in 1992, when the system was evenly divided between district contests and party list PR, there was little difference in the rate of female nomination between the two portions of the system; and in fact more women were actually elected through SMD than through the PR path (see Table 14.4). Out of five female MPs, three were elected from districts—all from the ruling HDZ, which received the lion's share of district seats. In 1995, when the number of district contests and the total number of seats in the chamber declined, only one woman was nominated to contest a district seat, and she lost. All of the women in parliament were recruited from the PR party lists.

If we looked only at 1995, the total failure of women in the SMDs would seem like an argument for the ticket balancing benefits of party list PR. We should bear in mind, however, a couple of things. First, all of the opposition parties (except the radical right HSP) ran together as a bloc in the SMDs in 1995,

Table 14.4. Distribution of women's mandates for the 1992 and 1995 elections

Party	PR portion			SMD portion			Total		
	Candidates	Women nominated	Women elected	Candidates	Women nominated	Women elected	Candidates	Women nominated	Women elected
1992									
HDS	60	3(5%)	0	60	3(5%)	3	120	6(5%)	3
HSLS	60	8(13.3%)	0	60	8(13.3%)	0	120	16(13.3%)	0
HSP	60	5(8.3%)	0	55	3(5.5%)	0	115	8(7%)	0
HNS	60	3(5%)	1	59	2(3.4%)	0	119	5(4.2%)	1
SDP	60	9(15%)	0	56	7(12.5%)	0	116	16(3.8%)	0
HSS	60	3(5%)	0	49	2(4.1%)	0	109	5(4.6%)	0
Regional	60	9(15%)	1	5	0(0%)	0	65	9(13.8%)	1
Total	420	40(9.5%)	2	344	25(7.3%)	3	764	65(8.5%)	5
1995									
HDZ	80	7(8.8%)	3	28	0(0%)	0	108	7(6.5%)	3
4 + Coal.	80	5(6.3%)	0	12	0(0%)	0	92	5(5.4%)	0
HSLS	80	13(16.3%)	1	10	0(0%)	0	90	13(14.4%)	1
SDP	80	18(22.5%)	3	4	0(0%)	0	84	18(21.4%)	3
HSP	80	3(3.8%)	0	28	1(3.6%)	0	108	4(3.7%)	0
Total	400	46(11.5%)	7	82	1(1.2%)	0	482	47(9.8%)	7

so the supply of those seats was extremely low. There were only 82 nominees for 28 seats to be divided among six to seven parties and a couple of independents. There were no safe seats, except for the HDZ. This was the worst possible scenario for women, so it is perfectly logical that only one woman was nominated to contest a district seat.

Although the overall proportion of female nominees increased in 1995 (partly a product of the reduced chamber size), the actual number of women nominated went down, in spite of the greater proportion of PR list seats. The number and proportion of women elected went up, but this appears to have been due mostly to the improved fortunes of the SDP. The HDZ, for its part, nominated only one more woman in 1995 than it had in 1992; and it elected precisely the same number (3). Two of those women were returning faces for the HDZ; the only difference is that they were shifted from the districts where they ran in 1992 onto party lists in 1995.

It is difficult to draw conclusions from such a small sample of women in such a small legislature. The figures in Table 14.4, however, suggest that the increased use of party lists in 1995 did not so much encourage the HDZ to reach out and balance the ticket with new women as to preserve the entrenched position of key party players, a few of whom just happened to be women. The SDP appears to be a different story. It increased the number of women it nominated in 1995, even as the size of the chamber shrank; but like the HDZ it shifted its female nominees to the party list.

❖ IDEOLOGY OF THE PARTY IN POWER

Based on the simulation results and the electoral data reported above, it could be argued the main obstacle to women's access in Croatia prior to 2000 was the success of the nationalist and conservative HDZ, not the electoral rules per se. That party's dominance of the legislature and its ideological reluctance to place women in the public realm dampened the possibilities for women to gain access to power. In fact, the increase in female representation over time and most notably in 2000 concides with the decay of HDZ hegemony.

Figure 14.1 shows the share of women nominated by each party arrayed from left to right.[8] There is little question that parties of the left have consistently nominated more women across elections. The only notable exception is the 4 + Coalition, which has been slating a lower number of female candidates than its ideological placement might suggest. That may be due to internal ideological differences. On the one hand, there are elements in the 4 + Coalition that are more left wing than HSLS; but on the other hand, the conservative Peasant Party (HSS) plays a very dominant role within the grouping. Perhaps more importantly, a coalition of four parties must satisfy

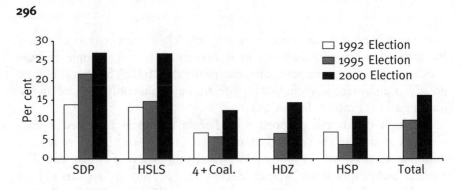

Figure 14.1. Per cent of female candidates by party and election

the need to maintain multiple party leaderships in power using the same number of seats available to other single parties. To the extent that those leaderships are comprised of men, the women in the coalition parties will have great difficulty getting nominated.

Given that leftist opposition parties have more woman-friendly recruitment practices, it would be safe to assume that the level of women's parliamentary representation would have been significantly lower in 2000 if the HDZ had not stumbled. The data support this. In fact, if the balance of popular support between HDZ and the opposition had remained precisely the same in 2000 as it was in 1995, the proportion of women in parliament would have dropped from 20 per cent to around 12–14 per cent.[9] That figure is still significantly higher than the 6.5 per cent of women elected in 1995 or the 4.2 per cent in 1992, so we may conclude that the ideology of the party in power does matter. But a changing of the guard by itself would not have produced the phenomenal increase of 2000.

There has been a steady increase over time in the proportion of female candidates across the party spectrum (Fig. 14.1). The HDZ is no exception to that trend. While it still nominates fewer women overall than the SDP and HSLS, the magnitude of increase in the proportion of female candidates within the HDZ rivals that of any other party in the spectrum. When we look at the distribution of nominations by type and gender in Table 14.5, it is clear that the expansion of the female candidate pool over time does not represent the use of women as fodder for ornamental positions on party lists. Not only has the proportion of female nominees steadily risen, so has the ratio of women nominated for winnable (mandate and fighting) seats. In 1992, two per cent of all mandate seats across parties went to women; in 1995 that figure increased to seven per cent; and then in 2000, it surged to 20 per cent.

In 2000, due to the elimination of SMD seats and the more balanced party competition, there were more mandate and fighting seats to go around. There were certainly more than ever for the opposition parties. But, data suggest

Table 14.5. Distribution of nominations by type and gender

Election	Mandate		Fighting		Ornamental	
	Women (%)	Men (%)	Women (%)	Men (%)	Women (%)	Men (%)
1992	2.1	97.9	9.4	90.6	9.4	90.6
1995	7.2	92.8	8.0	92.0	10.5	89.5
2000	20.0	80.0	18.6	81.4	14.3	85.7

that even the HDZ gave 13 per cent of its mandate seats and 20 per cent of its fighting seats to women in 2000, a marked increase over prior elections. The 'mandate' women were top party leaders the party wanted to preserve in power, including: the Deputy Prime Minister and Minister of European Integration, the Deputy Speaker of the House of Representatives (also president of the HDZ women's organization and a member of the party's Central Committee), the mayor of Dubrovnik, and a personal advisor to the president. But, the HDZ also offered women four of its fighting nominations. Two of those women had long histories of party service, one as an MP, the other as a former mayor of Zagreb and a former minister of construction and development. The other two were relative newcomers.

Taken together, these data provide some circumspect evidence for the ticket balancing incentives of party list PR: the preference rankings of parties do seem to change with changes in the electoral rules. Specifically, parties reach out to women when they can expect to send larger delegations to parliament, when the zero-sum nature of political competition is reduced. The number of women recruited will increase the most when opportunities to balance the ticket are available to parties that are ideologically amenable to female recruitment. Interviews further suggest that women were selected for more winnable nominations in 2000 due to their improved intra-party positions. In short, parties began recruiting women, because women had demanded and achieved important roles within their parties.

❖ INSTITUTIONALIZATION OF WOMEN'S INTRA-PARTY POSITIONS

One study dealing with the 2000 election party programmes concludes that, had the electoral success of women in 2000 depended on their parties' programmes—there simply would have been no success to speak of (Ženska Infoteka (b)). Compared with previous elections, the 2000 election programmes actually show a significant drop in parties' interest for issues concerning the position of women in society. While most parties' programmes for the 1995 election featured special sections devoted to women, issues of gender equality received very little attention in 2000.

The conservative Peasants' Party (HSS) and nationalist Croatian Democratic Union (HDZ) stayed true to their ideologies and featured a traditional family-related women's agenda in their electoral programmes. But even leftist SDP, in its joint electoral declaration with HSLS, devoted only two sentences to the issue of women's equal access to power:

> 'For SDP and HSLS, gender equality is one of the key determinants of a democratic and just society—a society in which power and responsibility are equally distributed, a society in which women equally participate in the decision-making process. We support legally guaranteeing women's equality in the workplace and in political life'. (Social-Democratic Party of Croatia (d), 7–8)

This statement, however brief, signifies a potentially important factor in the electoral success of women in 2000. Although we can only speculate about what the authors meant by 'legally guaranteeing women's equality in political life', there is strong evidence that at least the SDP wanted it to indicate a support for the institutionalization of women's representation in the form of quotas. Indeed, SDP's political program outright proclaims that the Social Democrats support intra-party women's quotas: 'SDP supports mandatory gender quotas in its executive bodies. We hold that this is the only way to expand the present horizons, forms and means of action and to establish developmental programmes that are practical and in tune with reality'. (Social-Democratic Party of Croatia (c), 10.)

According to *Be Active, Be Emancipated* (BaBe), a group for promotion and protection of the human rights of women in Croatia, the SDP, HSLS, and HDZ *all* claimed to have informal gender quotas prior to the 2000 election.[10] From what we know about male party leaders in Croatia and elsewhere, we can reasonably conclude that, if they truly did pledge support for informal gender quotas, they must have been faced with some strong pressures. There is compelling evidence that the drive for change came from women themselves.

Arguably the greatest difference between the nomination processes for the 2000 and previous elections was that women were significantly better organized. In fact, at least three of the four major parties—SDP, HDZ, and HSS—formed intra-party women's organizations. Obviously, the agenda of these organizations differ depending on their parties' ideologies. However, all three put significant emphasis on improving women's positions within their parties and the society as a whole.

SDP's Social-Democratic Women's Forum (SDFŽ) is arguably the strongest of these three organizations. It was formed in January of 1995 under the motto 'We are taking what is ours: half of heaven, half of earth, half of power'! As Ms. Dubravka Biberdžić, SDFŽ's vice-president and member of SDP's central committee claims, the main reason for forming SDFŽ was to unite women in a common goal of improving gender equality within SDP and society in general. Ms. Biberdžić further claims that SDFŽ has been extremely successful, particularly in training and lobbying for female candidates within the party and promoting female candidates to the public.

The Peasants' Party's (HSS) women's organization, Croatian Heart, was also formed with a goal of placing more women into positions of power within the party. As Croatian Heart's president Dr. Ružica Radović claims, the male conservative grip on power within HSS was, and still is, extremely strong. That is why a joint approach of all women within the party was absolutely essential for enabling any kind of improvement in intra-party gender equality. The organization was formed in 1998 and has so far had more success in organizing educational, cultural, and humanitarian activities for women than in exerting any recognizable pressure on the party leadership during elections. However, Dr. Radović claimed that the women of HSS were to have a much greater say in the 2001 local elections and were to actually seek implementation of a 30 per cent quota.[11]

HDZ's Union of Women 'Katarina Zrinski' is the youngest of the three women's organizations. It was formed in December of 1998 for the same reasons as SDFŽ and Croatian Heart—to activate women in pursuing their political interests through the Union and the party. The greatest achievements of the Union of Women, however, have not been in the sphere of elections, but rather in organizing campaigns on issues 'of the interest to the nation', as the Union's vice-president Jadranka Cigelj proclaims. In fact, Ms. Cigelj acknowledges that, although the Union of Women did exert some organized pressure on the party leadership during the formation of the party lists, the most important reason why there was an increase in the proportion of women among HDZ's candidates in the 2000 election was the strong leadership of the Union of Women president Jadranka Kosor, who, through her membership in the party's executive council, managed to greatly influence the nomination process. The relatively strong showing of HDZ's women in the 2000 election, however, generated some backlash from the party's established male leadership. Thus it is questionable whether women will be able to maintain their positions in the future.

All three female party leaders, disregarding their broader ideological differences, spoke with the same contempt for the post-independence re-traditionalization movement and with similar vigor for working towards change. The interviews made clear that politically active women of *all* parties worked together towards the achievement of a common goal of higher representation. Dr. Radović, Ms. Cigelj, and Ms. Biberdzic all stressed the important role non-governmental organizations played in connecting women across political lines, training female candidates, raising the awareness of a need for greater gender equality in politics, and exerting substantial additional pressure on predominantly male party leaderships to work towards change.

One of the most prominent women's organizations working for the advancement of women in society is the already mentioned *Be Active, Be Emancipated* (BaBe) group formed in 1994 in Zagreb. According to its coordinator Martina Belić, the group developed not only from anti-war and POW mothers' organizations from the early 1990s, but also as a continuation of a string of feminist organizations that were active in Croatia in the 1970s and 80s. The feminist movement in Croatia was actually one of the strongest in Eastern Europe during those two decades (Renne 1997: 166). Although its activities were redefined and weakened in the early 1990s due to the war, it was rejuvenated with financial assistance from non-governmental organizations from the West during the mid-1990s, and was hence able to return to its core activities of raising women's consciousness about their rights and improving the level of gender equality in all spheres of the society, particularly politics.

The organization BaBe, for example, formed the Women's Ad Hoc Coalition for monitoring political parties' attitudes towards women and their electoral performances. It also tried pushing for a model of parliamentary gender quotas. Although it was unsuccessful in that endeavour, it managed to bring the attention of the parties and the public to the issue of gender equality. Finally, and most importantly, BaBe organized training programs for women of all parties and ideologies on matters such as public speaking, running campaigns, consensus building, and lobbying. It therefore comes as no surprise that Ms. Belić, as well as the other interviewees, identifies BaBe and other women's organizations as a primary reason for the dramatic increase in women's representation in 2000.

❖ CONCLUSIONS

Both 'players' and 'rules' served a role in Croatia's leap toward parliamentary gender equality in 2000. The change of electoral rules allowed parties to go further into their preference rankings and probably also elevated women within those rankings, by providing party leaders with incentives and opportunities to reach out to female candidates. This is evidenced by the rise in nominations and winnable nominations for women across parties. At the same time, parties that have consistently nominated more women were, for the first time, able to take control of the parliament. The newfound success of the SDP in particular appears to have helped women. Of at least equal importance, however, is the fact that from the mid-1990s onward women became more organized and better able to pressure party gatekeepers to recruit women. They forged intra- and inter-party connections with significant assistance from women's non-governmental organizations; they moved women into positions of authority within the parties; and they achieved, in some instances, formal or informal quotas for female recruitment. No matter how many ticket-balancing incentives are created by the electoral rules, parties will only balance their tickets with women, if women form a significant constituency within the party. In Croatia, women were achieving that status just as the electoral system changed to provide greater incentives for ticket balancing and just as more ideologically amenable parties were coming to power.

Although this particular combination of conditions might seem serendipitous and unlikely to repeat itself, all of the women interviewed seemed to believe that what happened in 2000 was not an anomaly but a sign of a trend that will bring even greater gains for women in Croatian politics. There is certainly compelling evidence that suggests they are right. First of all, women that were elected to the parliament in 2000 were not elected by accident or simply placed on lists to give parties a 'female face'. As Ms. Biberdžić rightfully claims, they were capable, educated, recognizable candidates with long service to their parties,[12] who took on leadership roles in the parliament. Female MPs currently preside over seven out of 24 parliamentary committees, including the Committee for Internal Affairs and National Security, the Committee for the Economy, Development and Restoration, and the Lawmaking Committee. These three are widely considered to be among the most important parliamentary bodies.[13]

Secondly, although women of HDZ are experiencing some backlash from the party's male leaders, women in other parties have made significant progress since the 2000 election. The SDP followed its intra-party quota of 40 per cent, which is now firmly embedded in the party statute, and elected 50 women to the party's 122-member central committee. These women will, in turn, be well placed to press for greater female representation. Similarly, Article 68 of the new HSLS Statute proclaims that 'the nominations of the president of HSLS for the party's central bodies cannot contain more than two thirds of the members of the same gender'. These gains may be expected to have a contagion effect. Dr. Ružica Radović of HSS claims that women of her party were planning on 'making a stand' at 30 per cent for the 2001 local elections, to a great extent because they could point to the successes of women of SDP. Even the Sabor itself has recently started addressing the issue of gender equality, particularly through the newly formed Committee for Gender Equality.

These are deep structural changes that should transcend the conditions of a single election. It is obviously still too early to make firm conclusions about the permanency of the change brought by the 2000 election. Naturally, the success of women in the upcoming elections will depend on the shifts in the balance between leftist and rightist parties. Women's success will also depend on their ability to maintain and further their level of organization and to place pressure on the party centre. Nevertheless, the evidence appears

CROATIA'S LEAP TO POLITICAL EQUALITY ❖

strong enough to suggest that Croatia is on the path to greater gender equality in politics.

❖ NOTES

1 The author would like to extend his gratitude to Dr. Ružica Radović (HSS), Ms. Jadranka Cigelj (HDZ), Ms. Dubravka Biberdžić (SDP), and Ms. Martina Belic (BaBe) for allowing me to interview them; Ms. Karolina Leaković (SDP) and Mr. Domagoj Tonković (HSS) for supplying me with invaluable party-level data; and Ljubica Glaurdić who coordinated fieldwork by collecting data and setting up the interviews.

2 The proportion of women in the last parliament of the SFR Yugoslavia was about 18% (IPU).

3 It is important to note that all three elections had special provisions for the election of minorities and participation of Croatia's diaspora in the electoral process. However, for the purposes of this study, those particular provisions were not addressed. They would have unnecessarily skewed the results because diaspora and minority elections were conducted under completely different rules and with different balances between political actors.

4 This assumption is empirically supported. For example, the Croatian Democratic Union's nomination process for the 2000 election basically consisted of a party executive board 'retreat'. Article 29 of the SDP Statute proclaims that nominating powers rest with the Central Committee, upon 'proposals of the party president'. Article 51 of the HSLS Statute outlines almost identical powers for its president.

5 For SMDs, a mandate seat is one in which the party won by more than 10% of the votes; fighting seats are those where the party's candidate was within $+/-$ 10%. Ornamental are all others. In the mixed electoral systems of 1992 and 1995, the calculation is based on the Central Electoral Commission's calculations for the d'Hondt method of translating votes into seats on the national lists. For 1992, this resulted in mandate seats for the top fifty candidates of all parties (50 out of 420 total candidates). Fighting seats were 51–70; ornamental were any below 70. In 1995, the calculation came out as mandate (1–65), fighting (66–95), and ornamental (96–400). In 2000, fighting seats are the last to win and the first to lose, so for a list that won 8 seats, the fighting seats would be 8 and 9. Mandate seats are everything above (1–7), and ornamental seats are everything below (10–14).

6 For example, in the 1992 election, all 120 of HDZ's candidates (60 from the national list and 60 from the SMDs) were ranked according to the nature of their nominations (mandate, fighting, ornamental) and formed a new, 120-candidate-long 'party centre preference list', which represents a sort of a ranking list of all nominees the party centre used when assigning nominations.

7 When the 1995 electoral rules were applied to the 1992 votes of the electorate, for example, it was determined that HDZ would have had 33 mandate, 17 fighting, and 30 ornamental nominations from the national list portion, and 22 mandate, 4 fighting,

and 2 ornamental nominations from the SMD portion of the election. Therefore, their new list of nominations ranked by competitiveness would consist of 55 mandate, 21 fighting, and 32 ornamental nominations.

8 SDP's and HSLS's candidates were analysed separately for the 2000 election. For the 1992 election, candidates of parties that in subsequent elections joined the 4+ Coalition were analysed jointly. HSP's figure for 2000 is for its joint lists with HKDU. Also, although HSLS experienced a significant turn to the right *after* the 2000 election, it was placed further to the left than the 4+ Coalition to capture its ideological orientation in the 1992, 1996, and 2000 elections.

9 This is a rough estimate, based on the 1995 popular vote.

10 In their 20 December 1999 *Elektorine* publication, BaBe claims that SDP's informal quota was 40%, HSLS's 35%, and HDZ's 25%. If those figures are correct, not one of those parties actually fulfilled its promise: about 27% of both SDP's and HSLS's candidates, and only 14% of HDZ's candidates were women.

11 The local election results suggest it is highly unlikely that the women of HSS actually managed to push for the implementation of the 30% quota because only 10.3% of those elected from HSS lists were women. The proportion of women among all nominees was likely somewhat higher, but that data was unavailable.

12 Ms. Biberdžić claims that an ideal (and typical) female candidate for SDP is between 30 and 40 years old, has at least a university education, and at least 5 years of party service.

13 The Lawmaking Committee Chairman Ingrid Antičević-Marinović has recently been moved from that position and appointed Minister of Justice.

15 ❖ Women's Legislative Representation in Post-Communist Bulgaria

Tatiana Kostadinova

One of the characteristic features of socialist Bulgaria's national assembly was the relatively high percentage of women members. The research literature has broadly explained this in terms of the dominant Marxist-Leninist ideology that recognized complete equality of men and women (Meyer 1985: 22; Kenworthy and Malami 1999). The Bulgarian Assembly passed a special bill in October 1944 proclaiming equal opportunities regardless of gender (Kostova 1998: 250). The consequences of this proclamation were quite remarkable for the time: a majority of Bulgarian women were drawn into the labour force and a large group of them entered politics. In 1945, women entered the national parliament as deputies for the first time in the country's history (Kostadinova 1995: 110). Since then and until 1989, female legislative representation was determined by the ruling Bulgarian Communist Party (BCP) which set a recruitment rate in the 20–30 per cent range; in the last election under communist rule in 1986, 21.8 per cent of the seats went to women. Changes began with the start of the democratic transition in 1989 and the abolition of Article 1 of the Constitution, providing for the leading role of the Communist Party in society.

The first competitive multi-party elections held in June 1990 resulted in a dramatic drop in female representation down to 8.8 per cent of the seats. The high level of uncertainty, reinforced by the introduction of a new mixed electoral system and the extremely competitive nature of this first test of the distribution of voters' support, contributed to the election of a parliament composed predominantly of men. Women's representation increased by 5 per cent in 1991, to 13.8 per cent, but declined slightly in the course of the next two elections, first to 12.9 per cent in 1994 and then to 10.4 per cent in 1997. Finally, in 2001 there was a dramatic jump up to 26.3 per cent, making Bulgaria the leader in women's representation in Eastern Europe.

Kostova (1998: 256) suggests a significant number of female candidates in 1990 were nominated by parties that failed to meet the 4 per cent threshold imposed by the election law. It was rare, however, for women to be nominated by the larger parties and even rarer for them to be near the top of the party lists, which is necessary for success in winning seats. In the following sections I discuss possible explanations for this phenomenon. I focus on the legislative recruitment process looking at the determinants of women's willingness to run for office, their ability to get nominated by parties, and chances for election as deputies in the Bulgarian parliament. The analysis points to the importance of the transitional context and developments in the party system in particular. Although institutional choices that promote female representation were made by the Bulgarian political elites, the dynamics of economic and political transition shaped the behaviour of potential female aspirants and party gatekeepers in a way that seriously hurt women's legislative recruitment. Women's resurgence in the 2001 parliament shows that women's representation can be improved within the Bulgarian electoral system when parties with women in their leadership structures have an opportunity to use party lists to promote them. Unfortunately, for reasons discussed below, the circumstances that placed the Bulgarian Women's Party (BWP) in a position to do this may prove ephemeral.

❖ THE PROCESS OF SELF-NOMINATION

The post-war social changes in Bulgaria resulted in women's increased political awareness and involvement in public life. At the same time, political participation and association were closely directed and controlled by the BCP. The characteristic features of the previous system had important consequences for women's entry in the Bulgarian National Assembly after 1989.

❖ *Employment*

In the post-war period, one of the themes in the BCP's social program was the need to establish equal rights for men and women to study, work, and participate in the party's political and professional organizations (Ananieva and Razvigorova 1991). In Bulgaria, with its semi-feudal economy and deeply rooted traditional values, industrialization and urbanization brought significant changes in both women's opportunities and society's perceptions about emancipation. By 1982, the mass entry of women in the labour force reached 49 per cent of all employees, 53 per cent of those working in the field of science, and 51 per cent employed in public administration (Statisticheski Godishnik 1982: 110). Moving out of the house and into salaried employment helped many women to develop skills and the self-confidence that could be valuable in the political sphere.

Since 1989, unemployment has become a major concern for all households in Bulgaria. From 1989 to the mid-1990s, between 52 and 55 per cent of the total unemployed labour force in the country were women (Yearbook of Labour Statistics; 2000: 483). While the burden of unemployment falls somewhat disproportionately on women's shoulders, it is also clear that Bulgarian women are continuing to work. Women constituted 48 per cent of the adult labour force in Bulgaria in both 1994 and 1996 (The World's Women 1995: 141; Yearbook of Labour Statistics 2000: 93 and 449). There has not been a broad retreat into the private sphere, as that would not be economically feasible for most families; at the same time, women have not improved their professional status (Lippe and Fodor 1998).

World statistics on gender inequality show that in 1988, when both paid and unpaid labour are considered, Bulgarian women worked nine hours per week more than men; the time they spent doing unpaid labour was twice as much as that spent by men (The World's Women 1995: 105). This severe double burden has only intensified in the transitional period. Bulgaria's delaying of necessary reforms with regard to privatization and restructuring of the economy has resulted in severe economic problems. As the state's ability to provide social welfare has diminished and household living standards have declined, women have had to spend even more time and energy on the 'second shift', work at home. For a great number of women, the exigencies of family survival have simply supplanted the desire and opportunity to devote time to political participation.

❖ Education

Education is another factor that shapes women's ability to run for office and party leadership's decisions to nominate them. In socialist Bulgaria, there was free access to education for all groups of society. In 1982, 52 per cent of all university students were women (Statisticheski Godishnik 1982: 415). Educated equally as well as men, but assumed to split attention between the workplace and the home, Bulgarian women have often been deprived of advancement to high-ranking positions in the workplace. According to 1990 census data, the number of Bulgarian female workers in the professional, technical, clerical, and sales sectors exceeded that of male workers. In administrative or managerial positions, however, there were only 44 women per 100 men (The World's Women 1995: 99 and 141). In the present context of an emerging market economy, for many party gatekeepers, experience in profit-oriented enterprises, rather than ideological considerations, is seen as a crucial attribute for possible candidates. Therefore, Bulgarian men will often be preferred when selecting candidates.

❖ Mass culture

The socioeconomic developments that followed the introduction of the Soviet socialist model in Bulgaria caused changes in the way society perceived the role of women. Industrialization and collectivization in the agricultural sector

❖ TATIANA KOSTADINOVA

forced masses of people to move to the cities. While in 1946 only 25 per cent of Bulgaria's total population lived in towns, this number continued to grow through the entire post-war period and reached more than 70 per cent in 1994 (Statisticheski Godishnik 1982: 27; World Development Report 1996: 175). Urbanization weakened traditional values, including previous understandings that women's, especially wives' and mothers', place is only in the home. Expectations of a more active public role for women were developing in society, and women held significant numbers of public offices. In 1980, the percentage of women in the leadership of the Fatherland Front, the Bulgarian Trade Unions, and the Communist Youth Organization varied between 40 and 52 per cent (Kostova 1998: 252). In the late 1980s, 34 per cent of the members of the local elected government bodies were women (Ananieva and Razvigorova 1991). This active involvement was to a great extent the result of the BCP's dictates; yet, positive effects on women's experience with organizational activities and changes in traditional culture did occur.

According to survey data, Bulgarian women are as interested as men are in political issues. They devote a comparable amount of time to reading the news, watching political programmes broadcast on television, and participating in political discussions (Kostova 1998: 253). Thus, the levels of political knowledge and interest in current societal problems create conditions favorable for having significant numbers of women willing to run for office. Given their high levels of education, active involvement in local and municipal organization leadership, and interest in politics, many Bulgarian women might be expected to aspire for nominations. This willingness is constrained, however, by the difficulties of economic transition that generate a need to devote more time to the family.

There were, of course, limits to the changes in people's perspectives on women. True decision-making positions were dominated by men, and after the fall of the old system, traditional values re-established themselves in Bulgaria and other Eastern European countries (see Chapter 3). The rhetoric of directive emancipation did have some effects on women's position in society, but there was still a considerable gap between the rhetoric of true equality and the societal reality.

Table 15.1 presents demographic data regarding the Bulgarian parliamentary representatives in the last three parliaments. In terms of occupational status, most of the female representatives work in the liberal professions or are lawyers. The numbers are consistent over time and we see there are few differences when comparing the occupations of male and female representatives. The one significant difference is in the share of lawyers. The percentage of MPs in the three assemblies with a legal background is noticeably higher among the female MPs than among male MPs. Note also that Bulgaria differs from the rest of Eastern Europe in that there has not been a noticeable influx of new representatives from the business sector. Nevertheless, we see that workers have slowly disappeared from parliament; present-day MPs are overwhelmingly

Table 15.1. Sociological profile of Bulgarian members of parliament, 1994, 1997, and 2001 (per cent)

	1994		1997		2001	
	Women	Men	Women	Men	Women	Men
OCCUPATION						
Liberal professions[1]	48.4	49.5	44.0	51.6	55.7	55.9
Lawyers	29.0	16.3	24.0	9.6	23.0	14.0
Engineers	12.9	15.4	24.0	27.7	18.0	25.1
Government	9.7	11.5	4.0	3.3	1.6	0.6
Workers	—	4.8	—	2.8	—	—
Business	—	1.0	—	1.4	1.6	3.9
PARTY POSITION						
Party official[2]	58.1	60.6	36.0	50.2	29.5	43.0
MARITAL STATUS						
Single[3]	25.8	11.1	36.0	10.8	27.9	11.2

[1] This category includes scientists, school teachers, university professors, physicians, and musicians.
[2] Members of local or central party councils.
[3] Include divorced and widows/widowers.

Source: Adapted from data from the Bulgarian National Assembly <http://www.parliament.bg/-deputati>.

socioeconomic elites. In addition, as a part of an emerging overall trend towards electing rank-and-file candidates, almost two-thirds of the 1997 female winners and an even higher proportion of the 2001 female winners were not members of local or central party councils.

The most substantial difference in the social profile of male and female members of Parliament, however, is in their marital status. The share of single men is much smaller than that of single women. In 1997, over one-third of all female MPs, but fewer than 11 per cent of men elected to the assembly were unmarried. In 2001, the proportion of female MPs who were single dropped slightly, but they were still 2.5 times more likely to be single than men. That single women in Bulgaria are more likely to become members of Parliament gives us insight into the female self-nomination process. Many married women lack the time and other resources necessary to pursue a political career. Party gatekeepers and voters may also see married women as belonging primarily in the private sphere, taking care of their families, and therefore they are more hesitant to consider their candidacies.

❖ PARTY NOMINATIONS

To the extent that some Bulgarian women have the skills and desire to run for office, the next hurdle they face is at the nomination stage. They must be able to convince party leaders, usually men, that they can bring important resources, first and foremost votes, to the party ticket. The history of women's organization in Bulgaria provides some evidence regarding women's relative ability to accomplish this.

The first women's associations were established in the second half of the nineteenth century to provide help for women to study and to draw women into the liberation movement against Ottoman domination. After the liberation and until the communists' take-over, several important women's organizations, developed whose main goal was to achieve equal social and political rights and opportunities. During this period, women could not vote or run for parliament. The franchise was extended to women in 1937, but women did not actually compete for assembly seats until 1945. Under communist rule, women had the formal right to freely associate. In practice, however, they were not able to form any group or organization that was not initiated and monitored by the BCP. The Committee of the Bulgarian Women's Movement was established in the 1960s to coordinate various social and cultural activities approved by the Party. The organization survived after 1989, but lost popularity and is still attempting to develop a new image and gain legitimacy.

In contrast, the events leading to the fall of the communist regime in November 1989 can be traced to the organized actions of a remarkable group of women. Disappointed with the government failure to deal with the severe air pollution in the city of Ruse, in September 1987 women rallied in the first open public protest in Bulgaria after decades of communist rule (Desai and Snavely 1998). This gave a strong impetus to the emergence of various environmental, labour, and human rights groups that included women's rights problems in their programs. The major goal pursued by these groups was to push the regime for political and social changes towards democratization and the development of civil society. Women actively participated in the formation of opposition organizations, but failed to establish viable organizations of their own or to define women's problems as distinct from broader issues of human rights and the formation of civil society.

❖ THE POST-1989 PARTY SYSTEM

At the time of the first post-communist elections in June 1990, two major political forces dominated the Bulgarian political arena. Those were the leftist Bulgarian Socialist Party (BSP), the successor party to the former BCP, and the opposition centre-right coalition, Union of Democratic Forces (UDF). Initially, the BSP was better organized with a well-established network of local structures that covered the entire country. The UDF, a loose coalition of groups and parties, did not possess the organizational capacity of its main rival but enjoyed the prestige of being an anti-communist pro-democratic political alternative. From 1990 up to 2001, these two political organizations repeatedly won the largest portion of the vote in four Bulgarian legislative elections. In addition, a smaller but recognizable party of the Turkish minority group, the Movement for Rights and Freedoms (MRF), competed for seats and was successful mainly in districts with mixed ethnic composition.

Internal divisions within the two dominant parties over the speed and the scope of reform produced fragmentation and separation of smaller groups as independent parties (Kitschelt *et al.* 1999: 203). Of the latter, only a few achieved brief parliamentary representation. Among the UDF splinters, the Democratic Party, in a coalition with the Agrarians, won representation in 1994; in the next elections their coalition ran together with the UDF. A group of social-democratic, pro-western activists split from the BSP and won assembly seats in 1997 under the Euroleft label. It failed, however, to attract sufficient numbers of leftist voters and was unable to maintain its electoral success in 2001.

A major change in the structure of the party system occurred in 2001. The former king, Simeon II Saxe-Coburg-Gotha, returned to Bulgaria and decided to run in the June parliamentary election. Relying on the support of large segments of the population disappointed with the previous policies of BSP and UDF governments, Simeon organized a movement around an ambiguous populist platform. After the Sofia City Court refused to register his party, the former king forged a coalition with two small and unknown parties, the Bulgarian Women's Party (BWP) and the Movement for National Revival, in order to participate in the election.[1] The National Movement Simeon II (NMSII) won half of the contested seats and emerged as the largest parliamentary group in the thirty-ninth National Assembly. This success occurred without Simeon actually presenting an explicit party program of specific policy goals.

In spite of the BWP's recent success within NMSII, the establishment of Bulgarian women's organizations in the country's political structures after 1989 has been very difficult. Once the regime collapsed, Bulgarian women struggled to find a vehicle for active involvement in politics. Alternative groups proclaiming themselves successors of the old female unions from the beginning of the twentieth century were formed. Not surprisingly, their basic goals were formulated using much of the rhetoric of the past. Priority was given to 'women's self-realization within the family' and 'observing the laws guaranteeing the protection of mothers and children' (FBIS-EEU 19 March 1990: 16). The few women's associations that formed after 1989 have been organizationally weak and underdeveloped (Kostova 1998: 251). Furthermore, they tend to concentrate on issues within civil society and not within the formal political channels. All of these characteristics of the women's movement, in general, have applied to the BWP as well. The BWP does not characterize itself as feminist, nor does it promote or draw support from feminist groups.

❖ TATIANA KOSTADINOVA

In several other Eastern European countries major parties have established women's organizations within their parties. In Bulgaria, neither the UDF nor the BSP have established separate women's affiliates.[2] In the elections of 1990–7, there were no organizations, internal or external to the parties, that were able to exert serious pressure on the Bulgarian political parties to nominate women as candidates.

The extraordinary circumstances of 2001 provided, quite unexpectedly, the opportunity to negotiate the nomination of a much larger number of female candidates. The BWP was not a junior partner in a coalition; it was a partner Simeon's movement needed to run in the election. This placed the small women's party in a very good position to push for more nominations in winnable slots on the party lists. In other words, a party with women in the leadership structure was finally in a position to exploit the relatively woman-friendly electoral system.

❖ The electoral system

The need to change the Bulgarian electoral system was recognized early in the transitional process. Quotas were (and continue to be) explicitly rejected as an element of the old BCP's policies; the electoral rules that emerged in the democratic transition, however, provided parties with opportunities to recruit women if they chose to do so. The BCP and the UDF negotiated a new electoral law at the National Round Table sessions from January–March 1990. The most difficult part of the bargaining process was choosing the type of electoral districts. The BCP preferred single member districts relying on its strong local support; the opposition believed that a proportional representation (PR) system would better suit the emerging but organizationally underdeveloped non-Communist parties (Kolarova and Dimitrov 1996: 192). A mixed system was introduced as a compromise. Half of the assembly seats were to be contested in single-member districts with majority run-off and the remaining seats in 28 multi-member districts were to be allocated according to PR.

The electoral system was changed once again on the eve of the second Bulgarian multiparty election in the fall of 1991. The splits within the UDF and the growing mass public disapproval of the ex-Communist party increased the uncertainty of the election outcome. A pure PR system was introduced that closely resembled the PR part in the previous mixed system. According to the new formula, all 240 assembly seats are contested in 31 multi-member districts on closed lists using the d'Hondt method to calculate seat allocations. The district magnitude was kept almost the same, 7.74 as compared to 7.14 in the PR part in 1990. The 4 per cent threshold for representation was also retained to prevent excessive fragmentation and eventual cabinet instability. This system has proven to function satisfactorily and is still in force.

Two institutional elements important for female representation were established in the 1991 Bulgarian electoral system, a moderate average district magnitude and a legal threshold. Combined, these factors create conditions for few and bigger winners who can afford to include women and minorities when success is not at risk (Matland and Taylor 1997). Indeed, the number of elected parties in Bulgaria has been relatively low.[3] The major parties win several seats in many districts which results in an average party magnitude favourable to the election of female MPs. The empirical question is the following: 'If the institutional structure is favourable to Bulgarian party leaders including women, do party leaders in fact do so'?

❖ Nominations in practice

In general, the candidate nomination process in the bigger Bulgarian parties is centralized with some modest increase in local organizations' participation in the most recent elections (Kostova 1998: 256). The practice has been to reserve the top of regional lists for high-ranking party leaders in order to ensure their election. Local nominees are ranked lower on the ballot. Thus, women had to overcome two hurdles: first, to be approved by the central leadership as candidates, and second, to be placed high on the list to overcome tensions between central and local councils. In addition, the UDF leadership, a coalition of more than 15 parties and groups, had to solve the problem of intraparty conflict of interests.[4] For example, there is evidence to suggest that when lists are negotiated, compromises to include representatives of all unions are often made at the expense of female candidates. In the early stages of transition, the opposition's main goal was to defeat the former Communist Party in the election arena. Maintaining organizational unity and coherence has overshadowed a desire to ensure representation of women's interests. Table 15.2 shows the nomination choices made by major parliamentary parties from 1991 to 2001.

Nominations are important, but nomination to a party list does not, by itself, ensure election to the legislature. The data clearly show that, with the exception of the NMSII in 2001, a small proportion of parties' top nominations were female candidates. Those were given to a few women with positions in the party leadership. Initially the BSP, which had more women in its organizations and a history of women in leadership positions, slated a larger number of women on its lists than did the centre-right UDF. A substantial portion of these nominees, however, were placed low on the ballot, where chances to get elected strongly diminish. Overall, most of the female nominations made by the two leftist parties, the BSP and the Euroleft, were not in winnable positions. According to previous research, one characteristic feature of the post-1989 Socialist party elite and especially after 1994 was the increasing trend of exclusion in the recruitment process (Kostova 2000: 206). As the table shows,

Table 15.2. Position of nominated women on party lists (% of party candidates), 1991–2001

Party election	Position on party list					
	1	2	3	4	5	6 and lower
BSP						
1991	25.8	12.9	22.6	9.7	13.3	13.9
1994[1]	12.9	16.1	9.7	12.9	19.4	20.6
1997[2]	3.2	9.7	29.0	9.7	17.2	25.3
2001[3]	6.5	12.9	12.9	19.4	12.9	23.1
UDF						
1991	9.7	22.6	9.7	12.9	3.3	11.2
1994	9.7	9.7	16.1	22.6	10.3	10.1
1997[4]	19.4	0.0	9.7	12.9	19.4	15.1
2001[4]	19.4	19.4	12.9	19.4	12.9	23.0
MRF						
1991	15.4	7.7	8.7	28.6	0.0	8.3
1994	16.1	9.7	7.1	26.1	17.7	8.2
1997[5]	6.5	6.5	22.6	12.9	28.6	32.2
2001[6]	12.9	16.1	16.1	22.6	27.6	28.0
BBB[7]						
1994	6.5	16.1	8.0	22.2	42.9	11.1
1997	6.5	9.7	12.9	22.2	20.8	19.4
2001	6.5	16.1	23.3	30.8	25.0	29.3
EUROLEFT						
1997	9.7	16.1	16.1	19.4	22.6	21.3
2001	16.1	12.9	25.8	22.6	25.8	35.0
NMSII[8]						
2001	48.4	38.7	54.8	27.6	25.9	30.4

[1] In coalition with Bulgarian Agrarian Union 'Al. Stamboliiski' and Political Club 'Ecoglasnost'.
[2] In coalition with Political Club 'Ecoglasnost'.
[3] Coalition for Bulgaria.
[4] In coalition with the People's Union (the Bulgarian Agrarian Union and the Democratic Party).
[5] In coalition with Bulgarian Agrarian Union, Nikola Petkov, the Green Party, Party of the Democratic Centre, Union New Choice, and Federation Kingdom Bulgaria.
[6] In coalition with the Liberal Union and Euroroma.
[7] Bulgarian Business Bloc.
[8] National Movement Simeon II in coalition with the Bulgarian Women's Party and the Movement for National Revival.

Sources: Byuletin (1991); Matematicheski Kolektiv. 'Izbori'. (Mathematical Team. 'Elections') <http://izbori.math.bas.bg>; Bulgarian National Assembly. 'Danni za Deputati' ('Data on Members of Parliament') <http://www.parliament.bg>.

the share of women holding top positions on the BSP ballot dropped dramatically from 25.8 per cent in 1991 to 3.2 per cent in 1997 and 6.5 per cent in 2001.

The centre-right UDF put fewer women at the very top of the party lists in 1991 and 1994. The split of the Democratic Party and some branches of the Radical Democratic Party from UDF and the formation of the People's Union in 1994 increased the uncertainty and the risk of placing female candidates in top positions. In the next two elections, after sufficient knowledge about the district-level strength of the party was accumulated, 10 per cent more women were nominated in the first position on the UDF ballot. This significant increase coincides with the organizational transformation of the UDF from a broad umbrella party containing multiple smaller parties to a single unified party. It appears that party consolidation facilitated the nomination of women once the pressure on the UDF National Coordination Council to nominate leaders of various member groups diminished.

The case of the Turkish minority party, the MRF, suggests another interesting story about the link between women's positioning on the ballots and party coalition policies. In 1991 and 1994, women held 15–16 per cent of the party's top nominations. In these years, MRF ran on its own. In 1997, however, the MRF joined a broader electoral coalition. The number of women in the top slots (first and second) dropped precipitously from previous elections. At the same time, the proportion of fifth, sixth, and lower-placed female candidates significantly increased. What appears to have happened is the need to accommodate pre-electoral partnership with a number of other organizations brought a decrease in the share of women's top nominations.

The highest figures for women's nominations are reported for the debut of the NMSII. Almost one-half (48.4 per cent) of the first and over half (54.8 per cent) of the third slots were filled with female candidates. The BWP was able to bargain with Simeon and get the greatest representation of women among the first, second, and third positions on the list, which are the most attractive because they entail the greatest likelihood of election. The more symbolic fourth, fifth, and lower positions have noticeably fewer women in them. Future elections will show just how committed the NMSII really is to the recruitment of women to serve as the people's representatives in the assembly. The NMSII was balancing its ticket with the leaders of its constituent parties—a well-established practice. It just so happened that in 2001, one of the constituents was a women's party.

❖ Nominations and party magnitude

Some preliminary evidence from Table 15.2 suggests that if parties are only able to elect one or two representatives in a district there will be limited numbers of women elected; it is first when parties reach down to the third, fourth, and fifth place on the lists that women will start to receive significant

❖ TATIANA KOSTADINOVA

proportions of the nominations. In other words, it appears as if party magnitude should affect women's access to parliament. I examine this association using district level data for the three major parties, the BSP, the UDF, and the MRF, for the four electoral cycles between 1991 and 2001. The correlation between the proportion of elected female candidates and number of party seats won in the election, is positive and statistically significant for three of the four elections.[5] This suggests higher party magnitude covaries with higher proportions of elected women. The combination of reasonably high district magnitude along with the relatively limited number of parties leads to high party magnitudes. The data provide support for the idea that women are more likely to be nominated in winnable positions in those electoral constituencies where parties can expect to send multi-member delegations to parliament.

❖ FEMALE REPRESENTATION AND PARTIES

In the context of a transitional environment with a changing party system configuration, politicians responsible for the nomination process must act under the pressure of uncertainty. Potential shifts in voters' support make parties feel insecure about the electoral outcome even in the traditionally safest districts. All parties in Bulgaria have experienced the difficulties of working under conditions of information deficiency. Yet, they have registered varying levels of success with electing women on their ballots. Theoretically, these levels are expected to vary by party ideology. Looking at the results from the first democratic election in 1990, we find the former Communist Party was most supportive of female representation. Thirteen per cent of the BSP seats won at the first round belonged to women, while the centre-right UDF elected barely half that (see Table 15.3). The MRF did not elect any women in 1990. Note the data also support the institutional hypothesis that more women get elected in a PR than in a majoritarian system. For both the BSP and the UDF,

Table 15.3. Women elected to the Bulgarian Grand National Assembly, 1990, first round

Allocation rule	BSP		UDF		MRF	
	Total	Per cent female	Total	Per cent female	Total	Per cent female
PR	97	17.5	75	8.0	12	0
Majority	72	6.9	31	3.2	0	0
Total	169	13.0	106	6.6	12	0

Source: FBIS-EEU 13 June 1990, 7–8; FBIS-EEU 22 June 1990, 3–4.

women made up a substantially larger portion of the delegation elected via proportional representation than they did of the proportion elected via majoritarian districts.

Looking at subsequent elections, we see a gradual decrease in female representation in the BSP parliamentary group (see Table 15.4). This trend is observed regardless of how well the party as a whole performs on election

Table 15.4. Women in the Bulgarian National Assembly by party and by election year, 1991–2001

Party	1991	1994	1997	2001
BSP				
Per cent women MPs	18.9	16.8[1]	10.3[2]	10.4[3]
Total # seats	106	125	58	48
UDF				
Per cent women MPs	10.0	8.7	11.7[4]	17.6[4]
Total # seats	110	69	137	51
MRF				
Per cent women MPs	8.3	13.3	5.3[5]	9.5[6]
Total # seats	24	15	19	21
BBB[7]				
Per cent women MPs	—	7.7	0.0	—
Total # seats		13	12	
PEOPLE'S UNION				
Per cent women MPs	—	5.6	—	—
Total # seats		18		
EUROLEFT				
Per cent women MPs	—	—	14.3	—
Total # seats			14	
NMSII[8]				
Per cent women MPs	—	—	—	40.0
Total # seats				120
TOTAL				
Per cent women MPs	13.8	12.9	10.4	26.7
Total # seats	240	240	240	240

[1] In coalition with Bulgarian Agrarian Union 'Al. Stamboliiski' and 'Political Club E'coglasnost'.
[2] In coalition with Political Club E'coglasnost.
[3] Coalition for Bulgaria.
[4] In coalition with the People's Union (the Bulgarian Agrarian Union and the Democratic Party).
[5] In coalition with Bulgarian Agrarian Union, Nikola Petkov, the Green Party, Party of the Democratic Centre, Union New Choice, and Federation Kingdom Bulgaria.
[6] In coalition with the Liberal Union and Euroroma.
[7] Bulgarian Business Bloc.
[8] National Movement Simeon II in coalition with the Bulgarian Women's Party and the Movement for National Revival.

Sources: Matematicheski Kolektiv 'Izbori'. (Mathematical Team. 'Elections') <http://izbori.math.bas.bg>. Bulgarian National Assembly. 'Danni za Deputati' ('Data on Members of Parliament') <http://www.parliament.bg>.

❖ TATIANA KOSTADINOVA

day.[6] One of the possible explanations for these developments is the various groups' continuing intra-party struggle with the new role of the party. The split that led to the Euroleft group leaving the party and establishing its own party in 1996 contributed to this trend as well; many of the forces within the BSP that might have been sympathetic to women's representation departed with the Euroleft. The Euroleft could be expected to be sympathetic to women's representation as it is expressly interested in ties to Western European social democratic parties. In 1997 it did have the highest proportion of women of any delegation, but it failed to win representation in the 2001 parliamentary elections. While the UDF failed to improve female representation in the 1994 elections, it did somewhat better in 1997 and much better in 2001 with close to 18 per cent of its assembly group consisting of women.

The MRF, as an ethnic party appealing to the Muslim sector of the electorate, can be expected to be, culturally and religiously, less supportive of women's participation in politics. Yet, in 1994, it was more successful than the UDF in increasing female representation in its parliamentary group. At that time, the Turkish party maintained its organizational coherence and felt more confident in its electoral support. In 1997 and in 2001, however, the MRF had to give some of the safe positions on the ballot to several of its coalition partners instead of promoting women. In two of its 'safest' districts (Kurdjali and Razgrad), no women in 1997 and only one in 2001, party Vice-chairwoman E. Etem, obtained seats.

The NMSII's rate of female nomination in 2001 was clearly atypical for post-communist Bulgaria, or for a major party anywhere in Eastern Europe, and does much to account for the abrupt increase in the number of women elected to the National Assembly. The accomplishment was large in both absolute and relative terms: 48 seats and a 40 per cent share in the movement's parliamentary group. The magnitude of this success affected women's overall legislative representation, which, for the first time, rose above the levels seen in the last communist-dominated legislature.

It remains to be seen whether women's gains in 2001 were epiphenomenal, the product of a marriage of convenience between an upstart movement and a Bulgarian Women's Party that did not run in the 1991 and 1994 elections, and polled only 0.38 per cent of the vote (around 16,000 votes) in 1997. The BWP's leader, Vesela Draganova, became known for the first time when Simeon announced his intention to run in a coalition. Simeon wanted weak coalition partners and the BWP, which had never won a seat in the Assembly, provided that. Simeon's need for the party, however, placed the BWP in the position to pressure Simeon into placing its personnel into top list positions at an unprecedented rate. If the Simeon movement folds, or if it finds another minor party to take the BWP's place, it may well be that women's representation in the Assembly will fall to the rates seen between 1989 and 2001.

WOMEN'S REPRESENTATION IN BULGARIA ❖

As to whether this was strictly a symbolic victory for women, there are conflicting signals. Despite being 40 per cent of the NMSII parliamentary delegation, women have only two of 17 (12 per cent) ministerial posts. This is a drop from the previous UDF cabinet in which women filled three ministerial posts. Women do hold a higher proportion of committee chairmanships than in previous parliaments, although the numbers are still quite modest (3 of 20 committees, 15 per cent, are chaired by women).[7]

On the other hand, developments within Simeon's coalition indicate that he has been forced to consider the BWP's wishes. The BWP vigorously opposed an attempt made by Simeon's people to form and finally register their party in January 2002. They feared the Women's Party would be marginalized if Simeon's group no longer relied upon them. Holding a position in the leadership of the coalition, BWP party leader Draganova basically threatened not to accept the new party as a legitimate parliamentary party. Simeon was forced to postpone the founding meeting of his new party in order to avoid a split in the group. If the BWP is able to maintain its key position in the coalition, women's representation should continue to benefit. Also, given the composition of the NSMII coalition in parliament, it is likely that even if Simeon does eventually establish his own independent party, a large proportion of its sitting representatives would be women who were elected as part of the original coalition.

❖ CONCLUSION

Bulgarian women are well educated and interested in political issues. Their previous involvement in local and national structures of political and social organizations affiliated with the Communist Party, however, has had a dubious effect on access to power in the post-communist period. On the one hand, it has made them skillful and knowledgeable in the public arena. On the other, women have remained relatively passive with regard to competing for and winning public office. What emerges as a plausible explanation for women's diminished presence in politics is the diminished interest, not in politics per se, but in investing time and energy in public life, when the family needs to be protected against the hardships of economic transition. Autonomous organized women's groups have been slow to take root. Hence party gatekeepers, in the absence of pressure to recruit more women and to place them in top leadership positions within the party, have balanced their lists on the basis of other concerns. For the broad party coalitions that have dominated post-communist Bulgarian electoral politics, the chief concern has been party leaders' perpetuation in parliament. Top-list positions have been apportioned among the leaders of the parties that make up these coalitions, and, until Simeon's coalition with the BWP, those leaders have disproportionately been male.

❖ TATIANA KOSTADINOVA

There is good reason to be concerned that the gains made in the last election could be quickly reversed. There are, however, reasons to believe that women are establishing a more permanent presence. The outcomes of the 1990–7 multi-party competitive elections in Bulgaria did not promote female representation in an outstanding manner. Yet a group of women was able to cross the hurdles and participate in the work of the national legislature. Since the first transitional election in 1990, 83 Bulgarian women have been elected to Parliament. Twenty-two of them (26.5 per cent) have been re-elected. Furthermore, individual women have held prominent positions. The deputy prime minister in the sitting NSMII government is a female, as is true of the foreign minister in the previous UDF government. The emergence of a group of professional female legislators is a significant step towards the expansion of women's presence in political life. The post-1989 female members of the Bulgarian parliament have been well qualified for, and strongly devoted to, public work. The consequences of this have started to appear. Since the UDF unified as a single party, several women have become powerful at the highest level of the party leadership. Two women have been nominated to compete for the highest post in the party at the upcoming national conference.

The broader lesson of Bulgaria's 2001 election appears to be twofold: women benefit when parties become clearly unified organizations and when women achieve leadership positions in the parties. On paper, the existing electoral institutions ought to be woman-friendly. Even reasonably large party magnitudes, however, do not ensure the recruitment of women where party gatekeepers have no incentive (internal or external pressure) to place women in competitive slots. The volatile party system, and the uncertainty it generates in terms of voter support, has made parties hesitant to nominate women in competitive list positions. With women dedicated to establishing equitable representation in central positions, these concerns can be overridden.

As optimistic as the most recent election results are with regard to legislative representation of women in Bulgaria, it is still too early to say how strong and consistent the trend will be in the future. In many ways, the 2001 election was unique—the BWP got involved in the race almost accidentally. We do not know how stable the NMSII coalition will be, and whether the ex-king's party will register and next time run on its own. Even if he does, we do not know whether he will suffer the fate of each of the previous democratically elected governments: being turned out at the polls by a dissatisfied electorate. At the same time, diffusion effects are possible in future elections when other parties may choose to nominate more women to compete with the NMSII. However, the BWP was not electorally successful because voters wanted women; and the party itself does not maintain an explicit commitment to promoting gender equality. Bulgarian women's representation will only improve if women associate and press for a permanent place in national politics.

WOMEN'S REPRESENTATION IN BULGARIA ❖

❖ Notes

1 The city court's decision to refuse to register the king's party was based on irregularities in the registration documents.

2 It is worth noting that these parties formally had established youth groups, but no such organizations within the parties exist for women.

3 Measured through the formula developed by Laakso and Taagepera (1979), the effective number of elected parties in Bulgaria is: 2.42 in 1990, 2.41 in 1991, 2.73 in 1994, 2.52 in 1997 (Dawisha and Deets 1999), and 2.92 in 2001 (author's calculations).

4 Pre-election coalitions such as the Coalition of the Democratic Left and the Union for National Salvation faced the same problem in 1997.

5 There are 93 cases for each test (3 parties × 31 districts). In 1991, the bivariate correlation is 0.265 (sig. < 0.01, 2-tailed test). In 1994, the bivariate correlation is 0.226 (sig. < 0.03, 2-tailed test). In 1997, the bivariate correlation is 0.173 (sig. < 0.17, 2-tailed test). In 2001, the bivariate correlation is 0.277 (sig. < 0.01, 2-tailed test).

6 The BSP lost the 1991 election by a small margin, won over 50% of the seats in 1994, and lost again in 1997 when the UDF won an absolute parliamentary majority. The BSP failed to emerge as the victor in the 2001 elections as voters turned to Simeon after rejecting the sitting UDF party.

7 In the 1994 parliament women held 2 of 20 committee chairmanships (10%) and in 1997 they held only 1 of 15 (6.7%). With respect to deputy chairs, there was a significant increase in the new parliament. Nineteen per cent (11 of 58) of the deputy chairs were women. This is up from 10% in 1997 and 5.6% in 1994.

16 ❖ Women's Representation in Post-Communist Europe

Richard E. Matland

At the outset, we set two goals. First, to test a set of theories developed from studies of women's access to political power in Western Democracies. We wished to see how those theories fared in a significantly different context, the newly developing democracies of Central and Eastern Europe. Second, to develop a better understanding of how women were faring in the newly established democracies of Central and Eastern Europe. While we have not studied all of the new democracies, the eleven countries considered represent a broad cross-section and we believe the lessons drawn from these countries are useful in understanding women's access to political power in other post-communist European countries and, more generally, in democratic polities.

❖ An Overview of Levels of Representation

One of the clearest results in the chapters presented is the great diversity across countries. While all of these nations share a legacy of a communist past, they have set off in markedly differing directions and there is considerably greater diversity today than a dozen years ago. Where the various countries are today has relatively little to do with where they were as a group ten or fifteen years ago. Internal conditions, that vary across the countries, are determinative of women's representation.

While there is great diversity, we can start to establish tentative groupings in terms of women's representation. Figure 16.1 divides the countries in this study, and a handful of additional post-communist European states, into four quadrants based on the absolute level of women's representation and the change in women's representation from the first post-communist election to the most recent election.[1] By dividing the sample into four quadrants, we see some distinct differences.

Understandably, the first quadrant, which represents a significant increase in representation and low absolute levels of representation, has few countries

Absolute level of representation/ change in representation	0–5 per cent	5–10 per cent	10–15 per cent	15–20 per cent	>20 per cent
10% or greater increase in representation	I		II	Estonia² (PR)	West Germany (MMP) Bulgaria (PR) Croatia (PR)
5.1–10.0% increase in representation		Moldova² (PR)	Romania² (PR)	Czech Republic (PR)	Poland (PR)
2.6–5.0% increase in representation	IV	Bosnia-Herzegovenia² (PR) Macedonia (MMP)		III	
0.0–2.5% increase in representation	Ukraine (MMP)	Hungary (MMP) Albania² (MMP) Georgia² (MMP)	Lithuania (MMP) Slovenia (semi-PR) Slovakia² (PR)	Latvia² (PR)	
A decrease in representation		Russia (MMP)			

[1] The electoral systems used in the various countries are also identified, MMP = mixed member proportional system; PR = Proportional Representation only; semi-PR = Slovenian system of PR with individual districts.
[2] Countries in Eastern and Central Europe not included in our study.

Figure 16.1. Women's representation: absolute levels and change over time[1]

in it. None of the countries included in this book, and only Moldova of the other post-communist European countries, fits these criteria. The other three quadrants, however, all include several countries.

The second quadrant houses the 'success stories'; those countries with substantial representation of women where there has been a marked increase in representation since the first post-communist election. A couple of these cases are best understood as anomalies. The GDR joined a stable functioning democracy, and while the fusion led to important changes in German politics, the system is still easily recognizable as an evolutionary change in the old West Germany polity; as such, there are limited lessons for other countries. In addition, the case of Bulgaria is highly unusual, with the rise of a charismatic leader, the former king, Simeon II, leading to a huge increase in women's representation. It is too early to tell whether the gain for women in Bulgaria is a temporary blip or part of a more permanent improvement in women's participation in the halls of power. On the other hand, in Croatia, Poland, and to a lesser degree the Czech Republic, women's representation has risen to a point where there has been a substantial improvement since the initial elections and women control a sufficient bloc of parliamentary seats that they figure prominently in national politics.

These three countries have a number of traits in common, that combined form a picture that is distinct from the rest of Central and Eastern Europe. The political institutions, the issues on the political agenda, and the level of mobilization together produce relatively attractive outcomes for women. In terms of political institutions, all of these countries have party list PR systems. Another factor that is found in these three countries is that a major issue on the political agenda is the desire to 'join' Western Europe. All are leading candidates for membership in the European Union. They all have had extensive contacts with Western European countries and, more importantly, many of their parties have close ties to sister parties in Western Europe. In designing party institutions, it has been natural for these newly established Eastern European parties to copy what they found in their sister parties in the West. In several cases, this 'design borrowing' has led to the development of explicit party institutions, quotas, for example, that help insure access for women. Even when explicit institutions are not established, merely the desire for these new parties to establish themselves as modern European parties has helped women. Finally, and crucially, women have organized and mobilized to take advantage of favorable institutions, both inside and outside the parties. For example, Siemeńska notes that the dramatic increases in women's representation in Poland first occurred in the 2001 election, after a cross-party movement aimed at increasing representation had campaigned actively in Poland.

In the third quadrant, we find countries where there was some initial representation, but relatively little growth in women's representation has occurred over the more than a decade since liberation. These include Lithuania and Slovenia. The relatively high starting point, comparatively speaking, provides reason to believe these are countries where women should be able to break through, but they have been unable to for various reasons. In the case of Lithuania, Krupavičius and Matonytė suggest the last election was a high water mark for those parties that have been least open to women, resulting in a significant drop (6.9 per cent) in women's representation. Lithuania has system characteristics that could lead to significant improvements in women's representation in a relatively short period of time, but the spark has yet to occur.

Slovenia is a case where the desire to join Europe has been strong, where there has been an active women's movement (although it is less clear that women have been particularly active inside the parties), but where the political institutions have been extremely unfavourable, especially the electoral system. While Slovenia is officially a PR system, as Antić describes the way the system functions, with individual party candidates running in individual districts, it acts much more like a single member district system, in which parties often perceive strong incentives not to nominate women. As long as the existing electoral system remains, women will continue to struggle to gain representation.

In the fourth quadrant, are countries where representation is low and there has been small or no improvement over the past decade: Ukraine, Russia, Hungary, and Macedonia. These are countries where women have had a very difficult time gaining access and there has been no noticeable change in access in the past decade. These countries represent two distinct groups. First, Russia and the Ukraine represent countries that have struggled to develop stable party systems and democratic institutions. The evaluation of a number of scholars is that the transplantation of democracy into Russian and Ukrainian soil has succeeded only partially. Unlike several of the other Eastern European countries, these political systems have not developed stable democratic systems. Both Russia and Ukraine have been described as having non-party party systems. Furthermore, unlike several of the other Eastern European countries, where politics concerns distinct policy choices on a limited number of major issues in society (Kitschelt *et al.* 1999), politics in these countries has revolved around extracting rents from the political system. Issues of western integration have not penetrated the agenda, or at best, they have played a very minor role. Parties are organized around personalities and patronage is the order of the day. Furthermore, sexism on the part of party leaders has often frozen out women who might be viable candidates. These countries have developed systems where breaking in has been extremely difficult for women.

The remaining countries in this category are Macedonia and Hungary. In these countries, democratic institutions have developed, but women have been left behind. In both cases, the chapters make clear that the electoral system is a significant problem for women. Ristova notes that Macedonia uses a mixed system, but the system awards more than 70 per cent of the seats through single member districts. Montgomery and Ilonszki note the complicated three tier electoral system used in Hungary functions so as to discourage the ticket balancing expected in PR systems. For both of these countries the electoral system is enough of a barrier that it will be difficult to produce significant improvements in women's representation.[2] In addition, women have been unable to mobilize effectively to push parties to pay more attention to the issue of representation in these countries.

❖ Richard E. Matland

❖ LEGISLATIVE RECRUITMENT IN EASTERN EUROPE

In Chapter 2 we presented a model of the legislative recruitment process and suggested it would be a useful tool in understanding access to political power in Eastern Europe. Let us review some of the findings in the context of that model. The first step in the model was the move from eligible to aspirant. We suggested this move was affected by a candidate's political ambition and by the resources a possible candidate could generate. The decision to move from eligible to aspirant was also seen as being affected broadly by societal culture.

In Eastern Europe, as in Western Europe, women represent a majority of the eligibles. There are, however, some uniquely Eastern aspects of moving to be an aspirant. As Wilcox *et al.* document, there is considerably less support for Western style feminism. Public opinion is much more patriarchal in its view of the proper role of women. These views may affect all stages of the legislative recruitment process and are likely to lead to diminished political ambition on the part of women. Because the opportunity structure will appear poorer for many women in the East, the aspirant pool may be smaller in the East than in the West. However, while public opinion data seems to show uniformly that Eastern European countries are highly patriarchal, there is still *substantial* variation in the level of representation in Central and Eastern European countries. Public opinion does serve to depress supply, but a series of other important factors affect supply and demand at the other stages of the process.

Societal culture will not only affect women's overall willingness to aspire to office, but it may differentially affect groups of women who could be possible aspirants. This was shown quite strikingly in several of the chapters where the authors described the characteristics of nominees and MPs. Kostidinova notes, for example, that female MPs in Bulgaria were far more likely to be single than were their male counterparts. This outcome is probably both a result of societal culture affecting possible aspirant's evaluation of how viable they are politically and the fact that women with children, especially young children, are seen as lacking in another crucial political resource, time.

With respect to other resources, women have several of the resources traditionally emphasized in Western Democracies, such as high education and visible positions in society, but they are hurt *vis-à-vis* men in terms of additional assets valued by party gatekeepers. Several of the authors mentioned the importance of being able to bring economic resources to the table when being considered as a possible candidate. An increase in the number of candidates who have their base in private industry, where they often can use private economic resources to promote both their candidacies and those of their parties, has been noted in several countries and this has had a direct negative effect on the recruitment of women candidates.

Perhaps the most striking example of this was the Russian regional data where Nowacki found women won a higher proportion of legislative seats in rural regions than in urban regions. She suggests this occurs because in the rural regions, the resources women candidates had, that is, being local notables, were sufficient to counteract the disadvantage they faced in terms of economic resources. In the more urban districts, however, money mattered more, and where money mattered, fewer women were chosen as candidates or elected.

The second stage of the legislative recruitment model is moving from being an aspirant to being a candidate. At this stage, the possible aspirant must face party gatekeepers. Most of the Eastern European parties were interested in candidates with characteristics also found attractive to party gatekeepers in Western democracies. Candidates with high education levels, high socio-economic status, prominent positions in the local community and previous service to the party were all seen as attractive.

What several of the authors did note is the bar was set higher for possible female candidates. In their interviews with women serving in the Hungarian parliament, Montgomery and Ilonszki were repeatedly told that women had to have superior credentials to those of men. They would not have been chosen if they were merely men's equals. For women to be considered as attractive candidates they needed more education, more party service, or a very prominent position in society. Ristova documents this explicitly in Macedonia, showing that while most men in parliament had university degrees, *all* the women in parliament had university degrees. She also notes that while several of the men who served as government ministers had doctorates, *all* of the women who served as government ministers had doctorates. In short, to be considered a man's equal, women had to be more than a man's equal.

In our initial description, we stated that parties and party gatekeepers were interested in winning votes and aspirants would be evaluated in that light. If we modify this assertion slightly, we present a picture of parties that is both more realistic and allows for a more complex set of party goals. A more complex view of party goals is also consistent with the results found in the case studies. There are a variety of parties and difference in emphases among party goals.

In considering parties in Eastern Europe, Kitschelt (1995) describes three ideal types (charismatic, clientellistic, and programmatic). Charismatic parties are built around an individual leader who engenders intense loyalty. These parties are inherently unstable.[3] Clientellistic parties are patronage based with an emphasis on providing rewards to those members who are loyal to the organization. Programmatic parties have as their basis an ideological vision of how the good society should function; the goal of the party is to implement that broader vision. Across countries there were clear differences in the frequency with which these various party types appear.[4]

The evaluation of possible candidates by party gatekeepers is affected by these additional elements of concern. Party officials were interested in votes, but they had a number of other, often internal party concerns that influenced their evaluation of candidates. In some cases, these additional concerns hurt women. In several of the countries, including Ukraine, parties are largely clientellistic in form, and loyalty to a patron is valued above all. Party gate-keepers are first and foremost concerned about maintaining personal control over the party. Relatively little concern is shown for the vote consequences of one candidate vs. another, instead, loyalty is paramount. In these clientellistic parties, women rarely are part of the inner circle or seen as the loyal foot soldier that is the preferred candidate of the party leadership. Furthermore, the philosophical arguments concerning greater representation for women, tend to fall on deaf ears as the ideological or philosophical basis on which these arguments are made are unimportant to the party's primary goals.

In other cases, especially in programmatic parties, these additional party concerns help women. One of the concerns that newly established parties have is establishing their organizational identity or affirming their party's ideology. For several parties there was a conscious desire to emulate Western European parties and norms, a desire that was explicitly and actively encouraged by Western European parties that offered resources and support to parties in several Eastern European states. Especially in parties that were consciously trying to emulate parties they saw as their 'sister parties' in Western Europe, one way to legitimize oneself as a 'modern European party' was to establish procedures and internal party organizations that were similar to those found in the Western European parties.

We see this effect clearly in the Baltic Nations, where there was extensive contact between fledgling parties and parties in the Scandinavian countries. As a result, women's auxiliaries were established quite early in several parties and quotas were a legitimate topic for intra-party discussion. Those lobbying for quotas were quick to point out they were not discussing establishing Soviet style quotas, but instead social democratic style quotas à la the Swedish or Norwegian Labour Parties. While the effect on party lists might be virtually the same, the source of the idea was from Western parties and therefore far more palatable than when the idea was aired ten years earlier. Then it was seen as a relic of the Communist past. In several countries, women were adept at using the opening provided by the ties to Western parties to strengthen their positions and to lobby for improved representation, so the party could 'prove' that it was modern.

These effects were not uniform, however. There is a distinct geographical element to these effects. Those countries with extensive borders to Western

Europe were clearly more strongly influenced than those with borders that are more distant. Furthermore, the effects were distinct across parties too. They were most effective in parties that styled themselves social democratic and carried less weight in the more traditional conservative parties.

Putting pressure on gatekeepers, based on fidelity to the party's ideology, is one way women lobbied parties to open up to greater representation of women. Such efforts were most effective in programmatic parties. Another important tool, given the nomination process is open to the party rank and file, is to simply pack the meetings. Women mobilizing to make an issue of the levels of representation, both within the parties and outside of the parties, are an important part of the process of improving access.

When they were selected, most women candidates did not behave distinctly differently from the male candidates of the same parties. They carried the party banner, emphasized the party program, and promoted the party leaders. Being female was neither a positive nor a negative in terms of the projected message. There were, however, exceptions where being female was an important part of the message of the party, either explicitly or implicitly. Parties in some cases consciously chose to use women as the vehicle for sending a message as to the party's goals. Several examples of this strategic use of women by parties are described in the case study chapters.

Perhaps the most obvious case of this is various Women's Parties that sprung up in several countries. These parties, however, have tended to do poorly. In Bulgaria, *prior* to the coalition with NMSII, and in Ukraine, the Women's parties failed to gather even one per cent of the vote. In Lithuania, despite having a former prime minister as their leader, the Women's Party gained only one seat when they ran independently (in 1996). Only in Russia, where Women of Russia broke the five per cent barrier and entered the parliament with a substantial delegation following the 1993 parliamentary elections did a Women's party develop a parliamentary presence. Women of Russia, however, failed to clear the electoral threshold in 1995 and 1999 and have therefore failed to return to parliament.

The net effect of these parties on women's access has probably been negative. First, women's parties, with the one time exception of WOR in Russia, have not won seats. Second, they have drained away from more mainstream parties, activists who could have worked to improve women's positions in major parties.[5] Third, women's parties have probably influenced the strategies adopted by other parties. The other parties have 'learned' there is not significant diffuse demand for greater representation of women. If the parties that actively promote women as women do quite poorly, then other parties can feel safer in ignoring demands for greater representation.

Women's parties, however, were not the only parties to use women as an important part of their message. Perhaps the major party with the highest proportion of women parliamentarians in the world was the PDS in Germany.

❖ RICHARD E. MATLAND

Women were over 60 per cent of their MPs. The PDS commercial described in Brzinski's chapter, where a woman forcefully strides forth to stop the escalator where the working class and disadvantaged in society are being relegated to the bottom floors builds precisely on an image of women as protectors of the social welfare state. While the other parties are busy dismantling what is left of the social welfare state the PDS *women* are working hard to maintain equal goods for all. PDS women will act as the protectors of the welfare state is the explicit message in the advertisement.

Women, qua women, are also an important part of the message of the League of Polish Families in Poland. In this case, the message is one of building on the traditional role of women as protectors of traditional Polish values. The League of Polish Families is interesting in that it shows that parties with a heavy nationalist program need not be anti-women. In this case, a nationalist party is able to consciously use women to forward the image of protection of national values.

Women have also been touted as especially good candidates at fighting corruption. With an image as an outsider, women can be seen with brooms sweeping out the corruption that still exists in the halls of power. To the degree a party wishes to emphasize these messages they often find it useful to include women in their appeals and among their candidates.

In considering the public opinion polling, Wilcox *et al.* found there was considerable support for the 'women's movement', but very little support for policies that would appear to be at the core of Western feminism. Both Eastern parties and women have adapted to this environment. Women bring special strengths to a political party and a party's ticket, but their message has not been built around issues that energize feminists in the West. Rather, they have been quite consciously built around issues that are more relevant in the East and a message that is far less threatening and off-putting than a Western feminist message might be.[6]

While the issues where women are used to project an image are legitimate and important issues, they have tended to be secondary issues. They have taken a back seat to major issues, which can dominate the political agenda. For example, when the new states of Eastern Europe were being established, issues of marketization and democratization took primacy. Ristova notes that in Macedonia the threat of civil war has completely dominated the political agenda and has made it very difficult to raise issues of women's representation or policies. As stable political systems start to develop and the crucial issue of establishing a functioning democracy recedes, it is likely the issues on which women have a comparative advantage will become more prominent.

Krupavičius and Matonytė suggest the saliency of both representation concerns and issues on which women may be seen as having a special expertise are inversely related to conditions in the economic sphere. Women have had the hardest time gaining access in those countries where the economy has failed to turn around. In several countries, the economy is in worse shape today than it was a decade ago. When a country's economy is moving in a positive direction, then issues of representation and social issues have the opportunity to move up the political agenda and women's chances are enhanced. When the economy takes a serious downturn, or fails to move forward, that issue will dominate the political agenda and women's access will be diminished.

The final step in the legislative recruitment model is moving from candidate to elected MP. This is where candidates must face the voters. For most candidates, male or female, the success of their party and their position on the party lists determines the outcome of this meeting. Despite the apparent sexism found in the public opinion polling, there is exceedingly little evidence that voters actively refuse to vote for women. In deciding who to vote for voters have a wealth of impulses that can be used. Party platforms, evaluations of party leadership, evaluations of the job done by the sitting government, and other aspects of the various candidates are all likely to be more salient than candidate gender to voters.

Several authors examined the voter-candidate nexus. Birch notes in the Ukraine that candidate gender was listed as a principal factor influencing citizen's vote by only 0.5 per cent of her sample survey, 99.5 per cent of the voters emphasized other factors. Furthermore, regression analysis of candidate vote share found that candidate gender had no effect on the vote winning ability of candidates in the Ukraine. Moser notes that in Russia women running for single member district seats have a higher probability of winning than women on PR lists, or men running for single member district seats. This is hardly an indication that voters are the primary obstacle for female candidates. Siemieńska presents public opinion polling data from Poland showing that when the SLD/UP adopted explicit rules to guarantee women representation, 90 per cent of the voter's said this was irrelevant to their evaluation of the party. Among those for which it did matter, more said it would be a favorable than an unfavourable factor in their evaluation. In short, as in much of the Western literature on voting, candidate gender (or most commonly the fact there were a few women among a large number of candidates on the party list) was not a particularly salient factor when voters evaluated political candidates. Policy or patronage-based loyalty mattered much more.

❖ POLITICAL INSTITUTIONS AND WOMEN'S REPRESENTATION

❖ Electoral system effects

We wished to test Western theories of access in the newly developing democracies of Eastern and Central Europe. One of the consistent findings among the industrialized democracies is that women enjoy wider access to parliamentary positions in proportional representation systems than in majoritarian systems. The results in Eastern Europe, taken as a whole, support this assertion. The overall picture shows women do better in pure proportional representation systems. Furthermore, the results in Eastern Europe show that women do better in systems that are pure proportional representation systems than in mixed systems where some seats are based on single member districts and others based on PR lists. As noted there are four countries in our sample that have pure party list proportional representation. They rank as the top four countries in the sample in women's representation. The countries with mixed electoral systems all lag behind. Figure 16.1 shows this pattern is also replicated among those countries we did not study. Those with MMP have consistently lower levels of representation than those that are purely proportional.

Furthermore, there are six cases involving five countries where there has been a change in the electoral system in our sample during the 1990s. All have moved in the direction of greater proportionality. In five of the six cases (Bulgaria, Croatia (twice), Macedonia, and Ukraine) there was an increase in women's representation when the electoral system was changed as would be predicted; only in Lithuania did the change to a more proportional system not lead to an increase in representation.[7]

For those countries with mixed electoral systems, individual authors investigated the effects of the electoral system. The effects found within the individual countries are summarized in Table 16.1.[8] The pattern is consistent. First, the results affirm Moser's suggestion that Russia is a 'strange case'. In Russia, women do consistently better in the single member district. Almost everywhere else, however, women do better in the PR portion of the mixed systems. In twelve of thirteen non-Russian cases, we find a higher percentage of women being elected in the PR portion of the electoral system than in the single member district portion of the system. With such a uniform result, we can assert that having a PR portion of the electoral system helps women.[9] It is worth noting, however, that the effect is generally not strong. In only about one-quarter of the cases where the effect was in the expected direction was it statistically significant. In the stronger cases the effect is up near 7–8 per cent more women elected in the PR portion of the system. However, a large number of cases show small effects in the 3–5 per cent range. Effects in this range are clearly well below those found in Western Democracies with mixed member electoral systems (Moser 2001).

Part of the explanation for these modest results are that, when there are significant differences across parties in their support of women, the electoral system results are sensitive to where parties win their seats. This occurs if the mixed system is compensatory. In Hungary, for example, when the Socialists

Table 16.1. Comparison of single member and PR portions of mixed member proportional system elections

Country	Year	Total # of seats (N)	Number of SMD seats	Number of women elected SMD	% of SMD seats held by women	Number of PR seats	Number of women elected PR	% of PR seats held by women	Difference between PR and SMD (%)	Chi-square	Phi	p-value	Expected direction	Statistically significant
Slovenia	1992	88	69	7	10.1	19	5	26.3	16.2	3.31	0.194	0.07	Yes	Yes
Croatia	1995	108	28	0	0.0	80	7	8.8	8.8	2.62	0.156	0.11	Yes	No
Hungary	1990	385	176	6	3.4	209	22	10.5	7.1	7.18	0.137	0.01	Yes	Yes
Bulgaria	1990	287	103	6	5.8	184	23	12.5	6.7	3.24	0.106	0.07	Yes	Yes
Lithuania	1996	137	67	9	13.4	70	14	20.0	6.6	1.06	0.088	0.33	Yes	No
Macedonia	1998	120	85	5	5.9	35	4	11.4	5.5	1.10	0.096	0.31	Yes	No
Hungary	1994	386	176	15	8.5	210	28	13.3	4.8	2.24	0.076	0.15	Yes	No
Lithuania	2000	141	71	6	8.5	70	9	12.9	4.4	0.72	0.071	0.41	Yes	No
Russia	1993	450	225	26	11.6	225	34	15.1	3.6	1.23	0.052	0.27	Yes	No
Ukraine	1998	445	220	14	6.4	225	21	9.3	3.0	1.35	0.055	0.24	Yes	No
Hungary	1998	385	175	12	6.9	210	20	9.5	2.7	0.89	0.048	0.37	Yes	No
Lithuania	1992	141	71	5	7.0	70	5	7.1	0.1	0.00	0.002	0.93	Yes	No
Croatia	1992	120	60	3	5.0	60	2	3.3	-1.7	0.21	0.042	0.65	No	No
Russia	1999	450	225	20	8.9	225	15	6.7	-2.2	0.77	0.041	0.40	No	No
Russia	1995	450	225	31	13.8	225	15	6.7	-7.1	6.20	0.117	0.01	No	Yes

did well, they won large numbers of SMD seats, and consequently they won very few national list seats. National list seats went largely to the opposition. Under these conditions, the electoral system appears to have limited effect, but in fact, the effect does show up in the individual parties. These modest results also indicate that women have not been able to use the PR portion of the system anywhere near as effectively as women in industrialized democracies. Women have been unsuccessful in convincing parties they need to use their lists to provide for greater representation of women.

The other electoral system attributes presented in the theory chapter were district and party magnitude. We were interested in testing whether party magnitude, or the related concept of district magnitude, had an effect on women's representation. The individual tests of the effects of district or party magnitude present results that are reasonably unambiguous. In her work on the Russian regions, Nowacki found that district magnitude had a statistically significant and positive effect on the proportion of the delegation that was female. Siemieńska found a positive, but not statistically significant, effect for district magnitude in the Polish case.

Brzinski considers the effect of party magnitude across parties in the German case and she finds that party magnitude does have a strong positive effect for women's representation among the more conservative parties (FDP and CDU/CSU), a smaller effect within the SPD, and it has no noticeable effect among the Greens and PDS. In the Lithuanian case, women are better represented among the parties that win sufficient votes to be able to participate in the division of party list seats. In the Czech Republic, Hungary, and Bulgaria authors present individual statistical tests across elections for the effect of party magnitude. In all nine individual elections considered, the effect is in the expected direction, as party magnitude increases, the proportion of the delegation that is female increases. In five of these nine cases, the results are statistically significant.

The picture that evolves is similar to the results for the mixed member electoral systems. Women can be helped by party magnitude, but as we emphasized at the outset, an advantageous set of institutions does not automatically result in strong representation. It may affect the incentives of the actors involved, but additional elements need to be in place for women to take advantage of the institutional structure. Increases in party magnitude are expected to improve the position of groups that are organized within parties who are lobbying for greater representation. It is especially important for those groups that are important within the parties, but are not at the centre of power. The German case shows that in parties where women are at the centre of power in the party structure, with sufficient influence to ensure that concerns about equitable gender representation are prominently considered, women do not need high party magnitudes. There is no evidence that women have anywhere near the level of prominence and internal power in the parties in the rest of post-communist Europe to assure this outcome. It is certainly possible, however, that in some Eastern parties women are in such a weak position that even with advantageous institutions, women are unable to use the institutions to improve their position or that the assistance provided is very limited.

This does not mean, the electoral institutions do not matter. Electoral systems with relatively large numbers of members in the national assembly, relatively few electoral districts, and thresholds to keep small parties out, generate greater party magnitudes and these help women. The improvements, however, will not necessarily be immediate and dramatic.

❖ Party institutions

We suggested in Chapter 2 that an additional institutional variable of importance was the process by which parties selected the candidates running under the party label. This presumes that voters would not systematically discriminate against women as candidates, and sufficient numbers of women would aspire to politics that any party interested and willing to nominate women could do so in substantial numbers. The crucial question is: are parties willing to nominate women, and under what nomination procedures are they most likely to nominate women?

In reviewing the individual country chapters, the most consistent finding is that what is truly crucial is presence. Regardless of the institutions, without an active presence in the forums where decisions are being made women are unlikely to make significant gains. When they are present, *and make a conscious decision to promote the issue of greater representation*, they can lobby effectively. This is true, even in parties one might not expect to be particularly sympathetic to women. For example, Glaurdic notes that in Croatia despite the HDZ being a conservative-nationalistic party with very tight central control over nominations, because Jadranka Kosor was on the party's executive council and she lobbied extensively to improve women's position in the party, there were noticeable improvements in women's list placements in the last election.

On the other hand, Saxonberg, quite tellingly, describes the differences between the Club of Leftist Women, which is independent but affiliated with the Czech Communist Party (KSČM) and the Club of Christian Women, which is affiliated with the KDU–ČSL. In the former case the organization actively urged members to go to the caucus meetings, to actively support women candidates and to actively raise the issue of equal representation. The Christian Democratic women on the other hand very clearly did not see themselves as a faction that needed to fight to insure equitable representation of its members. They did not try to operate as a coherent bloc when the party was selecting candidates. Not surprisingly, given the distinct differences in the internal pressure to nominate women across the two parties, women are much better represented among the KSČM candidates, than among the KDU–ČSL candidates.

Nevertheless, while presence is crucial there are variations across parties in nomination procedures and the institutions can either help or hinder women candidates. One critical dimension on which nomination processes vary is centralization. Centralization of the candidate selection process can be thought of as a continuous scale, where we can identify four distinct points of local input. At one extreme, there is no local input into the process; the party leadership makes all decisions in terms of list construction and candidate selection. A second point exists when the local level has the right to make proposals as to possible candidates, but list construction is done at the central level. A third possibility is the lists are actually constructed with explicit ordering at the local level, but the central party authorities have the right to review and amend the local decisions. A final point is where final decisions are made at the local level, without a right of review by central authorities. We find all of these variations among the parties studied, but in most of the Eastern and Central European countries the process trends heavily towards the centralized end of the scale. While programmatic parties were slightly more likely to encourage local input than clientellistic parties, even among programmatic parties there was considerable centralization.

Centralization has at least a couple of origins. In clientellistic parties centralization goes hand in hand with a heavy emphasis on patronage. Processes are strongly centralized to insure the party bosses control access to a valuable resource: parliamentary seats. Even in programmatic parties, however, there is considerable centralization. In studying developing parties in Eastern Europe, Ishiyama (2000) suggests a parallel between these newly developing parties and the development of Western European parties in a previous era. Rokkan (1970) argued that Western European parties were initially created around small groups of urban elites. Over time, in order to remain competitive, these urban based parties were forced to expand their base, to 'mobilize the countryside' as it were. Ishiyama argues a similar process is occurring in Eastern European parties as they consider opening up selection processes to a broader group of party members.

Democratizing processes within a party, including turning over the power to select candidates for the national parliament to the local level, can lead to an energizing of the party's base and be an effective way of reaching out to possible electoral constituencies. Democratizing processes also hold out the danger, however, of losing control of internal party processes. Repeatedly Eastern European parties, even those with considerable programmatic elements, have preferred to take the route of retaining control of the party within a small group. One clear example is the Czech ČSSD experiment with direct elections to select their candidates in the 1996 elections. This provided a number of surprises in terms of who would be the party's candidates. The party quickly changed its rules to a caucus system with greater control by the party hierarchy. The result in 1998 was greater party control and a drop in the number of women nominated.

We also suggested that candidate selection procedures could be distinguished on whether they were patronage based or tended towards a more bureaucratic form. These elements are partially independent of the degree of centralization, but not entirely. As parties open up for greater input from the local level, they tend to develop rules and regulations to structure local input. Nevertheless, there is independent variation on this dimension. Some parties with considerable central control do this via formal rules and regulations, while in other cases, it is as if the list of candidates magically appears, with no one being able to explain exactly where it came from.

Interestingly, among the parties most likely to have a procedure that included significant elements of local constituency input were many of the communist successor parties. In several of the communist successor parties, there was a genuine effort to involve local party organizations in choosing candidates. For example in Slovenia, the ZLSD holds internal party votes that determine which individual's will be nominated. When women organized to lobby within these procedures they could have substantial effects (in Croatia for example). In other countries, however, even if the formal procedure allowed for the possibility of input, when women were poorly organized, little representation occurred (Ukraine).

That successor communist parties may be more democratic than most parties in terms of internal procedures for selecting candidates has a certain irony to it. There are several plausible roots to this result. First, in some cases the party had formal procedures in place for input from the local levels. With the change in regime, these formal procedures for local input stayed in place and started to take on a more meaningful role. It is also true, that unlike many of the newly established parties where membership was often concentrated in the nation's capital, the communist party had viable local parties that believed they had a legitimate right to influence decisions. Finally, one of the ways successor communist parties could disassociate themselves from the past regime was by establishing internal democratic processes.

We initially suggested that open processes, with explicit rules for selecting candidates, would help women. We still believe this is true. A review of the results across countries, however, shows the effect of institutions is very much dependent upon the degree to which women are organized to take advantage of the institutions. The same 'it depends' conclusion must be drawn in terms of whether centralization helps or hurts women. While local level input may

❖ RICHARD E. MATLAND

allow women at the local level to lobby at the grass roots, it is also true, as Saxonberg describes when discussing the Czech Social Democrats, that a localized procedure can dissolve into log rolling among small communities to get the most prominent person from their locality near the top of the list of candidates. These local notables are overwhelmingly male, and to the degree the district caucuses think in terms of ticket balancing it is often in terms of geography and not in terms of candidate sex. Furthermore, both Ristova, in her discussion of Macedonia, and Montgomery and Ilonszki, in their discussion of Hungary, note that party leaders at the local level can often be very conservative and very traditional in their views of the proper role of women. Therefore, it might appear that greater local input may be disadvantageous for women.

On the other hand, when party executive committees end up with the final say on which candidates will be nominated, then the decision may wind up in an arena where women are very poorly represented and where the under representation of women may not be seen as an important issue. Centralized decision making does allow for a comprehensive consideration of the whole slate of candidates a party presents and as such the under representation can be visible, but it also has to be seen as a legitimate concern by the central level before it is likely to lead to actions. The breakthrough of Polish women in the 2001 election is very much tied to the ability of women within the Democratic Left Alliance (SLD) to convince the centralized party body that there was a need to establish quotas to insure equitable representation. In the Polish case, the result was the central party actively working, via quotas, to insure there was equitable representation of women.

❖ Party ideology

An important part of the explanation for changes across time in women's representation is tied to changes in the political fortunes of parties that vary in the degree to which they nominate women. In general, women do best with parties that have a leftist orientation. As already noted in most countries the successor Communist parties were generally more open to women than the nationalist and conservative parties, although just 'how open' they were varied from country to country. In Croatia, Czech Republic, and Germany they were quite open and clearly the leaders in their country on the issue of representing women. In several other countries, the Communist successor parties were leaders even when women only received a modest level of support, because they received virtually no support in any of the other parties.

The parties where women did best were leftist parties that consciously tried to model themselves upon Western European social democratic parties, for example, the Lithuanian Social Democratic Party, the Euroleft in Bulgaria, or the SDP in Croatia. There are several reasons for this. First, in trying to develop an explicitly Western European message, many of these parties received support and advice from Western European social democratic parties. Part of that advice included an emphasis on opening up to women. Furthermore, one way to portray a party image of being modern and 'Western' to voters was to prominently promote women. Also, because these parties were adopting social democratic policies from Western parties, the ideas of creating women's auxiliaries and establishing quotas were seen as adopting Western and modern practices rather than returning to old communist mechanisms. In several of these parties, women have been able to get the party to institute quotas and they have led to women holding a significant portion of the party's seats in parliament.

While women tended to do best with parties of the left, there was also significant representation in some parties on the right. The Lithuanian Conservatives (Homeland Union) are a clear example of a broad-based conservative party where women were represented at least as well as they were among the other Lithuanian parties. Krupavičius and Matonyte suggest that for the Lithuanian Conservatives advice and support from Western conservative parties were also important in creating an opening for women. We see differences in women's access in centre-right parties across countries based on how the party systems developed. In some countries, for example Lithuania and Bulgaria, the centre-right has more or less remained a coherent whole including significant numbers of intellectuals. These parties have shown considerable willingness to nominate and elect women. In Hungary, on the other hand, Fidesz effectively exited their liberal, university-based supporters in the early 1990s, and with them went most of a possible base for a significant women's representation in Fidesz. Fidesz has become very conservative on issues of gender and it has one of the lowest levels of women's representation among major parties in Eastern Europe. Similarly, in Poland the most liberal elements of the Solidarity movement broke off and formed the much smaller Democratic Union, which later became the Freedom Union. Women did very well in these parties, but did poorly in the much larger and dominant Solidarity Election Alliance (AWS).

The League of Polish Families also represents a conservative party where women did extremely well. The League of Polish Families is a different party on the Eastern European landscape. It is a conservative party in the sense of emphasizing traditional values and there are strong nationalist tones to it, but the party has a strong base in women's organizations and therefore women have been well represented in the party.

The parties where women did worst over the eleven-country sample were the Agrarian Parties. These parties had their centres of strength in the rural areas with traditional cultures. We see in the Russian regions, in Poland, and in Croatia, the Agrarian parties have the very lowest levels of representation.

❖ RICHARD E. MATLAND

These are parties where the party leadership is often extremely traditional in its views on the proper role for women. Women also did poorly in several parties that described themselves as Liberal parties. This was especially true in parties where the liberal message had less to do with issues of civil liberties and a limited state, and more to do with support for radical economic reform. Parties who were most strident in supporting the move to marketization tended not to provide women with significant opportunities to be elected to parliament. These parties overwhelmingly drew their leadership, their candidates, and even their voters from the new business class—a class where women are dramatically underrepresented in all Central and Eastern European countries.

❖ Looking forward

Women continue to be significantly underrepresented in the newly established democracies of Central and Eastern Europe. They face significant challenges, including overt discrimination and a patriarchal culture that sees politics as a primarily male domain. A cursory glance at the data in Wilcox *et al.*'s chapter shows that while there are some variations across countries, this picture is consistent across post-communist Europe and diverges dramatically from views on the same questions in Western Europe. Despite this background, if we return to Table 16.1, we see the countries of Eastern Europe are almost evenly split. The countries in the second quadrant represent a group where there has been real progress. Women make up a significant portion of the parliament and there has been a noticeable increase in representation. For most of these countries, representation has risen by more than 10 per cent since the initial post-communist elections. Representation compares favourably with many industrialized democracies. These are also the countries in which stable democracy has taken root and political issues have moved beyond discussions of developing democratic institutions and market mechanisms. There is reason for optimism. In the future there should be greater space in the policy environment for issues of representation and women in many of these countries seem well organized to raise these issues.

In the other set of countries, however, despite several elections, and more than a decade since the regime shift, women have made very little headway in gaining access to political power. Women face a variety of barriers in these countries. In some cases the existing political institutions, especially electoral institutions, form an enormous barrier. Until these institutions are reformed, it is unlikely there will be significant gains. There has been some movement on this front. Both in Macedonia and Slovenia, there has been considerable discussion of changing the electoral systems in a direction that would be more woman friendly.[10]

The countries that show relatively little gains for women distinguish themselves from those countries where there have been advances in a number of other ways. Politics is dominated more by clientellistic parties than by programmatic parties in several of these countries. This hinders the development of a political dialogue where the issue of representation is a legitimate concern. Economic development also has been slow to occur in several of these countries. Therefore, economic issues dominate the issue agenda, making it difficult for issues where women would be seen as having a comparative advantage to rise on the agenda.

There are also clear differences across these two groups of countries in terms of women's mobilization. While women form more than 50 per cent of the voters, if they fail to become active in the existing political parties, either because access is denied or because they see party politics as an ineffective use of their resources, it is extremely unlikely the parties will respond spontaneously by promoting greater representation. One of the biggest steps that has to occur is that women both inside and outside the parties need to organize and need to see improved representation as a legitimate issue on which they must demand fairer treatment.

The model presented at the outset has proven to be a useful tool in organizing our understanding of women's access to political power in the newly developing democracies. Our expectations in terms of political institutions have also largely been confirmed. As such, it is worth reiterating one of the points we made at the outset. The countries of post-communist Europe are best seen as a sample of developing democracies. The outcomes in terms of women's representation are determined by a variety of factors, but they are factors that are readily recognizable with the theories developed in democratic polities.

There are a number of interesting research questions that remain to be investigated. There is a need to evaluate factors that affect the supply of female candidates and women's willingness to take the first step from being eligible to aspiring to political office. Siemieńska notes an optimistic trend in the public opinion polling data from Poland, where attitudes concerning the appropriateness of women in politics seem to be moving in a more liberal direction. These trends should be followed up. The role of non-governmental organizations in getting women to aspire to office and getting parties to take representation seriously also deserves more careful study. Greater consideration of how voters evaluate female candidates can give us an important understanding of some of the dynamics concerning voting and whether a candidate's sex affects the way voters evaluate a candidate in Eastern Europe.

In addition, we need to know more about what leads to successful mobilization of women within a party, and what leads to parties being willing to open up to demands for greater representation. We suggested earlier that

❖ RICHARD E. MATLAND

programmatic parties are more sensitive to such demands than clientellistic parties; this should be investigated further. We also suggested candidate selection processes are highly dynamic and changing rapidly. Some theorists suggest over time parties should open up to greater external influences. These countries should be followed up to see if these effects appear.

Above and beyond questions of access, there are a whole series of fascinating questions about how differences in levels of representation can affect policy outputs. As noted, feminism and support for women in politics in Eastern Europe has a different hue than it does in the West. This difference may have effects on policy outputs in manners that differ from those found in the West. Hopefully, future research can provide insight into these matters.

In short, there is a wealth of questions that deserve closer investigation. We believe this volume has provided a strong foundation on which to build future empirical studies of women's representation. As democratic development continues to unfold in post-communist Europe new data will be generated and there will be new opportunities to test our theories and enhance our understanding of the processes of democratic development and women's representation.

❖ Notes

1 Data for individual countries are presented in Table 1.1.

2 Macedonia had elections using a pure PR electoral system in the fall of 2002 (after this chapter was written). With the new electoral system there was a significant jump in women's representation to 18.3 per cent. Macedonia would now be placed in the second quadrant.

3 NMSII, the National Movement for Simeon the II, in Bulgaria is probably the best example of a charismatic party in Eastern Europe, although in this case Simeon has created a coalition of other parties rather than establish his own.

4 Kitschelt (1995) suggests the timing of industrialization, institutional features such as the existence of a presidential as opposed to a parliamentary system, the type of democratic transition that occurred, and the number of free elections since the transition determines the likelihood of programmatic parties.

5 This may be an unfair criticism. As Moser notes, in the case of Women of Russia they only established their own party after virtually all of the other parties failed to show any interest in the issues they were concerned about. The same is true in Lithuania where starting the Women's Party was one of the few options left open to Kazimiera Prunskienė after she was effectively squeezed out of Sąjūdis. In other words, one can question if other parties would have been open to pressure from women on these issues.

6 The messages that may be most effective for Eastern women are similar to those of the first wave feminists in the United States and United Kingdom. Addams (1915),

for example, in arguing for the vote in the United States, noted that a woman's responsibilities were first and foremost to her family, to keep them healthy, well fed, and to teach them properly. Addams notes, however, that in a modern urban society (Chicago in the early 1900s) these responsibilities required women to be publicly active in a whole series of public arenas to insure effective public health care, efficient public sanitation, food inspection, and modern schools. In other words, to fulfill their traditional role in a modern world, women must be active in politics.

7 In the Croatian chapter, Glaurdic runs simulations that appear to show the results in Croatia would have been largely the same regardless of the system. In running these simulations, however, Glaurdic assumes that everyone who has a mandate (safe) position on the party list in the PR system would be given a safe position if there were a change to a single member district system. As he points out himself, it is quite possible that this assumption overestimates, dramatically, how well women would have done in a single member district system.

8 We have not included Germany as West Germany dominates the results and the effects for Germany are already well known, women do much better on the party list portion of the system. Slovenia is included because the district portion of PR functions as if they were single member districts, formally, however, it is not a mixed member system.

9 If the outcomes were random, then we would expect about half of the cases to show women doing better in PR and about half where women were doing better in the SMD portion of the system. If the true probability were 0.50, the likelihood of getting a distribution where 12 or more of 13 cases all showed up in the same direction is 00.02%.

10 As noted above, these changes have occured in Macedonia and the consequences were as predicted here. An impressive 11 per cent jump in women's representation.

❖ RICHARD E. MATLAND

❖ Bibliography

Abramson, Paul R., John H. Aldrich, and David W. Rohde. (1987). 'Change and Continuity in the 1984 Elections.' *American Political Science Review*, 81.

Adamik, Maria (1993). 'Feminism and Hungary', in Nanette Funk and Magda Mueller (eds), *Gender Politics and Post-Communism: Reflections From Eastern Europe and the Former Soviet Union*. New York: Routledge, 207–12.

Addams, Jane (1915) 'Why Women Should Vote' pamphlet reproduced in George, Klosko and Margaret, Klosko (eds), *The Struggle for Women's Rights: Theoretical and Historical Sources*. New York: Prentice-Hall, 147–55.

Ágh, Attila (ed.) (1994). *The Emergence of East Central European Parliaments: The First Steps*. Budapest: Hungarian Centre of Democracy Studies.

Ananieva, Nora and Evka, Razvigorova (1991). 'Women in State Administration in the People's Republic of Bulgaria'. *Women and Politics*, 11: 31–40.

Andersen, Kristi (1975). 'Working Women and Political Participation, 1952–72'. *American Journal of Political Science*, 19(3): 439–53.

Anderson, Christopher (1993). 'Political Elites and Electoral Rules, 1949–1990', in Christopher Anderson, Karl Kaltenthaler, and Wolfgang Luthardt (eds), *The Domestic Politics of German Unification*. Boulder, CO: Lynne Riener Publishers, 73–116.

Andorka, Rudolf (1999). 'Dissatisfaction and Alienation', in Rudolf Andorka, Tamàs Kolosi, Richard Rose, and György Vukovich (eds), *A Society Transformed: Hungary in Time–Space Perspective*. Budapest: CEU Press, 147–54.

Antić, Milica (1991). 'Democracy Between Tyranny and Liberty: The situation of women in the Post-"socialist" nation state', in *Shifting Territories: Feminism, Socialism, Europe*, Feminist Review 39.

B.a.B.e.—Be Active, Be Emancipated, 'Ciljevi i program rada'. Goals and Program of Activities, www.babe.hr.

Ballington, Julie (1998). 'Women's Parliamentary Representation: The effect of List PR'. *Politikon*, 25(2): 77–93.

Banaszak, Lee Ann, and Eric Plutzer (1993a). 'Contextual Determinants of Feminist Attitudes: National and Subnational Influences in Western Europe'. *American Political Science Review*, 87(1): 147–57.

—— (1993b). 'The Social Bases of Feminism in the European Community'. *Public Opinion Quarterly*, 57(1): 29–53.

Belin, Laura and Robert Orttung (1997). *The Russian Parliamentary Elections of 1995*. Armonk, NY: ME Sharpe.

Benoit, Kenneth (1996). 'Hungary's Two-Ballot Electoral System'. *Representation*, 33(4): 162–70.

Bilous, Artur O. (1993). *Politychni ob'yednannya Ukraïny*. Kiev: Ukraïna.

Birch, Sarah (1995). 'The Ukrainian Parliamentary and Presidential Elections of 1994'. *Electoral Studies*, 14(1): 93–9.

—— (1996). 'The Ukrainian Repeat Elections of 1995'. *Electoral Studies*, 15(2): 281–2.

—— (1998). 'Party System Formation and Voting Behaviour in the Ukrainian Parliamentary Elections of 1994', in Taras Kuzio (ed.), *Contemporary Ukraine: Dynamics of Post-Soviet Transformation*. New York and London: ME Sharpe, 139–60.

—— (2000). *Elections and Democratization in Ukraine*. Basingstoke: Macmillan.

Bochel, John and David Denver (1983). 'Candidate Selection in the Labour Party: What the Selectors Seek', *British Journal of Political Science*, 13(1): 45–69.

Bohachevsky-Chomiak, Martha (1995). 'Practical Concerns and Political Protest in Post-Soviet Ukraine', in special issue on 'Women: Changing Roles'. *Transition*, 1(16): 12–17.

Bojcun, Marko (1995). 'The Ukrainian Parliamentary Elections in March–April 1994'. *Europe–Asia Studies*, 47(2): 229–49.

Bollobás, Eniko (1993). ' "Totalitarian Lib": The Legacy of Communism for Hungarian Women', in Nanette Funk and Magda Mueller (eds), *Gender Politics and Post-Communism: Reflections From Eastern Europe and the Former Soviet Union*. New York: Routledge, 201–6.

Bourdieu, Pierre (1984). *Questions de Sociologie*. Paris: Minuit.

Bratton, Kathleen and Leonard P. Ray (2002). 'Descriptive Representation, Policy Outcomes, and Municipal Day-Care Coverage in Norway'. *American Journal of Political Science*, 46(2): 428–37.

Breaux, David and Malcom Jewell (1992). 'Winning Big: The Incumbency Advantage in State Legislative Races', in Gary F. Moncrief and Joel A. Thompson (eds), *Changing Patterns in State Legislative Careers*. Ann Arbor: The University of Michigan Press, 87–106.

Brichta, Avraham and Yael Brichta (1994). 'The Extent of Impact of the Electoral System Upon the Representation of Women in the Knesset', in Wilma Rule and Joseph F. Zimmerman (eds), *Electoral Systems in Comparative Perspective: Their Impact on Women and Minorities*. Westport, Connecticut: Greenwood Press, 115–26.

Brown, Archie (2001). 'Vladimir Putin and the Reaffirmation of Central State Power'. *Post-Soviet Affairs*, 17(1): 45–55.

Brunner, Georg (1990). 'Elections in the Soviet Union', in Robert K. Furtak (ed.), *Elections in Socialist States*. New York and London: Harvester Wheatsheaf, 20–52.

Buckley, Mary (1992). 'Political Reform', in Mary Buckley (ed.), *Perestroika and Soviet Women*. Cambridge: Cambridge University Press, 54–71.

—— (1997). 'Women and Public Life', in Stephen White, Alex Pravda, and Zvi Gitelman (eds), *Developments in Russian Politics 4*. Durham: Duke University Press, 189–207.

Bullock, Charles S. III and Loch K. Johnson (1992). *Runoff Elections in the United States*. Chapel Hill and London: University of North Carolina Press.

Burmistenko, Milada (1996). 'Female Unemployment: Ukraine and Great Britain— A Comparison'. *The Ukrainian Review*, 43(2): 13–20.

Bystydzienski, Jill (1994). 'Norway: Achieving World-Record Women's Representation in Government', in Wilma Rule and Joseph F. Zimmerman (eds), *Electoral Systems in Comparative Perspective: Their Impact on Women and Minorities.* Westport, Connecticut: Greenwood Press, 55–64.

Byuletin: Izbori '91 (Bulletin: Elections '91) (1991). Sofia: Tzentralna Izbiratelna Komisiya. Sofia: Central Electoral Commission.

Cain, Bruce, John Ferejohn, and Morris Fiorina (1987). *The Personal Vote.* Cambridge, MA: Harvard University Press.

Carroll, Susan J. (1989). 'The Personal Is Political: The Intersection of Private Lives and Public Roles Among Women and Men in Elective and Appointive Office.' *Women and Politics,* 9(51):67.

—— (1994). *Women as Candidates in American Politics,* 2nd edition. Bloomington: Indiana University Press.

Caul, Miki (1999). 'Women's Representation in Parliament: The Role of Political Parties'. *Party Politics,* UC Irvine: Center for the Study of Democracy, 5(1): 79–98.

Čermáková, M. (1995). 'Women in the Czech society: Continuity or Change', in M. Čermáková (ed.), *Women, Work and Society.* Prague: The Sociological Institute of Czech Academy of Sciences.

Čermáková, Marie (1997a). 'Zaměstnanost žen a vzdělání jako faktor sociální diferenciace,' *Sociální Politika,* 5:9–10.

Čermáková, Marie (1997b). 'Postavení žen na trhua práce,' *Sociologický časopis,* 33(4):389–404.

Chamberlayne, Prue (1995). 'Gender and the Private Sphere: A Touchstone for Misunderstanding Between Eastern and Western Germany'? *Social Politics,* 2(1).

Chudíková, A. (1998). 'Uplatneniežien vo verejnom živote'. *Roľnícke noviny,* 23: 6.

Cichomski, Bogdan and Pawel Morawski (1996). *Polish General Social Surveys, 1992–1995: Cumulative Codebook.* Warsaw: Institute for Social Studies, University of Warsaw.

Clem, Ralgh S. and Peter R. Craumer (1997). 'Urban-Rural Voting Differences in Russian Elections, 1995–1996: A Raion-Level Analysis'. *Post-Soviet Geography and Economics,* 38: 379–95.

Cook, Elizabeth Adell (1994). 'Voter Response to Women Senate Candidates', in Elizabeth Cook, Sue Thomas, and Clyde Wilcox (eds), *The Year of the Woman: Myths and Realities.* Boulder, CO: Westview, 217–36.

Cook, Elizabeth Adell, and Clyde Wilcox (1992). 'A Rose by Any Other Name: Measuring Support for Organized Feminism'. *Women and Politics,* 12(1): 35–52.

Corrin, Chris (ed.) (1992). *Superwomen and the Double Burden: Women's Experiences of Change in East Central Europe and the Former Soviet Union.* London: Scarlet Press.

—— (1993). 'People and Politics', in Stephen White, Judy Batt, and Paul G. Lewis (eds), *Developments in East European Politics.* Durham, NC: Duke University Press.

—— (1994a). *Magyar Women: Hungarian Women's Lives 1960s–1990s.* Basingstoke: MacMillan.

—— (1994b). 'Women's Politics in "Europe" in the 1990's'. *Women's Studies International Forum,* 2: 289–97.

Croatian Democratic Union, 'Statute of the Croatian Democratic Union'. www.hdz.hr/hr/onama/statut d.htm.

Croatian Democratic Union's Women's Union Katarina Zrinska. 'Statute of the Women's Union'.

Croatian Peasants' Party. 'Electoral Declaration 2000'.

Croatian Social Liberal Party. 'Statute of the Croatian Social Liberal Party', www.hsls.hr/statut.html.

ČSSD (Czech Social Democratic Party) (1997). Information from their Internet address: http://www.cssd.cz.

Czudnowski, Moshe (1975). 'Political Recruitment', in Fred I. Greenstein and Nelson W. Polsby (eds), *Handbook of Political Science: Micropolitical Theory*, vol. 2. Reading, MA: Addison-Wesley.

Dahlerup, Drude (1988). 'From a Small to a Large Minority: Women in Scandinavian Politics'. *Scandinavian Political Studies*, 11(4): 275–98.

Dalton, Russell (1993). *Politics in Germany*, 2nd edition. New York: Harper Collins College Publishers.

—— and Wilhelm Bürklin (1996). 'The Two German Electorates', in Russell Dalton (ed.), *Germans Divided: The 1994 Bundestag Elections and the Evolution of the Germany Party System*. Oxford: Berg, 183–208.

Darcy, R. and Sarah Slavin Schramm (1977). 'When Women Run Against Men', *Public Opinion Quarterly*, 41: 1–12.

—— Susan Welch, and Janet Clark (1994). *Women, Elections, and Representation*, 2nd edition. Lincoln, Neb: Nebraska University Press.

—— (1985). 'Women Candidates in Single and Multi-Members Districts: American Legislative Races'. *Social Science Quarterly*, 66: 945–53.

Davis, Rebecca Howard (1997). *Women and Power in Parliamentary Democracies: Cabinet Appointments in Western Europe, 1968–1992*. Lincoln: University of Nebraska Press.

Dawisha, Karen, and Stephen Deets (1999). 'The Divine Comedy of Post-Communist Elections', *Paper Presented at the Annual Meeting of the American Association of Slavic Studies. St. Louis, MO*.

Delli, Carpini, Michael, X. and Scott Keeter (2000). 'Gender and Political Knowledge', in Jyl Josephson and Sue Tolleson-Rinehart (eds), *Gender and American Politics: Women, Men, and the Political Process*. Armonk, NY: ME Sharpe.

DELO (1996). March 2nd.

Desai, Uday and Keith Snavely (1998). 'Environmental Nonprofit Organizations in Bulgaria'. *Paper Presented at the Annual Meeting of the American Political Science Association. Boston, MA*.

Dodson, Debra L. (1998). 'Representing Women's Interests in the US House of Representatives', in Sue Thomas and Clyde Wilcox (eds), *Women and Elective Office: Past, Present, and Future*. New York: Oxford University Press.

—— and Susan J. Carroll (1991). *Reshaping the Agenda: Women in State Legislatures*. New Brunswick, NJ: Center for the American Woman and Politics.

Downs, Anthony (1957). *An Economic Theory of Democracy*. New York: Harper & Row.

Duerst-Lahti, Georgia (1998). 'The Bottleneck: Women Becoming Candidates', in Sue Thomas and Clyde Wilcox (eds), *Women and Elective Office: Past, Present, and Future*. New York: Oxford University Press, 15–25.

Duverger, Maurice (1955). *The Political Role of Women*. Paris: UNESCO.

Einhorn, Barbara (1993). *Cinderella Goes to Market: Citizenship, Gender, and Women's Movements in East Central Europe*. London: Verso.

Eisenstein, Zillah (1993). 'Eastern Europe Male Democracies: A Problem of Unequal Equality', in Nanette Funk and Magda Mueller (eds), *Gender Politics and Post-Communism: Reflections from Eastern Europe and the Former Soviet Union*. New York: Routledge, 303–17.

Fisher, Mary Ellen (1985). 'Women in Romanian Politics: Elena Ceausecu, Pronatalism, and the Promotion of Women', in Sharon Wolchik and Alfred Meyer (eds), *Women, State, and Party in Eastern Europe*. Durham: Duke University Press.

Fodor, Eva (1985). 'The Political Woman? Women in Politics in Hungary', in Sharon Wolchik and Alfred Meyer (eds), *Women, State, and Party in Eastern Europe*. Durham: Duke University Press.

—— (1994). 'The Political Woman? Women in Politics in Hungary', in Marilyn Rueschemeyer (ed.), *Women in the Politics of Postcommunist Eastern Europe*. New York: ME Sharpe, Inc.

Fowler, Linda and Robert D. McClure (1989). *Political Ambition: Who Decides to Run For Congress New Haven*. CT: Yale University Press.

Fox, Richard Logan (1997). *Gender Dynamics in Congressional Elections*. Thousand Oaks: Sage.

Funk, Nanette and Magda Mueller (eds) (1993). *Gender Politics and Post-Communism: Reflections from Eastern Europe and the Former Soviet Union*. New York and London: Routledge.

Gal, Susan (1994). 'Gender in the Post-Socialist Transition Period: The Abortion Debate in Hungary'. *Eastern European Politics and Societies*, 8(2): 256–87.

Gal, Susan and Gail Kligman (2000). *The Politics of Gender after Socialism*. Princeton, NJ: Princeton University Press.

Gallagher, Michael and Michael Marsh (eds) (1988). *Candidate Selection in Comparative Perspective: The Secret Garden of Politics*. London: Sage.

Gibson, John (1999). *Parties and Voters: The Effects of the Polish Electoral System on Women's Representation*, paper prepared for presentation at the *Conference on Women's Political Representation in Europe: 10 Years After the Fall*. Norway: Bergen.

Gigli, S. (1995). 'Toward Increased Participation in the Political Process', in *Transition: Events and Issues in the Former Soviet Union and East Central and Southeastern Europe*. Prague: Open Media Research Institute.

Gluchowski, Peter M. and Ulrich von Wilamowitz-Moillendorff (1998). 'The Erosion of Social Cleavages in Western Germany, 1971–1997', in Christopher J. Anderson and Carsten Zelle (eds), *Stability and Change in German Elections: How Electorates Merge, Converge, or Collide*. Westport, CT: Praeger, 13–32.

Goskomstat, Rossii (1998). *Regiony Rossii: Statisticheskii sbornik*, Tom II. Moscow: Goskomstat.

Goven, Joanna (1993). 'Gender Politics in Hungary: Autonomy and Anti-feminism', in Nanette Funk and Magda Mueller (eds), *Gender Politics and Post-Communism: Reflections from Eastern Europe and the Soviet Union*. New York: Routledge, 224–40.

Goven, Joanna (1994). 'The Gendered Foundations of Hungarian Socialism: State, Society, and the Anti-Politics of Anti-Feminism, 1948-1990.' Berkeley: University of California.

—— (2000). 'New Parliament, Old Discourse? The Parental Leave Debate in Hungary', in Susan Gal and Gail Kligman (eds), *Reproducing Gender: Politics, Publics, and Everyday Life After Socialism*. Princeton, New Jersey: Princeton University Press, 286–306.

Grad, France (1997). *Volitve in Volilni Sistemi* (Elections and electoral systems). Ljubljana: Inštitut za javno upravo.

Grofman, Bernard and Arend Lijphart (eds) (1986). *Electoral Laws And Their Political Consequences*. New York: Agathon Press.

Guadagnini, Marila (1993). 'A "Patritocrazia" Without Women: the Case of the Italian Party System,' in Joni Lovenduski and Pippa Norris (eds), *Gender and Party Politics*. London: Sage.

Hahn, Jeffrey W. (1997). 'Regional Elections and Political Stability in Russia'. *Post-Soviet Geography and Economics*, 38(5): 251–63.

Hahn, Jeffrey W. (ed.) (1996). *Democratization in Russia: The Development of Legislative Institutions*. Armonk, NY: ME Sharpe.

Haney, Lynne (1997). ' "But We are Still Mothers": Gender and the Construction of Need in Post-Socialist Hungary'. *Social Politics*, 4(2): 208–44.

Hankiss, Elemer (1990). 'East European Aternatives.' New York: Oxford University Press.

Havelkova, Hana (1996). 'Abstract Citizenship? Women and Power in the Czech Republic'. *Social Politics*, 3(2–3): 243–60.

—— (1997). 'Transitory and Persistent Differences: Feminism East and West', in Joan W. Scott, Cora Kalan, and Debra Keates (eds), *Transitions, Environments, Translations*: Feminisms in International Politics. New York: Routledge, 56–64.

Heinen, Jacqueline (1992). 'Polish Democracy is a Masculine Democracy'. *Women's Studies International Forum*, 15(1): 129–38.

Heinrich, Hans Georg (1986). *Hungary: Politics, Economics, and Society*. Boulder, CO: Lynne Reiner Publishing, 217.

Heitlinger, Alena (1979). *Women and State Socialism: Social Inequality in the Soviet Union and Czechoslovakia*. London: MacMillan Press.

Hellevik, Ottar and Tor Bjørklund (1995). 'Velgerne og kvinnerepresentasjon' (Voters and Women's Representation), in Nina Raaum (ed.), *Kjønn og politikk (Gender and Politics)*. Oslo, Norway: Tano Press.

Hesli, Vicki L. and Arthur H. Miller (1993). 'The Gender Base of Institutional Support in Lithuania, Ukraine and Russia'. *Europe–Asia Studies*, 45(3): 505–32.

Hickman, John (1997). 'The Candidacy and Election of Women in Japanese SNTV Electoral Systems'. *Women and Politics*, 18(2): 1–26.

Htun, Mala and Mark Jones (2002). 'Engendering the Right to Participate in Decision making: Electoral Quotas and Women's Leadership in Latin America', in Nikki Craske and Maxine Molyneux (eds), *Gender and the Politics of Rights and Democracy in Latin America*. London: Palgrave.

Hughes, James (1997). 'Sub-National Elites and Post-Communist Transformation in Russia: A Reply to Kryshtanovskaya and White'. *Europe–Asia Studies*, 49(6): 1017–36.

Iankova, Elena (1996). 'Women's Participation in Post-Communist Social Dialogue', in Barbara Wejnert and Metta Spencer (eds), *Research on Russia and Eastern Europe*, vol. 2: *Women in Post-Communism*. London: JAI Press, Inc.

Ilonszki, Gabriella (1999). 'Legislative Recruitment: Personnel and Institutional Development in Hungary 1990–1994', in Gábor Tóka and Zsolt Enyedi (eds), *Elections to the Hungarian National Assembly*. Berlin: Edition Sigma.

Inglehart, Ronald (1990). *Culture Shift in Advanced Society*. Princeton: Princeton University Press.

—— (1997). *Modernization and Postmodernization*. Princeton: Princeton University Press.

International Labour Office-Central and Eastern European Team [ILO-CEET] (1995). *The Ukrainian Challenge: Reforming Labour Market and Social Policy*. Budapest: Central European University Press.

Inter-Parliamentary Union (1997). *Men and Women in Politics: Democracy Still in the Making*. Geneva, Switzerland: IPU.

Inter-Parliamentary Union [IPU] (2000). *Women in Parliament: World Classification*. http://www.ipu.org/wmn-e/classif.htm.

Ishiyama, John T. (1996). 'The Russian Proto-Parties and the National Republics'. *Communist and Post-Communist Studies*, 29(4): 395–411.

Ishiyama, John T. (2000) 'Candidate Recruitment, Party Organisation and the Communist Successor Parties: The Cases of the MSzP, the KPRF, and the LDDP'. *Europe–Asia Studies*, 52(5): 875–96.

Izborna komisija Republike Hrvatske (Electoral Commission of the Republic of Croatia) (1992*a*). 'Državne liste stranaka' (National Party Lists), Zagreb, July 7.

—— (1992*b*). 'Izvješće br. 30, Izbori 1992' (Report No. 30, 1992 Elections), Zagreb, August 11.

—— (1995). 'Državne liste stranaka' (National Party Lists), Zagreb, October 7.

Izborna komisija Republike Hrvatske (Electoral Commission of the Republic of Croatia) (1995). 'Izvješće o provedenim izborima za zastupnike u Zastupnički dom Sabora Republike Hrvatske', Report on the Elections for the House of Representatives of the Croatian Parliament, Zagreb, November.

Jancar, Barbara Wolfe (1978). *Women Under Communism*. Baltimore, MD: Johns Hopkins University Press.

Jaquette, Jane S. and Sharon L. Wolchik (eds) (1998). *Women and Democracy: Latin America and Central and Eastern Europe*. Baltimore, MD: The Johns Hopkins University Press.

Jones, Mark A. (1996). 'Increasing Women's Representation Via Gender Quotas: The Argentine Ley de Cupos'. *Women and Politics*, 16(4): 75–98.

—— (1998). 'Quotas in South American Legislatures'. Paper presented at the 1998 Midwest Political Science Association Meetings. Chicago, IL.

Judge, David (1994). 'East-Central European Parliaments: The First Steps', in Attila Ágh (ed.), *The Emergence of East Central European Parliaments*. Budapest: Hungarian Centre of Democracy Studies.

Kapitány and Kapitány (1999). 'Az 1998-as választási kampányműsorok szimbolikus értéküzenetei' (Symbolic Values and Messages in the Electoral Campaign Films in

1998) in S. Kurtán *et al.* (eds), *Magyarország politikai évkönyve*. Budapest: Centre for Democracy Studies, 148–61.

Kasapi, Gulumsere (1994). 'The Role of the Albanian Woman in the Development of the Macedonian Society' in *The Status of Woman in the Contemporary Social Trends, Organization of Women in Macedonia*. Skopje.

Katzenstein, Mary Fainsod, and Carol McClurg Mueller (1987). *The Women's Movement in the United States and Western Europe*. Philadelphia: Temple University Press.

Kaukėnas Jonas (1995). Tiesos ir meilės keliu (Road of the Truth and Love), Vilnius: Diemedis p. 169.

Kenworthy, Lane and Melissa Malami (1999). 'Gender Inequality in Political Representation: A Worldwide Comparative Analysis'. *Social Forces*, 78(1): 235–68.

Kitschelt, Herbert (1989). *The Logics Of Party Formation: Ecological Politics In Belgium And West Germany*. Ithaca: Cornell University Press.

——(1995). 'Formation of Party Cleavages in Post-communist Democracies: Theoretical Propositions'. *Party Politics*, 1: 447–72.

——Zdenka Mansfeldova, Radoslaw Markoswski, and Gábor Tóka (1999). *Post-Communist Party Systems: Competition, Representation, and Inter-Party Cooperation*. Cambridge: Cambridge University Press.

Kolarova, Rumyana and Dimitr Dimitrov (1996). 'The Roundtable Talks in Bulgaria', in John Elster (ed.), *The Roundtable Talks and the Breakdown of Communism*. Chicago: The University of Chicago Press, 178–212.

Kolinsky, Eva (1996). 'Women and the 1994 Federal Election', in Russell Dalton (ed.), *Germans Divided: The 1994 Bundestag Elections and the Evolution of the Germany Party System*. Oxford: Berg, 265–92.

——(1998). 'Women and Politics in Western Germany', in Marilyn Rueschemeyer (ed.), *Women in the Politics of Postcommunist Eastern Europe*, Revised and Expanded Edition. Armonk, NY: ME Sharpe, 64–88.

Kostadinova, Tatiana (1995). *Bulgaria 1879–1946: The Challenge of Choice*, East European Monographs, No. CDXXIX. New York: Columbia University Press.

Kostova, Dobrinka (1998). 'Similar or Different: Women in Postcommunist Bulgaria', in Marilyn Rueschemeyer (ed.), *Women in the Politics of Postcommunist Eastern Europe*. Armonk: ME Sharpe, Inc., 249–66.

——(2000). 'Bulgaria: Economic Elite Change During the 1990s', in John, Hingley and Gyorgy, Lengyel (eds), *Elites After State Socialism: Theories and Analysis*. Lanham: Rowman & Littlefield Publishers, Inc., 199–207.

Krisch, Henry (1996). 'The Party of Democratic Socialism: Left and East', in Russell Dalton (ed.), *Germans Divided: The 1994 Bundestag Elections and the Evolution of the Germany Party System*. Oxford: Berg.

Kruks, Sonia, Rayna Rapp, and Marilyn Young (eds) (1989). *Promissory Notes: Women in the Transition to Socialism*. New York: Monthly Review Press.

Krupavičius Algis (1998). The Post-Communist Transition and Institutionalization of Lithuaniana parties in Hofferbert R. (ed.) *Parties and Democracy: Party Structure and Party Performance in Old and New Democracies*. Oxford: Blackwell Publishers, 43–69.

——(1999). Party Systems in Central East Europe: Dimensions of System *Stability*. Glasgow: University of Strathclyde, 178.

KSČM (1995a). 'Návrh nominace kandidátç za KSČM do sncmovny PCR na kandidátní listiny ve volbeních krajích.'

—— (1995b). 'KSČM Ústfední operativní volební štáb: Návrh kriterií a providel pro vébcr kandidátç na poslance za KSČM do Paramentu …eské republiky a zásad jejich pfípravy.'

Laakso, Markku and Taagepera Rein (1979). 'Effective Number of Parties: A Measure with Application to West Europe'. *Comparative Political Studies*, 12(1): 3–27.

LaFont, Suzanne (1999). 'Male Economies and the Status of Women in the Post-Communist Countries'. www.geocities.com/suzannelafont/eewomen.htm.

—— (2001). 'One Step Forward, Two Steps Back: Women in the Post-Communist States'. *Communist and Post-Communist Studies*, 34(2): 203–20.

Lampland, Martha (1994). 'Family Portraits: Gendered Images of the Nation in Nineteenth Century Hungary'. *East European Politics and Societies*, 8(2): 287–316.

Lancaster, Thomas D. (1998). 'Candidate Characteristics and Electoral Performance: A Long-term Analysis of the German Bundestag', in Christopher J. Anderson and Carsten Zelle (eds), *Stability and Change in German Elections: How Electorates Merge, Converge, or Collide*. Westport, CT: Praeger, 281–300.

Lapidus, Gail (1993). 'Gender and Restructuring: The Impact of Perestroika on Soviet Women', in Valentine Moghadam (ed.), *Democratic Reform and the Position of Women in Transitional Economies*. Oxford: Oxford University Press, 137–61.

Leduc, Larry, Richard Niemi, and Pippa Norris (1996). *Comparing Democracies: Elections and Voting in Global Perspective*. London: Sage Publications.

Lehmann, Susan Goodrich (1998). 'Inter-Ethnic Conflict in the Republics of Russia in Light of Religious Revival'. *Post-Soviet Geography and Economics*, 39(2): 461–93.

Lemke, Christiane (1993). 'Old Troubles and New Uncertainties: Women and Politics in United Germany', in Michael G. Huelshoff, Andrei S. Markovits, Simon Reich (eds), *From Bundesrepublik To Deutschland: German Politics After Unification*. Ann Arbor: University of Michigan Press, 147–66.

Liborakina, Marina (1998). 'The Unappreciated Mothers of Civil Society'. *Transitions*, 5(1): 52–7.

Lijphart, Arend (1991). 'Debate-Proportional Representation: III. Double Checking the Evidence'. *Journal of Democracy*, 2(1): 42–8.

—— (1993). 'Constitutional Choices for New Democracies', in Larry, Diamond and Marc F. Plattner (eds), *The Global Resurgence of Democracy*. Baltimore and London: Johns Hopkins University Press, 146–58.

Lipovskaia, Olga (1997). 'Women's Groups in Russia', in Mary Buckley (ed.), *Post-Soviet Women: From the Baltic to Central Asia*. Cambridge: Cambridge University Press, 186–200.

Lippe, Tanja van der and Eva Fodor (1998). 'Changes in Gender Inequality in Six Eastern European Countries'. *Acta Sociologica*, 41(2): 131–49.

Loewenberg, Gerhard (1994). 'The New Political Leadership of Central Europe: The Example of the New Hungarian National Assembly', in Thomas F. Remington (ed.), *Parliaments in Transition: The New Legislative Politics of the Former USSR and Eastern Europe*. Westview Press Inc.

Loewenberg, Gerhard and Samuel C. Patterson (1979). *Comparing Legislatures*. Boston: Little Brown.

Lovenduski, Joni (1986). *Women in European Politics: Contemporary Feminism and Public Policy*. Amherst: The University of Massachussets Press.

Luker, Kristin (1984). *Abortion and the Politics of Motherhood*. Berkeley: University of California Press.

Maisel, Sandy L. and Walter J. Stone (1997). 'Determinants of Candidate Emergence in US House Elections: An Exploratory Study'. *Legislative Studies Quarterly*, 22(1): 79–96.

Mannila, Elina Haavilo (1988). *Unfinished Democracy: Women in Nordic Politics*. Oxford: Pergamon Press.

Marody, Mira (1993). 'Why I Am Not a Feminist: Some Remarks on the Problem of Gender Identity in the United States and Poland'. *Social Research*, 60(4): 853–64.

Marsh, Rosalind (ed.) (1996). *Women in Russia and Ukraine*. Cambridge: Cambridge University Press.

Matland, Richard E. (1993). 'Institutional Variables Affecting Female Representation in National Legislatures: The Case of Norway'. *Journal of Politics*, 55(3): 737–55.

—— (1995). 'How the Election System has Helped Women Close the Representation Gap', in Lauri, Karvonen and Per Selle (eds), *Closing the Gap: Women in Nordic Politics*. Aldershot: Dartmouth.

—— (1998a). 'Legislative Recruitment: A General Model and Discussion of Issues of Special Relevance to Women', in Azza M. Karam, Cehan Abu-Zayd, and Frene Ginwala (eds) *Women in Parliament: Beyond Numbers*. Stockholm, Sweden: International IDEA.

—— (1998b). 'Women's Representation in National Legislatures: Developed and Developing Countries'. *Legislative Studies Quarterly*, 23(1): 109–25.

—— (1998c). 'The Two Faces of Representation', Paper Presented at the European Consortium for Political Research workshops in Warwick, England, March 23–8.

—— and Donley T. Studlar (1996). 'The Contagion of Women Candidates in Single-Member District and Proportional Representation Electoral Systems: Canada and Norway'. *The Journal of Politics*, 58(3): 707–33.

—— (1998). 'Gender and the Electoral Opportunity Structure in the Canadian Provinces'. *Political Research Quarterly*, 51(1): 117–40.

—— and Michelle A. Taylor (1997). 'Electoral System Effect on Women's Representation: Theoretical Arguments and Evidence from Costa Rica'. *Comparative Political Studies*, 30(2): 186–210.

Matynia, Elzbieta (1994). 'Women After Communism: A Bitter Freedom'. *Social Research*, 61(2): 351–77.

McFaul, Michael and Nikolai, Petrov (1997). 'Russian Electoral Politics After Transition: Regional and National Assessments'. *Post-Soviet Geography and Economics*, 38(9): 507–49.

McFaul, Michael, Nikolai Petrov, and Andrei Ryabov (1999). *Primer on Russia's 1999 Duma Elections*. Moscow: Carnegie Endowment for International Peace.

Meier, Petra (1999). 'Necessary but Not Sufficient: The Belgian Gender Quota Law'. Paper presented at the Conference on Women: Citizens of Europe C.E.L.E.M., Toledo, Spain, May 8–9.

Melnikienė, Rasa (1997). 'Lietuvos Moterų Dabartis ir Problems' (Life and problems of Lithuanian women), paper presented at the Women's conference, May 17, Druskininkai, Lithuania, unpublished, p. 198.

Meurs, Mieke (1998). 'Imagined and Imagining Equality in East Central Europe: Gender and Ethnic Differences in the Economic Transformation of Bulgaria', in John Pickles and Adrian Smith (eds), *Theorizing Transition: The Political Economy of Post-Communist Transformations*. London and New York: Routledge.

Meyer, Alfred G. (1985). 'Feminism, Socialism, and Nationalism in Eastern Europe', in Sharon L. Wolchik and Alfred G. Meyer (eds), *Women, State, and Party in Eastern Europe*. Durham, NC: Duke University Press, 13–30.

Mishler, William and Richard Rose (1994). 'Support for Parliaments and Regimes in the Transition Toward Democracy in Eastern Europe'. *Legislative Studies Quarterly*, 19(1): 14–18.

Moghadam, Valentine M. (ed.) (1992). *Privatization and Democratization in Central and Eastern Europe and the Former Soviet Union: The Gender Dimension*. Oxford: Clarendon Press.

Mojanovski, Cane T. (1996). Socijalniot I politickiot profil na politickite partii vo Makedonija, Skopje: Liber.

Molyneux, Maxine (1985). 'Mobilization Without Emancipation? Women's Interests, the State, and Revolution in Nicaragua'. *Feminist Studies*, 11(2): 227–54.

—— (1990). 'The "Woman Question" in the Age of Perestroika'. *New Left Review*, 183: 23–49.

—— (1991). 'Marxism, Feminism, and the Demise of the Soviet Model', in Rebecca Grant and Kathleen Newland (eds), *Gender and International Relations*. England: Open University Press.

—— (1998). 'Analyzing Women's Movements'. *Development and Change*, 29(2): 219–45.

Moncrief, Gary and Joel Thompson (1991). 'Urban and Rural Ridings and Women in Provincial Politics in Canada: A Research Note on Female MLA's'. *Canadian Journal of Political Science*, 24(4): 831–40.

Montgomery, Kathleen (1997). *Explaining the Puzzle of Women's Representation in the Hungarian National Assembly*. Chicago, IL: Palmer House.

—— (1996). *Crafting Representation In A New Democracy: The Case Of Hungary*. Ph.D. Dissertation, Emory University.

Montgomery, Kathleen and Thomas F. Remington (1994). 'Transitions from Communism: the Case of the 1990 Soviet Republican Elections.' *Journal of Communist Studies and Transition Politics*, 10(1).

Morgan, April and Clyde Wilcox (1992). 'Anti-Feminism in Western Europe, 1975–1987'. *West European Politics*, 15(4): 151–69.

Morondo, Dolores (1997). 'The Situation of Women in Hungary, Poland and the Czech Republic'. Working Paper of the European Parliament Directorate General for Research FEMM 102 EN. Luxembourg: European Parliament.

Moser, Robert G. (1998). 'The Electoral Effects of Presidentialism in Russia', in John, Lowenhardt (ed.), *Party Politics in Post-Communist Russia.* London: Frank Cass, 54–75.

Moser, Robert G. (1999). 'Independents and Party Formation: Elite Partisanship as an Intervening Variable in Russian Politics,' in *Comparative Politics*, 31(2):147–65.

Moser, Robert G. (2001). *Unexpected Outcomes: Electoral Systems, Political Parties, and Represenation in Russia.* Pittsburgh: University of Pittsburgh Press.

Národný akčný plán pre ženy v Slovenskej republike. (Document).

Najcevska, Mirjana, Arifi Teuta, and Gaber Natasa (1997). Ucestvoto na zenata vo sovrementite trendovi vo Republika Makedonija (Fondacija Fridrih Ebert).

Nechemias, Carol (1994). 'Soviet Political Arrangements: The Representation of Women and Minorities', in Wilma Rule and Joseph F. Zimmerman (eds), *Electoral Systems in Comparative Perspective: Their Impact on Women and Minorities.* Westport, CN: Greenwood Press, 89–101.

—— (1996). 'Women's Participation: From Lenin to Gorbachev', in Wilma Rule and Normal Noonan (eds), *Russian Women in Politics and Society.* Westport, CN: Greenwood Press, 15–30.

—— (1998). 'Women and Politics in Post-Soviet Russia', in Marilyn Rueschemeyer (ed.), *Women in the Politics of Postcommunist Eastern Europe.* Armonk, NY: M.E. Sharpe, 8–23.

Norrander, Barbara K. and Clyde Wilcox (1998). 'The Geography of Gender Power: Women in State Legislatures', in Susan Thomas and Clyde Wilcox (eds), *Women in Elected Office: Past, Present, and Future.* New York: Oxford University Press.

Norris, Pippa (1985). 'Women's Legislative Participation in Western Europe'. *Western European Politics*, 8(4): 90–101.

—— (1987). *Politics and Sexual Equality.* Boulder, CO: Rienner.

—— (1996). 'Legislative Recruitment', in Lawrence LeDuc, Richard G. Niemi, and Pippa Norris (eds), *Comparing Democracies: Elections and Voting in Global Perspective.* Thousand Oaks, CA: Sage, 184–215.

—— (1997). 'Choosing Electoral Systems: Proportional, Majoritarian, and Mixed Systems'. *International Political Science Review*, 18(3): 297–312.

—— (1997). *Passages To Power: Legislative Recruitment In Advanced Democracies.* Cambridge: Cambridge University Press.

—— and Ronald Inglehart (2000). 'Cultural Barriers to Women's Leadership: A Worldwide Comparison'. Paper for Special Session 16 'Social Cleavages and Elections', delivered August 3, at the International Political Science Association World Congress. Quebec City.

Norwegian Institute of International Affairs, Centre for Russian Studies (http//www.nupi. no/Russland/Database/start.htm).

Oates, Sarah (1998). 'Party Platforms: Toward a Definition of the Russian Political Spectrum', in John Lowenhardt (ed.), *Party Politics in Post-Communist Russia.* London, Portland, OR: Frank Cass, 76–97.

'Obrazovanie naseleniia Rossii (po dannym mikroperepisi naseleniia 1994 g.' (1995). Moscow: Gosudarstvennyi komitet Rossiiskoi Federatsii po statistike [Goskomstat Rossii].

Odbor za zakonodavstvo Zastupničkog doma Sabora (Lawmaking committee of Sabor's Lower House) (1993). 'Pročišćeni tekst Zakona o izborima zastupnika u Sabor Republike Hrvatske' (Full text of the Law for the Election of Members of Parliament). Zagreb, March 22.

Okruhlicová, A. (1998). 'Barriers and Carriers in Politics—the Heritage of Socialism?'. Presented at the conference *Losers of the 'Wende'—Winners of the EU? Participation of Women: Chances and Effects of the Transformation Process.* Vienna: Austrian Political Science Association: Politik und Geschlecht, Forum Für Feministische, Diskussionen 1998.

Olson, David and Philip Norton (1996). *The New Parliaments of Central and Eastern Europe.* London: Frank Cass.

'Open Women's Line': www.owl.ru/win/winet/Russian/Organiz/Contents/Area/main.html.

Panorama: www.glasnet.ru/~panorama/IZBIR/.

Pateman, Carol (1989). *The Disorder of Women.* Cambridge: Polity Press.

Paxton, Pamela (1997). 'Women in National Legislatures: A Cross-National Analysis'. *Social Science Research,* 26(4): 442–64.

Pavlychko, Solomea (1997). 'Progress on Hold: The Conservative Faces of Women in Ukraine', in Mary Buckley (ed.), *Post-Soviet Women: From the Baltic to Central Asia.* Cambridge: Cambridge University Press, 219–34.

—— (1996). 'Feminism in Post-Communist Ukrainian Society', in Rosalind Marsh (ed.), *Women in Russia and Ukraine.* Cambridge: Cambridge University Press, 305–14.

Peto, Andrea (1994). ' "As He Saw Her": Gender Politics in Secret Party Reports in Hungary During the 1950s', in Andrea Peto and Mark Pittaway (eds), *Women's History: Central and Eastern European Perspectives.* Budapest: Central European University, 107–17.

Petrov, Nikolai (2001). 'Consolidating the Centralized State, Weakening Democracy and the Federal System'. *Russian Regional Report,* 6(22): 19 (East West Institute).

Phillips, Anne (1993). *Democracy and Difference.* University Park, PA: Penn State University Press.

Pigniczky, Reka (1997). 'The Making of a Women's Movement in Hungry after 1989', in Tanya Renne (ed.), *Ana's Land: Sisterhood in Eastern Europe.* Boulder: Westview, 121–32.

Poguntke, Thomas (1994). 'Parties in a Legalistic Culture: the Case of Germany', in Richard S. Katz and Peter Mair (eds), *How Parties Organize: Change and Adaptation in Party Organizations in Western Democracies.* London: Sage, 185–215.

Politicheskii almanakh Rossii 1997. (1998). Moscow: Carnegie Center.

Politychni partii Ukraïny, Kiev: KIS. (1998). 276.

Potichnyj, Peter J. (1992). 'Elections in the Ukraine, 1990', in Zvi Gitelman (ed.), *The Politics of Nationality and the Erosion of the USSR.* Basingstoke: Macmillan, 176–214.

Potucek, Martin (1996). 'How Czechs Reflect the Tasks and Transformation of the Public Sector,' paper presented at the NISPACEE fourth annual conference 'Developing Organizations and Changing Attitudes: Publish Administration in Central and Eastern Europe,' Tirana, Albania, March 27–30.

Press and Information Office (1985). *Facts and Figures: A Comparative Survey of the Federal Republic of Germany and the German Democratic Republic*. Bonn: Federal Republic of Germany.

Prinz, Timothy S. (1993). 'The Career Paths of Elected Politicians: A Review and Prospectus', in Shirley Williams and Edward L. Lascher, Jr. (eds), *Ambition and Beyond: Career Path of American Politicians*. Berkeley, CA: Institute of Governmental Studies Press.

Prunskienė, Kazimiera (1995). 'I Was Regarded as an Exception'. *Lithuania: Women in the Changing Society* 16. Vilnius: UNDP.

Purvaneckienė, Giedrė and Rasa Ališauskienė (1998). Moterų ir lyčių lygyblės klausimai Lietuvos politinių partijų rinkimų į Seimą programose (Women and gender equality issues in the Lithuanian electoral party programs), the in Purvaneckienė Giedrė (ed). Moterys ir rinkimai (Women and elections), Vilnius: Moterų nformacijos centras, 37, 194.

Raciborski, Jacek (1997). *Polskie wybory. Zachowania wyborcze społeczeństwa polskiego 1989–95 (Polish Elections: Electoral Behaviors of Polish Society 1989–95)*. Warsaw: Scholar.

Racioppi, Linda and Katherine O'Sullivan See (1995). 'Organizing Women Before and After the Fall: Women's Politics in the Soviet Union and Post-Soviet Russia'. *Journal of Women in Culture and Society*, 20(4): 820–50.

——(1997). *Women's Activism in Contemporary Russia*. Philadelphia: Temple University Press.

Rae, Douglas W. (1971). *The Political Consequences of Electoral Rules*, 2nd edition. New Haven, CT: Yale University Press.

Rahat, Gideon (1999). 'Intraparty Candidate Selection Methods: An Analytical Framework'. Paper presented at European Consortium for Political Research Workshop. 'The Consequences of Candidate Selection'.

Regulska, Joanna (1998). ' "The Political" and its Meaning for Women: Transition Politics in Poland', in John Pickles and Adrian Smith (eds), *Theorizing Transition: The Political Economy of Post-Communist Transformations*. London and New York: Routledge.

Remington, Thomas F. (1997). 'Democratization and the New Political Order in Russia', in Karen Dawisha and Bruce Parrott (eds), *Democratic Changes and Authoritarian Reactions in Russia, Ukraine, Belarus, and Moldova*. Cambridge: Cambridge University Press, 69–129.

Renne, Tanya (ed.) (1997). *Ana's Land: Sisterhood in Eastern Europe*. Boulder, CO: Westview Press.

Republika Hrvatska, Državno izborno povjerenstvo (Republic of Croatia, National Elections Commission) (2000). 'Izvješće o provedenim izborima za zastupnike u Zastupnički dom Sabora Republike Hrvatske'. Report on the Elections for the House of Representatives of the Croatian Parliament, Zagreb, January.

Reynolds, Andrew (1999). 'Women in the Legislatures and Executives of the World: Knocking at the Highest Glass Ceilings'. *World Politics*, 51(4): 547–73.

Rokkan, Stein (1970). *Citizens, Elections, Parties*. New York: David McKay Company.

Rose, Richard, Neil Munro, and Stephen White (2001). 'Voting in a Floating Party System: The 1999 Duma Election'. *Europe–Asia Studies*, 53(5): 419–43.

Rubchak, Marian J. (1996). 'Christian Virgin or Pagan Goddess: Feminism Versus the Eternally Feminine in Ukraine', in Rosalind Marsh (ed.), *Women in Russia and Ukraine*. Cambridge: Cambridge University Press, 315–30.

Rueschemeyer, Marilyn (ed.) (1998*a*). *Women in the Politics of Postcommunist Eastern Europe*. Revised and Expanded Edition. Armonk, NY: M.E. Sharpe.

—— (1998*b*). 'Women in the Politics of Eastern Germany: The Dilemmas of Unification', in Marilyn Rueschemeyer (ed.), *Women in the Politics of Postcommunist Eastern Europe*. Revised and Expanded Edition. Armonk, NY: M.E. Sharpe, 89–115.

Rule, W. (1981). 'Why Women Don't Run: The Critical Contextual Factors in Women's Legislative Recruitment'. *Western Political Quarterly*, 34(1): 60–77.

—— (1987). 'Electoral Systems, Contextual Factors and Women's Opportunity for Election to Parliament in Twenty-Three Democracies'. *Western Political Quarterly*, 40(3): 477–98.

—— (1990). 'Why More Women Are State Legislators: A Research Note'. *Western Political Quarterly*, 43(2): 437–48.

Rule, Wilma and Nadezhda Shvedova (1996). 'Women in Russia's First Multiparty Election', in Wilma Rule and Norma C. Noonan (eds), *Russian Women in Politics and Society*. Connecticut: Greenwood Press, 40–62.

Sabor Republike Hrvatske (Parliament of the Republic of Croatia) (1992). 'Ukaz o proglašenju Zakona o izborima zastupnika u Sabor Republike Hrvatske'. Law for the Election of Members of Parliament, Zagreb, April 15.

Saint-Germaine, Michelle A. (1989). 'Does Their Difference Make a Difference? The Impact of Women on Public Policy in the Arizona Legislature'. *Social Science Quarterly*, 70(4): 956–68.

Sapiro, Virginia (2002). *It's the Context, Situation, and Question, Stupid: The Gender Basis of Public Opinion in Understanding Public Opinion* (2nd edition). Washington, D.C.: CQ Press.

Satre Ahlander, Ann-Mari (2001). 'Women's and Men's Work in Transitional Russia: Legacies of the Soviet System'. *Post-Soviet Affairs*, 17(1): 56–80.

Saxonberg, Steven (2000). 'Women in East European Parliaments'. *Journal of Democracy*, 11(2): 145–58.

Scarrow, Susan (1998). 'Political Parties and the Changing Framework of German Electoral Competition', in Christopher Anderson and Carsten Zelle (eds), *Stability and Change in German Elections: How Electorates Merge, Converge, or Collide*. Westport, CT: Praeger Publishers, 301–22.

Schlesinger (1966). *Ambition and Politics: Political Careers in the United States*. Chicago: Rand McNally.

Schmitt, Karl (1998). 'The Social Bases of Voting Behavior in Unified Germany', in Christopher J. Anderson and Carsten Zelle (eds), *Stability and Change in German Elections: How Electorates Merge, Converge, or Collide*. Westport, Connecticut: Praeger, 33–54.

Schmitter, Philippe C. (1998). 'Contemporary Democratization: The Prospects for Women', in Jane S. Jaquette and Sharon L. Wolchik (eds), *Women and Democracy: Latin American and Central and Eastern Europe*. Baltimore and London: Johns Hopkins University Press, 222–38.

Scott, Hilda (1973). *Does Socialism Liberate Women?* Boston: Beacon Press.

—— (1976). *Women and Socialism: Experiences from Eastern Europe.* London: Allison and Busby.

Sebestény István (1999). 'Az 1998-as magyar parlamenti választások képviselőjelölt-jeinek társadalmi jellemzői' (The Social Characteristics of the Parliamentary Candidates in 1998), in S. Kurtán *et al.* (eds), *Magyarország politikai évkönyve.* Budapest: Centre for Democracy Studies.

Seltzer, Richard A., Jody Newman, and Melissa Voorhees Leighton (1997). *Sex as a Political Variable: Women as Candidates and Voters in U.S. Elections.* Boulder: Lynne Reinner.

Shlapentokh, Vladimir, Roman Levita, and Mikhail Loiberg (1997). *From Submission to Rebellion: The Provinces Versus the Center in Russia.* Boulder, CO: Westview Press.

Siemieńska, Renata (1990). *Płeć, zawód, polityka. Udział kobiet w życiu publicznym w Polsce (Gender—Profession—Politics: Women's Participation in Public Life).* Warszawa: Instytut Socjologii Uniwersytetu Warszawskiego.

—— (1994). 'The Contemporary Dilemma of the Polish Family and Its Genealogy'. *The European Journal of Women's Studies,* 1(2): 207–27.

—— (1996a). 'Women's Political Participation in Central and Eastern Europe: A Cross-Cultural Perspective', in Barbara Wejnert and Metta Spencer (eds), *Research on Women in Russia and Eastern Europe,* vol. 2: '*Women in Post-Communism*'. Greenwich: JAI Press Inc.

—— (1996b). *Kobiety: nowe wyzwania. Starcie przeszłości z teraźniejszością (Women: New Challenges: Clash of the Past and the Present).* Warsaw: Institute of Sociology—University of Warsaw.

—— (1997). *Płeć a wybory. Od wyborów parlamentarnych do wyborów prezydenckich (Gender and Elections: From Parliamentary to Presidential Elections).* Warsaw: ISS UW and F. Ebert Stiftung.

—— (1998). 'Consequences of Economic and Political Changes for Women in Poland' in J.S. Jaquette, S. Wolchik (eds), *Women and Democracy.* Latin America and Central and Eastern Europe. Baltimore and London: The John Hopkins University Press.

—— (1999). 'Elites and Women in Democratizing Post-Communist Societies'. *International Review of Sociology,* 9(2): 197–219.

—— (2000). *Nie mogą, nie chcą czy nie potrafią? (They Have No Opportunities, They Do Not Want, They are Unable. Do They?).* Warsaw: Institute for Social Studies—University of Warsaw and F. Ebert Stiftung.

—— 2002. 'The Political Culture of Elites and Public: Building Women's Representation in Post-Communist Poland' in T. Klonowicz, G. Wieczorkowska (eds), *Social Change, Adaptation and Resistance.* Warsaw: Warsaw University.

Šiklová, Jirina (1996). 'McDonald's, Terminators, Coca Cola Ads—and Feminism? Imports From the West', in Tanya Renne (ed.), *Ana's Land: Sisterhood in Eastern Europe.* Westview Press, 76–81.

—— (1998). 'Why Western Feminism Isn't Working: The New Presence'. *The Prague Journal of Central European Affairs,* 8–10.

Simon, Janos (1993). 'Post-Paternalist Political Culture in Hungary: Relationship Between Citizens and Politics During and After the "Melancholic Revolution" (1989–91)'. *Communist and Post-Communist Studies,* 26(2): 226–38.

Skjeie, Hege (1991). 'The rhetoric of difference. On women's inclusion in political elites'. *Politics and Society*, 19: 233–63.

Slider, Darrel (1996). 'Elections to Russia's Regional Assemblies'. *Post-Soviet Affairs*, 12(3): 243–64.

SLS Programme, Slovenian People's Party.

Smejkalova, Jirina (1994). 'Do Czech Women Need Feminism? Perspectives on Feminist Theories and Practices in Czechoslovakia'. *Women's Studies International Forum*, 17(3): 277–82.

Social-Democratic Women's Forum of SDP. 'Program: We are Taking What is Ours: Half of Heaven, Half of Earth, Half of Power!'

Social-Democratic Party of Croatia (1999). 'Pošteno, pravedno, pametno: izborni program SDP' (Fair, Just, Smart: Electoral Program of SDP). Zagreb, November.

—— (2000). 'Statute of the Social-Democratic Party of Croatia'. Zagreb, December.

—— 'Political Program of SDP', www.sdp.hr/prog.html.

—— 'Electoral Declaration of the Social-Democratic Party of Croatia and the Croatian Social-Liberal Party'.

Solnick, Steven L. (1998). 'Gubernatorial Elections in Russia, 1996–97'. *Post-Soviet Affairs*, 14(1): 48–80.

Sperling, Valerie (1999). *Organizing Women in Contemporary Russia: Engendering Transition*. Cambridge: Cambridge University Press.

Statisticheski Godishnik na Narodna Republika Bulgaria (Statistics Yearbook of the People's Republic of Bulgaria) (1982). (Sofia: Komitet po Edinna Sistema za Sozialna Informaziya pri Ministerski Suvet).

Statistics Finland (1997). *Kunnallisvaalit 1996* (Municipal Elections 1996). Helsinki: Suomen virallinen tilasto.

Statistische Bundesamt [Federal Statistics Agency] (ed.) (1999*a*). 'Der Bundeswahlleiter: Bundestagswahl', [WWW] http://194.95.119.6/wahlen/.

—— (1999*b*). 'Monatliche Wirtschaftsindikatoren: Arbeitsmarktdaten der Bundesanstalt fuer Arbeit', [WWW] http://194.95.119.6/indicators/d/d_arb.htm.

Statistisches Amt der DDR (1990, 1989, 1979, 1969). *Statistisches Jahrbuch der DDR*. Berlin: Rudolf Haufe Verlag.

Stoner-Weiss, Kathryn (1997). *Local Heroes: The Political Economy of Russian Regional Governance*. Princeton, NJ: Princeton University Press.

—— (1999). 'Central Weakness and Provincial Autonomy: Observations on the Devolution Process in Russia'. *Post-Soviet Affairs*, 15(1): 87–106.

Strømsnes, Kristin (1995). 'Kjønn og politisk kunnskap' (Gender and political knowledge) in Nina C. Raaum (ed.), Kjønn og politikk (Gender and Politics). Oslo, Norway: Tano Publishing.

Sundberg, Jan (1995). 'Women in Scandinavian Party Organizations,' in Lauri Karvonen & Per Selle (eds), *Women in Nordic Politics. Closing the Gap*, Aldershot et al.: Dartmouth Publishing Company, 83–111.

Taagepera, Rein (1994). 'Beating the Law of Minority Attrition', in Wilma Rule and Joseph F. Zimmerman (eds), *Electoral Systems in Comparative Perspective: Their Impact on Women and Minorities*. Westport, CN: Greenwood Press, 235–47.

Taagepera, Rein and Matthew S. Shugart (1989). *Seats and Votes: The Effects and Determinants of Electoral Systems*. New Haven, CT: Yale University Press.

Tamerius, Karen L. (1995). 'Sex, Gender, and Leadership in the Representation of Women', in Georgia Duerst-Lahti and Rita Mae Kelly (eds), *Gender Power, Leadership, and Governance*. Ann Arbor: University of Michigan Press, 93–112.

The World's Women: Trends and Statistics (1995). Social Statistics and Indicators Series, No. 12. New York: United Nations.

Thomas, Sue (1991). 'The Impact of Women on State Legislative Policies'. *Journal of Politics*, 53(4): 958–76.

—— (1997). 'Why Gender Matters: The Perceptions of Women Officeholders'. *Women and Politics*, 17(1): 27–53.

Thomas, Sue, and Clyde Wilcox (eds) (1998). *Women and Elective Office: Past, Present and Future*. New York and Oxford: Oxford University Press.

Togeby, Lise (1994). 'Political Implications of Increasing Numbers of Women in the Labor Force'. *Comparative Political Studies*, 27(2): 211–40.

Trinkūnienė, Inija and Jonas Trinkūnas Jonas (1999). 'Patriarchalizmo apraiškos lietuviškoje tradicijoje' (Manifestations of paternalism/ patriarchalism in the Lithuanian tradition) in Purvanecikienė Giedrė (ed.). Moterys: tapatumo paieškos (Women: search of identity), Vilnius: Moterų informacijos centras (Women information center), 169.

Tóka, Gábor (1995). 'A Short History of the Hungarian Parties of the Transition', in Gábor Tóka (ed.), *The 1990 Election to the Hungarian National Assembly: Analyses, Documents, and Data*. Berlin: Edition Sigma.

Turčániková, K. (1998). 'Nerovnomerné zastúpenie žien', Hospodárske noviny, 25.11.97 Výborná, L., 'Muži nedôverujú ženám', Práca, 1.9.

Urban, Michael and Vladimir Gel'man (1997). 'The Development of Political Parties in Russia', in Karen Dawisha and Bruce Parrott (eds), *Democratic Changes and Authoritarian Reactions in Russia, Ukraine, Belarus and Moldova*. Cambridge: Cambridge University Press, 175–219.

Ured Predsjednika Republike Hrvatske (Cabinet of the President of the Republic of Croatia) (1994). 'Zakon o izmjenama i dopunama Zakona o izborima zastupnika u Sabor Republike Hrvatske' (Law Regarding the Changes to the Electoral Law for the Parliamentary Elections), February 8.

Valen, Henry (1988). 'Norway: Decentralization and Group Representation', in Michael Gallagher and Michael Marsh (eds), *Candidate Selection in Comparative Perspective* London: Sage.

—— (1998). 'Introduction: Women and Elective Office: Past, Present, and Future', in Sue Thomas and Clyde Wilcox (eds), *Women and Elective Office: Past, Present and Future*. Oxford: Oxford University Press, 1–14.

Vianello, Mino and Renata Siemieńska *et al.* (1990). *Gender Inequality: A Comparative Study of Discrimination and Participation*. London: Sage Publications.

Wanner, Catherine (1998). *Burden of Dreams: History and Identity in Post-Soviet Ukraine*. University Park, PA: Pennsylvania State University Press.

Watson, Peggy (1993). 'The Rise of Masculinism in Eastern Europe'. *New Left Review*, 198: 71–82.

—— (1997). 'Civil Society and the Politics of Difference in Eastern Europe', in Joan Scott, Cora Kalan, and Debra Keates (eds), *Transitions, Environments, Translation: Feminism in International Politics*. New York: Routledge, 21–9.

Waylen, Georgina (1994). 'Women and Democratization: Conceptualizing Gender Relations in Transition Politics'. *World Politics*, 46(3): 327–54.

Wejnert, Barbara (1996). 'Introduction' and 'Political Transition and Gender Transformation in the Communist and Post-Communist Periods', in Barbara Wejnert and Metta Spencer (eds), *Research on Women in Russia and Eastern Europe*, vol. 2: '*Women in Post-Communism*'. Greenwich: JAI Press Inc.

Welch, Susan (1977). 'Women as Political Animals? A Test of Some Explanation for Male–Female Political Participation Differences'. *American Journal of Political Science*, 21(4): 711–30.

—— and Donly Studlar (1990). 'Multimember Districts and the Representation of Women'. *Journal of Politics*, 52(2): 391–412.

—— (1986). 'British Public Opinion Toward Women in Politics: A Comparative Perspective'. *Western Political Quarterly*, 39(1): 138–52.

—— and Sue Thomas (1991). 'Do Women in Public Office Make a Difference?' in Debra Dodson (ed.), *Gender and Policy Making: Studies of Women in Office*. New Brunswick, New Jersey: Center for the American Woman and Politics, Rutgers University.

Wesołowski, Włodzimierz and Przemysław Mielczarek (1999). 'Zmienność i stabilizacja warstwy politycznej: cztery Sejmy okresu transformacji' (Changes and Stability of Political Class: Four Sejms of the Period of Transformation). *Studia Socjologiczne*, 3: 37–82.

White, Stephen (1988). 'Reforming the Electoral System'. *Journal of Communist Studies*, 4(4): 1–17.

—— Alex Pravda, and Zvi Gitelman (1997). *Developments in Russian Politics 4*. Durham: Duke University Press.

White, Stephen, Richard Rose and Ian McAllister (1997). *How Russia Votes*. Chatham, NJ: Chatham House.

Wilcox, Clyde (1991a). 'Support for Gender Equality in West Europe: A Longitudinal Analysis'. *European Journal of Political Research*, 20(1): 127–47.

—— (1991b). 'The Causes and Consequences of Feminist Consciousness in West Europe'. *Comparative Political Studies*, 23(4): 519–39.

Wilson, Andrew and Artur Bilous (1993). 'Political Parties in Ukraine', *Europe–Asia Studies*, 45(4): 693–703.

—— and Sarah Birch. 'Virtual Democracy in Ukraine: The Political Economy of Party Politics Under Post-Communism' (working title), unpublished manuscript, n.d.

Wolchik, Sharon L. (1981). 'Ideology and Equality: The Status of Women in Eastern and Western Europe'. *Comparative Political Studies*, 13(4): 445–76.

—— (1985–1986). 'The Precommunist Legacy, Economic Development, Social Transformation, and Women's Roles in Eastern Europe', in Sharon L. Wolchik and Alfred G. Meyer (eds), *Women, State, and Party in Eastern Europe*. Durham, NC: Duke University Press.

—— and Alfred G. Meyer (eds) (1985). *Women, State, and Party in Eastern Europe*. Durham, NC: Duke University Press.

'Women in Politics: Post-Election Reflection' (1997). Typescript of the report from the conference held at the University of Warsaw, November 3.

Women in Slovenia in the 1990s, Women's Policy Office, Ljubljana.

World Development Report: From Plan to Market (1996). World Bank: Oxford University Press.

Yearbook of Labour Statistics (2000). Geneva: International Labour Office.

Yoder, Jennifer (1999). *From East Germans To Germans?: The New Postcommunist Elites.* Durham, NC: Duke University Press.

Zastupnički dom Sabora Republike Hrvatske (Lower House of the Parliament of the Republic of Croatia) (1999). 'Zakon o izborima zastupnika u Hrvatski državni Sabor' (Electoral Law for the Parliamentary Elections), November 3.

Zelle, Carsten (1998). 'Factors Explaining the Increase in PDS Support After Unification', in Christopher J. Anderson and Carsten Zelle (eds), *Stability and Change in German Elections: How Electorates Merge, Converge, or Collide.* Westport, CT: Praeger, 223–46.

Zenska Infoteka (a). 'Izborni rezultati 2000—Election Results 2000 Study', http://www.zinfo.hr/hrvatski/stranice/istrazivanja/izbori2000/izborni-rezultati-2000.htm.

——(b). 'Zene i izbori: stranački programi- Women and Elections: Party Programs', www.zinfo.hr/hrvatski/stranice/istrazivanja/izbori2000/stranacki-programi-2000.htm.

Zlotnik, Marc (1996). 'Russia's Governors: All the President's Men?' *Problems of Post-Communism,* 43(6): 26–34.

❖ Index